W9-BTS-687

BUSINESS DEPARTMENT
BIRMINGHAM PUBLIC LIBRARY
2100 PARK PLACE
BIRMINGHAM, AL 35203

THE NEW MARKETING
RESEARCH SYSTEMS

#255089993

THE NEW MARKETING RESEARCH SYSTEMS

How to Use Strategic Database Information for Better Marketing Decisions

David J. Curry

John Wiley & Sons, Inc.

New York • Chichester • Brisbane • Toronto • Singapore

BUSINESS DEPARTMENT
BIRMINGHAM PUBLIC LIBRARY
2100 PARK PLACE
BIRMINGHAM, AL 35203

658.830285

In recognition of the importance of preserving what has been
written, it is a policy of John Wiley & Sons, Inc. to have
books of enduring value published in the United States
printed on acid-free paper, and we exert our best efforts
to that end.

Copyright ©1993 by David J. Curry
Published by John Wiley & Sons, Inc.

All rights reserved. Published simultaneously in Canada.

Reproduction or translation of any part of this work
beyond that permitted by Section 107 or 108 of the
1976 United States Copyright Act without the permission
of the copyright owner is unlawful. Requests for
permission or further information should be addressed to
the Permissions Department, John Wiley & Sons, Inc.

This publication is designed to provide accurate and
authoritative information in regard to the subject
matter covered. It is sold with the understanding that
the publisher is not engaged in rendering legal, accounting,
or other professional services. If legal advice or other
expert assistance is required, the services of a competent
professional person should be sought. *From a Declaration
of Principles jointly adopted by a Committee of the
American Bar Association and a Committee of Publishers.*

Library of Congress Cataloging-in-Publication Data

Curry, David J., 1944–
    The new marketing research systems : how to use strategic database
information for better marketing decisions / by David J. Curry.
        p.   cm.
    Includes index.
    ISBN 0-471-53058-1
    1. Marketing research—Statistical methods—Data processing.
    I. Title.
    HF5415.2.C87   1992
    658.8'3'0285—dc20   92–9811

Printed in the United States of America

10 9 8 7 6 5 4 3 2 1

This book is dedicated to my wife, Patricia, with love

Trademarks Mentioned in the Book

Coca-Cola
Holiday Inn
Polk
Walt Disney World (DisneyWorld)
Kraft
McDonald's
Citibank
Sears
Clairol
Metromail
Lesp
Spice Islands
Kraft USA
ClusterPLUS
MicroVision
InfoScan
Promotion Scan
Infomark
VALs

Diet Coke
Revlon
Pepsi-Cola
K mart
L.L. Bean
Cheerios
Sanka
Wal-Mart
Fresca
Metaphor
Durkee
Micro-merchandising
ACORN
PRIZM
SCANTRACK
BehaviorScan
Ad Tracker
Metaphor

Acknowledgments

This book bears the imprint of many persons. Several of my colleagues at the University of Iowa, including Penny Baron and Dan Moore of efficient market services and Gerald Eskin of Information Resources, Inc., were instrumental in creating the new marketing research systems. These individuals have provided inspiration, direction, and extensive material for the book. Their help is deeply appreciated. I also want to thank two of my former students, Edward Sachs and Susan Helfers Brady, both of whom are now with A. C. Nielsen, for keeping me informed about current events in the single-source industry and providing material for many of the examples used in the book.

I am indebted to a number of colleagues and associates whose reviews provided insightful suggestions and contributed to the conceptual framework of the book: David Aaker, University of California, Berkeley; Gary Gaeth and John Mittelstaedt, University of Iowa; Tim Heath, University of Pittsburgh; Avijit Ghosh, New York University; John McCann, Duke University; Srinivas Reddy, University of Georgia; Doyle Weiss, University of Iowa; and Franklin Houston, Rutgers University. I also want to note the valuable research assistance of Subir Bandyopadhyay (McGill University) and Catherine Hanson Short. Their dedication to the project is gratefully acknowledged.

Examples and graphics are the result of the cooperation of firms in both the single-source and geodemographic research sectors. I want to thank the individuals at these firms who devoted their energy and time to fulfilling requests for material: Daniel Huck and Carol Passero, CACI–Federal; Patricia Bromm, Jeri Towner Denniston, Louis Tazioli, and Jon Voorhees, Equifax–National Decision Systems; April James and Kevin Lourens, Claritas Corporation; Julie Brierly and Kim Smith, Donnelley Marketing Information Services; David Chapman, National Planning Data Corporation; John Totten (while at IRI) and Travis Whitlow, A. C. Nielsen; Jody Holtzman, Information Resources, Inc. Willard Bishop, Willard Bishop Consulting, Ltd.; Judith Kozacik, the Food Marketing Institute; Mike Thran, Washington National Insurance Company; and Joy Klemencic, Procter & Gamble Company. Special thanks are extended to Frank Hightower and

Todd Wade of Equifax–National Decision Systems for numerous examples, the use of an Infomark system at the University of Cincinnati, and personalized system training.

My thinking about various topics in this book has been strongly influenced by discussions with certain individuals. Robert Herbold (Procter & Gamble Company) and John Burwick (Kroger Company) have clarified institutional practices in the consumer packaged goods industry. Anthony Power of Information Advantage helped me to better understand the role of decision support systems in the modern business enterprise. Arthur Helmicki of the University of Cincinnati tutored me in linear system theory. My mentor at the University of California at Berkeley, John Myers, contributed more to this work than he may realize. My thanks to each of these gentlemen.

Other individuals provided detailed help in specific chapters, including Johannes Ledolter, University of Iowa (Appendix 8A): Jim Spaeth, Viewfacts, Inc. (Chapter 11); Barbara Clayton, U.S. Bureau of the Census (Appendix 12A); Kelly Tritz, Toro Company (Chapter 15); George Moore, Equifax–National Decision Systems (Chapter 16); Helen Lawson, CACI, Ltd., London (Chapter 16); Maureen Johnson, Research International, Ltd., London (Chapter 16); and Steven Burt, Institute for Retail Studies, Stirling, Scotland (Chapter 16).

Chapter 17 was originally drafted as a cooperative effort between myself, Darryl Hales, and Monika Torrence (formerly of Kraft USA, now with Spectra Marketing Systems). Darryl and Monika, with support from Eric Deaton, formulated the micro-merchandising concept and successfully implemented it at Kraft. Monika has since become my primary contact at Spectra, along with her colleagues Tom Daly and John Larkin. Their cooperation is gratefully acknowledged.

Chapter 18 represents a collaborative effort with Charles Whiteman, University of Iowa; Suresh Divakar, SUNY, Buffalo; and Sharat Mathur, Australian Graduate School of Management. It was a pleasure to work with these energetic and talented individuals. We depended on RATS software and frequent guidance from its designer, Tom Doan at ESTIMA. Our thanks for use of a superb product.

The talented staff at John Wiley & Sons and Publication Services deserve praise for their shaping of the manuscript. From Wiley, I am indebted to John Mahaney, Editor, Gloria Fuzia, editorial assistant, and Linda Indig, Managing Editor. Ted Long, Greg Martel, and Leslie Trimmer at Publication Services masterfully coordinated the final production process. My thanks to them and to their able staff, including Dave Mason, copy editing, Tonja S. Prodehl, typesetting programming, and Kristin L. Humbargar, graphics production. I thank Rawly Burns and George Mathew for their help in creating graphics in the late stages of the project. The word-processing efforts of Karen Mueller of the University of Cincinnati and those of the entire staff at the University of Iowa who worked on the manuscript during its "early years" are warmly appreciated.

Among those who provided technical support, two people have been with the project from the beginning: Barbara Yerkes and Linda Knowling. In addition to expert editing, Barbara provided constant encouragement and good humor. She is a pleasure to work with and a genius at rephrasing, reorganizing, and reframing. Linda managed to take my crude ideas and random scribblings and turn them into informative graphics. I very much appreciate her creative skills and her untiring dedication to quality.

For supporting my research and writing efforts I want to thank Bob Dwyer, the Center for Direct Marketing; my department chairman, Fritz Russ, and his assistant Toni Briscoe; Dean George Daly, University of Iowa; and Dean Jerome Schnee, University of Cincinnati. These individuals provided resources and an intellectual climate in which lengthy projects of this type can be completed.

Finally, and foremost, I thank my wife, Patricia, who spent long hours proofreading and editing the manuscript. I am indebted to her for this help, but more so for the love, inspiration, and encouragement she has given me throughout the book's preparation. The book is truly ours.

Preface

In 1986, when this book was conceived, the gap between marketing research practice and the research principles offered in standard texts was very clear. Standard texts typically devoted only a few pages to the developments brought about by UPC scanner data and geodemographic data. They defined a few terms, provided some examples, and studied several cases. Rarely was there more than a hint that the new technology had given birth to a distinct research philosophy or that major clients were consuming millions of dollars in scanner research reports annually.

As was suspected then and is known now, the single-source industry would grow to be the dominant force in packaged goods marketing research. This growth brought with it new jargon, new analysis techniques, and new reporting methods. Even more critical for marketing executives, single-source technology shifted institutional power in packaged goods marketing from manufacturers to retailers and created a host of new management issues. Managers must use the enormous quantity of transaction-level data to make complex decisions about strategic focus (national, regional, or local?), communications mix (promote or advertise?), and activity timing (weekly features?). The results they achieve with electronic data, which are more costly than survey data, will determine whether these data are also more valuable than those previously available.

Practitioners faced with day-to-day management pressures are not the only ones confused and frustrated with the volume and detail of data available from electronic databases. Academic researchers today must possess computer and statistical skills far surpassing those needed in the prescanner era. Although data are often supplied "free" to interested researchers, their cost is ultimately measured in the person-years needed to set up, run, and interpret analyses. Today's marketing scientists must resolve complex questions about data aggregation, model effects pooling, and market dynamics that marketing researchers rarely encountered before 1980.

These developments—their fast pace, their far-reaching impact, their vast economic importance—make the lack of published guidance particularly frustrating. Academics attempting to integrate modern techniques into the classroom find little help in available texts. Managers are equally perplexed by students with four to six years of marketing education who draw a blank about terms such as "shelf-keeping unit," "all commodity volume," and "slotting fee" and whose idea of a marketing research problem is to decide whether to do a mail or a phone survey.

With these issues as its principal motivation, this book summarizes the more than 10 years of concepts, procedures, and discoveries that are missing from standard texts. The primary goals are to chronicle the impact of new technologies on packaged goods marketing in particular and on marketing practice more generally, and to offer a coherent management/research philosophy that makes full use of electronic information. UPC scanner data and the resulting single-source industry are covered in depth along with critical developments in geodemography, a companion field to single-source technology. The book reviews how both scanner technology and refined census geography have altered our view of research. It identifies the products and methods used by key firms in these two industries and illustrates solutions that successfully integrate data, models, reports, and strategy delivery tools.

The book also addresses major shortcomings of current practice. After 10 years of experience with detailed, real-time data, we are still information-age novices seeking to understand the data we mass-produce. The volume of data not only overwhelms managers and their information specialists, but also reveals marketplace dynamics that are far more complex than previously realized. To date, results have often been disappointing, despite a huge investment in powerful computers, sophisticated software, and high-priced consultants.

To address these issues, this book is divided into four parts. Part I highlights major changes affecting the practice of marketing research. Part II discusses single-source systems, primarily those based on scanner and electronic data. Part III reviews geodemography and the major geodemographic systems available in the United States and Europe. Part IV concentrates on two types of integrated systems: systems that interlock scanner, trade area, and geodemographic data, and systems that analyze scanner data using forecasting and control models. A more detailed description of each section follows.

PART I: CHAPTERS 1–5

Chapters 1 through 5 introduce the book's central theme, marketing research systems, and discuss nine shifts that have led to their development. Two of these shifts have altered our strategic perspective: the shift from macro- to micromarketing and the shift from risk redemption research to opportunity identification research. The other seven shifts reflect important technological changes that have dramatically affected marketing practice, including the shift from aggregate to disaggregate data, the shift from surveys to observation, and the shift from separated to integrated databases.

Part I also criticizes the project orientation that dominates existing marketing research texts. Numerous examples illustrate failures of the project approach and its heavy reliance on inferential statistics. Subsequent sections are designed to motivate the reader to adopt a new style of thinking about the role of technology in modern marketing research systems.

Because it attempts to sell a certain viewpoint rather than describe procedures, Part I raises a number of arguable points, points that may disturb some readers but that will pique the interest of others and lead to further discussion. Chapter 5 in particular contrasts the systems philosophy presented in this book with the traditional project philosophy. Chapter 5 should be of interest to executives whose firms rely heavily on project-oriented research and to university faculty who want to present an alternative to the project orientation.

PART II: CHAPTERS 6–11

Part II describes modern single-source systems, especially those offered by A.C. Nielsen and Information Resources, Incorporated. Chapter 6 reviews elements of these systems, defining terms and summarizing main applications.

Chapter 7 provides detail on the main suppliers of single-source data. Measures that these firms make available to their clients are discussed in light of established theories of pricing, repeat buying, and brand loyalty. These theoretical frameworks illustrate why single-source data suppliers choose to gather and report certain facts and not others and how manufacturers, retailers, and advertising agencies can best use these facts.

Chapter 8 deviates from the substantive content of the other chapters in Part II. It reviews conceptual issues and corresponding terminology relevant for understanding and creating single-source reports. The framework permits a reader to categorize output from any marketing research system (or any other decision support system, for that matter), and it helps to clarify how an analyst can more effectively create reports and a user more effectively read them.

Chapters 9 through 11 describe the three principle user groups for single-source reports: manufacturers, retailers, and advertising agencies. These chapters provide case studies that illustrate concepts discussed in Chapters 6 through 8 and preview developments that are likely to materialize in the next five years.

In Part II as elsewhere, chapter appendixes introduce supplemental material or technical detail. For example, the appendix to Chapter 6 provides a stylized history of marketing research concentrating on ideas that led to modern single-source systems. The appendix to Chapter 7 discusses important deficiencies encountered with single-source systems despite their size and technical sophistication. The appendix to Chapter 8 discusses advanced topics in reporting— for example, how automatic control theory is linked to modern reporting techniques and how to recognize and solve problems typically encountered in a marketing research system.

PART III: CHAPTERS 12–16

Part III of the book reviews the second major practical innovation in modern marketing management: geodemographic systems. Although geodemographic systems were developed before single-source systems, their value in conventional marketing applications (not just direct/database marketing) has only recently become evident.

Single-source systems and geodemographic systems are natural complements. Single-source systems deliver market information to management, and geodemographic systems deliver management strategy to the market. Working systems that combine the best features of single-source technology and geodemography are now emerging, and examples of this fusion are provided at several points in the book.

Part III follows the format established in Part II. Chapter 12 gives a conceptual overview of geodemography, describes how GD systems are built from census data, and illustrates one of their most basic applications: list qualification. Conceptual preliminaries done, Chapter 13 then discusses the four major geodemographic systems available in the United States: ACORN, ClusterPLUS, PRIZM, and MicroVision. A complete overview of each system is provided, along with precise descriptions of the standard (mainframe) factor analysis and cluster analysis results available from each vendor.

Chapter 14 presents detailed applications of geodemography. These include list qualification, direct marketing, media selection, retail site selection, product positioning, and product optimization. Modern geodemographic systems also interlock with other commercial databases. These links are reviewed in detail, including those with VALS, Simmons, National Family Opinion, Nielsen, and Arbitron media services.

Whereas Chapters 12 through 14 concentrate on mainframe GD systems, Chapter 15 discusses the emerging class of desktop systems, which permit a manager to integrate geodemographic data with sensitive internal data concerning site location, market share, competitor intelligence, dealer cooperation, and new products. Examples from Toro Company's successful application of desktop geodemography illustrate these applications.

The concluding chapter in Part III, Chapter 16, reviews European GD systems; U.S. companies interested in penetrating the post-1992 European common market can refer to this chapter to be well informed about the technical support available in Europe. Chapter 16 also outlines how to build double-tiered GD systems designed for a common rather than splintered European environment. These systems support both inter- and intracountry targeting and will link with pan-European broadcast and print media to provide unified strategy delivery tools for the continent.

A GD system's key ingredients—U.S. census data and cluster analysis—are discussed in separate appendixes to Chapter 12. Census data constitute a powerful business resource when supported by software from third-party vendors that take advantage of the TIGER system. Developed expressly for the 1990 census, TIGER supplies the raw ingredients for the application of multivariate statistical tools, such as cluster analysis, that put census data to work in microsegmentation.

The appendix to Chapter 15 reviews Lorenz curves and other measures of customer concentration, including the Gini index, used in geodemographic segmentation analyses. The discussion is reasonably nontechnical, although sufficient detail is supplied for comprehension, application, and computation.

PART IV: CHAPTERS 17–18

Part IV treats two advanced topics: micromerchandising systems and category management systems. Micromerchandising systems combine scanner data, geodemographic data, and trade area data to help resolve the manufacturer/retailer power struggle. Such systems operationalize the relationship philosophy advocated by several well-known marketing scholars, including Philip Kotler. Although the systems discussed here are intended for packaged-goods marketing, similar systems are expected to develop in a variety of industries where strict vertical integration is impossible but where channel members must cooperate to succeed.

Chapter 17 first reviews traditional merchandising systems and discusses their limitations. It defines the micromerchandising concept and outlines its benefits. The chapter then describes how to build a micromerchandising system and closes by reviewing two working systems and discussing empirical tests of their performance.

Although real-time feedback and control of the marketing mix have long been mentioned in academic circles, not until now has the juxtaposition of weekly scanner data, high-speed microcomputing, and developments in mathematical theory created an environment in which real-time control can be implemented. Chapter 18 discusses real-time control of the marketing mix and reviews applications of this powerful approach. The chapter concentrates on category management in packaged goods, where problems amenable to real-time control are particularly pressing.

SOURCES OF EXAMPLES

This book relies on information supplied by a number of commercial firms. To balance the treatment, I use proportional numbers of examples from various companies and resist explicit evaluations of competing products. In fact, available single-source and geodemographic systems differ on so many dimensions that a comprehensive evaluation could only be incomplete and misleading. All of the systems discussed in this book are supplied by firms with excellent reputations for quality, technical expertise, and client support. Readers interested in further detail are urged to contact industry representatives.

USES OF THE BOOK

The book is designed to serve three readership segments: practicing managers, their marketing science specialists, and university faculty. Standard advice would direct brand managers to the single-source chapters and retail managers to the sections on geodemography. However, I hope that simultaneous coverage of these two topics will encourage managers to consider creative mixtures of single-source and geodemographic concepts. For example, retailers may gain insight about how to combine single-source data with their own point-of-sale data. Packaged goods brand managers may appreciate how geodemographic segmentation can link diverse elements of overall corporate strategy.

Marketing science specialists supporting line management often find that their interactions with commercial data suppliers are clouded by sales content. Specialists will find that the conceptual, explanatory style of the book helps them separate "fatty" sales language from "leaner" descriptive content.

The book may also hasten the penetration of these technologies into other industries. Single-source systems were originally created to serve packaged goods marketers—for example, those selling non-durables—and geodemographic systems were created primarily to serve durable goods marketers. However, the POS data available for many durable products can now be linked to in-store and nonstore causal data to improve marketing programs for clothing, appliances, electronics, and sporting goods, among others. Managers in these industries can benefit from advances in data collection, data analysis, and reporting borrowed from the packaged goods industry. In return, packaged goods firms can borrow the best applications of geodemography to coordinate local area marketing programs that take advantage of nationwide economies of scale.

Finally, although the book is positioned for the trade, it may serve as a supplemental text or a source of examples for business-school courses in marketing technology, database marketing, direct marketing, business demography, and the design of decision support systems. Prepublication versions of the book have been used as the main text in separate courses on single-source and geodemographic systems and to supplement a more traditional MBA marketing research course. More generally, graduate level business students in marketing and information systems will find the book to be a valuable source of information.

David J. Curry
Forest Lake, Wisconsin
September 1992

Contents

THE NEW MARKETING
RESEARCH SYSTEMS

PART ONE

MARKETING RESEARCH SYSTEMS

1 THE NEW RESEARCH FOCUS

The purpose of business is to get and keep a customer.

Theodore Levitt, "The Globalization of Markets"

INTRODUCTION

New technology permeating all business institutions combined with imaginative application and surprisingly systematic corporate liaisons has borne a new species of marketing research. The new breed is more powerful and sophisticated than the old. It relies on observation, not intuition; it employs integrated research systems, not isolated projects; and it uses disaggregate data to place the individual consumer at the focal point of strategy.

The new research has emerged so rapidly that it represents a discontinuity in the evolutionary pattern rather than a natural extension of previous practices. The appearance of scanner data, cable television, and upstart direct marketing firms signaled this change. By 1983 even the popular press carried news of an electronic revolution in marketing research.[1] But revolutions had also been promised by the demographers, the motivation researchers, the physiologic specialists, and others with a novel measurement device or a new modeling

3

approach. Although useful, these ideas led only to profitable niches for a few specialist firms.

The fertile ground of technology has produced not simply a collection of novel research techniques but a more complicated organism that portends the death of traditional methods and the extinction of the institutions that teach and apply those methods. The ideas compiled in current research texts—the 10 steps in a research project; simple random sampling; mail, telephone, and personal interviewing; hypothesis testing; and regression analysis—are dinosaurs. They represent a project philosophy that no longer makes sense, they require expertise that is often irrelevant, and they focus on technical issues rather than business problems.

Nine fundamental shifts in the business climate are responsible for spawning the new order of research.[2] These shifts fall into three major categories. First, technology is returning the individual to the focus of marketing strategy. Technology permits the collection, storage, and use of disaggregate data in integrated databases, which has fostered a shift from macro to micro marketing. Second, technology supports, supplements, and in some cases supplants management decision making. Managers are able to access data collected via observation, not surveys; data stored in dynamic research systems, not static project reports; and data transformed into knowledge, not processed, dehydrated, and compressed into statistics. Finally, technology is reshaping business institutions globally, structurally, and permanently. Independent research firms are yielding to information conglomerates. Universities are no longer the source of research innovation and talent. Marketing research is identifying business opportunities, not simply reducing business risk.

In this chapter we discuss the first two of these shifts—mass to micro marketing and aggregated to disaggregated data—and the research innovations that support them. These two trends have one major idea in common: a focus on the individual consumer rather than on a market or markets. Markets, the focus of most economic study, are illusory. Markets do not make decisions, exhibit brand loyalty, or react to price changes; people do. All aggregate economic behavior begins at the level of two-party exchange: Someone sells, and someone buys. Intelligent marketing strategy is based on a sound "bottom-up" understanding of the players who carry out these exchanges.

THE SHIFT FROM MASS TO MICRO MARKETING

The first shift precipitating the demise of traditional research methods is a shift in the fundamental institutions and philosophy of the business world. The mass-marketing technique used with so much success by retail conglomerates such as Sears, JC Penney, and Safeway gave way to a more precise, sensitive philosophy referred to as micro marketing. Micro marketers found ways to locate smaller and smaller segments, down to the level of single individuals—segments whose profitability could be assured and whose reachability was enhanced by novel channels of distribution, promotional vehicles, and tailored messages made possible by technology that was unavailable only a decade before. Key indicators of this shift are shown in Table 1.1.

Mass Marketing

Mass marketing was epitomized by majority strategies, efforts by manufacturers to find the largest group of people with similar needs and buying habits who could be attracted to retail outlets by messages in the mass media and convinced to buy replicates of mass-produced items. Economies in production, media buying, and central warehousing drove this approach, which thrived on a "bigger is better" rationale. Mass marketers sought compromise in product design, channel selection, and sales message to reach and sell to a few demo- or geographic collectives.

The main problem with mass merchandising was captured succinctly by Rapp and Collins in their book *MaxiMarketing:* "Remember what Gertrude Stein said about California? 'There is no there there.'" [3] The labels "elderly consumer," "heavy user," "upscale suburbanite," "price-sensitive," and "loyal repeat buyer," although convenient and often clever, conveyed a false sense of unity to target segments that could be refined further. The surface was being scratched, but the substratum was richer and more diverse than the mass marketer could imagine.

By 1975 computerized, databased technology revealed the promise of addressing individual consumer needs and the unsettling consequences of ignoring them. The possibility of directing the advertising dollar to a specific buyer ended the days of shotgun strategies. Marketing could employ more cost-efficient, personal, and accountable techniques and could be guided not only by targeting, but also by predictions of behavior. And the efforts could be scored by an investment mentality that had no trouble with concepts such as lifetime value or relationships with individual human beings. Micro marketing returned the individual to the marketing equation. [4]

Research Innovations

Certain innovations in marketing research were at the foundation of this shift, and these and even more recent innovations are bubbling with potential. The key ideas include geodemographic and advanced list segmentation; customer databases, online databases, accessible databases, and real-time databases; electronic exchange operations such as cable shopping, kiosk shopping, and videotext catalogs; telemarketing and integrated offering systems;[5] specialized media such as direct mail, addressable taps, and cable networks; person-to-person marketing, business-to-business marketing, and marketing by linking in-store and nonstore efforts.

These innovations mean that marketing managers know about television viewing habits and shopping behavior on a household-by-household or person-by-person basis. They know each household's makeup, location, and demographic

TABLE 1.1. The Shift from Mass to Micro Marketing

Time Period	Era	Meaning and Methods	Symptoms
1950s–1960s	Mass marketing	The mass marketer sold replicates of the same product to everyone and employed mass merchandising, mass communications, mass media, and mass production.	Coca-Cola offered one kind of cola, Clairol sold hair dye, and Holiday Inn was the only motel chain. The Norman Rockwell family prevailed: mother, father, and 2.4 children. Sellers used majority strategies and compromised in product design, channel of distribution, and sales message.
1970s	Segmentation and line extension	The segmenter sought homogeneous subgroups that were reachable, measurable, and sizable and offered them variations on a product theme. Segmenter employed demographic, psychographic, and sociographic approaches; lifestyle, volume, and benefit segmentation.	Coca-Cola offered diet cola and Fresca. The family evolved: 54% of mothers worked, 53% of all households contained only one or two people, singles headed 24% of all households.
Early 1980s	Intensified niche marketing	The niche marketer sliced markets into smaller and smaller groups of consumers and satisfied the needs and wants of each group. The era of demassification, begun in the 1970s, clearly gathered momentum.	Colas became finely differentiated into diet, caffeine-free, caffeine-charged, and cherry. Nine Lives offered 23 kinds of cat food. Revlon made 157 shades of lipstick, 41 of them pink. Markets were deregulated, including utilities, banking, and the airlines.
Late 1980s and 1990s	Micro marketing	The micro marketer directs programs at census tracts, mail carrier routes, single households, or individuals and employs sophisticated technology, targeted lists, profiled media, and integrated databases.	GM's Saturn plant will allow each car to be designed by its owner. Brand loyalty declines; information blossoms. Network TV slips; cable TV grabs hold. Channels multiply; new products proliferate. Coupons, catalogs, and databases explode.

Source: The New Direction in Advertising and Marketing Strategy, Based on ideas from Stan Rapp and Thomas L. Collins, *Maxi Marketing,* New York: McGraw-Hill, 1987.

profile. They can experiment with split-cable messages or multitap messages. They can replace national commercials with ones tailored to meet the objectives of a single city, census tract, or ZIP+4 neighborhood, or they can use multiple catalogs positioned and assembled for the tastes of a particular census block group or even a single family. The new research means that marketers can learn precisely how many cents off on a coupon will do the job, what rebate will close the sale, or what interest rate will guarantee an investment switch. Micro-marketing research allows a marketer to direct promotion to consumers who have demonstrated adventurous buying habits or to target those who use a competitor's product. The marketer can decide between a heavier ad schedule and one with a wider variety of commercials.[6]

In summary, earlier visionaries were clearly correct in asserting that technology would finally allow business to transcend the economies of mass production and return to a preindustrial world where individual tastes and values matter.[7] Ironically, there are so many of us now that even our most idiosyncratic needs are shared, (see Table 1.2). Postmodern technology is capable of locating, sizing, and serving individuals via a vast micro-marketing machine that is beyond the view of most consumers. One capability of this machine is to keep records about each of us.

FROM DATA AGGREGATION TO DATA DISAGGREGATION

Marketing research data have habitually been stored in aggregate form due to the vestiges of a file-cabinet mentality and to unimaginative strategists who are fascinated by the whole market but intimidated by the parts behind the sum. Figure 1.1 illustrates a data aggregation system. The system gathers sales and customer profile data on a customer-by-customer basis from scanner checkouts at each store. Weekly totals are organized by store within a geographic territory. Quarterly reports for management aggregate the weekly entries across all stores within a specific territory.

In this case there are four distinct points at which the data are compressed: Individual customer information is compressed into a store total, daily store data are compressed into a weekly figure, weekly figures are added to form a quarterly summary, and information from individual stores is condensed to represent sales in a geographic territory. Data aggregation clumps together particular observational units, such as "customer," to form a vector or profile of information for a larger observational unit, such as "store." In the process, however, the system's ability to trace activity back to an individual customer is destroyed.

Until recently, destroying detail was a practical necessity because of storage and access limitations of computer systems. But this technological constraint gave rise to an abhorrent analysis philosophy: Total and summarize. Data stored in chunks reveal large-scale statistical regularities but treat market chaos as "white noise," as statistical perturbations unamenable to further study and unrevealing of further insight. Although the data reduction process can be extremely useful for extracting "macro regularities" from market activity, it precludes the possibility of analyzing small-scale differences, of viewing the data from different

TABLE 1.2.   Shared Traits Yield Cost-Effective Microsegments

New Movers	Over 50
Households that have recently moved to a new address Size: 3 million households annually (*Source*: Metromail)	Individuals more than 50 years of age, on lists typically compiled from census data; also known by other labels, such as *mature market* Size: 21 million households (*Source*: Metromail; Cadwell Davis Partners, New York)
F.L.Y.E.R.S.	**College Students**
Fun-loving youth en route to success with $200 billion in discretionary income to spend on records, blue jeans, junk food, and movie tickets Size: 41 million individuals, ages 13–25 (*Source*: Graham and Hamdan (1987); Flyers Consulting, Inc., Cambridge, MA)	Full-time college students who can be selected by class, school type, major, and other factors; typically compiled from student directories; apartment and dorm rooms are "minihouseholds" Size: 7.5–12.4 million individuals (*Source*: Metromail; Marketing and Financial Management Enterprises)
Newlyweds	**Foreign-Born Americans**
Couples who have recently married Size: 550,000 households (*Source*: Metromail)	U.S. citizens currently living in the United States but who were born elsewhere; subgroups include Hispanics, Eastern Europeans, Latin Americans, Asian Americans, and others Size: 14 million individuals (*Source*: Market Development Inc.; Claritas Corporation)

perspectives, and of verifying patterns between customers rather than between stores or territories. The principle behind the rationale, often implicit, for data aggregation is that any differences that exist at finer levels of detail can be ignored because they do not or cannot influence marketing strategy.

In contrast, disaggregated data are stored, analyzed, and interpreted at their finest level of detail—at the customer level, in this example. Systems that use disaggregate data adhere to the following principle: All macro-level phenomena such as sales, market share, and public opinion originate at the level of micro-activity, micro-function, and micro-action. Thus, for a full understanding of market forces, micro-level activities must be acknowledged and modeled in a system that links the behavior of a single person to a product's market

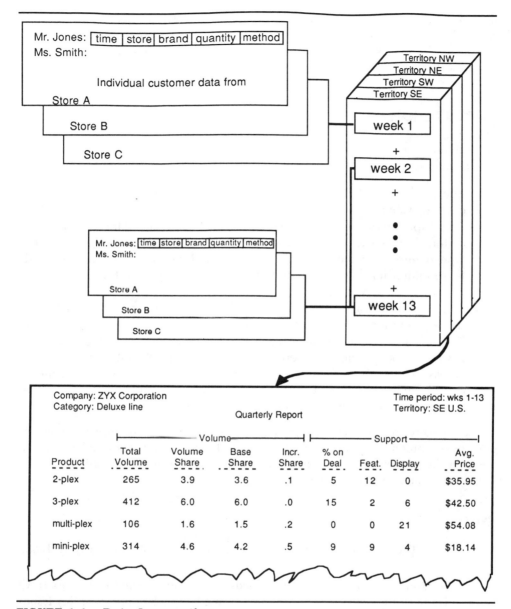

FIGURE 1.1. Data Aggregation

performance. The effects of action and strategy, designed to improve bottom-line performance measures such as market share, must be traceable to the individual or household.

To put this principle into practice requires data that are stored and analyzed at their finest level. In other words, more information is better. More information at greater levels of disaggregation allows information users to construct and reconstruct their own indices, baselines, and models. It allows strategists to resolve questions whose importance was not apparent when the project was started or when the system was put in place. Although summary reports should be issued regularly, the philosophy of storing disaggregate data is based on flexibility in response to market phenomena.

CONCLUSION

Several forces are responsible for the shift from aggregated to disaggregated data. These include:

- The availability of cheap, high-capacity data storage devices and megaprocessing systems.
- The displacement of manual data collection and manual data entry by automated devices such as laser scanners, hand-held scanners, voice-activated tape recorders, remote "people meters," audimeters, and other methods that monitor marketing activities at their source and speed their entry into an electronic system.
- The availability of increasingly sophisticated marketing models that assist managers in interpreting large quantities of data.
- The feasibility of implementing micro-level marketing strategies to take advantage of individual differences. Thus corporate strategists now have access to innovative distribution channels, sales techniques, pricing mechanisms, and promotional options that, contrary to their counterparts in earlier eras, do not foreclose ingenious marketing programs.

These forces represent important changes occurring at both the input and output ends of the pipeline linking customer activity to marketing strategy. They make possible the conceptualization and implementation of refined, flexible programs largely unimaginable prior to 1985.

Notes

1. See "The New Magicians of Marketing Research," *Fortune* 25 (July 1983), p. 73.

2. See John C. Webber, "Packaged Goods Marketing Research—Where's It All Going," Transcript Proceedings, Special Advertising Research Foundation Key Issues Workshop, New York (July 1986), pp. 34–40.

3. Stan Rapp and Thomas L. Collins, *Maximarketing: The New Direction in Advertising and Marketing Strategy*, New York: McGraw-Hill, 1987, p. 1.

4. See John Stevenson's book review of *MaxiMarketing: The New Direction in Promotion, Advertising, and Marketing Strategy* (January 1987), pp. 31–32; Leonard M. Lodish and David J. Reibstein, "Keeping Informed," *Harvard Business Review* (January–February 1986), pp. 168–182; and F. Robert Dwyer, "Customer Lifetime Valuation to Support Marketing Decision-Making," *Journal of Direct Marketing* 3(4) (Autumn 1989), pp. 8–15.

5. See Larry J. Rosenberg and Elizabeth C. Hirschman, "Retailing without Stores," *Harvard Business Review* 58 (4) (July–August 1980), pp. 103–112.

6. Stevenson, op. cit., p. 31.

7. For further details, see Alton F. Doody and William R. Davidson, "Next Revolution in Retailing (Thinking Ahead)," *Harvard Business Review* 45(3) (May–June 1967), p. 4; William R. Davidson and Alice Rodgers, "Nonstore Retailing: Its Importance to and Impact on Merchandise Suppliers," in *The Growth of Non-Store Retailing,* New York: New York University, Institute of Retail Management, 1979; and Rosenberg and Hirschman, op. cit.

2 THE NEW TECHNOLOGY

It was possible, Burton thought, to live in this world and only wonder about the how. But a complete human, one trying to realize all his potential, would also probe the why. This situation demanded the why and the how. Lacking the first, he could not function properly without the second.

Philip Jose Farmer, *Gods of Riverworld*

THE SHIFT FROM SEPARATED TO INTEGRATED DATABASES

Two interrelated phenomena are influencing the shift to integrated databases, one conceptual and the other technical. The technical force is the development of software that replaces a flat file or a data matrix with a data vault of virtually infinite volume. The basic principle is that a single data field on one record can serve as a link to a related field on a second record, even though the two come from different flat files based on completely different types of observation units.

For example, in Figure 2.1, the record for an individual contains an address field in addition to fields based on other information such as age, income, and marital status. Another file contains a wealth of information about census tracts, including the street addresses contained within each tract. Since the address field is common to both files, it can be used to relate individual addresses and census tracts—in either direction—thus telescoping the amount of information available for both types of observation units. For example, a direct marketer might want to locate all census tracts where the average age for married men is less than 42. Another goal might be to identify counties in which at least 60 percent of households consist of married couples. Because the television stations serving a given census tract are listed, the census tract data also can be linked with the information contained for each station, including its coverage area, programming format, and rate structure.

Relational databases allow the efficient storage and integration of information about a wide variety of observation units. The database can be entered from nearly any perspective, and as management issues expand, the information needed to address them can be tracked and brought to bear immediately.

Integrated Data Systems

Complementary databases in conjunction with a single relational database can be integrated into a marketing research system. Two cases are shown (Figure 2.2A

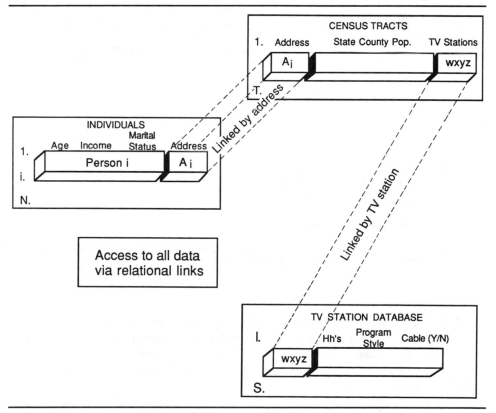

FIGURE 2.1.   A Relational Database

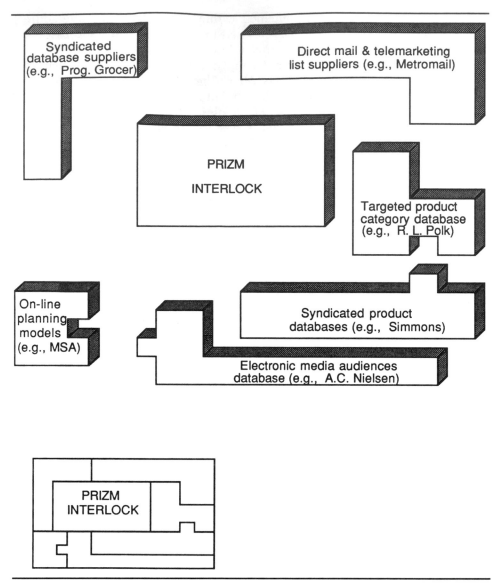

FIGURE 2.2A.   PRIZM: Geodemographic System

and 2.2B), one from a large-scale geodemographic system (PRIZM) used by direct marketers and a second from an integrated scanner-panel system (InfoScan).[1] Both cases show how a central concept, such as geodemographic market segmentation or scanner tracking, is supplemented by data needed for formulating overall business strategy.

For example, a direct marketer such as L.L. Bean wants to know which geodemographic segments can be projected as major responders, which lists contain the majority of such households, and to what magazines these households

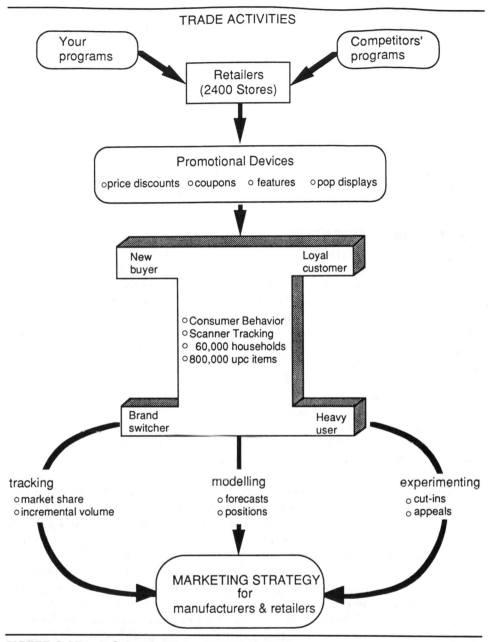

TRADE ACTIVITIES

Your programs

Competitors' programs

Retailers
(2400 Stores)

Promotional Devices

o price discounts   o coupons   o features   o pop displays

New buyer

Loyal customer

o Consumer Behavior
o Scanner Tracking
o 60,000 households
o 800,000 upc items

Brand switcher

Heavy user

tracking
o market share
o incremental volume

modelling
o forecasts
o positions

experimenting
o cut-ins
o appeals

MARKETING STRATEGY
for
manufacturers & retailers

FIGURE 2.2B.   InfoScan: Integrated Data System

subscribe. Therefore, PRIZM's geodemographic clusters of census block groups are supplemented by (1) list supplier databases from companies such as Metromail, (2) syndicated databases such as those from Simmons, and (3) electronic media databases such as those from A. C. Nielsen media services. Although these databases do not have a common owner, they form an ensemble—via contractual agreements—that interlocks them in a unified, problem-solving network.

The major packaged goods companies that purchase scanner data from Information Resources, Inc. and A. C. Nielsen desire to integrate store movement data, promotion tracking data, consumer purchase data, and television viewing data. The InfoScan system provides this integration via its access to 49 InfoScan markets (60,000 households in major metropolitan areas) linked to store-level data and to other tracking services. These data are accessible via a relational database keyed by UPC scanner code, week, product style, product type, category, or brand, according to metro market, region, or the total United States.

The best systems are able to take advantage of both the technical superiority of relational data structures and the conceptual flexibility of large-scale integration of diverse information reserves. This store of information must, however, be intelligently brought to bear on marketing problems.

FROM DATA PROCESSING
TO DECISION AIDING

The shift from data processing to decision aiding has been substantially influenced by technical developments and, more importantly, by increased management acceptance of decision support systems, expert systems, and artificial intelligence. Acceptance of these approaches may be the most crucial factor for a firm attempting to bridge the old and the new orders in marketing research.

The research function traditionally has been staffed with technical experts who assist managers by providing project results. The researcher's task was to collect data from primary or secondary sources and to submit computer output or summary reports to managers, who assumed responsibility for formulating strategy. Managers integrated and interpreted processed data, a task considered too complex and too broad to trust to machines or technical specialists.

As computer software became more sophisticated and hardware permitted plans to become reality, cleverly coded quantitative models began assisting the decision-making process. Although marketing information systems and decision support systems were the topic of texts 15 years ago, these systems are just now becoming standard management tools.

Decision support systems permit a manager to answer "what if" questions about sales, market share, product positioning, and trading areas. These scenarios are carried out in an interactive environment in which the computer provides structure while the manager provides intuition and creativity. In many cases, graphics are on call to aid this creative process. Standard reports suggest certain strategic questions and then assist the manager in finding and analyzing the data needed for answers.

Data from an integrated system—such as PRIZM or InfoScan—can be downloaded to a manager's personal computer to provide privacy, fast turnaround, and links to experience and past analyses not available on a company's mainframe.

According to management studies cited by the American Marketing Association's Task Force on Great Ideas, decision support systems increase an ex-

TABLE 2.1.   Metaphor and LESP

Metaphor Brand Management Applications	
Monitoring	Routine monitoring of shipments, distribution, featuring, and pricing
Troubleshooting	In-depth analysis of 75 causal relationships that may influence business performance
Brand management	Brand tracking to analyze top-line, trend, and performance reports
	Planning assistance for scheduling, forecasting, and budgeting
	Identifying competitive advantages

Dialog Systems Logistics Expert Systems Programs (LESP)	
Purpose	To increase productivity within the materials, production, and distribution functions
Features	An interactive knowledge base, automatic question generation, question and answer interaction, automatic answer generation, plus rational capabilities that allow consideration of uncertainty
Applications	Sales and market audits, packaging, customer service programs, vehicle routing and scheduling, inventory planning and control

ecutive's productivity from about 5 to 20 percent and influence the quality of decisions in ways that cannot be quantified.[2] The Metaphor Decision Support System and Dialog System's expert systems (the LESP package), shown in Table 2.1, help managers to identify and capitalize on sometimes hidden opportunities. They assist in allocating scarce corporate resources to the various elements of the marketing mix. Top management is relieved of the arduous task of collecting data and organizing them for decision-making purposes.

Such systems are beginning to incorporate artificial intelligence. An AI system is accessible to everyone in an organization, speeds training, and accelerates knowledge transfer. Artificial intelligence captures and codifies specialized human knowledge and makes it available to others.[3]

The subfield of artificial intelligence known as knowledge engineering appears to have the most potential. A knowledge or expert system is a computer program that uses data and inference to solve problems that usually require significant human expertise. The knowledge in the system consists of data, facts, and heuristics. Data are numbers, codes, or other bits of information from public or private sources. A system's facts are verifiable statements that are usually based on a consensus among knowledgeable experts in the field. A system's decision heuristics are rules of good judgment or good guessing that characterize the decision making of those individuals considered to be most qualified.[4] These systems provide a way of codifying both the results and the reasoning from past research.

Although comprehensive applications of knowledge engineering began to appear in the 1980s, the field holds promise for a variety of standard marketing problems that now rely on conventional research and often uninformed or inconsistent human judgment for their resolution. These problems include selecting optimal retail product assortments, finding profitable product positions, determining short-run pricing policy, and choosing appropriate advertising vehicles, among others. For example, the LESP package solves a broad range of materials, production, and distribution problems, such as vehicle routing and scheduling, freight rate negotiation, customer service evaluation, and product packaging. Like other knowledge systems, LESP interrogates its user in English-language sentences in an effort to learn what the user knows about a specific problem. The system can offer recommendations based on incomplete or uncertain knowledge and can explain the reasoning behind its questions and recommendations.

The rules that an expert system employs can be easily changed or deleted, and new rules as well as more facts can be routinely added. The flexibility of knowledge systems to change and learn, their capability to command volumes of facts, and their systematic integration of all the evidence bearing on a particular problem result in superior decision-making capabilities.

FROM AD HOC STUDIES
TO MARKETING RESEARCH SYSTEMS

Ad Hoc Marketing Research

An ad hoc study is designed to solve a particular problem or to address a single major issue that might consist of several related subissues. This is marketing research in its paradigmatic form. Beginning researchers tend to think of research as one or several ad hoc studies, and this is also the way that many executives think about the research function. The key components of this view are:

- The role of marketing management is to solve a series of independent, isolated problems.
- The research function is therefore time-discrete. A project starts, is executed, and ends.
- The data necessary to solve one problem are separable from (or are more useful if separated from) the data needed to solve another problem.
- Different managers have different responsibilities and hence must use different approaches and different information to solve problems.
- Marketing as a business function should be separated from finance and manufacturing.

The ad hoc view thus builds walls around those engaged in marketing research. Perhaps more disastrously, research is wrapped in a cloak of mathematical-statistical-computer expertise that is inaccessible to managers, who must make the decisions.

Research Systems

A research system is not only integrative and encompassing; it is also flexible and open, permitting access to those who have neither the skills, time, nor inclination to become engrossed in technical detail but are responsible for directing the course of a business. A research system has the following characteristics:

- *A research system's planning horizon is infinite.* A system is built and remains built and operable thereafter.
- *A system evolves.* Once the system is built, its capabilities, tasks, and objectives are periodically reviewed to allow the system to adapt to the changing needs of the business function. Thus what may start as a marketing information system can become a decision support system and, eventually, part of a larger, integrated system linking marketing, manufacturing, and finance.
- *A system is flexible.* An ad hoc project obtains data from one or a limited number of sources for a fixed period of time. A system obtains data in real or near-real time, from certain standard secondary sources as well as from a variety of primary sources.
- *A research system promotes common, fundamentally sound approaches to decision making because it contains decision models, data-processing models, and strategic support models that can be applied to a wide variety of business problems.* An ad hoc approach commonly rests on a single methodology, such as conjoint analysis, nonmetric multidimensional scaling, or logit analysis. This inflexible tie to a particular method prevents a thorough understanding and review of the information contained in the data.
- *A research system promotes a holistic approach rather than a functional approach to solving business problems.* Marketing, manufacturing, and finance are linked by access to common databases, common objectives, and increasingly common standards of performance.
- *A research system resides in the enterprise.* Ad hoc projects are often commissioned from outside firms. The most important implications and results can be lost because the data used to create a consulting report and other vital elements reside with the consulting firm rather than with the client. Accumulated data, experience, and insights about a project and, equally important, insights about the process of conducting research remain outside of and inaccessible to the business firm that needs them. Knowledge transfer is blocked. A research system does not preclude the use of outside consultants, but it provides a place to keep disaggregate data (for later review and reuse if necessary) and provides a common store of accumulated experience.

The time-honored reasons for commissioning periodic research projects have lost their meaning. Equipment prices, service, and support have improved to the point where any firm can afford to have in-house computer services. The assortment of hardware and the greatly expanded availability of software eliminates the financial and technical necessity of hiring an external service.

There remains a distinction in skills, available time, and primary orientation between the line manager and research experts. Lodish and Reibstein suggest that technical requirements have increased to the point where a management scientist must be on call to assist the line manager in executing marketing strategy.[5] However, line managers should play an integral role in the development, maintenance, and evolution of a research system, even if technical problems are solved by management science experts. In contrast to the project philosophy, these experts should not ride to the rescue, slay the dreaded lack-of-data dragon, and depart in glory. They should be considered part of the system, whether their paycheck is printed inside or outside the firm.

Finally, although commissioned research seems to hold the promise of fresh insight, primary data collection is characterized by high costs, long delays, and disappointing results due to a failure to clearly visualize the decision process and its requirements. (Andreasen's "backward marketing research" approach, which starts where the process usually ends—with action and implementation—and then works backward to a project's beginning, can help to avoid this disappointment.[6]) Many aspects of the problem-solving process may no longer lie in the domain of commissioned research. Several years of experience with ad hoc projects usually reveals a core set of strategy issues, information, and modeling requirements. The idea of a research system is to capture this core, to permanently trap those actionable elements that seem to disappear when a project is over but that should remain in a firm's collective memory.

FROM SURVEYS TO OBSERVATION

Traditional data collection used written questionnaires, personal interviews, and other techniques that concentrated on what people thought, believed, or talked about. Now observational methods concentrate on what people do—what products they buy, what television programs they watch, and what they say (not what they say they say).

The development of unobtrusive, miniaturized, and accurate data collection devices has changed the rules. Unobtrusive devices such as scanner checkout systems, people meters, and system monitors record who, what, when, and for how long. Unobtrusiveness has been aided by better engineering, miniaturization (allowing precise measurement of difficult-to-measure processes), and accurate monitoring from a distance of people, places, and activities. For example, improved telemetric devices record eye movements, brain wave patterns, and physiological functions more accurately and in more realistic settings than ever before. A hospital beeper system finds doctors, registers their movements, and serves as a remote data collection terminal that records patient diagnoses. A television connected via cable becomes an order center and, therefore, a data collection device detailing who orders what and when.

Certain developments in data collection vividly illustrate the shift from surveys to observation—what is available now and what the future holds. Marketing research has long been the prognosticator for management decision, but management has been forced to use a relatively dirty crystal ball. The new technologies are cleaning the crystal's surface so that management can see farther, with more clarity, and sometimes in full color. Improved vision (for example, more data) places added stress on management to make full use of what is known. We return to this theme later in the book to provide as much guidance as possible.

Changes Affecting Traditional Methods

Telephone interviewing, personal interviews, and mail surveys have been dramatically affected by the shift to high technology. Telephone interviewing is now conducted by computer-assisted software that dials automatically, records a call's status, and checks for quota fulfillment. These systems automatically schedule callbacks and display questions on screen to an interviewer-operator, who keys responses and is aided by automatic branching, skipping, and prompting protocols that depend, sometimes in complicated ways, on preceding response patterns. Question foils are automatically rolled over to protect against order bias and to guarantee correct data entry. These systems download each interview to a central file without human intervention; files can be processed to provide top-line results (percentage response patterns per foil) in real time, or they can output more sophisticated analyses in a matter of hours.

Face-to-face interviewing has been replaced by several types of self-interviewing in electronic centers situated in strategic locations. In these centers CRT stations are programmed to hail passersby in digitized voices that invite cooperation. A touch-sensitive screen displays questions that can be programmed in a variety of foreign languages. Extra-large letters on a color display encourage useful responses. For example, systems collect ZIP code information from a respondent via a numerical keypad. The ZIP code information is linked by a relational database to census tract or ZIP+4 data, to electronic media data, and to other databases in an integrated system to provide complete and actionable results.

Laser disc technology is available for questions regarding product, store, restaurant or menu design, or packaging research, or for testing a large number of visual options. For example, Maritz's Interactive Videodisc Interviewing System, MIVIS, consists of four basic elements: a videodisc player that accesses and displays information, a microcomputer that interfaces with the videodisc system, a touch-sensitive screen used as the respondent's input device, and special software to control system operation.[7] The system can access up to 54,000 individual pictures or, equivalently, two hours of continuous programming. The laser disc approach also generates clean output requiring neither data entry nor editing. In addition, it provides complex skip and branching patterns that allow much more detailed responses than are possible with competing techniques. Like most other electronic survey systems, MIVIS also keeps track of quotas, ensuring that sample requirements are met. Finally, MIVIS results can be interlocked with those captured in other systems.

Mail surveys that elicit responses to closed-end questions can be read by optical scanning machines and can be delivered to potential respondents in novel places and in novel ways. Magazine inserts and warranty cards are examples, but more innovative is Trade-Off Research's use of Sawtooth's Ci2 and Adaptive Conjoint Analysis systems, which deliver a computer disc questionnaire to would-be respondents.[8] A respondent simply places the disc in an IBM-compatible microcomputer and keys in responses. Completed discs are then mailed back to Trade-Off Research. This method permits administration of very complicated surveys, shifts the task of data entry to respondents, and typically achieves a response rate of 50 percent or higher.[9]

Unobtrusive Data Collection

Some recent developments are interesting as much for their implications as for their current application. For example, Lee Weinblatt of the Pretesting Company in Englewood, New Jersey, has designed a wristwatch that is activated when it is within 9 inches of a microchip embedded in a magazine page. The "watch" stops when moved further away. The device's memory can be programmed to delete "reading sessions" lasting less than a minute (or some other browsing cutoff), and the information can be downloaded at the end of a test period using an electronic decoding device.[10] Mr. Weinblatt suggests that the device could be distributed to respondents unaware of its dual function who could be chosen to fulfill certain demographic, geographic, or lifestyle quotas. The resulting readership information would be more accurate than that available with conventional techniques, such as Starch Reports, and would not be subject to a variety of social or awareness biases.

Another example of an unobtrusive remote monitoring technique is the use of satellite receiving capabilities to record the signals from third-party processors of advertising messages (for example, radio, television, cable). This system uses pattern recognition technology on a real-time basis to record which ads run on these media. The system's contents can then be linked via an integrated system to ratings data, ad content data, and consumer purchase data to provide a precise and complete picture of what specific communities see and do with regard to products advertised electronically. One such system, offered by Broadcast Advertisers Reports (BAR), Inc. of New York, currently monitors signals in Philadelphia, Chicago, New York, and Los Angeles and plans to expand to 16 full-time markets by the mid-1990s.

Whether or not the enormous volume of information that can be collected with observational devices will prove useful for strategic decisions depends on other trends, especially the availability of large-scale integrated decision support and expert systems. At present our ability to collect data has outstripped our ability to use data intelligently. The most pressing needs in the near future are for intelligent processing, assimilation, and modeling of these data and for their systematic use in organized research systems.

Notes

1. PRIZM and other geodemographic systems are described in detail in Chapters 12–16. InfoScan and other single-source systems are described in detail in Chapters 6–11.

2. See *Marketing News* 20(11) (May 23, 1986), pp. 1, 16.

3. See Henry Winston, *Artificial Intelligence*, 2d ed., Reading, MA: Addison-Wesley, 1984.

4. See Paul Harmon and David King, *Expert Systems,* New York: John Wiley & Sons, 1985, p. 5.

5. Leonard M. Lodish and David J. Reibstein, "Keeping Informed," *Harvard Business Review* No. 1 (January–February 1986), pp. 168–181.

6. See Alan R. Andreasen, "Backward Market Research," *Harvard Business Review* (May–June 1985), pp. 176–182.

7. See *Marketing News* (February 13, 1987), p. 17.

8. See Harrison Goldstein, "Computer Surveys by Mail," in Carol Potera, ed., *Sawtooth Software Conference on Perceptual Mapping, Conjoint Analysis, and Computer Interviewing,* Encino, CA: Trade-Off Research July 20, 1987, pp. 55–59.

9. Ibid., p. 59.

10. See *Marketing News* 20(8) (April 11, 1986), p. 1.

3 INFORMATION CONGLOMERATES

INTRODUCTION

Chapters 1 and 2 reviewed six shifts in marketing research that can be traced either directly or indirectly to improved technology. For example, the shift from mass marketing to micro marketing depended on improvements in mainframe mass-storage devices and data retrieval time, which enabled efficient access to large databases. The shift from data aggregation to data disaggregation was supported by the development of UPC scanners and distributed computer networks. This chapter concentrates on a shift driven more by competitive forces than by technology: the shift from independent research firms to information conglomerates, a shift that has undermined the role of universities as industry's primary source of marketing science specialists.

Information conglomerates have become a major force in modern marketing practice because they can satisfy all of a client's information needs. These giants develop large, specialized databases and then integrate the databases in an information network that can focus on any aspect of a client's business problem. The resulting networks are intricate report production machines that require huge investments in electronic technology and operators with specialized skills.

This chapter presents examples of information conglomerates from both the single-source and the geodemographic industries. For single-source firms, we summarize the growth and development phases of A. C. Nielsen and Information Resources, Inc., the undisputed leaders in this field. In terms of geodemography, we discuss the Dutch firm VNU, which owns Claritas Corporation (PRIZM), and the Equifax Corporation, owner of National Decision Systems (MicroVision). These examples illustrate how information conglomerates form, and they provide important background for later descriptions of single-source and geodemographic research systems.

The second major section of the chapter focuses on how the demise of smaller research firms has dramatically altered the relationship between the academic community and industry. This section discusses the widening gap between the skills acquired in most academic institutions and those needed to perform successfully in today's high-tech environment. The discussion provides a basis for more precise arguments in Chapter 5 about deficiencies of certain classroom research approaches.

THE SHIFT FROM INDEPENDENT RESEARCH FIRMS TO INFORMATION CONGLOMERATES

The Single-Source Industry

Despite its youth—the first single-source system was officially launched in 1986—the single-source industry has already gone through a major acquisition phase.[1] Figure 3.1 shows the takeover patterns of A. C. Nielsen and IRI before 1987, when Dun and Bradstreet (already the owner of A. C. Nielsen) nearly acquired IRI. These two firms were involved in eight mergers, joint ventures, buyouts, or acquisitions between 1984 and 1988. For example, in November 1986 Nielsen purchased the Majers Corporation, a specialist in evaluating promotions that influence retail sales. Just two years earlier, Majers had acquired TRIM, a 10-year-old company that supplied electronic point-of-sale data collected from 750 stores in 32 states. In 1987 Nielsen also formed a joint venture with National Panel Diary to combat IRI's InfoScan, launched the year before.[2]

Information Resources began its own acquisition phase in June 1985, when it bought Management Decision Systems, Inc., a privately held consulting firm specializing in custom software for product and marketing management. IRI continued to supplement its integrated scanning and testing services with companies specializing in complementary products and skills: Marketing Advancements, Inc. and Keystrokes, Inc., for coupon fulfillment; ABA Groups, Inc. and Data Group, Inc., which offered specialized computer services such as APOLLO for the retail trade.

Although both Nielsen and IRI are dominant firms in the marketing research industry, their gross revenues are far less than those of true information conglomerates, whose economic domain typically encompasses many such firms in several industries. As Figure 3.1 shows, the Dun & Bradstreet information conglomerate owns Donnelly Information Publishing, Moody's, and several other information firms serving a variety of industries. Thus, even without the addition of IRI, Dun & Bradstreet is today the focal point for a substantial concentration of information power.

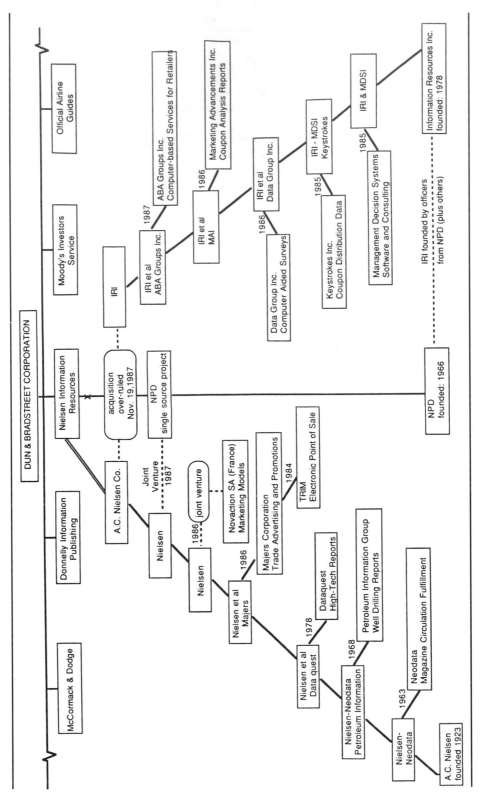

FIGURE 3.1. Information Conglomerates

26

The Geodemographic Industry

Smaller firms supplying geodemographic data are also being swept up by information conglomerates, some of them foreign-owned. Two examples illustrate this trend.

Claritas, which supplies geodemographic data through its PRIZM system, was purchased in 1985 by Verenigde Nederlandse Uitgeversbedrijven (United Dutch Publishing Companies). As Figure 3.2 shows, Claritas is just one of many U.S. acquisitions by VNU, an international power in publishing and information services.[3] The others include respected U.S. marketing research firms such as Birch Radio, Scarborough Associates, and Market Metrics. The company's U.S. affiliates combined with its global power make VNU a formidable worldwide competitor.

As a second example, consider the Equifax Corporation, one of Dun & Bradstreet's direct competitors in a variety of industries—including geodemography, where D&B owns Donnelly (ClusterPLUS). In July 1988, Equifax acquired National Decision Systems, whose sales were then approximately $18 million. Although this acquisition rounded out Equifax's Marketing Services Division and positioned the company as a leader in geodemography (for example, NDS sells MicroVision in a mainframe version and via its desktop system called INFOMARK), it was only one of 24 acquisitions made by Equifax in the years 1988 to 1990. During this same period, Equifax's corporate returns from operations rose from $894 million in 1988 to over $1 billion in 1990. These impressive figures justify Equifax's self-description as "the information source" and indicate that the company is fulfilling its corporate mission "of turning information into income through the process of value-added automation."[4]

Lessons for Marketing Research Practice

What can we learn from this recent history about the practice of marketing research and the marketing research industry? First, although technology and large investments are needed to buy into the industry, these two elements alone are insufficient for success. Firms must have intimate knowledge of clients' marketing information needs, in addition to the specialized software that can create and deliver reports to fulfill these needs. For example, IRI's initial investment in BehaviorScan in 1978 was more than $6 million for checkout facilities, television cut-in devices, computer hardware, and other equipment needed to collect and process data and to control advertising experiments for its BehaviorScan clients.[5] Even though this investment was substantial, it would not have been sufficient had IRI not evolved from a supplier of diary panel data. Due to its link with NPD (three of IRI's founders—Gerald Eskin, John Malec, and William Walters—had been employed by NPD), IRI had substantive expertise in coding, entering, and analyzing panel data. It could therefore concentrate its investment in data-capturing devices and signal transmission networks rather than in hiring key personnel, writing custom software, or developing sophisticated models.

The longer-term effects of the growth of information conglomerates are unclear. However, in the packaged goods industry, the retail pharmaceutical industry, and many other industries, it appears that these giants may replace local,

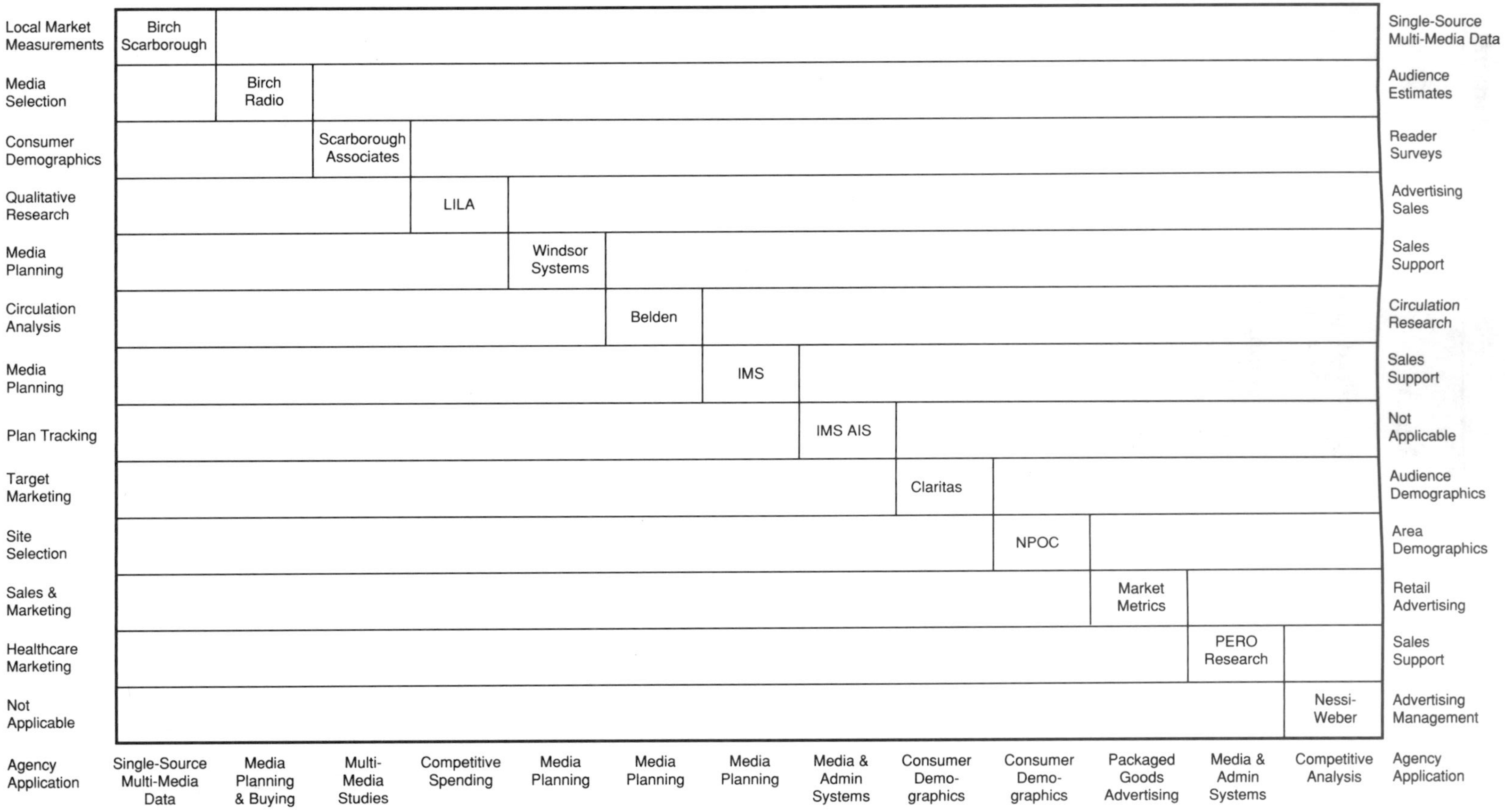

FIGURE 3.2. VNU's Presence in the U.S. Research Industry

Source: VNU brochure

The figure is a matrix relating VNU's business units (companies) to agency applications and market functions. The diagonal entries are:

Agency Application (left axis)	Company	Market Segment (bottom axis)	Function (right axis)
Local Market Measurements	Birch Scarborough	Single-Source Multi-Media Data	Single-Source Multi-Media Data
Media Selection	Birch Radio	Media Planning & Buying	Audience Estimates
Consumer Demographics	Scarborough Associates	Multi-Media Studies	Reader Surveys
Qualitative Research	LILA	Competitive Spending	Advertising Sales
Media Planning	Windsor Systems	Media Planning	Sales Support
Circulation Analysis	Belden	Media Planning	Circulation Research
Media Planning	IMS	Media Planning	Sales Support
Plan Tracking	IMS AIS	Media & Admin Systems	Not Applicable
Target Marketing	Claritas	Consumer Demographics	Audience Demographics
Site Selection	NPOC	Consumer Demographics	Area Demographics
Sales & Marketing	Market Metrics	Packaged Goods Advertising	Retail Advertising
Healthcare Marketing	PERO Research	Media & Admin Systems	Sales Support
Not Applicable	Nessi-Weber	Competitive Analysis	Advertising Management
Agency Application		Agency Application	Agency Application

independent marketing research firms and in-house research departments. Because of advancements in data-capturing techniques, the growth of information conglomerates will also affect industrial, governmental, and international marketing research. ELCAP, Elrick and Lavidge's "single-source" service for durable products, is a good example, since Elrick and Lavidge is also owned by Equifax.

Whether or not smaller, innovative companies can continue to compete is a matter of concern. The market power of the giants often places them in a favored position with consumers of marketing research, even in areas where the services or skills of large firms may be inferior to those of a smaller, local company.

Two trends appear to counter the dominance of conglomerates: Retailers are increasingly using their own point-of-sale (POS) data, and more high-tech firms, such as efficient market services, are specializing in refined analysis and applications of single-source and geodemographic data. Each of these topics is pursued in more depth in later sections of the book. In regard to the first trend, note that local databases available from a retailer's POS transactions are insufficient for many business decisions, since causal data are absent and supply-side biases abound. In regard to the second trend, successful niche firms are not necessarily a countertrend to the formation of information conglomerates, since small firms are likely to be acquired once they demonstrate some success and a growing client list.

Next we examine another noteworthy effect of the growth of the information conglomerate: unlike smaller, independent research firms, conglomerates are depending less and less on universities as a source of skilled employees. This issue is of special interest to the academic institutions that train marketing research students, to those seeking employment in research, and to the firms that must hire research expertise.

FROM UNIVERSITIES TO SUPPLIERS AS THE SOURCE OF INNOVATION AND TALENT

The growth of the information conglomerate has immediate relevance for students and teachers of marketing research: We are out of date and out of touch. The academic community is teaching outmoded concepts; it is using conservative analysis techniques and relatively ineffective and often irrelevant models. It is being left in the dust of the new-age pioneers, who have achieved a level of competence far exceeding that offered in the typical classroom. Worse yet, many members of the academic community are unaware of the increasing skills gap between their students and industry requirements. As a result, the source of talent for the largest marketing research firms is other firms in the research industry.

The field has shaken out into a few identifiable kinds of skills, all of which require hands-on experience with the large, technically sophisticated systems mentioned earlier. These skills include real-time programming and database programming; statistical modeling, performed primarily by very experienced specialists with Ph.D.s in statistics, psychology, physics, and sometimes business; technical product development, carried out by teams of specialists; and client contact, accomplished by individuals who have superior communication and presentation skills.

The message for our educational approach is disconcerting at best. A strong foundation in probability theory and statistical inference, the focus of most research textbooks, is important for developing certain modes of problem solving, thinking, and logical analysis. However, a strong statistical background is far from synonymous with competence in today's marketing research systems. Teaching about large-scale integrated systems requires equipment that schools cannot afford. Without such equipment, foundation concepts that are "classroom-testable" are less and less relevant; skills are implemented in practice at such a high level of technological sophistication that their connection to the material discussed in the classroom is tangential at best. At worst, classroom discussions can be devoid of practical merit; key points often go unnoticed due to lack of hands-on reinforcement. Finally, the practical relevance of standard skills is declining:

- *The theory of simple random sampling.* Commercial systems do not use simple random samples and often lack any standard sampling frame. Instead, specialists develop a very large sample that accurately profiles the population of interest, usually the total United States, as well as smaller geographic areas such as metro-markets. Clients demand the understandability and deterministic qualities offered by matching. They are not particularly interested in confidence bounds or maximum-likelihood estimates, concepts traditionally taught in business school classrooms.

- *The very idea of sampling.* Sampling is being replaced in many cases by a complete census. For example, Claritas Corporation and CACI, Inc.– Federal offer products that use all observation units of a particular type from the U.S. census (all census block groups or all counties, for example). Similarly, although a single-source store panel uses a sample of scanner-equipped stores, it includes all data at the transaction level within each store. There is no sampling of customers or shelf-keeping units; all observations from these two universes are included. The old arguments that censuses cost more and contain destructive nonsampling errors are often invalid.

- *The concept of the research project.* Research designs, sampling frames, and lists of research steps are too strongly associated with a project orientation to marketing research rather than a systems orientation. A sample is a cross section of a process that can now, in many cases, be monitored in real-time. Because the objects of inquiry (consumers, stores, products, prices, and promotions) are dynamic, the research process and analytical frameworks must be equally dynamic.

- *Simplified decision models.* The multilayered decision support models used in practice bear little resemblance to the kinds of statistical models that can be taught in the classroom. Complex models such as SCAN*Pro, ASSESSOR, PROMOTER, and CoverStory[6] could each have an entire course devoted to their construction and theory; the focus in the classroom therefore shifts to their use instead. However, the academic community is trapped in a catch-22, knowing full well that the appropriate use of such models depends on an understanding of their logic and structure.

In the major research firms, specialists constantly use integrated databases and sophisticated models, learning their value, logic, and approach as much by experience as by conceptual assimilation or rational progression. The new breed of researcher, trained on the job, is street-smart, responsive, and intuitive in a way that the classroom product cannot equal.

CONCLUSION

This chapter has explored two interrelated shifts affecting marketing research practice: the shift from smaller, independent research firms to information conglomerates, and the shift from academia to industry as the main supplier of marketing research expertise.

To successfully build and operate the various databases and analytic models that characterize single-source and geodemographic firms requires specialized knowledge. Few U.S. universities train graduate students to fill these specialized roles. The argument of this chapter is that important conceptual debates are resolved by Ph.D. specialists when a system is built, not by system "operators" when the system is used. These particular points, which are likely to elicit strong counterarguments from the academic community, are explored in more detail in Chapter 5.

Finally, the brief discussion here of how these two shifts may affect marketing research practice foreshadows more detailed discussions that will appear throughout the book. Readers should find that the arguments made in this chapter will assume deeper meaning in relation to Parts II (on single-source systems) and III (on geodemographic systems). In addition to analyzing these problems, later sections of the book also provide actionable guidelines to help narrow the widening gap between marketing theory and industry practice in the specialized field of marketing technology.

Notes

1. The industry has subsequently gone through a major shakeout phase. Briefly, in late 1987 two competitive groups could be identified among firms supplying scanner panel data: those linking scanner data with TV cut-ins (such as BehaviorScan, ERIM, and AdTel) and those linking scanner data with a nationwide network of retail outlets and media services, but without TV cut-in capabilities (such as InfoScan, NABSCAN, SCANTRACK, and SAMSCAN). However, NABSCAN and ERIM were subsequently dismantled, and AdTel's TV cut-in service was subsumed by SAMI's SAMSCAN service. SAMSCAN was scheduled for nationwide expansion following the Arbitron Corporation's acquisition of SAMI, but due to competitive pressures, this liaison failed, and all SAMSCAN contracts were terminated in October 1990. See *Marketing News* 21(18)(August 28, 1987), p. 1.

2. NPD was an outgrowth of the Home Testing Institute, founded in 1951 by Henry Brenner, a pioneer of modern research practices. For further historical perspectives on these and other developments in the single-source industry, see the appendix to Chapter 6.

3. VNU is the largest publisher by far in the Netherlands and ranks among the top 10 in Europe. VNU companies publish 60 consumer magazines—roughly half of them in the Dutch language—and more than 70 professional and technical magazines, as well as 7 regional newspapers. (*Source*: Company documentation, VNU Business Information Services, 1990.)

4. The facts and figures for this paragraph were drawn from the following sources: *Equifax: 1990 Annual Report* (pp. 4, 7); a Shearson Lehman Hutton report entitled *Equifax* (November 1, 1988, pp. 10, 16); and a report published by First Boston Bank entitled *Equifax, Inc.* (December 28, 1989, p. 4).

5. IRI's subsequent investment to develop InfoScan is rumored to be on the order of $40 million, exceedingly high relative to traditional standards in the field of marketing research.

6. SCAN*Pro is the on-line report access system used with A. C. Nielsen's SCANTRACK service. ASSESSOR, PROMOTER, and CoverStory are registered trademarks of Information Resources, Incorporated.

4 THE STRATEGIC ROLE OF RESEARCH

THE SHIFT FROM RISK REDEMPTION TO OPPORTUNITY IDENTIFICATION

The purpose of business is to get and keep a customer.[1] The purpose of marketing research is to accumulate, assimilate, and transform customer knowledge into business strategy. This revised definition suggests a variety of new marketing research functions, many of which will be identified in later chapters, such as baselining, tracking, classifying, forecasting, and evaluating. The principal function of marketing research, however, is to deliver timely information to managers so that they can issue strategic instructions. This apparently simple idea, that management's job is to issue instructions, permits the linkage of marketing research to a general model of marketing management. The model clarifies exactly how marketing research supports management decision making in a modern business enterprise, and it offers a variety of new perspectives that enable research systems to be designed.

Two levels of management—middle and strategic—use research in different ways. Later arguments (see the Appendix to Chapter 8 and Chapter 18) will demonstrate that middle management is part of a cybernetic control loop whose primary function is to keep a firm on the course heading established by strategic management. Middle managers use research to assess whether the firm is deviating from this established course.

In their role as controllers, middle managers (brand or product managers in a packaged goods firm, for example) issue instructions to various support teams, who then translate these instructions into executable programs. To assist in control, a marketing research system must supply nearly continuous feedback about relevant process variables, such as sales and market share. Thus the baselining, tracking, and reporting functions of research are of keen importance at this level.

Strategic management sets the objectives for a firm and, in so doing, seeks opportunities. Marketing research systems support this function by monitoring both the competitive environment and the consumptive environment (past, present, and potential customers). The system indicates when and where certain weaknesses among competitors may appear, and where and when certain market opportunities may emerge.

OPPORTUNITIES IN DIRECT MARKETING: IN-STORE AND NONSTORE SALES

An instructive illustration of the use of marketing research to identify opportunities is provided by the in-store–nonstore synergy found in direct marketing. For example, direct marketing firms such as The Sharper Image and Banana Republic have followed impressive catalog sales by opening chains of retail stores. And there is a flip side, cases where traditional retail stores such as Laura Ashley and Bloomingdale's have expanded into direct marketing and catalog-generated businesses.

Although these two paths to success were created via imagination and hard work, at their core is a new form of marketing research, one that identifies opportunities rather than simply reducing risk. The driving force behind each of the in-store/nonstore success stories is the accumulation of information about current customers and prospects via a research system that monitors client behavior and client needs. This new role for marketing research is illustrated in Figure 4.1. The key steps are accumulating a customer database, creating a prospect mailing list, and searching the customer database. Each of these steps represents an important juncture in the development of sales through opportunity identification.

The Bloomingdale's Example: In-Store First

How does this approach work? Take Bloomingdale's, in the left path in Figure 4.1. Prior to 1978, Bloomingdale's was dominated by an in-store sales mentality based on decades of traditional retailing habits and practices. Due to a variety of factors,[2] the chain's retail sales began falling. Clearly, some sales were being taken by direct marketers. At that point the company had a choice between entrenching itself further in the shrinking pie segment of in-store sales or seizing the opportunities that were attracting the catalog users.

A major asset of a store such as Bloomingdale's is that, due to their long history, they have accumulated an extensive set of customer names, addresses, and, if their records have been well kept, buying patterns. These records serve two fundamental purposes. First, they provide a potential direct sales or catalog customer base of former clients, who clearly want what the chain has to offer but who live too far from a store to shop there regularly. This customer base, for example, identifies midwestern families who shop at Bloomingdale's during trips to New York but who are unable to return on a regular basis.

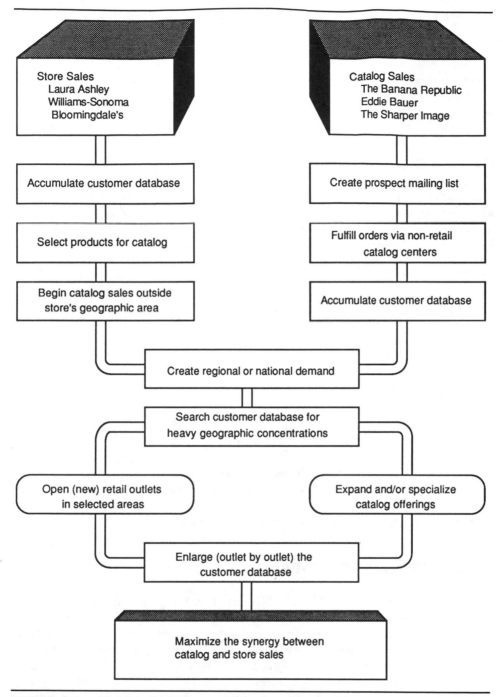

FIGURE 4.1.   Linking In-Store and Nonstore Marketing

Second, the store's customer database can be analyzed to determine the geodemographic profile among that range of customers and products that appears to be responsible for the bulk of Bloomingdale's profits. This is an example of the 80/20 principle in action, but facilitated and refined by today's high-speed computers and sophisticated analytical models. By enlisting the services of a national census profiler,[3] the store's management can develop a clear set of geodemographic target markets consisting of individuals scattered throughout the United States who, if they could, would shop regularly at Bloomingdale's.

Banana Republic: Nonstore First

The marketers in the right-hand path in Figure 4.1 also rely on research that identifies opportunities, but in this case the base is pure direct marketing—pure nonstore sales. For example, Banana Republic started by using conventional mailing list techniques to create their prospect base, and orders were filled by mail. However, after several years of operating as pure direct marketers, they accumulated an active customer database of significant size, one that could be analyzed to reveal large geographic concentrations of active customers. In essence, an analysis of Banana Republic's mail order base revealed a significant tally of customers in particular parts of the country, such as Chicago. A natural step, although one with striking implications at the time, was for Banana Republic to open retail outlets in the midst of these customer concentrations.

Synergy

The left path in Figure 4.1 (in-store sales first) and the right path (nonstore sales first) converge, so that when a company simultaneously markets by both methods, a certain synergy is realized. For example, Bloomingdale's by Mail, established by Barr Marchesault in 1978, had grown to nearly $70 million in sales by 1984.[4] Executives marketing by both methods can afford lavish catalogs that might not be justified by mail-order sales alone. These catalogs reinforce retail sales and enhance the store's image with retail shoppers.

RISK REDEMPTION RESEARCH

Traditional "risk redemption" research is based on the principles that the world is uncertain, that there is a single correct course of action, and that finding it is a gamble. The process is a crap shoot. A winning roll waits, but the odds of achieving it are not conditioned on human psychology, human behavior, tactics, or planning. According to this view, accumulated experience from prior efforts can place tighter bounds on one's uncertainty and can reduce but probably not eliminate the risk. Risk redemption assumes that an appropriate set of actions has been selected, and through logical (decision tree) analysis the best act-state combination can be found.

A static project view of research dominates risk redemption thinking because the creation of a decision tree or a payoff table puts the world on hold.

The real competitive complex continues while the risk reducers dally, working out the details of an act-state scenario. If the scenario is still valid following the two to six months it takes to decide, the risk reducers have been more lucky than smart.

OFFENSIVE MARKETING RESEARCH

With real-time monitoring, computer-assisted decisions, and comprehensive databases, research becomes an offensive weapon in an executive's arsenal rather than a defensive one. Most executives instinctively recognize the limitations of conventional risk redemption research and discard it in favor of marketing intelligence. The clear advantage they find is that marketing intelligence monitors competition and indicates when, where, and from whom certain weaknesses may appear or certain market opportunities may emerge due to changing consumer behavior patterns or changing tastes. As Davidson remarked in his book *Offensive Marketing,* "Most of the really successful new consumer products introduced in the past decade fulfilled relatively obvious needs, which the simplest form of investigation would have revealed. The critical reason for their success was not shrewd investigation, but skillful design and selling."[5] Davidson stresses that offensive marketing research should produce decisions and not data, should look for action, should see the people behind the numbers, and should be imaginative.[6]

The purpose of research is to assist in developing business strategies and to solve business problems. It is insight, not numbers. As Kotler and his colleagues note, traditional research methods are often reflexive; the analysis becomes an end in itself.[7] The process gains momentum so that analyses are performed and reports are written just to finish a project, whether or not the content bears on strategy and action. As these authors stress, research should be reflective, not reflexive. Companies should not wait for market opportunities. They need to know how to systematically search, choose, and manage them.[8]

NEEDED: A SHIFT FROM DATA TO MEANING

The changes affecting the world of marketing research are unfolding rapidly. Problems that were once at the core of good research—gaining respondent cooperation, securing sufficient data, and securing these data in a timely fashion—are now on the fringe. Data are collected routinely through electronic sales, distribution, promotion, and funds transfer systems. They are secured without the need to gain cooperation, without the need to sample, and without delay. Today data constitute a commodity. To quote John Costello, president of A. C. Nielsen's Market Research USA operation, "We need more insight, not more data. Technology is not an end in itself. Databases are critical, but know what you're looking for first. What happened to knowledge?"[9]

The data deluge requires that the emphasis of marketing research shift from statistical inference to strategic meaning. During the past 50 years, research textbooks have conveyed powerful insights from the literature of statistics. Almost all of these were variations on the same theme—that with a sufficiently well designed sample, one can make sharp leaps to a larger population.

Breakthroughs in inferential thinking have been adopted—obsessively, in many cases—due to their elegance and rigor. What most researchers forgot was that the leap from sample to population is not the most important one in the research process. The leap from data to meaning is at the center of marketing research. Useful research must travel the path from statistics to insight, from insight to action, and from action to success. The emphasis on inferential methods gave the impression that more data would invariably solve a problem. However, the new technologies have provided a welcome slap in the face. Even with all the data, available all the time, problems remain. Populations are heterogeneous, dynamic, and mysterious. The keys in business are meaning, action, and results, not representation.

Like the physicists, microbiologists, and other scientists steeped in high technology, marketing researchers can finally see the objects that they want to study. Today's instruments measure marketing communications, consumer populations, business functions, and sales transactions with unfailing accuracy and dogged determination. They monitor actual consumer behavior as well as an endless list of variables that intervene between stimulus and response, such as personal traits, lifestyle, political persuasion, and income. They keep track of the systems that support or constrain economic activity, such as distribution channels, government regulations, and consumer credit.

Our thirst for empirical sustenance should be quenched because we are awash in a riptide of data. What is needed now is a way to stay afloat. Precise and objective data are valuable for refuting long-held beliefs, but they cannot provide unifying principles. More often than not, masses of data discourage clarity of thought. Too many data drown, dilute, or waterlog the best ideas. Unifying principles are discovered by swimming against the current.

Marketing research systems are designed to provide a tasteful blend of theory, data, and action: theory about human behavior and the philosophy of consumption; data to guide theory development and to monitor plans put into practice; and action in the form of appropriate sales and marketing activities delivered precisely where they will be most effective. Although our high-tech instruments provide a better understanding of marketing systems, to prosper we must recognize and seize opportunities. Slow starts or incorrect guesses in today's fast-paced markets are fatal.

Notes

1. Theodore Levitt, "The Globalization of Markets," *Harvard Business Review* 61(3) (May–June 1983), p. 101.

2. See Stan Rapp and Thomas L. Collins, *MaxiMarketing: The New Direction in Promotion, Advertising, and Marketing Strategy,* New York: McGraw-Hill, 1987, pp. 240–245.

3. National census profilers such as National Decision Systems, Inc., Claritas Corporation, Donnelly Marketing Services, and CACI-Federal are discussed in Part III of this book.

4. See Rapp and Collins, op. cit., pp. 240–245.

5. Hugh Davidson, *Offensive Marketing*, 2d ed., Hants, England: Gower, 1987, p. 48.

6. Ibid., pp. 207–208.

7. Philip Kotler, Liam Fahey, and Somkid Jatusriptak, *The New Competition*, Englewood Cliffs, NJ: Prentice-Hall, 1985, p. 62.

8. Ibid., p. 85.

9. See Howard Schlossberg, "Balance Urged Between Technology and Judgment," *Marketing News* 24 (23) (November 12, 1990), p. 11.

5 RESEARCH PROJECTS VERSUS RESEARCH SYSTEMS

*The fallacy of progressive summarization: Data processing often
tries to serve the needs of managers with summaries of data. The
higher the level of management, the greater the degree of
aggregation or summary. In fact, higher-level managers often have
questions more subtle or complex than those which can be
answered by preplanned summaries. What they really need is the
ability to have questions relating to the data answered when they
arise.*

James Martin,
An Information Systems Manifesto

INTRODUCTION

The vast majority of marketing research is conducted using a project format
tailored to the requirements of a particular marketing problem. Project research is the lifeblood of thousands of small and medium-sized marketing
research firms, and it is the approach most often taught in university marketing research courses. Although the approach has merit, it is encumbered by
a variety of weaknesses inherited from the technological constraints and research climate in effect during its period of refinement, 1950 to 1975. Today the

40

academic and commercial practice of marketing research remains saddled by investment in outdated technology and overdependence on traditional problem analysis techniques.

This chapter discusses the weaknesses of project-based research and offers an alternative view of the research function in modern business practice. The weaknesses fall into three broad categories corresponding to the validity, the speed, and the quality of marketing research's response to management information requests. For example, a project tends to falsely isolate one business problem from interrelated problems faced by the same firm, thereby damaging the validity of project recommendations. Similarly, a project's data collection and analysis phases often require so much time that the project's recommendations are outdated before they can be implemented.

After discussing criticisms of the project approach, the chapter outlines features of an alternative view associated with marketing research systems. The systems approach is appealing because it harnesses the power of relational databases, expert systems, and model building to generate high-quality, fast responses to management's information requests. If used properly, information can even shape a firm's business strategy, elevating the acquisition and use of information from a supporting role to a line productivity tool.

MARKETING RESEARCH PROJECTS: A CRITIQUE

A marketing research project requires a single individual, a small group, or a team to fulfill a series of steps in three phases, as shown in Figure 5.1.[1] In the first phase, situation analysis, researchers identify a particular problem, refine the problem definition, establish a need for certain information, and specify research objectives. In the second phase, researchers collect relevant primary and/or secondary data. In the final phase, they process and analyze these data, extract insights, and present a project report.

Research projects are either exploratory, conclusive, or performance-monitoring, labels that roughly correspond to projects undertaken before, during, and after a strategy has been developed to solve a particular marketing problem. Exploratory research concentrates on situation analysis in order to refine management's understanding of a problem's scope. Conclusive research evaluates the courses of action developed during an exploratory phase. Once a strategy has been selected and implemented, monitoring research tracks its performance, examining changes in key variables such as sales, market share, and brand-name recall.

There is nothing inherently wrong with the step-by-step approach used to execute a traditional marketing research project. The steps serve as a framework for organizing ideas, as reference points for monitoring progress, as insurance against major omissions, as an indexing system for research methodologies, and as abstractions for what in practice are complex networks of interlocking activities. However, few projects actually adhere to each step in the list, and worse, the simplicity of such lists diminishes the potential impact of the overall research process.

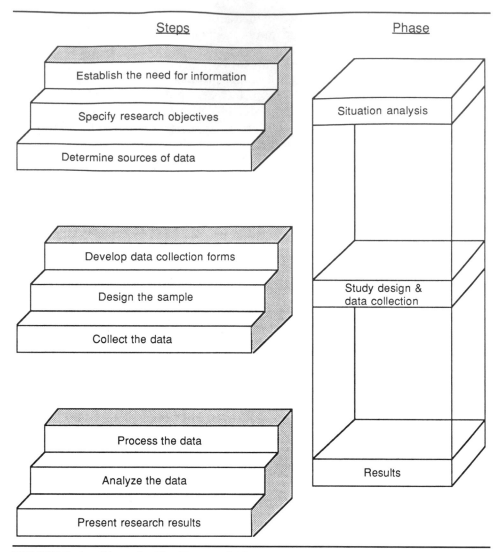

FIGURE 5.1.   Steps in the Research Process

PHASE 1: SITUATION ANALYSIS

The purpose of a situation analysis is to establish the need for information, specify research objectives, and determine sources of data. In the process of achieving these goals, a project usually exhibits three fundamental weaknesses. It focuses on a single business issue, it uses research as a passive rather than an active business tool, and it fails to anticipate management's information needs.

Single Issue Focus

Project research typically ignores the interrelationships between business activities both inside and outside the firm. As Wind and Robertson suggest, project research is dedicated to optimizing a component of the marketing mix.[2] It may give some attention to the interdependency between mix components, especially advertising and pricing, yet it ignores the synergistic effect $(2 + 2 = 5)$ that may result from particular combinations of marketing variables. In essence, focusing on a single problem simplifies the research task, providing a false sense of security in today's multidimensional, competitive marketing environment.

Defensive Approach

Situation analyses are also defensive: Research is kept in storage until needed, and it is then unleashed to do its job. Offensive marketing research is proactive rather than reactive. It searches for weaknesses in competitive programs, emerging niches in consumer demand, and changes in the economic environment that might propel certain programs forward and launch others into oblivion. In contrast, a project situation analysis is static; it assumes that opportunities are not perishable and that the competitive environment is stable. In other words, no matter how quickly an exploratory study can be done, its execution puts marketplace activity on hold. Depending on when the study begins, it may miss the most critical aspects of an unfolding situation.

Failure to Support Management's Information Needs

As Figure 5.1 indicates, one of the key parts of a situation analysis is to establish the need for information. However, business decisions always require information. The more pertinent questions are what information is needed and why is it valuable? The project approach operates on the premise that a limited quantity of information—usually assembled during a relatively brief time period—will solve a problem. However, executives typically need information support, that is, information that flows on request, not a discrete packet of information supplied once and discontinued thereafter. True decision support means management interaction with a marketing research system. The manager is responsible for requesting information in light of the needs of a particular business problem, and the system supplies facts and data, along with algorithms that integrate the facts and data into informative reports.

Establishing information needs just prior to data collection is also particularly risky since insufficient time may be devoted to collecting and processing relevant data. An alternative philosophy recognizes that a fairly standard set of marketing problems faces all firms. These problems must be anticipated as part of a firm's charter. For example, every firm must position its product(s), set prices, create and revise promotional appeals, introduce new products, select target segments, penetrate new markets, and phase out existing products. Good management should know these core marketing tasks and systematically identify—long before a specific problem arises—the information needed to accomplish each task.

PHASE 2: STUDY DESIGN AND DATA COLLECTION

Project data collection is often ad hoc, requires an inordinate amount of a firm's time and resources, and is typically executed poorly. Although a vast array of secondary and syndicated data are available, in the view of many executives marketing research is still synonymous with primary data collection. A single method—phone, mail, or personal interview—is likely to be used. Such data are ad hoc because they are collected for a single purpose rather than for multiple purposes and because results from separate projects on behalf of the same firm cannot usually be connected.

Timing and Quality Control Problems with Primary Data Collection

Collecting primary data involves the coordinated activities of a research team that has been trained to execute the various phases of a research design: constructing the instrument, interviewing, editing, controlling, and reporting. Most manufacturing firms and, a fortiori, most retailers are poorly equipped for these tasks. If the data are collected by an in-house team, the job is likely to be poorly executed and incomplete. Moreover, data collection, not decision analysis, will account for most of the time devoted to a project. Since in-house research is typically a staff function, line management will be separated from the research process and will likely exert little influence on the methods used.

Even hiring a data collection agency or a full-service marketing research firm is no guarantee of quality data or actionable results. For example, although many data collection firms imply that they use random or stratified random sampling, sampling frames that result in appropriate inferential statistics are seldom found in research practice. True inferential methods are too costly and require more technical expertise than most independent research firms possess. What may be offered is qualitative research, a convenience sample, or a firm's "tried and true" quasi-probability method, none of which can be adequately evaluated even under the best of circumstances.

The Role of Statistical Inference

Project research, with its emphasis on statistical inference, tends to present a static view of a dynamic marketplace. Inferences are usually presented in terms of summary statistics, such as means, variances, cross-tabulations, or regression coefficients, or in a diagrammatic summary, such as a multidimensional scaling perceptual map or a cluster dendogram. Due to decades of emphasis in the classroom, it is easy to forget that valid statistical inference is *not* the goal of marketing research. The goal is to help management formulate strategy that will sell products and establish client relations. Accurately summarizing a population, for example, accurately estimating certain population parameters—no matter how adequately or cleverly that population has been identified—may do little to achieve a firm's business goals.

PHASE 3: RESULTS

The final phase of a research project typically consists of data processing, data analysis, and results reporting. Even though these phases are at the "action end" of a research project, poorly conceived data processing may remove important content, data analysis is often misleading, and traditional project reports—even if well-executed—tend to summarize what happened rather than tell what to do.

Overprocessed Data

Once the natural links between facts, events, and issues are broken, they cannot be accurately reconstituted—certainly not by processing technology and data processing software designed to pick data apart rather than unify them. Traditional data processing typically removes meaning and insight from data, flattens many dimensions into one or two, and freezes competitive dynamics into market statics. Processed data lack natural cohesion. They are an amalgam of separate, low-quality parts that together do not form a decision-sustaining whole.

Research as an End in Itself

Data analysis can also misdirect. That is, project researchers may become infatuated with analyzing data rather than supporting management's decisions. And no matter how statistically sophisticated, data analysis may lead to exactly the wrong conclusion. For example, when Sony researched the market for a lightweight portable cassette player, results showed that consumers wouldn't buy a tape recorder that didn't record. Company chairman Akio Morita decided to introduce the Walkman in the face of these negative prospects. Morita's business instincts were correct, partly due to his ability to consider important aspects of the situation that escaped the research team.[3]

A related problem occurs when a research team becomes so obsessed with finishing a project that they lose sight of its original purpose. This is especially true if research staff are responsible for projects ordered by different line managers with separate or, worse, conflicting goals. Under such stressful conditions, the research staff's natural reaction is to avoid deep commitment to the business problem and to take refuge in the research process itself. Consequently, results are delayed and may be only tenuously connected to line management's decision support needs.

Selective Analysis

Finally, data analysis too often depends on one technique, such as regression analysis, conjoint analysis, multidimensional scaling, or correspondence analysis. Such techniques can reduce large quantities of data to a more manageable size in order to highlight certain features of a situation. However, each technique exhibits particular biases in terms of which features are highlighted and which are subdued. An executive must remember that a given technique merely pushes data through a black box of deterministic, rule-based transformations. Only he or she can add real value to data via human insight, inductive logic, and imagination.

PROJECT REPORTS: ANSWERS OR DEAD ENDS?

A report is typically the final product of a marketing research project. Traditionally, the reporting process divides a firm's personnel into two camps that might be designated as reporters and readers or, alternatively, as presenters and listeners. However logical this division may be from a skills standpoint, it effectively separates the research function from decision-making responsibility. For example, report writers devote considerable effort to absorbing facts, integrating them, and articulating ideas and may have a stronger sense of appropriate strategy than report readers. By sheltering line management from actively participating in research activities, a project may deny them actionable insights.

Of course, there are strong arguments for separating research doers from research users, including differences in skills, objectives, interests, and available time. The idea is that research can be performed "off-line" without bothering management with the details. Research staff is charged with the responsibility to effectively transfer knowledge back to line management by means of written or oral reports.

However, oral reports put the listener in an extremely passive role; indeed, better prepared, more entertaining presentations usually create the most passive listeners. The audience simply enjoys the show. Although written reports require some action (reading) on the part of the audience, they have no interactive features. Unlike an oral presentation, the reader cannot interrupt with a question, call for a clarification, or add new data. Therefore, at their best, traditional reports are neither "user-friendly" nor dynamic; at their average, they can be destructive. Decision makers may seize only a few points highlighted in a presentation rather than grasp a broader picture.

MARKETING RESEARCH SYSTEMS

The criticisms discussed thus far are summarized in Table 5.1 along with the corresponding features of a marketing research system. For example, a project has a distinct beginning and end, whereas a system continues to evolve. A research system stores data that portray the marketplace from a variety of perspectives to support business decisions that cut across functional lines. Since the system resides in-house, it protects a firm's sensitive internal data, such as sales and market share by region, product, and salesperson. Most important, a system delivers reports that are customized for the decision before management.

The remainder of this chapter discusses marketing research systems in more detail and summarizes some common features of the systems to be reviewed in later chapters. Although no existing system satisfies all the requirements of a complete marketing research system, existing systems take advantage of today's technological environment and indicate (by their weaknesses) how future systems can be improved.

TABLE 5.1. Projects versus Systems: An Overview

	Project	System
Planning horizon	Finite: A project starts and stops	Infinite: A system starts, continues, evolves
	Cross-sectional focus	*Longitudinal focus possible*
	• Cannot (routinely) track trends • Seasonal or time-dependent patterns may be misread	• Trends in key variables • Seasonal or other time-dependent patterns can be isolated and observed
Objective	To solve a (single) problem	To support management decision making to achieve a desired state of affairs
	Defensive: A project is initiated to react to a problem	*Offensive:* A system can search for opportunities
	Functional isolation: A project is usually done for a given department	*Functional interaction:* A system supports business decisions that cut across department lines
Who is involved	Typically outside consultants	Corporate management
	• Who often rely too heavily on a single methodology • Who know less about the organization's needs than does management • Who are a security risk • Who take knowledge with them when they leave	• Who use appropriate data and models • Who quickly identify critical issues • Who keep sensitive data in the organization • Who are motivated to disseminate data to colleagues
Modus operandi	• Projects are time- and labor-intensive • Projects are often designed and executed poorly • Projects are subject to errors at each stage	• Systems are capital-intensive • Systems reduce the chances of certain types of errors • System costs are spread over time, markets, customers, and users
Report delivery	Projects tend to produce hard-copy reports or oral presentations that:	Systems deliver reports electronically that:
	• Arrive slowly • Separate users from doers • Report "what was" • Are inflexible	• Are timely • Are customized for the decision problem at hand • Are dynamic and predictive • Are flexible (*by context*)

Definition of a Marketing Research System

Consider the following definition of a marketing research system, or MRS.

> A marketing research system uses naturally occurring transaction data—supplemented by census data, media data, client lists, and data from other sources—as a basis for operational control and strategic planning. The key problems in such systems concern data collection, data management, report delivery, modeling, and model management.

There are a number of key points in this definition. First, a marketing research system relies primarily (but not exclusively) on naturally occurring transaction data rather than on data generated from surveys. Transaction data include UPC scanner data, financial data, TV viewing data, and a variety of data that can be captured electronically as part of customary marketplace activities. Note that a transaction is the observable component of a two-party exchange, the atomic unit of all economic activity. In other words, transaction data can be collected unobtrusively because they are the electronic manifestations of important marketplace activities, including competitive dynamics, buyer behavior, and supply-side/demand-side interactions.

Other Aspects

Not all data in a marketing research system are collected directly from transactions. For example, census data, the cornerstone of modern geodemographic systems, are collected by traditional mail and personal interviews. Similarly, data about cognitive processes—attitudes, opinions, and purchase intentions—must be collected by direct questioning of human subjects. However, unlike a traditional project, a MRS stores these data in relational databases to link them to other data at management's disposal. Survey data stored in this manner are also regularly updated using standard operational definitions and research instruments. For example, as Chapter 15 explains, geodemographic research systems gain much of their power from relational links between census data and survey data collected by Simmons, National Family Opinion, and other traditional data suppliers. The suppliers agree to link members of their sample to electronic data via the postal ZIP code so that people's attitudes and opinions can be integrated with their purchase habits and conditions in the local marketing environment to allow a more thorough understanding of the forces influencing market behavior.

A MRS is designed to routinely satisfy management's requests for information, especially information that facilitates operational control. For example, in packaged goods marketing, brand managers must regularly recalibrate a brand's marketing mix. Certain mix elements, such as pricing and in-store promotions, are executed on a weekly basis. Therefore, a MRS must be able to routinely monitor marketplace activities (provide feedback) to guarantee that these activities are carried out as planned and to track trade and consumer response to them. System models must also provide valid short-term forecasts (feedforward) of key measures, including the volumes sold and marketing mix levels of a brand's direct competitors. Ideally, the system should automate routine decisions through the application of principles from real-time, optimal control. (Specific methods for doing this are discussed in Chapter 18.) In other words, the system should perform three basic functions, listed here in order of increasing sophistication: (1) monitoring, (2) forecasting, and (3) optimal control.

Of course, a MRS cannot automate strategic planning. Its function in this regard is to support human decision makers. However, unlike a research project, a MRS provides information support on request, and it delivers the information using the most effective technique available, that is, in reports generated by the system, not by human report writers. If properly developed, the system offers management a strategic advantage through its combination of rapid response speed, superior validity, and accurate modeling. This combination permits a firm to anticipate competitive actions and marketplace opportunities, allowing research to contribute directly to the bottom line as a productivity tool rather than as a fixed cost or line-item expense.

CONCLUSION

This chapter has presented detailed criticisms of project-based marketing research, the approach that has served as an academic and industry standard for more than 60 years. The chapter briefly reviewed the three major phases in a research project and critiqued fundamental activities associated with each phase. Among the most important criticisms are the following: Traditional project research typically uses a predetermined methodology to resolve a single business problem. Inordinate amounts of time and money are devoted to a project's data collection, analysis, and report-writing phases. Findings may have little bearing on the business situation that exists at the project's end and may not suggest action steps or appropriate business strategy.

The criticisms are not intended to disparage the tremendous contributions to marketing research made by scholars in associated disciplines such as statistics and psychology or to insult the thousands of dedicated project researchers in both academia and industry. However, experience suggests that without forceful arguments, habits persist despite strong evidence of their inefficiency. The key idea underpinning the criticisms expressed here is that the technical tools of the information age have (1) eliminated the need for many of the steps in a traditional research project, (2) replaced other steps with more efficient approaches, and (3) nullified many of the fundamental precepts on which traditional project research is based.

Although other marketing scholars have reflected on the criticisms presented in this chapter, most university professors teaching marketing research feel compelled to stress what existing research texts stress. As more and more supporting material becomes available and as large, working systems become more widely used, academics will systematically explore the benefits (and costs) of this alternative view of the marketing research function in modern business practice.

Notes

1. See Thomas C. Kinnear and James R. Taylor, *Marketing Research*, 3d ed., New York: McGraw-Hill, 1987, p. 20. A similar list can be found in virtually every available marketing research text.

2. Yoram Wind and Thomas Robertson, "Marketing Strategy: New Directions for Theory and Research," *Journal of Marketing* (Spring 1983), pp. 12–25.

3. See Johny K. Johansson and Ikujiro Nonaka, "Marketing Research the Japanese Way," *Harvard Business Review* (May–June 1987), pp. 16–22.

PART TWO

SINGLE-SOURCE SYSTEMS

6 THE SINGLE-SOURCE CONCEPT

At its simplest, the concept of single-source data is the measurement of marketing cause and market place effect using the same data source. This enables the marketer to observe the causal relationship.

Jim Spaeth and Mike Hess, "Single-Source
Data . . . the Missing Pieces"

Social Science research aims to develop causal propositions supported by data and logic.

1. $X \rightarrow Y$ *X might influence Y but Y does not influence X,*
2. $X \leftarrow Y$ *Y might influence X but X does not influence Y,*
3. $X \leftrightarrows Y$ *X and Y might influence each other,*
4. $X \leftrightarrow Y$ *X and Y might show statistical coordination.*

The word might *appears in each formulation. It is not necessary to know that X does cause Y, it is only necessary that causation is conceivable or possible. Thus an arrow indicates potential flows of causation, not necessarily actual flows. The situation is like a street map indicating one-way streets. It does not tell us whether there are any cars on the streets, but if there are any, it tells us which way they can move.*

James E. Davis, *The Logic of Causal Order*

INTRODUCTION

The single-source system represents a natural stage in the evolution from impressive but disconnected research databases to fully integrated marketing research systems. Disconnected databases have often defined market areas, product categories, and market facts differently. Older systems typically collected data manually, responded slowly, and delivered market-level reports rather than reports disaggregated to a region, store, or household. In contrast, single-source suppliers assemble data for UPC-scannable items in supermarkets and drug stores, augment these data with data from household panels, and produce reports so that clients can baseline, track, forecast, and optimize important sales and marketing variables.

This chapter discusses InfoScan and SCANTRACK, the two major single-source systems offered, respectively, by Information Resources, Inc. and A. C. Nielsen.[1] Both systems evolved from less sophisticated, less integrated research products. InfoScan followed BehaviorScan, IRI's flagship television cut-in service. SCANTRACK grew out of A. C. Nielsen's Food Index Store Audits service and its ERIM Testsight project. ERIM was designed to compete with BehaviorScan but was abandoned in 1988 as demand for television cut-in services diminished.[2] (See the appendix to this chapter for a brief history of developments in marketing research that produced today's single-source systems.)

This chapter is designed to provide a general but complete overview of the single-source concept. Key terms such as *store panel, household panel, active city, passive city, scanner universe,* and *trade environment* are defined and illustrated using InfoScan, SCANTRACK, or both. However, detailed comparisons between the two existing systems are postponed until Chapters 7–11 in order to first develop a top-down understanding of these complicated systems.

WHAT IS THE SINGLE-SOURCE CONCEPT?

In their published literature, Nielsen and IRI understandably emphasize their respective system's unique strengths and operational characteristics, focusing on commercial differences rather than on their conceptual common ground. The characteristics these systems share suggest the following definition of a single-source system:[3]

> A single-source system records each marketing signal that impacts a household either directly (in-home) or indirectly (through the retailer), traces the route and medium these signals took to reach that household, and partitions the household's purchase behavior in a way that links it with signal content.

In other words, the objectives of a single-source system are:

1. To measure causal factors (price, product, promotion) at their point of effect (in the home or in-store)
2. To trace how and when these factors affect consumer behavior

3. To identify where each signal originates (with the manufacturer or with the retailer)
4. To collect data at strategic points in the product movement pipeline (factory, warehouse, retail, and home)
5. To analyze these data to identify how marketing forces interact with household geodemographics and retail trade behavior to influence consumption patterns
6. To deliver actionable information to management in three client segments: manufacturers, retailers, and advertising agencies

To obtain the data, each system's in-store scanners monitor prices and price promotions for all UPC-scannable items; in-store audits monitor selected product placements and merchandising displays weekly; in-home meters monitor television viewing in certain panel households; and audits monitor magazine and newspaper advertising in panel cities.

DATA COLLECTION

The two major single-source suppliers collect and integrate data somewhat differently. Figure 6.1 shows five primary nodes in the packaged goods channel and the data that can be collected between nodes. However, not all of these data collection points are actually used. For example, A. C. Nielsen collects data using in-store scanners and supplements these with in-home scanning, but it does not monitor factory or warehouse withdrawals. IRI relies exclusively on in-store scanners; that is, it uses only the third link of the four possibilities.

In-store scanning, the critical component in these systems, is used in two ways. First, the data are summarized and reported at the store level. Second, store data are coordinated with data on individual consumers, obtained from a household panel dispersed among a system's "member" cities.

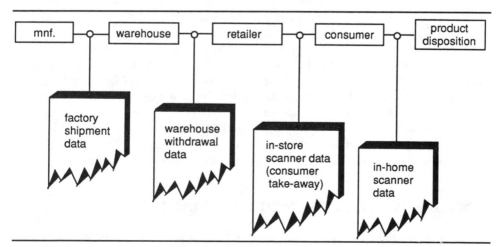

FIGURE 6.1. Data Collection Points

TABLE 6.1.   Single-Source Systems: Summary[a]

	InfoScan	SCANTRACK
Major markets	49	50
Other markets	17 (optional)	25 (projection areas)
Panel households		
In-store (grocery)	60,000	14,000
In-store (Rx)	15,000	—
In-home	—	15,000
Retail store panel		
Total stores	2,253	2,675
Total chains	66	50

[a] Latest available data as of June 1, 1991.

Table 6.1 indicates the relative sizes of the (grocery) household panels in the two systems. IRI's system has 60,000 households spread among 49 standard and 17 optional markets, and Nielsen has 29,000 households in 50 cities. Panel households are samples from the larger U.S. population of all households, and the store panels are samples from the population of U.S. grocery stores. Properties of these samples and characteristics of the respective populations from which they are drawn are discussed in detail later in this chapter and in Chapter 7.

Databases

Data from both households and stores are accumulated in five primary databases: a household database, a store database, a retail factors database, a promotion factors database, and an advertising database. As Figure 6.2 shows, these databases fall into three environments: the consumer environment, the trade environment, and the promotion environment. The power of a single-source system is generated by a complex set of interactions among these three environments. In the simplest of terms, the system must track what products were sold (the trade environment); who bought these products (the consumer environment); and why these products were bought (the promotion environment).

The remainder of this chapter is devoted to developing a thorough understanding of each of these environments as well as the data collection methods associated with each and the databases so formed. Examples from each system are provided to illustrate concepts, but a detailed comparison of the systems is postponed until Chapter 7. This chapter and Chapter 7 focus on the supply side of single-source systems; Chapters 9, 10, and 11 focus on the demand side, presenting three client segments that use single-source data. Chapter 8 introduces the framework used in Chapters 9–11 to classify single-source report types.

SINGLE-SOURCE CONSUMER ENVIRONMENTS

The household database stores information from a panel of thousands of households divided into a small active panel and a much larger passive panel. House-

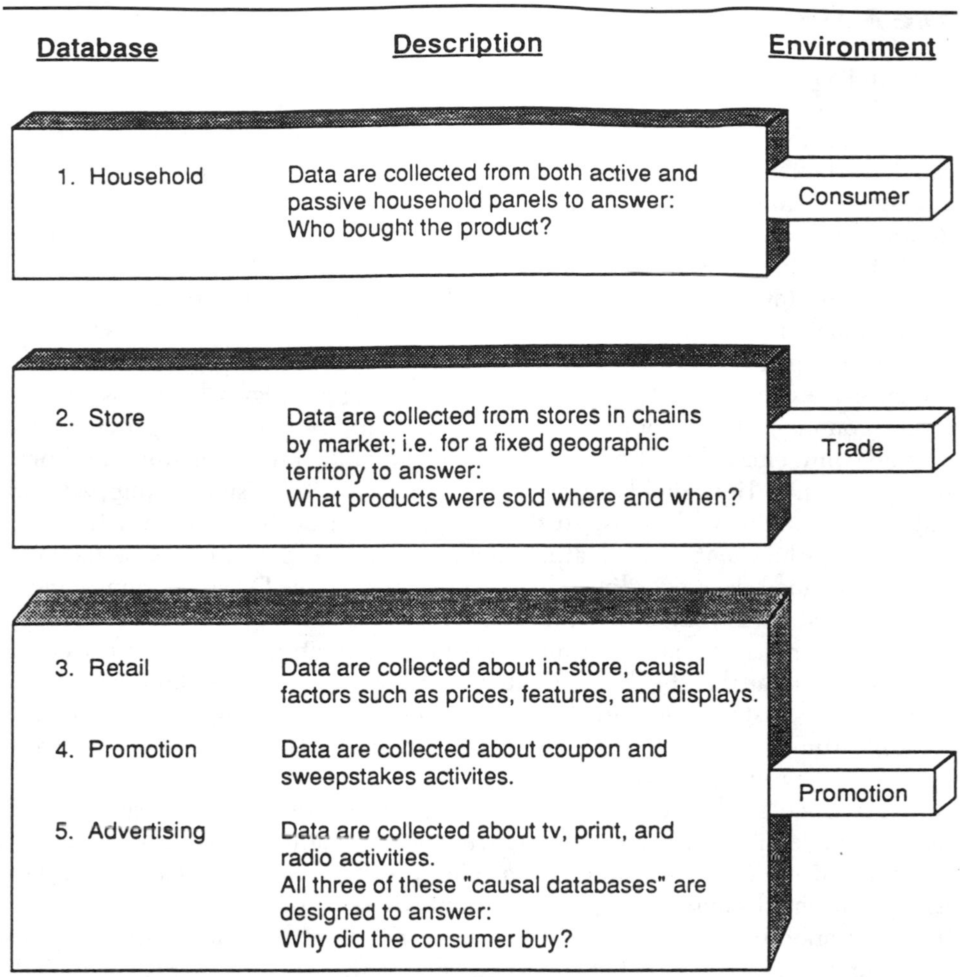

Database	Description	Environment
1. Household	Data are collected from both active and passive household panels to answer: Who bought the product?	Consumer
2. Store	Data are collected from stores in chains by market; i.e. for a fixed geographic territory to answer: What products were sold where and when?	Trade
3. Retail	Data are collected about in-store, causal factors such as prices, features, and displays.	Promotion
4. Promotion	Data are collected about coupon and sweepstakes activites.	
5. Advertising	Data are collected about tv, print, and radio activities. All three of these "causal databases" are designed to answer: Why did the consumer buy?	

FIGURE 6.2. Databases in a Single-Source System

holds in both panels grant the research firm permission to store and retrieve information about their purchase behavior and geodemographic makeup. The key difference between the active and passive constituents is summarized in the following definitions.

Active panel: A collection of households in which *every* significant marketing influence is monitored for each member household

Passive panel: A collection of households in which only *selected* marketing influences (such as coupon redemption) are monitored

Data are collected primarily by in-store UPC scanners but also by hand-held scanning devices operated either at the point-of-sale or at home by panel members.

The Active Panel

To form its active panel, a single-source supplier contracts with individual households in a town, with the town's available media, and with the town's major retailers in order to control all sources of marketing influence on a household's purchase behavior. To ensure control, an active panel is typically distributed among 10 or fewer small towns (population 70,000 to 200,000; see Table 6.2 for details), each served exclusively by cable television or else sufficiently isolated so that over-the-air signals can be protected from spillover from neighboring cities. These towns must also meet a number of other criteria in their retail and promotional environments.

Active panels were originally developed for TV cut-in experiments. In a TV cut-in, a client tests two competing advertising strategies,[4] such as two different commercials or (more commonly) two campaigns consisting not only of unique commercials but also of a battery of coupon, print-ad, in-store, and pricing treatments. Households in an active panel have televisions equipped with individually addressable taps, so that a test ad can be inserted in a time slot reserved by the client. Participating families are also exposed to a newspaper ad or a direct mail flyer coordinated with their particular TV ad. A household is unaware that its ad may differ from that of its neighbor.

The purchase behavior of members of each treatment group is traced via UPC scanning at the checkout counter (or later, in the home), and reports are delivered to assist the client in choosing between the competing campaigns. Tests typically run for a period of six months to a year, depending on the repurchase cycle of the product category.

Packaged goods manufacturers employ active panels for three reasons. First, using a single-city test drastically reduces the contaminating effects of nonsampling factors or geodemographic mismatches prevalent in traditional test markets using household samples from different cities.[5] Second, there is less likelihood that a competitor can sabotage a test, since the client has considerable control over the promotion and retail environments in the test city. Third, with individually addressable taps, subsequent treatments in a town can be applied to a completely new randomization of the household panel. Thus there is little fear of bias due to sampling error, learning, or buildup effects.

The Passive Panel

The passive part of a single-source panel is much larger than the active part; participants reside in most major metropolitan areas in the United States, and testing involves neither total urban coverage of media nor retail coordination. TV viewing by passive panel members is monitored in some cases, but the promotional environment does not permit TV cut-ins or coordination with other media.

Table 6.3 provides a sketch of the major differences between an active panel and a passive panel. The main purpose of a passive panel is to track product movement among packaged goods and pharmaceuticals rather than to ensure experimental control. Passive households numbering several thousand in a single city are clustered in a few neighborhoods chosen carefully for their demographic

TABLE 6.2. Single-Source Systems: Active Panels[a]

Location	Town (000s)		Panel	
	Population	Households	Households	TV[b]
InfoScan (BehaviorScan)[c]				
Cedar Rapids, IA	188	73	3,000	cbl addr 2,000
Eau Claire, WI	117	42	3,000	cbl addr 2,000
Grand Junction, CO	113	42	3,000	cbl addr 2,000
Marion, IN	78	28	3,000	cbl addr 2,000
Midland, TX	116	42	3,000	cbl addr 2,000
Pittsfield, MA	92	35	3,000	cbl addr 2,000
SCANTRACK				
Sioux Falls, SD[d]	89	35	3,000	ota addr 2,000
Springfield, MO[d]	211	79	3,000	ota addr 2,000
Nielsen/ NPD[e]				
Chicago				
Los Angeles				
New York				
Philadelphia				
San Francisco				

Key: addr: Individually addressable
  cbl: Cable television
  ota: Over-the-air television

[a] This information is valid as of January 1, 1991, but is subject to change. Figures were obtained from company brochures, discussions with corporate personnel, and the *Rand McNally Commercial Atlas and Marketing Guide,* 119th ed. Chicago, New York, and San Francisco: Rand McNally, 1988.

[b] Individually addressable TVs can be placed in different treatment groups for different tests. Split-cable markets have two fixed treatment groups used for all tests. Note that not all panel households have addressable TVs. For example, of the 3,000 panelists in a BehaviorScan market, only 2,000 are addressable.

[c] BehaviorScan consisted of nine markets in 1989. However, three of these—Rome, GA; Salem, OR; and Williamsport, PA—were phased out early in 1990.

[d] Sioux Falls and Springfield were formerly part of Nielsen's ERIM project but are now part of SCANTRACK's active panel.

[e] Local market samples range in size from 300–1,700 households all equipped with in-home scanners. Of the 15,000 households in the Nielsen/NPD sample, 5,000 have TV meters using over-the-air technology, with this figure rising to 7,500 by 1995. Nielsen's Monitor-Plus system will be associated with each of these households. See Chapter 11 for details on Monitor-Plus. See also Lewis C. Winters, "Home Scan vs. Store Scan Panels: Single-Source Options for the 1990s," *Marketing Research* 1(4) (December 1989), pp. 61–65.

representativeness and for their patronage of participating stores.[6] For example, the Nielsen SCANTRACK panel in Los Angeles consists of 4,000 households patronizing 16 stores. Nielsen uses area probability sampling to ensure that projections are statistically sound within each trading area.

TABLE 6.3. Active versus Passive Panels

Criterion	Active Panel	Passive Panel
Main objective	Controlled experiments	Product movement tracking
	Test marketing	National and regional coverage
City type (number of cities)	Small, demographic profile similar to general U.S. (few, 2–10)	Major metro area (many, 35–50)
TV cut-ins (cable or network)	Yes	No
Retail coverage (stores)	Nearly complete; all major grocery and Rx	Partial; small proportion of city total in selected neighborhoods
Promotional environment	One newspaper: coordination with direct mail, radio, in-store promotions	Varies; no coordination with media or in-store promotions

Aggregation and Reports

The most powerful aspect of single-source data is that they are disaggregate. They can be presented to management from virtually any point of view to address a wide range of questions. Furthermore, household data are more powerful than store-level data because they are more disaggregate. Household data are nested within store data. Nesting means that household-by-household transactions can be aggregated upward to the store level. For example, household data can be reported by demographic split (such as men versus women), by ethnic group, or by loyal versus nonloyal buyers—three perspectives unavailable at the store level. Store-level data can be presented by shelf-keeping unit (SKU) within brand,[7] by brand within category, by store department, by retail chain, and by time period. But store-level data cannot be partitioned by consumer demographics, brand-loyalty measures, or any other characteristic that refers to a household rather than a store. For example, using sales receipts for an entire store for a given week, a system cannot report what percent of those sales or which particular sales were made to Hispanic households. Store data per se are not "tagged" to household characteristics. In sum, store-level sales are the aggregate of individual transactions in that store. Individual transactions offer a finer level of resolution and, consequently, more reporting possibilities.

It would seem, then, that the best single-source database is the one that collects the most household data. In practice, however, this is not a valid conclusion. A client firm must choose among single-source services based on a variety of strategic considerations and information needs. Single-source suppliers differ with respect to their flexibility and willingness to customize reports, the types of standard reports they offer, their promptness in replying to inquiries, their expertise in setting up and integrating databases, their willingness to provide training in the analysis of scanner data, and their analytic capabilities. Competition between A. C. Nielsen and IRI is fierce on each of these dimensions. Details about differences between these two suppliers are provided in Chapters 7–11.

SINGLE-SOURCE TRADE ENVIRONMENTS

Trade refers to both retail and wholesale trade in the packaged goods sold in supermarkets, drug stores, and mass-merchandise stores. The term *retail environment* means the collection of major retailers, smaller chains, and independents included in a system's trading areas. A single-source system samples from the population of all such stores. This sample can be characterized by the total number of stores included, the cities in which these stores are located, the neighborhoods within each city, and the geodemographics of this store-by-city combination. The major cities in each system's store panel are shown in Table 6.4.

Different trade environments can be compared on several attributes: the in-store versus out-of-store environment, the market type (such as active versus passive city), and the data collection technique(s) employed.

In-Store versus Out-of-Store

The in-store environment consists of shelf stock, the physical arrangement of a store, its size, the number of checkouts, and other characteristics, such as store hours and specialty departments. In contrast, the out-of-store environment is characterized by the geodemographics of neighborhoods within cities.

The in-store environment interacts with the consumer environment via the data collection process. For example, a single-source system that relies exclusively on in-store scanners cannot monitor trade activity in neighborhoods served by non-scanner-equipped stores. (Such stores are usually small and may exhibit definite ethnic patterns in both ownership and product lines carried.) Reports based solely on in-store scanners will underestimate the volume of certain items and misrepresent brand choice among certain demographic segments. Systems that supplement in-store scanners with in-home devices can capture information that would otherwise elude the system; they improve a system's "coverage." However, costs increase when in-home scanning techniques are used because this form of data collection is intrusive. It requires high incentives to gain and keep cooperation among panelists. In brief, the value of total retail coverage is not infinite, and the price that single-source clients are willing to pay for improved coverage is limited.

The Trade Environment in Active versus Passive Markets

The trade environment in active towns differs substantially from that in larger metropolitan areas where passive panels reside. These differences may impact market share and other measures extracted from single-source data. For example,

TABLE 6.4. Single-Source Store Panels

	InfoScan		SCANTRACK	
	Number of Stores	Percent ACV	Number of Stores	Percent ACV
Albany	30	78	31	80
Albuquerque	13	81	—	—
Atlanta	44	79	57	79
Baltimore	53	85	35	86
Birmingham	31	77	46	80
Boise	12	77	—	—
Boston	54	83	78	83
Buffalo	39	87	41	85
Charleston	14	77	—	—
Charlotte	30	76	31	76
Chicago	62	93	83	89
Cincinnati	36	85	50	83
Cleveland	35	86	59	81
Columbus	30	86	45	85
Dallas	51	76	67	83
Denver	44	84	56	87
Des Moines	14	77	32	75
Detroit	41	86	62	83
El Paso	13	74	—	—
Grand Rapids	30	86	34	83
Green Bay	13	81	—	—
Harrisburgh	12	82	—	—
Hartford	41	85	42	85
Houston	46	78	75	78
Indianapolis	31	88	59	85
Jacksonville	30	77	37	74
Kansas City	36	76	52	79
Knoxville	15	72	—	—
Little Rock	30	69	36	73
Los Angeles	78	92	114	92
Louisville	30	76	41	75
Memphis	31	68	39	69
Miami	45	86	60	83
Milwaukee	34	92	47	90
Minneapolis	37	78	54	81
Nashville	31	64	39	69
New Orleans	39	80	58	78
New York	86	88	124	88
Norfolk	—	—	—	—
Oklahoma City	39	75	50	75
Omaha	26	78	32	78
Orlando	32	82	37	79
Peoria	13	90	—	—
Philadelphia	54	83	66	84
Phoenix	41	80	40	83
Pittsburgh	38	82	59	81

TABLE 6.4. *(Continued)*

	InfoScan		SCANTRACK	
	Number of Stores	Percent ACV	Number of Stores	Percent ACV
Portland, ME	15	81	—	—
Portland, OR	55	83	62	85
Providence	30	83	—	—
Quad Cities	—	—	—	—
Raleigh	33	74	40	73
Richmond	34	79	35	76
Roanoke	13	79	—	—
Sacramento	32	84	38	85
Salt Lake City	34	84	43	80
San Antonio	31	79	41	76
San Diego	35	89	46	89
San Francisco	50	88	69	88
Scranton	15	87	—	—
Seattle	41	87	57	86
Shreveport	14	73	—	—
Spokane	13	85	—	—
St. Louis	42	79	60	83
Syracuse	16	82	33	82
Tampa	41	82	73	80
Toledo	13	91	—	—
Tulsa	18	74	—	—
Washington	—	—	60	84
Wichita	28	72	—	—
Total cities	66		50	
Total stores	2,253		2,675	

Notes:

"Number of stores" shows within each local market how many stores are included from the $2 million grocery universe.

"Percent ACV" indicates what percent of the total all-commodity volume in that market is accounted for by a system's store sample.

an active town is small and usually has only a few major grocery stores. A typical case is Eau Claire, Wisconsin, a BehaviorScan market that has eight supermarkets representing two major chains, three smaller chains, and three independents.

In passive cities the retail environment is much richer, more diverse, and embedded in a consumer mosaic that differs from that found in active towns. For example, the major supermarket chains in Nielsen's Los Angeles SCANTRACK location bear little resemblance to active-panel towns such as Eau Claire, Sioux Falls, and Springfield.

An important feature of the stores selected in major metropolitan areas is that they must have all-commodity-volume (ACV) sales exceeding $2 million annually.[8] InfoScan has consistently defined its scanner universe at this threshold, but Nielsen originally used $4 million annually for SCANTRACK, adding the $2–4 million store universe to its system in 1988.

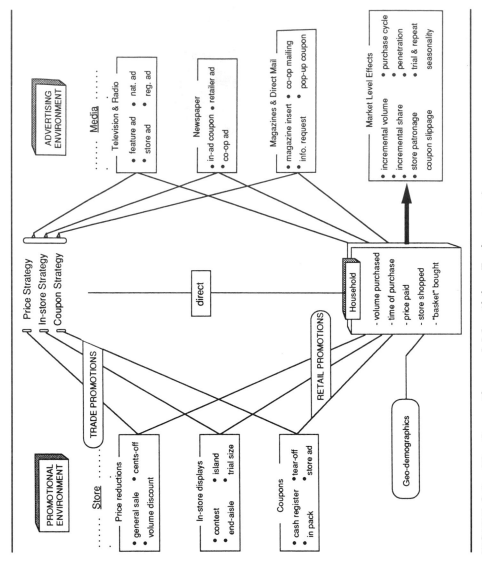

FIGURE 6.3. The Promotion and Advertising Environment

64

THE PROMOTION AND ADVERTISING ENVIRONMENT

Figure 6.3 provides an overview of the promotion and advertising environment in a single-source system. The promotion environment is shown on the left side and the advertising environment on the right. In either case, the strategy and tactics for a particular SKU, brand, or product line begin with a manufacturer and end with consumer demand at the household level.

Strategies can be implemented in five basic ways: (1) directly (manufacturer to household); indirectly through (2) the trade, (3) the retailer, or (4) both; and (5) indirectly through a particular advertising medium. For example, a manufacturer may offer a refund as an on-pack, mail-in coupon. This type of promotion is a direct link with a household, involving neither the retailer nor an advertising medium. A manufacturer might also offer a price cut to retailers as part of a trade promotion, and all or part of this cut might be passed on to consumers. Retail chains also act independently to offer price cuts, complimentary items, extra volume, and so forth; these promotional mechanisms may or may not be based on manufacturer incentives. Finally, certain strategies are implemented through broadcast media, print media, or direct mail. For example, a manufacturer might include a cash rebate coupon in one of its print ads.[9]

Each supplier has a proprietary name for its particular set of services that monitor promotional activity. IRI uses its PromotionScan System to analyze the effectiveness of trade and consumer promotions in generating incremental sales volume nationally, by market, and by retail chain. Nielsen's SCAN*PRO Monitor uses data gathered from the nearly 2,700 supermarkets in its system to analyze past, present, and future effects of in-store displays, price reductions, and newspaper advertising by retailers. Despite its sale of scanner contracts to IRI, SAMI still offers its FeatureFax and CouponFax systems. For example, the FeatureFax system tracks retailer features daily in 100 metro markets. FeatureFax was the first to score ads using a graded (1–4) quality index, but IRI and Nielsen have followed suit.

The effects of promotion variables are accounted for by partitioning sales, share, and profit into a base and an incremental portion. The base sales for a brand are determined by tracking its sales in all weeks that are free of promotional manipulations. Proprietary formulas are used to factor out the influences of seasonal patterns, competitive promotions, and economic trends in order to develop an accurate week-by-week forecast of what would happen if the market were left free to settle to a "natural" equilibrium.[10] Incremental sales are then defined as the difference between actual sales and this baseline. Incremental sales are divided further into various consumer segments (such as loyal buyers versus deal buyers), so that a brand manager gains a complete picture of the effects of strategy and tactics on sales, profit, and consumer behavior.

CONCLUSION

This chapter analyzed the main features of single-source research systems. These systems are designed to supply actionable reports to clients in three segments: manufacturing, retailing, and advertising. In a typical single-source system, reports are generated from five databases. The store database collects information on stores within fixed geographical reference frames to determine what products are bought, when, and where. The household database collects data, using both active and passive panels, to determine who bought these products. Three other databases—the retail factors, promotion factors, and advertising databases—accumulate information about causal influences on consumer purchase behavior, including the ads, prices, and features to which households are exposed in their local shopping environments.

Each major supplier of single-source data implements these generic concepts in different ways. Although some examples were provided here, the next few chapters provide considerably more detail about the unique characteristics of InfoScan and SCANTRACK and, to a lesser degree, about newer services such as Viewfacts. Because of the rapid change in this industry, new competitors are likely to enter, and existing competitors may soon start to diversify or seek specialized niches for their product offerings. Anticipated changes are discussed in other sections of the book.

Notes

1. A third system, SAMSCAN, offered by Arbitron/SAMI Corporation, was discontinued in October 1990. At that time, the 200-plus SAMI contracts were assigned to Information Resources, Inc. After February 22, 1991, clients could sign with either IRI or Nielsen. See *Advertising Age* (January 14, 1991), p. 21.

2. SAMSCAN was an outgrowth of SAMI's warehouse withdrawal service and its corporate merger in 1986 with Burke Marketing Services Corporation. This merger was dissolved in July 1989.

3. See also David J. Curry, "Single-Source Systems: Retail Management Present and Future," *Journal of Retailing* 65 (Spring 1989), pp. 1–20.

4. Occasionally, but rarely, three-way or four-way splits are used. Higher-level splits seriously diminish the power of a test, making results difficult to interpret.

5. Since active panels are located in several towns, multiple test sites can be used if desired. Even so, the treatment groups for a given test do not correspond to cities but rather are randomly selected (and optimally matched) within and between cities.

6. The data suppliers report that the initial cooperation rate when panel members are recruited is about 40 to 50 percent for an in-store panel and about 10 percent for an in-home panel.

7. A shelf-keeping unit (SKU) is a narrowly defined category designed to capture the items among which a consumer might choose when making a single purchase decision. SKU categories are typically delineated by package size, product flavor, container type, and color.

8. Of the 30,400 supermarkets with 1991 sales exceeding $2 million, 20,672 or 68 percent were equipped with UPC checkout scanners. See *Nielsen's International Market Review Service,* Nielsen Marketing Research, Table 17.

9. For further details, see Robert C. Blattberg and Scott A. Neslin, *Sales Promotion: Concepts, Methods, and Strategies*, Englewood Cliffs, NJ: Prentice-Hall, 1990.

10. A baseline value is not a simple statistical average of a brand's sales or market share over time, but an estimate (usually the intercept term) from a comprehensive volume or share model. For example, to derive a baseline volume, InfoScan and SCAN*PRO use an Erlang (1,1) exponential smoothing model. SCAN*PRO makes two passes through the data to first identify and then eliminate the effects of anomalous data points. To determine the baseline for market share, Lee G. Cooper and Masao Nakanishi (*Market Share Analysis: Evaluating Competitive Marketing Effectiveness*, Boston: Kluwer Academic, 1988, pp 162–164) suggest several alternative models, all of which are special cases of either the multiplicative competitive interaction model or the multinomial logit model discussed in Chapter 18.

APPENDIX 6A:
SINGLE-SOURCE SYSTEMS: A BRIEF HISTORY

In late 1986, when it introduced InfoScan, IRI was the first to use the term "single-source" to describe an integrated, scanner-based research system.[1] This appendix reviews major developments in marketing research that led to the single-source concept. Divergent research lines are not discussed, but definitive histories of these topics can be found elsewhere.[2]

This retrospective is organized by marketing research era. As Table 6.5 shows, these eras roughly correspond to decades of the twentieth century. Sections in this appendix note key events in each era and suggest the relevance of these events to single-source systems. The years 1900 through 1950 are reviewed rapidly, with greater attention devoted to more recent developments, especially to the period of accelerated evolution following IRI's introduction of BehaviorScan in 1978.

The Early Years (1900–1950)

Single-source systems illustrate just how far marketing research has advanced in a remarkably brief time. Formal marketing research had its origins little more than 80 years ago, in 1911, when Charles Coolidge Parlin became the first professional marketing researcher. Parlin's early studies with Curtiss Publishing Co. were concerned exclusively with institutional practices. He concentrated first on problems in the agricultural implements industry and later on wholesaling and retailing activities in the textile industry. Because of the interest his early studies aroused, research departments were established at both U.S. Rubber in 1915 and Swift and Co. in 1917.

The A. C. Nielsen Company was founded in 1923 to conduct "performance surveys"—engineering and economic studies—of machinery manufacturers.[3] However, in 1928 the company began conducting surveys with customers of these companies, thereby shifting its research focus from institutional practices to consumer behavior.

After a decade of growing acceptance during the 1920s, marketing research blossomed in the 1930s with the widespread use of descriptive statistics, graphs, and charts and, in 1937, with Lyndon Brown's publication of the first marketing research text. During this period, researchers recognized the advantages of collecting data in longitudinal studies, and today's automated systems with their extensive tracking ability are traceable to these pathbreaking efforts. In fact, Nielsen's Food Index, a direct precursor of SCANTRACK, was created in 1933 using data from a national panel of retail food stores.

At the same time, researchers increasingly realized that in the absence of careful collection and analysis standards, data could be misleading. Significant developments in inferential statistics and experimental design began to strongly influence how research studies were conducted. Analysts of that era became aware of the need to construct sampling plans carefully, to control sources of error, and to report the standard errors of their estimates. Confidence intervals and hypothesis tests became widely used. And in 1949 Robert Ferber published *Statistical Techniques in Marketing Research*, an impressive volume that collected

TABLE 6.5. Eras in Marketing Research

Era	Dates	Relevance for Single-Source Systems	Key Events
Institutional Studies	1911–1920	First use of formalized marketing research	J. George Frederick establishes The Business Bourse (1911). Charles C. Parlin becomes market research professional at Curtiss Publishing Co. (1911). Research depts. are established at U.S. Rubber (1915) and Swift and Co. (1917). C. S. Duncan publishes *Commercial Research: An Outline of Working Principles* (1919).
Acceptance and Growth of Marketing Research	1921–1930	Focus shifts from firm behavior to consumer behavior	A. C. Nielsen is founded (1923) and conducts first market surveys (1928). First Census of Distribution (1929).
Descriptive Statistics and Surveys	1931–1940	Data are collected continuously rather than sporadically	Burke Field Services created (1931). Nielsen establishes a national panel of retail food stores, creating the Nielsen Food Index (1933). First research text published: *Marketing Research and Analysis* (1937) by Lyndon O. Brown.
Inferential Statistics and Experimental Design	1941–1950	Clients first recognize and account for errors in data	Robert Ferber publishes *Statistical Techniques in Marketing Research* (1949) (based on work by Fisher, 1935; Kempthorne, 1946; and many others).
Early Panels	1951–1960	Marketing variables are not only measured but tracked	Nielsen launches its Television Index Service (1950). Henry Brenner fulfills Scott Paper's request for a diary panel and starts the Home Testing Institute (1951). SAMI launches its warehouse withdrawal service (1966).
Normative Models and Econometrics	1961–1970	The research focus shifts from description to understanding	Developments in simulation, Markov models, game theory, time series, and multivariate statistics experience widespread application in marketing research. ADTEL links household purchase data and TV viewing (dual cable) data (1968).

(continued)

TABLE 6.5 *(Continued)*

Era	Dates	Relevance for Single-Source Systems	Key Events
Special Packages and Market Response Models	1971–1980	Clients see the value of "what-if" modeling	Conjoint analysis, multidimensional scaling, and cluster analysis are extensively applied in commercial research. IRI launches BehaviorScan (1978)
Scanning and TV Cut-ins	Early 1980s	Psychological constructs are replaced by behavioral data linked to causal factors	BehaviorScan creates research revolution. ERIM is launched and dies (1985–1988). POS scanners become widely used.
Single-Source Integrated Systems	Late 1980s to early 1990s	Clients demand that "all" causal factors be considered and that reports integrate household, store, and media data	InfoScan is launched (1986). SAMSCAN & SCANTRACK launched (1987). Nielsen tries People Meters (1987)

Sources: Paul E. Green and Yoram Wind, "Statistics in Marketing," Working Paper 82-014R (July 1982), University of Pennsylvania, p. 2–4; Lawrence C. Lockley, "History and Development of Marketing Research," in Robert Ferber (ed.), *Handbook of Marketing Research,* New York: McGraw-Hill, 1974, pp.1-3–1-15; Thomas C. Kinnear and James R. Taylor, *Marketing Research: An Applied Approach,* New York: McGraw-Hill, 1987, pp. 28–30.

important developments in statistics and showed how they could be applied in marketing research studies.

The Period 1950–1978

Following World War II, marketing research activity increased dramatically, paralleling the growing acceptance of the marketing concept. By 1950 there were more than 200 marketing research firms in the United States with total sales exceeding $50 million dollars per year.[4] By 1970 marketing research revenues had increased tenfold, to more than $500 million dollars annually.

Important Connections

Several important developments that bear directly on today's single-source systems occurred during the 1950s and 1960s. Two of the most important were Nielsen's Television Index Service, launched in 1950, and the Home Testing Institute, created in 1951.

In 1936 Nielsen acquired from two MIT professors—Robert Elder, an electrical engineer, and Robert Woodruff, a marketing instructor—the rights to a crude version of an audimeter. In 1942, after improving the device, Nielsen invited 1,000 families in nine states to be members of its first Radio Listeners Panel, thereby launching the Nielsen Radio Index, which continued until 1964.

Experience with the radio panel was so positive that Nielsen adapted its device to the emerging television technology. The company tested its new "telemeter" in 1948 and began using it on a full-scale household panel in 1950. The telemeter was the forerunner of today's high-tech devices, such as the People Meter and Passive People Meter, that collect detailed TV viewing data from single-source households.

The other relevant development of the 1950s, the Home Testing Institute, had multiple influences on today's single-source systems. First, the HTI was the origin of National Panel Diary (NPD) Research, a company that in 1987 formed a joint venture with A. C. Nielsen to contribute expertise to the SCANTRACK project. Second, another major player in the single-source industry, IRI, was started by three defectors from NPD and by a fourth party who throughout the 1980s consulted for A. C. Nielsen.

The Home Testing Institute was established in 1951 by Henry Brenner at the request of the Scott Paper Company, which wanted a household panel to systematically track the home use of paper products. The service was highly successful and was soon diversified to track a variety of other products sold in retail grocery outlets. To carry on activities for other clients, Brenner subsequently formed NPD Research in 1966.

John Malec, Bill Walters, and Gerald Eskin, three of the four founders of IRI, worked for NPD during the late 1960s and early 1970s. Although NPD became the country's premier creator and user of written diary panels, it was slow to accept scanner technology. Malec, Walters, and Eskin, however, saw the possibilities clearly. The fourth visionary and founder of IRI, Penny Baron, left the company in 1983 to start a private consulting firm that worked until 1991 with A. C. Nielsen on various SCANTRACK-related products, completing a complicated network that links HTI, NPD, IRI, and A. C. Nielsen.

During the 1960s and 1970s, marketing research seemed to be in a holding pattern as both client and supplier firms tried to digest the rapid developments from earlier eras. In retrospect, this period has proved to be a time of testing and experimentation to link emerging computer technology with more sophisticated mathematical models of marketing processes. These models came from two principal sources: developments in management science (including operations research and econometrics) in the 1960s and psychometrics in the 1970s.

Economists and operations researchers suggested applications of simulation techniques, Markov models, game theory, mathematical programming, logit analysis, and time series forecasting to marketing problems. These models not only extracted descriptive detail from longitudinal databases but also suggested how management could optimize, at least in theory, certain elements of the marketing mix.

From psychometrics, key developments in multidimensional scaling (MDS), conjoint analysis, and cluster analysis paved the way for enlightened understanding of consumer decision behavior. Highly theoretical axiomatic approaches to measurement in mathematical psychology gave way to practical algorithms in both nonmetric MDS and additive conjoint measurement. Computer power also increased to the point where large-scale cluster analyses could be conducted.[5]

Developments in normative models and special packages played a major role in the evolution of today's single-source systems, primarily through their impact on reporting philosophy. Researchers saw the value of linking empirical data to "if-then" models, so that managers could project sales and market share as functions of their own and competitors' marketing mix variables. Both of the major single-source suppliers now offer extensive market response capabilities to help clients position brands, price them, and determine other levels of marketing mix variables.

The Era of Scanning and TV Cut-ins: 1978–1985

Experts in the single-source industry agree that scanning and TV cut-ins were the immediate predecessors of single-source technology. The key product in this era—BehaviorScan—was introduced by IRI in 1978 and still accounts for a significant portion of IRI's business. BehaviorScan was the first service to link scanner data to a precise vector of promotional and demographic factors that might cause purchase behavior and to forge this link at the (disaggregate) household level. BehaviorScan integrated the notions of a household panel and scanned purchase data to objectively measure both input and output factors in consumer behavior. The UPC code, reliable laser scanners, and individually addressable taps for TV panel households made BehaviorScan possible.

The UPC and Laser Scanners[6]

The UPC now found on almost every product symbolizes the advances in production, packaging, handling, and distribution that are due to automation. These innovations did not occur overnight; they are the result of a steady application of automation techniques throughout the food retailing industry.

The first experimental laser scanner was used by the General Tracking Corporation, a regional grocery distributor in Carlstadt, New Jersey, in 1969.[7] But as recently as 1973 the grocery industry was still experimenting with five approaches to identifying labels: bar codes, matrix codes, pie chart codes, fluorescing inks, and magnetic stripes. In June 1974 one of the first scanners capable of reading the Universal Product Code (UPC) was installed in Marsh's supermarket in Troy, Ohio. The scanning system was added to the store's existing computer-driven cash register. By 1980 better than 90 percent of all grocery items carried UPC codes, and today this figure exceeds 99 percent.

Currently the UPC and its European counterpart, the European Article Numbering (EAN) system, are used for a wide variety of applications, including point-of-sale scanning in drug stores, mass-merchandise outlets, and other store types. The codes are applied to library referencing problems, equipment and product inventory problems, technical problems in medicine, and other problems in a wide variety of applications. Recently, the U.S. Postal Service even announced plans to put bar codes on all letter mail by 1995. These codes will facilitate the post office's mail-sorting task but will also find numerous applications in marketing research systems. Scanning technology is essential for single-source research systems, since it facilitates rapid, large-scale data entry.

The Individually Addressable Tap

The other essential constituent for BehaviorScan is the individually addressable tap, or IAT. The IAT is one part of an ensemble of so-called automatic program insertion devices. These devices attach to a household's TV set and permit a central computer to direct a signal to that set independent of the signal's other destinations.[8] With IATs, two TVs in adjacent households can receive two different messages at the same time on the same channel. This capability is absent in dual-cable TV, the technology used previously with household panels.

Individually addressable taps were critical to the success of BehaviorScan. For the first time a panel of households could be divided into two or more randomly selected experimental treatments without regard to household geography or time. In a dual-cable system, households proximate to one another must be affixed to the same cable. Thus one treatment may consist of households on the west side of town connected to cable A and the second treatment of households on the east side of town connected to cable B. With IATs, households next to each other can be in different treatments, and households tuned to a particular channel can receive different signals.

The combination of these two features produces a system with several important advantages. First, tests for different clients can use different randomizations of the same panel. As a result, systematic factors and carry-over effects can be randomized out differently in each test. Second, because the geographic composition of the treatment groups in a given city changes each time, retail shopping behavior, which is strongly determined by trade area geography, can be tracked consistently and cleanly. Bias due to spatial relations between a fixed household subpanel and a particular group of stores is ruled out. Finally, other factors related to panel member sensitization (discussions with neighbors, demographic characteristics, and so on) are statistically eliminated.

BehaviorScan struck an immediate chord in the marketing research community. Hercules Segalas of the investment firm Drexel Burnham Lambert said, "In 20 years, it's one of the most exciting things I've seen. It comes close to being a direct measurement of the advertising dollar." And Reg Rhodes, former president of Burke Marketing Research, admitted that "IRI has changed the game as we all knew it."[9]

The results were phenomenal. IRI's operating revenues, which were nonexistent in 1978, reached $400,000 in 1979, multiplied sevenfold to $2.8 million in 1980, doubled to $5.9 million in 1981, and doubled again to more than $12.3 million by fiscal 1982. The company had profits exceeding $2 million in 1982. Revenues were cycled back into BehaviorScan, which quickly grew from two test-market cities—Pittsfield, Massachusetts, and Marion, Indiana—to nine. From a historical perspective, BehaviorScan paved the way for IRI's introduction of InfoScan in 1986.

Single-Source Integrated Systems: 1986 to the Present

Although BehaviorScan was immensely successful, it was and is primarily a TV cut-in service designed to run sophisticated tests of new products and advertising campaigns. Clients soon wanted more. In addition to evaluating a specific ad or price-off deal, clients wanted to track their brand's market share not only at the national level but by store and by trade area. They also wanted to diagnose how each marketing variable affects sales and how these variables interact with household demographics.

During the second quarter of 1986 the company introduced InfoScan to satisfy these client demands. Standard & Poor's stock report describes InfoScan as a system "which tracks the weekly purchases of every UPC-coded product sold in supermarkets nationwide and all the promotional activities that motivate consumer spending."[10] At that time, InfoScan was the only available tracking service that integrated individual household purchase data with store sales data.

First A. C. Nielsen and then SAMI/Burke followed suit, introducing SCANTRACK and SAMSCAN, respectively, in 1987. Until October 1990, when SAMSCAN was phased out of business, the three systems constituted the single-source industry.

Conclusion

Single-source systems (1) track purchase behavior at the household and store levels, (2) measure marketing variables electronically rather than manually, (3) capture causal information, and (4) integrate and align all component databases. Because they take advantage of today's powerful electronic hardware, single-source systems have also resulted in a major data explosion. Eskin outlines four contributing factors to this explosion.[11] First, the number of time periods reported on has gone from bimonthly (6 per year) with manual audits to every four weeks (13 per year) with warehouse withdrawal data to weekly with scanners. Second, the geographic resolution has changed from 11 regions with Nielsen's NFI to about 70 metro-markets with scanner data. Third, more measures are now available, up from about 10 with handwritten diaries to more than 100 with scanner data. Finally, the level of reporting detail has gone from brand aggregations to the individual UPC.

The consequences of many of these changes are reviewed in Chapter 7, which discusses the unique characteristics of single-source systems in much greater detail. Chapters 8 through 11 concentrate on reports now available to managers as a result of single-source developments.

Notes

1. In his paper "Single-Source Data: The U.S. Experience," presented to the Special Joint ARF/MRS Research Leaders Conference (Boston, July 24, 1989), Gerald Eskin states (p. 3): "Certainly the term 'single-source' is not new. Eskin and Malec used the term in 1979 at an ARF conference where they announced the opening of the first electronic test marketing service, BehaviorScan. Earlier references are also known."

2. See, for example, Lawrence C. Lockley, "History and Development of Marketing Research," in Robert Ferber (ed.), *Handbook of Marketing Research*, New York: McGraw-Hill, 1974, pp. 1-3–1-15. See also Paul E. Green and Yoram Wind, "Statistics in Marketing," Working Paper 82-014R (July 1982), University of Pennsylvania, and many of the references therein.

3. Material on A. C. Nielsen is taken from corporate documents supplied to the author by the A. C. Nielsen Company.

4. See Thomas C. Kinear and James P. Taylor, *Marketing Research: An Applied Approach,* New York: McGraw-Hill, 1987, p. 31.

5. The key figures in these three lines of research were Roger Shepard and Joseph Kruskal in nonmetric MDS, R. Duncan Luce and John Tukey in conjoint measurement, and Robert C. Tryon in cluster analysis.

6. This section relies heavily on Craig K. Harmon and Russ Adams, *Reading Between the Lines: An Introduction to Bar Code Technology,* Peterborough, NH: Helmers, 1989, Chapter 2, pp. 5–11.

7. An optical bar code had been adopted by the North American railroad industry in 1967, but its development was crippled by organizational problems and disagreement about its features. The system was phased out by about 1976.

8. See Thomas F. Baldwin and D. Stevens McVoy, *Cable Communications,* 2d ed., Englewood Cliffs, NJ: Prentice-Hall, 1988, pp. 52–56, 295.

9. See "The New Magicians of Market Research," *Fortune* 25 (July 1983) p. 73.

10. See *Standard & Poor's Corporation Standard OTC Stock Report,* 54(13) (February 1, 1988), Sec. 24: Information Resources, Inc.

11. Eskin, op cit.

7 THE MAJOR SINGLE-SOURCE SUPPLIERS

[In the next 5 to 10 years there will be] an order-of-magnitude increase in the amount of marketing data used [and] a similar tenfold increase in computer power available for marketing analysis.

John D.C. Little, "Decision Support
Systems for Marketing Managers" (1979)

If there is a phrase that summarizes the situation, that phrase is "Data Explosion." The combination (of more time periods, geographic breakdowns, measures, and detail) results in over a one thousand–fold increase in information and related data storage, display and utilization requirements. Put another way, for every one number that someone had to deal with in 1979, there are now 1,420 numbers. These statistics refer to a single category. For the data vendor, who must deal with all categories, the problem is even larger.

Gerald Eskin,
"Single Source Data: The U.S. Experience" (1989)

INTRODUCTION

This chapter compares the two U.S.-based single-source systems with respect to their overall size, the products that they deliver to clients, the structure of their household and store databases, and their specific sources of data. The chapter first stresses how single-source systems differ from local area databases—databases accumulated by a single retailer such as Safeway or Walmart. A naive analysis might conclude that "scanner data are scanner data"; why should Safeway or any other retailer sell their data to IRI and then buy the same data back in some other form? Why should a manufacturer like Dracket Corporation buy Safeway data from IRI rather than directly from the Safeway chain? The discussion squarely addresses these questions by identifying four areas where single-source systems add value to POS data.

Next the chapter discusses why single-source suppliers choose to record their particular data items in the five key databases mentioned in Chapter 6. The rationale is developed by linking these data to accepted theories related to consumer behavior, repeat buying, and economics. For example, certain single-source data are used to generate reports about loyal versus deal-prone consumers (consumer behavior), about a brand's market penetration (repeat buying), and about its price elasticity (economic theory).

In the concluding section, limitations of the existing systems are discussed. One of the most important is that the high-tech image often masks problems of statistical inference associated with data collection in today's single-source systems. In other words, although these systems collect many times more data than traditional research methods can, they are still subject to sampling and related errors (such as nonresponse, noncoverage, and field errors), which can severely distort estimates of such parameters as a brand's market share or the timing and trend of its sales. Particular features of this problem are discussed near the end of the chapter and in the appendix.

SINGLE-SOURCE SYSTEMS VERSUS LOCAL AREA DATABASES

Single-source systems are one of three subclasses of marketing research systems. These three—single-source systems, geodemographic systems, and local area databases—play different roles in the overall scheme. Geodemographic systems are the subject of Part III of the book, and discussion of them is postponed to that point. Here we consider the differences between a single-source system and a local area database.

Local Area Databases

A local area database is created when a retail outlet (usually part of a chain) uses its point-of-sale scanning equipment to monitor transactions. Management reports on sales trends, new items, and potentially deletable items are generated from the resulting database. For example, the UKROPS supermarket chain in

Virginia, in cooperation with CitiCorp, operates a local area database involving several of its stores.[1] UKROPS uses its own database to track sales of all the items it carries, thereby obtaining market feedback more quickly and more cost-effectively than an outside firm such as IRI or Nielsen could.

Retail managers sometimes succumb to the argument that their stores' own POS data can satisfactorily fulfill their firms' information needs. But strategic management sees the value of a separate and complete view of the national marketplace. Only an independent data supplier that monitors across regions, product lines, and retail outlets can effectively integrate data nationwide in a particular industry, such as packaged goods. As the following section points out, reliance only on its own data may seriously misdirect a retailer's strategic planning.

Why Local Area Databases Are Not Enough

A local area database, whether generated from a single store or from a nationwide chain, cannot accomplish certain research objectives. First, a local area database cannot monitor sales of the same or similar products in competing outlet types. As a consequence, such a system cannot report realistic sales and market share figures or other key measures at the regional level, let alone at the national level. Data in the system represent only a portion of the transactions carried out for a given SKU; the other portions consist of sales for the SKU in competing retail chains. For example, an item may move slowly in the Walmart chain but very well in the Dominicks chain.

Second, local area databases typically do not monitor causal factors that may influence in-store consumer behavior. These influences—including competitive pricing, national print and broadcast promotion, and coupons—reach households by diverse channels that are not routinely captured by scanners in a single store or chain. One of the most important advantages of a single-source system is its ability to integrate causal data (such as features, displays, and price cuts) with effects data (sales) to trace significant sales changes to their source.

Third, a local area database cannot monitor sales of products or product categories not stocked by the sponsoring chain. Simply put, transaction activity in a single store cannot be divorced from that store's fixed environment, including the brands it carries, its location, and its image. For example, an item may move slowly in the Walmart chain because it is shelved near Walmart's low-priced, private-label substitute.

Finally, a local area database cannot monitor the behavior of households who do not frequent the store or chain. This problem is a variation of nonresponse bias encountered in survey research; regular customers of Walmart may be systematically different from regular customers of Dominicks or Kroger. These differences cannot be accounted for in analyses based on data from the Walmart chain alone.

Analyses Constrained by Supply-Side Policy

Each of the preceding points is a manifestation of the more general problem of "supply-side" biased research. Simply put, a firm's internal management information system cannot be used for legitimate competitive analyses, since the data contained therein reflect the policies of the firm rather than pure market forces. For example, a store that carries only one national brand of mouthwash in addition to its private-label brand cannot diagnose how the sales of either brand would fare in face-to-face competition with other national and private brands. As a second example, a chain that locates its stores only in shopping malls cannot, by analyzing its own database, determine the effect of (nonmall) location on store sales.

Examples that illustrate the supply-side fallacy abound. In general, understanding the behavior of parts of a market system—such as a single brand's sales, a single store's sales, or household consumption—requires examination of activity at the system level—the total mix of brands, stores, households, and promotions. This point, that the behavior of a part is a function of conditions in the whole, is frequently lost on managers who claim that since they manage only a single store, they need not be concerned with nationwide activity. This argument is incorrect.

Summary

Single-source systems monitor an entire market system—all the influences on sales activity for a certain class of products. They are the first organized research systems designed to comprehensively monitor influences on sales for nationally distributed packaged goods. The pioneering work of IRI and Nielsen (and Arbitron/SAMI) is admirable, even though clients are often frustrated that the systems do not yet fulfill all the promise of high technology.[2] Chapter 6 provided a brief overview of these companies; we now examine their various product offerings in more detail.

INDUSTRY SIZE AND DIMENSIONS

Industry Size

In 1988, when Arbitron/SAMI was still a player, the combined gross revenue for the three single-source firms exceeded $1.3 billion (see Table 7.1). A. C. Nielsen was the top-ranking marketing research firm in both 1987 and 1988. SAMI was second in 1987 and third in 1988, and Information Resources was in fourth position in each of those years.[3] On the client side, more than 100 of the Fortune 500 firms are packaged goods manufacturers. Consumer packaged goods producers account for 30 percent of all Fortune 500 revenues and spend an average of $1.4 million each annually on single-source data and reports.[4]

Databases

A single-source system comprises five key databases: household, store, retail factors, promotion factors, and advertising. (See Figure 7.1.) The store and the household databases are the largest and most costly. The other three generate

TABLE 7.1.   Gross Revenues Generated by the Major Suppliers of Single-Source Data

Company	Home Office	Parent or Major Interest	Research Revenue[a]			
			1987	1988	1989[b]	1990
A. C. Nielsen	Northbrook, IL	Dun & Bradstreet	730.3	880.0	426.0	468.6
Arbitron/SAMI	Minneapolis, MN Cincinnati, OH	Control Data	324.9	320.0	253.5	230.6
Revenue generated by Burke Marketing Research					27.1	25.2
Information Resources	Chicago, IL	Citicorp[c]	105.5	129.2	113.8	136.3
Total			1,160.7	1,329.2	829.8	835.5

[a]Sources: *Advertising Age,* June 5, 1989; June 11, 1990; and June 3, 1991. All revenues are in millions of U.S. dollars. The 1987 and 1988 figures for Nielsen are estimates.
[b]Unlike the figures for 1987 and 1988, the years 1989 and 1990 do not include Nielsen's worldwide revenues.
[c]Citicorp acquired a 10–15 percent interest in IRI ca. March 1990.

data for a system's promotion environment and are linked to both the household and store databases. These databases were discussed briefly in Chapter 6 and are reviewed carefully here to convey a precise understanding of their contents and purpose.

The household and store databases employ fundamentally different observation units. A store record summarizes all UPC activity in a store for a fixed time period. Sales to individual households are not recorded in this database.

The household database, on the other hand, accumulates information from a panel of households scattered across the United States. Members of these households shop in the stores located in their local markets, but the household is the unit of observation, not the store. Of course, household records can be aggregated upward to estimate sales in a given store or across all stores in a given market, but not all households are monitored. Thus estimates of store sales from a household sample are subject to sampling error, whereas sales records in the store database constitute a "sales census"—not subject to sampling error—for a given store.[5]

The household database also records causal factors influencing household purchase patterns. Part of the record for each household identifies the promotion signals arriving in that household from various sources, including television, newspaper, radio, and other national-level signals, as well as local signals such as in-store prices and retail coupons.

To construct a store database, one must define the scanner (ACV) universe(s) to which projections will be made, the characteristics of the sample, and the data collection methods on which these projections will depend. Some data recorded at the store level are also recorded in the promotion factors databases, including in-store features and displays, store format, and prices.

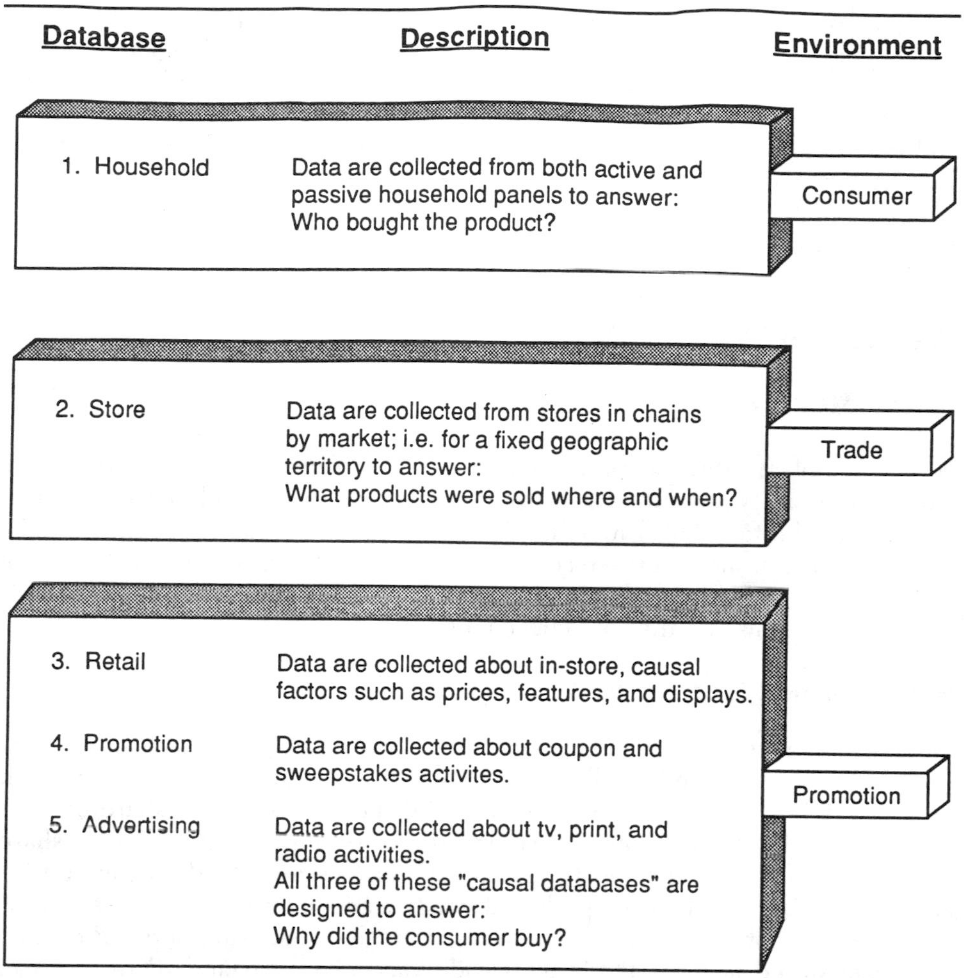

Database	Description	Environment
1. Household	Data are collected from both active and passive household panels to answer: Who bought the product?	Consumer
2. Store	Data are collected from stores in chains by market; i.e. for a fixed geographic territory to answer: What products were sold where and when?	Trade
3. Retail	Data are collected about in-store, causal factors such as prices, features, and displays.	
4. Promotion	Data are collected about coupon and sweepstakes activites.	Promotion
5. Advertising	Data are collected about tv, print, and radio activities. All three of these "causal databases" are designed to answer: Why did the consumer buy?	

FIGURE 7.1. Databases in a Single-Source System

The universe, sample characteristics, and collection methods for the household database differ from those for the store database. For a household sample, the sampling plan permits projections to the national level by loyal versus non-loyal buyer, by demographic split, and by other household characteristics. Data collection from households is also more complicated than that from stores: store data are simply written from a store's computer file to a central file, but household data come from panel members who must record their purchases either in the store or at home or both. Explicit cooperation is thus required from each member of each household included in the household panel.

Like the store database, the household sample provides a segment of the data needed for the retail factors, promotion factors, and advertising databases. But the household database focuses on signals that may differ by household, not by store. These include what TV programs are watched by various household members, what coupons they redeem, and at what stores they shop. Furthermore, a complete demographic profile is generated for each household so that researchers can analyze how demography interacts with causal signals to influence consumer decision making.

The three client segments for single-source data—manufacturers, retailers, and advertising agencies—demand different types of reports depending on the specific variables being measured during the data collection process. The household and store databases yield different sets of marketing measures of interest to clients in these segments. These measures are reviewed next.

MARKETING MEASURES

Store Measures

Four types of measures are reported from stores: sales volume measures, distribution intensity measures, in-store promotion measures, and price measures. The 47 possibilities shown in Table 7.2 are obtained by mathematical transformations of one or more of these core indices. Both IRI and Nielsen offer all 47 of these measures. Various subgroups are briefly reviewed next to point out their theoretical origins and their practical applications.

Sales Volume Measures

Sales volume is tracked by UPC in both units and dollars within each store. Thus volume can be reported at all levels from UPC up.[6] Since volume is tracked for every UPC, the volume for one UPC can be reported as a share of sales for any logically defined competitive group—for example, a given UPC's share of ready-to-eat cereal sales or its share of all cereal sales. Standard competitive groups have been defined by packaged goods manufacturers, and these groups are used in reports published by both major single-source suppliers. Of course, with data stored at the UPC level, a wide variety of nonstandard reports can also be constructed.

Distribution Intensity Measures

A second core group consists of measures of distribution intensity. Among these is the percentage of stores selling a particular item. As Table 7.2 shows, this percentage can also be weighted by ACV to account for store size. For example, if stores A and B carry item x and store C does not, then the distribution intensity for x is 67 percent, assuming that all three stores are of equal size (ACV). However, if store A has twice the ACV of either of the other two stores, then the appropriately weighted distribution intensity is $[(2/4)(A = 1) + (1/4)(B = 1) + (1/4)(C = 0)]$, or 75 percent, not 67 percent.

In-Store Promotion Measures

Each store's total ACV is broken down by various promotion categories, including feature, coupon, display, and price reduction for a given reporting period. (The shortest reporting period currently available is one week.) Thus if total store

TABLE 7.2.   Reported Measures: Store Database

Sales volume measures
  Unit volume
  Dollar volume
  Per million ACV
  Per store selling

Market share measures
  Dollar share
  Dollar share: merchandising "on"
  Dollar share: merchandising "off"

Distribution intensity measures
  ACV-weighted distribution
  Percentage of stores selling

In-store promotion measures
  Percent ACV with:
    Feature
    In-ad coupon
    Display
    Feature and display
    Price reduction
    Feature by feature ad size
    Display by display location
    Any merchandising

Cumulative measures
  Cumulative ACV-weighted weeks with:
    Feature
    Display
    Feature and display
    Price reduction
    Feature by feature ad size
    Display by display location
    Any merchandising

ACV-weighted share measures
  ACV-weighted share of:
    Features
    Displays
    Features and displays
    Features by feature ad size

Percent volume measures
  Percent of volume with:
    Feature
    Display
    Feature and display
    Price reduction
    Feature by feature ad size
    Display by display location
    Any merchandising

Price average measures
  Average:
    Price
    Price with feature
    Price with display
    Price with feature and display
    Price with price reduction
    Price with any merchandising
    Everyday regular price
    Percentage price reduction vs.
      regular price

Incremental volume measures
  Incremental:
    Volume due to trade promotions
    Dollars due to trade promotions

  Percent increase volume
    associated with:
    Feature
    Display
    Feature and display
    Price reduction

  Markdown dollars at retail

sales are $100,000 in a given week, and $12,000 of this total was sold on feature, then the percent ACV sold on feature is simply 12 percent. Because individual items are sold with several promotion variables "on," the promotion categories are not mutually exclusive. As Table 7.2 indicates, ACV is reported according to certain accepted standards, although other possibilities could be defined.

Price Measures

A single-source system records each item's base price as well as its actual sales price. The size and cause of any difference between these two prices is registered. The system can then average these data, sort them by UPC, and use other computations to report a variety of price statistics.

Other Measures

The other store measures shown in Table 7.2 are variations on those just described. A cumulative measure simply sums a basic statistic over several weeks. ACV-weighted share measures adjust for store volume. Percentage volume measures normalize other volume measures; for example, volume sold on feature is divided by a store's total volume. Finally, incremental volume measures compare the actual volume sold (by UPC) to an established baseline.

Household Measures

The household database contains four categories of measures based on four different theories: the theory of repeat buying, the theory of brand loyalty, economic theory, and marketing theory. The measures shown in Table 7.3 are variations on these themes.

Repeat Buying

The theory of repeat buying was formalized by Andrew Ehrenberg and other authors in the late 1960s and early 1970s.[7] This literature defines measures related to both trial and repeat purchasing of packaged goods, the two most basic measures being penetration and purchase frequency.

Penetration: The proportion of people who buy an item at least once in a given period (denoted b by Ehrenberg)

Purchase frequency: The average number of times buyers buy the item in the period, denoted w

Certain single-source statistics are empirical estimates of these constructs. For example, the household penetration measure shown in Table 7.3 is the proportion of households in a specified geographic market that purchased at least one unit of an item during a given period (Ehrenberg's b measure). The number of units bought on a particular purchase occasion is not an issue in the calculation of market penetration. Thus Pepsi-Cola is said to have penetrated a household whether that household bought one can or six.

Buying rate measures, the third group listed in Table 7.3, adjust for volume and purchase occasions. A purchase occasion is a store visit by a household mem-

TABLE 7.3. Reported Measures: Household Database[a]

Buyer penetration measures
    Household penetration
    Category penetration

Volume measures
    Volume per 1,000 households

Buying rate measures
    Average:
        Volume per buyer
        Purchase occasions per buyer
        Volume per purchase occasion
        Volume per deal/
            nondeal purchase occasion
        Purchase cycle
        Weekly grocery expenditure
           per buyer

Buyer loyalty measures
    Buyer loyalty within category
    Buyer loyalty within type
    Percentage buyers new to brand
    Percentage buyers new to brand
        on deal

Price measures
    Price paid per:
    Volume
    Volume: deal and nondeal
    Volume before coupon(s)

Dealing measures
    Percentage buyers or volume by:
        Any deal
        Manufacturer's coupon
        Trade deal
        Feature store coupon
        Display
        Price reduction
    Share of:
        Category deal volume
        Manufacturer coupon volume
        Trade deal volume

TV viewing measures
    Percentage households viewing
    Commercial exposure per viewing household
    Share of voice

Outlet measures
    By outlet type:
        Percent of sales
        Penetration
        Buying rate

[a] IRI does not scan in-home; thus its viewing measures are based on data from BehaviorScan (B-Scan) markets only. It cannot sort data by outlet type since all B-scan outlets are grocery stores. A. C. Nielsen's in-home scanning permits sorting by outlet type.

ber. On a single occasion an item such as Pepsi may or may not be purchased. If it is purchased, the number and size of units is at issue. These measures—such as volume per buyer, purchase occasions per buyer, and volume per purchase occasion—conveniently summarize important elements of trial and repeat purchasing.

    These measures are related to one another by various formulas. For example, using the following algebraic identity, researchers can demonstrate how changes in one variable in the marketing mix may affect repurchase rates.[8]

$$m = b \cdot w$$

$$\frac{\text{Mean}}{\text{(volume/total)}} = \frac{\text{Penetration}}{\text{(buyers/total)}} \cdot \frac{\text{Frequency}}{\text{(volume/buyer)}}$$

For example, a price reduction may increase a brand's average volume per buyer but leave the brand's penetration rate unaltered. That is, a manager's decision to reduce the price of a brand of cola, for example, can increase sales without inducing new households to purchase the product or to switch from competing brands. Ultimately, the price reduction strategy may be determined a failure because it simply increased the brand's volume among existing buyers rather than inducing Coke loyals to switch or non–cola drinkers to try a cola. Increasing sales to one's own customers at reduced prices may actually decrease revenues and profits rather than increase them. With an identity such as $m = b \cdot w$, sales changes from one period to another can therefore be decomposed into actionable constituents.[9]

Loyalty Measures

A second class of household measures is derived from the theory of brand loyalty. A brand-loyal household is operationally defined as one that buys the same brand in two successive time periods.[10] The key issue—the resolution of which is aided by single-source reports—concerns the effects of in-store promotions on loyal versus new customers of a given brand.

Single-source systems have made both retail and brand managers more aware of the short-run power of promotion. Consequently, the increased use of promotion tools has eroded brand loyalty.[11] According to a study by Needham and Harper, the percentage of customers who would stick with their brand in the face of competitor discounts fell from 80 percent to 60 percent during the 1980s.[12] Therefore, single-source systems measure brand loyalty at the category and SKU (item type) levels. In any given time period the total customer base Is divided into new and loyal buyers. Table 7.3 shows that new buyers in a given period are further divided into those buying on deal and those not buying on deal. Such decompositions aid management in diagnosing promotion effects. For example, featuring a brand may simply induce loyal customers to stock up, reducing the brand's own sales in future time periods rather than inducing trial on the part of new customers.

Economic Theory

The third category of household indices includes measures of total volume response to traditional "economic" variables such as base price and price discounts. A discount can be delivered to the household via coupon, in-store feature, or some other mode, each of which is highlighted in system reports.

Marketing Mix Variables

The last major category of household measures summarizes the extent of promotion and distribution activities and their effects on households in a panel. For example, to create television-related measures each household's total viewing time is recorded and apportioned by advertiser. Using its in-home panel, Nielsen's SCANTRACK supplements such supply-side measures with a demand-side behavioral measure: the percentage of each household's purchases by outlet type. IRI cannot yet match this capability because it uses in-store scanners exclusively and does not register household visits to nonscanner stores.

DATA DELIVERY

Single-source firms deliver standard printed reports, custom-designed printed reports, formatted data, and accessories such as factbooks and UPC dictionaries.[13] Each firm also offers extensive client support services, ranging from problem definition to strategy implementation and follow-up.

The physical products offered by single-source suppliers are delivered in the modes listed in Table 7.4: hard copy, magnetic tape, PC diskette (floppy disks), on-line query, and CD-ROM optical disk. The reader is assumed to be generally familiar with each of these. Here the differences between Nielsen and IRI in the area of data delivery are briefly highlighted.

Household Data

Both IRI and Nielsen deliver household data by hard-copy standard reports and data tapes. These traditional forms of product delivery have been used in the marketing research industry for more than three decades. IRI also supplies reports and data on PC diskette and on-line through its PC-EasyCast system; Nielsen's SCAN*Pro Monitor and SCAN*EXPERT systems are also on-line.[14] Before its demise, SAMI had moved to a more advanced form of delivery, CD-ROM, for its household data. Both IRI and Nielsen now offer data on optical disk.

Store Data

All three firms can deliver store data by hard copy, tape, and diskette; IRI and Nielsen also permit on-line access to a subset of their store databases. As of July 1989, Nielsen had 92 stores willing to release data, and IRI had 75.[15]

TABLE 7.4. Data Delivery

	InfoScan	SCANTRACK
Household data		
Hard copy	x	x
Tape	x	x
PC diskette	x	No
On-line access	x	No
Optical disk		No
Periodicity	Weekly	Weekly
Delay	1 week	1 week
Store data		
Hard copy	x	x
Tape	x	x
PC diskette	x	x
On-line access	x	x
Optical disk	x	x
Periodicity	Weekly	Weekly
Delay	3 weeks	3 weeks

SAMI developed and continues to deliver on CD-ROM three unique products called TradeMaster, DecisionMaster, and SalesMaster. Each of these products relies on the same operating principle: two years of data are stored on a CD-ROM along with a built-in query language. SAMI's approach gives clients considerable flexibility and independence. It frees them from the constraint of fixed formats and allows users to explore data on a desktop computer.

Periodicity

For the most part, household and store data are reported in weekly batches, with delays ranging from one to three weeks. Store data arrive uniformly later than household data.

COLLECTING DATA

Table 7.5 summarizes how data are collected from households and stores for the various databases in a single-source system. Both IRI and Nielsen rely heavily on in-store scanners to record the store shopped, units purchased, and prices paid household by household. Store promotions and coupon redemption activities are recorded by observers in each store. (See Table 7.6.)

Nielsen collects the most data from nonscanner stores through its portable scanner-equipped Shoppers' Panel. IRI uses BehaviorScan markets to monitor activity in drug stores, using in-store scanners like those in the supermarkets.

ISSUES IN SINGLE-SOURCE SYSTEM DESIGN

Statistical Inference

Statistical inference means generalizing to a whole after observing some of the parts. The problem of statistical inference is to quantify the relationship between the true (total population) value of a parameter, such as market share, and an estimate of this parameter based on data from a sample of the population. Single-source systems attempt accurate generalizations to at least four major populations, or "universes," as they are called in commercial brochures: a store universe, a household universe, a geographic (city/nation) universe, and a product (brand/category) universe. There are serious system design problems associated with each of these.

To illustrate, consider the following inquiries that a brand manager might pose to a single-source system, listed in order of increasing specificity. This example illustrates two important issues: (1) General queries are loaded with implicit assumptions, and (2) as queries become more and more specific, the relevant sampling frame grows smaller and smaller.

Q1: What is brand B's market share?   Averaged over all regions, all retail outlets, and all households in a fixed time period.

TABLE 7.5. Data Collection: Household Database

	InfoScan		SCANTRACK	
	In-Store	In-Home	In-Store	In-Home
Scanner grocery stores				
Store shopped	SS	na	SS	HS
Units purchased	SS	na	SS	HS
Price paid	SS	na	SS	DF/HS
Store promotions	SO	na	SO	SO/HS
Coupons redeemed	SO	na	SO	HS
Nonscanner stores				
Store shopped	na	na	na	HS
Units purchased	na	na	na	HS
Price paid	na	na	na	DF/HS
Store promotions	na	na	na	SO/HS
Coupons redeemed	na	na	na	HS
Other stores				
Store shopped	SS*	na	na	HS
Units purchased	SS*	na	na	HS
Price paid	SS*	na	na	DF/HS
Store promotion	SO*	na	na	SO/HS
Coupons redeemed	SO*	na	na	HS

Key:
HS = Home scanner   DF = Store data file
SS = Store scanner   * = Drug stores in BehaviorScan markets only
SO = Store observation

TABLE 7.6. Special Data Collection: Store Database

Displays

Lobby
Front-end aisle
Mid-aisle
Back-end aisle
Shipper
Trial size
Specialty

Feature ads

Four types coded

Manufacturer coupons

FSI
ROP
Sunday supplement
Woman's magazine
Direct mail

Q2: What is brand B's market share:
  a. In the Pacific Northwest? Averaged over all stores and households
  b. In the Kroger chain? Averaged over all regions and households
  c. In single-parent households? Averaged over all regions and stores

Q3: What is brand B's market share:
  a. In the Pacific Northwest and in the Kroger chain? Averaged over all households
  b. In the Pacific Northwest and single-parent households? Averaged over all outlets
  c. In the Kroger chain and single-parent households? Averaged over all regions

Q4: What is brand B's market share in single-parent households in the Pacific Northwest in the Kroger chain?

The value of the parameter "brand B's market share" differs within each of the universes implied by each question. An estimate of market share based on the sample offered by a particular single-source system will be in error. The magnitude and structure of this error depend on the sampling procedures used by the system and on other factors, such as the accuracy of data entry, the method used to analyze the data, and operational definitions (of "category" of "brand B"). Although this chapter is not an appropriate place to explore statistical issues in detail, the reader is cautioned that each system uses different methods for defining the sampling frame for each of these universes. Furthermore, as management inquiries become more focused, estimates become less reliable. In Q4, for example, only a small portion of the total sample applies. In such a case, sample properties are often unknown, and estimates are usually unstable because the effective sample size may be very small.

Universe Definitions

Even the definition of a particular "universe" can be problematic. For example, there are two store universes currently defined in packaged goods: the $2 million ACV scanner universe and the $4 million ACV scanner universe. The former includes only scanner-equipped grocery stores selling at least $2 million annually—approximately 21,000 stores in the United States. It excludes non-scanner stores of all types, including grocery stores, and any scanner-equipped store selling less than $2 million annually. (Such stores exist.)

Figure 7.2 illustrates one way to view store structure. Existing single-source systems address only a small portion of the possibilities.

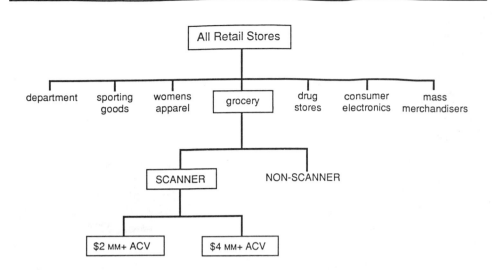

IRI uses in-store scanners exclusively and defines its store universe as $2MM ACV+. Its store sample of 2,175 stores in 66 cities (49 passive + 17 supplemental including 6 B-Scan markets) yields between 75–85% coverage in each city.

A.C. Nielsen issues separate reports for the $2MM and the $4MM ACV + universe. Its store panel consists of 2,675 stores in 50 cities that cover on average about 75–85% of total ACV volume in the $2MM universe and about 67–72% in the $4MM universe.

FIGURE 7.2. Possible Store Universes

CONCLUSION

Pointing out these issues is not meant to detract from the power of single-source systems, nor is it meant to denigrate system designers. The design problems they face are complex, and the amount of financial and human resources already devoted to solving these problems is staggering. The fact that today's systems are operational is a credit to the dedication of a relatively small number of industry founders and a very large number of technical support staff.

Despite the effort invested thus far in single-source systems, industry experts realize that improvements are needed in all phases from data collection to report generation. The most pressing need is to ensure that the millions of dollars invested in hardware yield dividends to practicing managers. Both of the primary single-source firms are improving their standard and custom reports in response to the criticism that emphasis has been placed on the technical development of these systems rather than on their ability to improve the timing and quality of management decisions.[16] The next four chapters deal more specifically with single-source reports.

Notes

1. See Roy Schwedelson, "New Wave Database," *Direct Marketing* (March 1988), p. 40; and Terrence V. O'Brien, "Decision Support Systems," *Marketing Research* (December 1990), pp. 51-55.

2. Weaknesses of single-source systems are reviewed in the following articles: Blair Peters, "The Brave New World of Single Source Information;" Verne B. Churchill, "The Role of Ad Hoc Survey Research in a Single Source World;" and Gale D. Metzger, "Single Source: Yes and No (The Backward View);" all appearing in *Marketing Research* 2(4) (December 1990), pp. 13–21, 22–26, and 27–33, respectively.

3. The other two firms consistently in the top five are IMS International and Research International. See *Advertising Age*'s annual special section on the research business.

4. This figure is taken from a 1989 study by Temple, Barker & Sloane, Inc. based on a survey of 50 leading consumer packaged goods manufacturers.

5. Note, however, that the stores included in a single-source system are still a sample of a larger store universe. This point is discussed further at the end of the chapter. In a single store, households from the household database constitute only a sample of all households shopping that store in a given time period; the store's "store record," however, contains sales for all transactions in that period.

6. Other possible reporting categories are SKU, variety (such as size or flavor), brand, category, department, store, and chain, to name just a few.

7. See A. S. C. Ehrenberg, *Repeat Buying*, New York: North Holland, 1972. See also Gerald J. Eskin, "Dynamic Forecasts of New Product Demand Using a Depth of Repeat Model," *Journal of Marketing Research* 10(2) (May 1973), pp. 115–129; and J. H. Parfitt and B. J. K. Collins, "The Use of Consumer Panels for Brand-Share Prediction," *Journal of Marketing Research* 5 (May 1968) pp. 131–146.

8. This is an algebraic identity rather than a "natural law" because b cancels in the numerator and denominator on the right-hand side: $v/t = (b/t) \cdot (v/b)$. Thus the formula is true by definition. For a formula to achieve the status of a natural law such as $e = mc^2$, all constructs must be independently definable and measurable; for example, m and c^2 are not simple algebraic factors of e.

9. Another useful volume identity is:

Sales = (Number of buyers) (Average number of occasions per buyer)
(Average number of units per occasion) (Average price per unit)

Various marketing programs affect each of these components differently. Program effects can be diagnosed more precisely using this decomposition.

10. The operational definition of loyalty may vary from supplier to supplier, but in no case does it include an attitudinal component. These definitions differ from the conventional interpretation that loyalty is both an attitudinal and a behavioral construct.

11. Gerard J. Tellis, "Advertising Exposure, Loyalty and Brand Purchase: A Two-Stage Model of Choice," *Journal of Marketing Research,* 15(2) (May 1988), pp. 134–144. Tellis' findings were also discussed in *The Wall Street Journal* (February 15, 1989), p. B6 and (March 1, 1989), p. B6.

12. See William C. Johnson, "Sales Promotion: It's Come Down to 'Push Marketing,' " *Marketing News* (April 1988), p. 2.

13. Various types of reports and reporting principles are discussed in Chapter 8. Reports for each client segment are discussed in Chapters 9 to 11.

14. For more detail, see Chapter 8.

15. Certain stores are unwilling to release sales for private-label and/or generic brands, and in some cases data are not available by week. See Advertising Research Foundation, "The ARF Scanner-Based Services Fact Sheet" (April 1989).

16. See, for example, "Technology Deals with Data Mass It Created," *Marketing News* (April 10, 1989), pp. 1–2.

APPENDIX 7A:
ERRORS IN SINGLE-SOURCE SYSTEMS

Introduction

This appendix is divided into four sections, each corresponding to an important type of error in single-source systems; (1) error in estimation, (2) error due to lack of respondent compliance, (3) error in system input, and (4) error in analysis. Errors in estimation occur for a variety of reasons. The first section concentrates on mismatches between a single-source system's intended sampling frame(s) and the sampling frame(s) achieved by the system's operating practices. The section outlines reasons for such mismatches and illustrates, using a simple example, that the resulting biases in estimated sales and market shares are more serious in some product categories than in others.

Noncompliance and nonresponse errors are closely linked to whether a system relies on in-store or in-home scanning to collect data from households.[1] IRI relies exclusively on in-store scanning, and Nielsen uses a mixture of data from in-home and in-store scanners. For example, UPCs and store IDs are scanned in the home, but prices are read from store files.

Measurement errors in single-source systems are due to malfunctioning equipment as well as human error. The third section describes a variety of errors in this class, including those due to "high cones," missing price data, and data misalignment.

The final section of the appendix concentrates on faulty analysis of scanner data. Using a simplified but well-structured example, the section shows how a common analysis practice can lead to serious errors regarding the relative effectiveness of various merchandising activities. The example points out that single-source data are not collected according to a controlled experimental design but rather using a design with unknown statistical properties. Results are sensitive to the effects of omitted variables, especially when omitted variables and included variables interact.

Errors in Estimation

The most basic requirement of a single-source system is that it accurately report a brand's market share in a variety of contexts, for example, in a given metro-market, among outlets in a particular retail chain, or among shoppers of a particular type. Accuracy is judged by how well the reported share agrees with the true (population) share. The problem is that different questions imply different populations, each requiring special attention to ensure that estimates based on a sample from that population are accurate. Because single-source systems are so complex, system designers were able to give special attention to only a relatively few such implied populations. For example, the population of all retail stores nationwide that are both scanner-equipped and have yearly (ACV) sales exceeding $2 million dollars is well defined. Each system's store panel is fairly representative of this nationwide population. However, these systems were not designed to respond well to ad hoc queries that demand an accurate estimate of a brand's market share among Kroger stores in Cleveland, for example, or among brand-loyal consumers shopping Walmart. Each ad hoc query implies a very special population. The match is often poor between a system's household and store sampling frames and sampling frames that could be justified theoretically. Resulting estimates therefore have unknown properties. They may be biased, they may have very large standard errors, or they may be quite good in some cases but grossly inadequate in others.

Studies that bear on these issues indicate that in certain product categories point-of-sale scanner data misrepresent sales volume and market share. Average errors are between ±3 percent and ±10 percent but can reach an order of magnitude of 100 or more (that is, true share may be 10 percent but reported share 0.1 percent).[2]

There are at least four reasons for these errors:

1. Different scanning approaches provide different degrees of market coverage.
2. The definition of the store universe builds in bias.
3. The sampling frame of stores within markets contributes to sampling error.
4. There is an interaction among the extent of an item's distribution, a system's coverage, and the sampling frame.

An Illustration

Table 7.7 uses the ground pepper product category to illustrate these points. In contrast to categories such as canned soup or air fresheners, in which nearly all stores carry all brands, two major pepper brands dominate each market: Durkee and Spice Islands. Private-label brands represent a significant share, and most retailers stock only one national brand.[3] For example, in the Randall's stores shown in Figure 7.3, one manager stocks Spice Islands (S), and the other stocks Durkee (D).

Warehouse withdrawal estimates are included in Table 7.7 as a comparative baseline to show how an alternative data collection approach would lead to different levels of market coverage and different estimates of market share. Moving from left to right in the exhibit, warehouse withdrawal data (column b) typically offer about 95 percent coverage and reflect shares fairly well at the market level.[4] A system that uses only in-store scanners and excludes stores with less than $2 million annual ACV might yield 74 percent coverage and would misrepresent shares. As column c shows (vs. actuals in column a), Durkee's market share is underestimated (16 estimated versus 24 actual), and P4's share is overestimated (23 versus 17 actual).[5] If in-home scanning supplements in-store scanning (column d), coverage and estimates improve considerably in theory as long as panel households are cooperative and representative. However, if the Randall's chain is excluded from the sampling plan (column e), either because the single-source supplier excludes it or because this chain does not want to participate, coverage is severely reduced, and market share estimates are more error-prone.

Column f shows the wide range of share estimates that might result in these varying situations. For example, Durkee's estimated market share ranges from a low of 9 percent with one system (in-store scanning, Randall's not participating)

TABLE 7.7.   Single-Source Systems: Volume and Share with Various Approaches

	Albertson's	(+2 MM) Eagle	(+2MM) Econofood	(−2MM) Randall's	(+2MM) Safeway	(−2MM) Nonscanner
Market 1	— —	S 5 P1 6	D 4 P2 4	S 4 P3 2	S 10 P4 10	D 4 P1 2
Market 2	(−2 MM) D 6 P5 5	— —	— —	(+2MM) D 8 P3 15	(+2MM) S 5 P4 7	(−2MM) D 2 P1 1
	(*a*)	(*b*)	(*c*)	(*d*)	(*e*)	(*f*)

Brand	True Share Volume = Share	Warehouse Withdrawal		Scanner Universe: In-store Scanning		Scanner Universe & In-home Scanning		In-store Scanning, Randall's Not Participating		Each Brand's Observed Share Range
		Volume	Share	Volume	Share	Volume	Share	Volume	Share	
D	24	24	25	12	16	24	24	4	9	9–25
S	24	24	25	20	27	24	24	16	34	24–34
P1	9	8	8	6	8	9	9	6	13	8–13
P2	4	3	3	4	6	4	4	4	9	3–9
P3	17	16	17	15	20	17	17	0	0	0–20
P4	17	16	17	17	23	17	17	17	35	17–35
P5	5	4	5	0	0	5	5	0	0	0–5
Total	100	95	100	74	100	100	100	47	100	100

Key: D: Durkee
     S: Spice Islands
     P1: Private label 1
+2MM: All-commodity volume exceeds $2 million annually

to a high of 25 percent with warehouse withdrawal data. The brand's true share is 24 percent. Each brand is affected differently; accuracy differs between sub-markets, and the timing of events differs across data collection methods.[6]

In-Home versus In-Store Scanning

A second controversy about data collection occurs at the other end of the product movement pipeline—in the consumer's home. Members of Nielsen's Shoppers' Panel use an in-home data-capturing device, and IRI panel members do not. Nielsen's hand-held scanners have sufficient random-access memory to store several days' worth of scanning, which can be downloaded through a panelist's phone to a central computer. Three issues dominate discussions about in-home scanning: panelist compliance, data capture, and retail coverage.

Compliance

IRI relies exclusively on in-store scanners because they collect data unobtrusively. Therefore panel members are easier to recruit, the resulting (household) sample is more representative, and causal factors (features, displays, and so forth) are more easily coordinated and integrated into system databases. Since experimental testing is not the primary focus of a single-source system, one can argue that passive data collection by means of in-store scanners is most sensible. After all, these systems were created to reduce the workload encountered with handwritten diaries. In-home scanners once again make panel members active participants in the research process and are subject to the attendant problem of noncompliance; a panelist simply refuses to scan certain items for one reason or another. One can also argue that demanding active participation in data entry increases the likelihood that certain demographic and ethnic groups will refuse to participate in a household panel. Thus nonrespondents tend to be systematically different from respondents, a fact that decreases the accuracy of estimates.

Retail Coverage

Another point of contrast between in-store and in-home scanning concerns each method's retail coverage. A system based on in-store scanners may miss purchases from nonscanner stores, large but nonparticipating scanner stores, or scanner stores with less than $2 million ACV. Assuming compliance, households using in-home scanning should record all of their purchases regardless of the retail outlet used. Nielsen argues that IRI's in-store scanners underestimate market share and sales volume for items whose sales come primarily from convenience stores. This argument has merit, as does IRI's counterargument that noncompliance and nonresponse bias in the home more than offset the coverage advantages. One thing is certain, however: Manufacturers attempting to make informed distribution decisions appreciate knowing the types of outlets in which their items sell best. Nielsen can offer sales and share figures by outlet type. IRI's capacity to do so is limited.

Measurement Errors

There are three classes of data capture problems: problems due to the scanning mechanism per se, problems due to other electronic errors, and missed causal data. With regard to scanning per se, in-store scanners are subject to misreading multi-item packages—for example, a six-pack of Coke might be scanned as one can—often because of the plastic band used in the packaging technique. Industry jargon refers to this as a "high-cone problem" in reference to the conelike form of plastic multipacks. High-cone problems are most prevalent in categories such as carbonated beverages, beer, canned juices, bottled water, and others where multi-item packaging is regularly used.[7]

Both single-source systems are subject to a variety of data capture problems due to retail electronic and data alignment problems. The most common problems are bad prices, no prices, bad volume, and data misalignment. Bad prices occur when a retailer's price differs from the price consumers paid. This usually happens when a store's price file is improperly updated, or when a price is simply misentered by the system operator. In some cases retailers completely neglect to send IRI or Nielsen a price for a given item.

Retailers also occasionally forward incorrect sales volumes because of data-processing errors. For example, a retailer may report sales in weeks 1 through 4 and then fail to report sales in weeks 5 and 6. In week 7 sales reporting resumes, but the retailer may send a cumulative sales report for an unknown number of weeks. When asked to reconstruct what actually happened during weeks 5 through 7, the retailer may be unable to respond.

There are two major kinds of data alignment problems: feature/display–volume misalignment and price–volume misalignment. In either case, the week an actual event occurs (a feature is turned "on" or a price is changed) is not the same as the week in which the corresponding volume is recorded. These problems can often be detected post hoc by noting a volume "blip" and aligning it with the closest promotion event. Obviously, inferential rules must be used to decide how to realign the data. Even cleverly designed rules can be in error.

Finally, missed causal data occurs when an item is featured or displayed but the merchandising event is not recorded at all. Both IRI and Nielsen capture causal data manually using in-store observers. Missed causal data is therefore due to human error.

Misuses of Scanner Data

A final class of problems stems from the way single-source data are used by retail and brand managers to make critical decisions. Although these problems come in a variety of forms, one common practice among manufacturers is to use single-source reports to gauge the effects of in-store merchandising activities on its brands' sales volumes. The practice involves three steps. First, select a sample of stores that show variation in merchandising activities.[8] Second, tally sales among stores with like merchandising conditions. For example, tally sales in stores in a given week where a brand is featured. Finally, compare the average sales in these stores with sales in stores where the brand is not featured.

There are two problems with this approach: (1) Sales of an item are influenced by *systematic* factors not controlled in this quasi-experimental approach, and (2) the "experimental design" does not account for interaction effects. Each of these problems is illustrated next using a simple numerical example.

The illustration involves a situation where the true effects are as shown in the following table. For simplicity, we assume that management is interested in estimating the effect of featuring on brand sales. Unknown to management, however, features and displays interact. That is, simultaneously featuring and displaying the brand causes sales to increase to 120 units, an increase that exceeds that expected from the sum of effects due to featuring and displaying alone.

	Display		
Feature	**On**	**Off**	**Feature Effect**
On	120	100	110
Off	90	90	90
Display effect	105	95	100

To calculate the sales response to feature, management may follow the procedure just outlined: Tally sales in stores featuring and compare them to stores not featuring. The main problem is that in any given week, a disproportionate number of stores featuring may come from column 1 rather than column 2 of the table. In an extreme case, all stores may come from column 1 (D on), and the following would result:

Store conditions	**Model**
F on, D on	120 + error
F off, D on	90 + error
Estimated effect of feature	30 (1.5 times actual)[9]

The actual effect of feature is 20 units, the value given in the row marginals $(110 - 90)$, which averages out the effect due to display. Although this is an extreme example, it is important to realize that *any* imbalance in the sample on which conclusions are drawn will bias management's view of the effectiveness of features and displays for this brand. Simply put, trying to estimate the effect of one merchandising variable without controlling for the effects of another leads to biased estimates. Errors are magnified when there are interactions between variables included in a design and variables omitted systematically from it. The main problem with standard single-source reports is that they virtually always omit critical variables, such as competitors' merchandising activities, that may systematically interact with analysis variables. Chapter 18 indicates how this problem can be avoided.

Conclusion

This appendix used a series of logical arguments and simple examples to illustrate various sources of error in single-source data and reports. Four error types are identified: (1) estimation errors, (2) compliance errors, (3) measurement errors, and (4) analysis errors. Measurement errors are probably the least important of these, and estimation errors are arguably the most important since they stem from the inherent complexity in a single-source system. Sadly, the various error sources compound one another, rendering the final error structure difficult to analyze with traditional statistical techniques.

Notes

1. Note that the *store panels* of both IRI and Nielsen rely on in-store scanning; thus both panels face equivalent measurement problems.

2. See Information Resources, Inc., "The Magnitude and Structure of Error Estimation in BehaviorScan Experiments" (January 1982) and the SAMI-Burke validation study (ca. January 1988).

3. This example draws on the findings from SAMI-Burke's study comparing warehouse withdrawal data with point-of-purchase scanner data. Ground pepper is not an isolated instance. Similar problems arise in a number of product categories.

4. The word *coverage* is used to indicate the percentage of total ACV that is tracked by a single-source sysetem as goods traverse the product movement pipeline. Thus 100 percent coverage means that a system monitors every item; that is, the system succeeds in collecting a real-time census of all items in transit. Adequate coverage is easier to attain in the early stages of product movement because goods are bundled in large units, such as truckloads, from warehouse to retailer. But as goods leave retail, they do so in small quantities dispersed among a large number of buyers. Hence attaining acceptable coverage becomes much more difficult. Note that low coverage does not imply poor share estimates, although it increases their likelihood. However, high coverge does imply accurate share estimates.

5. Durkee's volume in column *c* is estimated using Econofood's entry (D-4) in market 1 plus Randall's entry (D-8) in market 2. These two stores are the only ones that satisfy the logical conjunction (scanner store = yes and ACV ≥ $2 million).

6. Warehouse withdrawal data are prone to errors in trend lines, especially for seasonal items, items that will soon be promoted at retail, and new items. In all three cases, retailers tend to build their stock in anticipation of sales. The stock buildup is registered by warehouse withdrawls even though the goods may not yet have sold at retail.

7. Though both in-store and in-home scanners are subject to mechanical errors, read rates exceed 99 percent accuracy.

8. Note that this is a sample of either IRI's or Nielsen's store panel, which is in turn a sample from a particular store universe, such as the $2 million–plus ACV universe.

9. The model assumes that actual sales on feature may differ from 120 in different stores but that these "errors" will average out among stores featuring. A similar argument is made for nonfeaturing stores. Further, a statistician would average the differences in the row marginals to yield an effect of 10 rather than 20 for featuring. The recovered effect would also be averaged to 15 rather than 30, so that estimated sales would still be 1.5 times actual sales.

8 CONCEPTS IN SINGLE-SOURCE REPORTING

You can have all the facts and still not have any information. You can have lots of information and not know what it means. You can know exactly what it means but not know what to do.

Paraphrased from an A. C. Nielsen brochure
(1988)

INTRODUCTION

Chapter 7 introduced a small part of what is potentially a rich vocabulary for discussing research reports and the reporting process. The chapter used a few terms, such as *delivery mode* and *periodicity*, that have entered the marketing research vocabulary. This chapter systematically accumulates and integrates these and related ideas to form a comprehensive framework for discussions of single-source reports.[1]

The framework highlights important distinctions among report types, differences that affect the cost of preparing a report, its domain of applicability, and its inherent limitations. Most marketing research systems require a mixture of report types. The framework introduced in this chapter establishes parameters that define this mix and suggests both the strengths and weaknesses of reports that fit into each framework cell.

The chapter first defines each dimension of the framework and then uses these dimensions to classify the reports currently offered by single-source suppliers. Table 8.1 foreshadows this classification, showing one example in each of six main cells in the framework.

TABLE 8.1.   Prototypes for Each Report Possibility

	Market Status Reports		Market Response Reports	
	Standard	**Custom**	**Standard**	**Custom**
Procedure	Nielsen: Retail account reports	Nielsen: ADPRO reports	IRI: Apollo reports	IRI: Assessor
Model	Nielsen: SCAN*Pro Modeler	IRI: Apollo TotalStore		

THE MAJOR DIMENSIONS OF A REPORT

What are the principal dimensions of a report, aside from the medium on which it is delivered and the timing of its arrival? That is, what features might permit us to differentiate reports?[2]

The first dimension divides a report's content (its numbers, text, and graphs) into two parts: a focal portion and a contextual portion. Focal-analytic variables specify what is analyzed, for example, *market share*; contextual variables specify the circumstances under which the focal variable is reported, for example, market share for *brand B* in *region R*.

The second dimension identifies whether the report summarizes historical information or predicts future events. A market status report summarizes historical information—"what was" or "what happened"; it is postdictive. A market response report answers the question "what if" and is based on a strict set of assumptions about future conditions; it is predictive.

The third dimension identifies a report's operating premise, that is, the mechanism, whether a theoretical model or a procedure, that creates the information delivered in the report. Models are costly to develop and require more abstract thinking than do procedures. Most reports can be constructed by following the steps in a procedure without recourse to model-building principles. However, as will be shown, some reports—especially market response reports—must rely on a model in order to fulfill their preassigned function.

The final dimension identifies whether a report is standard or customized. Standard reports are "mass-produced" and delivered to a client at predefined times. They require little special programming or other extraordinary methods to prepare. Standard reports for different clients may contain identical focal-analytic and contextual variables, but since each client specifies the particular product or environment of interest, the results of the analysis are specific to the client's needs. The numbers, text, and graphs delivered in a standard report may differ by client, but the format is identical across clients. Custom reports, on the other hand, require special preparation, do not have a regular delivery schedule, and have contextual and/or focal-analytic variables uniquely defined to match a client's problem. These reports are usually delivered by a support team assigned to work closely with the client.

REPORT CONTENT: FOCUS AND CONTEXT

Defining Ideas

A report consists of two major parts: the primary subject matter, defined by a set of focal-analytic variables, and a context, defined by a set of contextual variables fixed at certain levels. For example, the SCAN*Pro Monitor report shown in Table 8.2 was constructed using three contextual variables (time period, city, and category) and two focal-analytic variables (total volume, in equivalent units, and baseline volume). The other printed variables—all focal-analytic, such as share of category—are simply transformations of these two.

Examples of contextual and focal-analytic variables are readily available in commercial software such as SAS or SPSS. For example, SAS uses *by* variables to define a report's context. Asking for sales reported *by city* generates a report with sales as the focal-analytic variable and city as the contextual variable. As another example, an analyst who asks for treatment means in an analysis of variance experiment is asking for a report with one focal-analytic variable—the dependent variable—reported at all levels on one or more contextual variables—the treatment variables in the experiment.

Contextual and focal-analytic variables are not mutually exclusive: A given variable can serve either function depending on reporting needs. For example, although sales is usually a focal-analytic variable, an analyst might design a report that shows market share of brand *b* in store chains with ACV $\geq$ \$4 million and

TABLE 8.2.   SCAN*Pro MONITOR: Total Volume and Share Report

From Week Ending 10/8/88
Through Week Ending 12/31/88

In Seattle

	Total Equivalent Unit Volume	Percent Volume Change vs. Year Ago	Share of Category	Share Point Change vs. Year Ago
Sparkling mineral water	6,578	(23.4)	6.1	(4.3)
Sparkling mineral water	0	*	0.0	0.0
Sparkling water	223	22,200.0	0.2	0.2

	Baseline Percent of Total Volume	Baseline Volume	Percent Baseline Change vs. Year Ago	Share of Category Baseline	Baseline Share Point Change vs. Year Ago
Sparkling mineral water	86.2	5,673	(25.4)	5.9	(4.9)
Sparkling mineral water	*	0	*	0.0	0.0
Sparkling water	93.3	208	20,700.0	0.2	0.2

Source: Copyright A.C. Nielsen Co.. Actual data are shown but the year and market are disguised.

in chains with ACV < \$4 million. In this case the sales variable (ACV) is used to define the report's context. Similarly, a report that shows mean price for brand b when it is "on feature," "on discount," and "on display" uses price as a focal-analytic variable. However, to report market share for brand b when it is "on a price deal" versus "not on a price deal" is to use price as a contextual variable.

Report Design Considerations

The distinction between focus and context provides a useful way to address issues in report design. A given report can always be partitioned into two mutually exclusive, exhaustive sections by means of this dichotomy. The designer's first step is to decide in which capacity the available variables might serve. Once this decision has been made, subsequent design decisions are far less complicated.

Variations on this dichotomy have been suggested by other authors. For example, McCann and his colleagues at Duke's Marketing Workbench Laboratory mention four parts of a report: context, data, observations, and conclusion.[3] The *context section* contains information about the category, brands, markets, and time periods; it states the context of the analysis. The *data section* contains numerical or graphical data that support or illustrate the observations and conclusions that follow. The *observations section* contains one or more sentences or phrases about the data. These observations are usually obtained directly from the data. The *conclusion section* goes beyond the direct observations and makes one or more broader statements about the situation. Thus for McCann and colleagues the data section comprises focal-analytic variables whose information content is interpreted in the observations and conclusion sections.[4]

REPORT PERSPECTIVE

The report perspective is based on whether a report describes "what is" or "what will be."[5] A market status report tells a manager the current state of affairs — "what is" the market share of brand B or the price of brand X. Such a report usually includes "what was" for comparative purposes.

Most reports currently offered by the two major single-source suppliers are market status reports.[6] For example, Nielsen's Market Sales Report (part of its Retail Accounts report series) shows total sales every four weeks in a given geographic market, by product category within department. (See Figure 8.1.) IRI's Category and Topline Report from its PromotionScan series is also a market status report. It details sales in a particular region, breaks nationwide volume and incremental volume down within a specific category, and shows the value of trade support for each SKU.

Even though market status reports seem rudimentary, they require a steady stream of disaggregate data largely unavailable from projects or traditional written diaries. Scanner technology has made market status reports more accurate, far more detailed, and available at far shorter intervals.

MARKET SALES REPORT

CURRENT: 4 WEEKS ENDING 01/31/87 (FROM WEEK ENDING 01/10/87)
PREVIOUS: 4 WEEKS ENDING 01/03/87 (FROM WEEK ENDING 12/13/86)
YEAR AGO FIGURES NOT AVAILABLE

	DOLLAR SALES		DOLLAR SALES PERCENT CHANGE		SHARE OF DOLLAR SALES			OPERATOR SHARE OF MARKET DOLLAR SALES		
	CURR 4 WEEKS	PREV 4 WEEKS	CURR VS PREV	CURR VS Y/A	CURR 4 WEEKS	PREV 4 WEEKS	Y/A 4 WEEKS	CURR 4 WEEKS	PREV 4 WEEKS	Y/A 4 WEEKS
TOTAL SALES DOLLARS Cincinnati	139,495,196	143,648,046	-2.9	N/A	100.0	100.0	N/A			
DRY GROCERY ITEM TOTALS Cincinnati	69,995,713	72,272,180	-3.1	N/A	50.2	50.3	N/A			
BABY FOOD Cincinnati	1,062,378	1,013,537	4.8	N/A	.8	.7	N/A			
BAKING MIXES Cincinnati	1,159,368	1,136,647	2.0	N/A	.8	.8	N/A			

COMPANY: XYZ CORPORATION
CATEGORY: PANCAKE SYRUPS
MARKET AREA

PromotionScan

Category and Brand Topline Report

Time Period: 06.23.86 to 12.15.86

	VOLUME						TRADE SUPPORT				
PRODUCT	Total Volume	Vol Share	Base Share	Incr Share	Incr Weeks	% ACV on Deal	Avg Wks Feat Only	Avg Wks Displ Only	Avg Wks F+D	Avg Wks Price Red Only	Avg% Price Red
Aunt Jemima	2.64890M	21.5	20.0	1.5	2.0	30.8	0.3	0.4	0.1	7.2	20.8
12 oz	242,304	2.0	1.9	0.1	0.8	1.3	0.0	0.0	0.0	0.3	15.9
24 oz	609,936	5.0	4.5	0.5	3.0	9.4	0.2	0.2	0.0	2.1	19.2
36 oz	119,232	1.0	0.9	0.1	2.2	2.4	0.0	0.1	0.0	0.5	16.4
Log Cabin	3.08927M	25.1	21.9	3.2	3.8	44.1	0.4	1.2	0.0	9.8	26.3
12 oz	345,360	2.8	2.7	0.1	1.2	5.4	0.0	0.1	0.0	1.3	27.8
24 oz	939,024	7.6	6.6	1.1	4.3	21.8	0.2	0.8	0.0	4.7	22.7
36 oz	306,108	2.5	2.3	0.2	2.2	7.5	0.1	0.0	0.0	1.9	20.4

FIGURE 8.1. Market Status Reports

Market status reports reflect an accounting philosophy, whereas market response reports answer a managerial question: If we take this action, what will happen? The if-then structure requires a model of the demand process. For example, Nielsen's SCAN*Pro Planner "supports your promotion decisions by simulating the market response to alternative strategies. With SCAN*Pro Planner you can find out the most likely results of your promotion decisions before you put plans into action."[7] Similarly IRI's Apollo system shows a store manager how a store section will look if it is rearranged to maximize direct product profitability or to accommodate a new item that requires a certain amount of shelf space.

REPORT OPERATING PREMISE

The third dimension in this framework, also suggested by Little, is the report's operating premise. The framework distinguishes a report based on a procedure from one based on a model. This distinction is based on two important new questions: How is the report created, and what *can* it mean?

As Little described the two operating premises, "a procedure is a way of calculating a result; a model is a set of assumptions about how something works."[8] For example, a child tying his or her shoes invokes a procedure—rules that will always result in a specific outcome if applied in an appropriate situation. Arithmetic operations such as addition and subtraction invoke procedures, and many solutions in more complicated disciplines, such as the relational algebra in database management systems, matrix algebra in mathematics, and computer programming in computer science, are sets of procedures.

Note that market status reports are premised on procedures. For example, historical totals, index numbers, and baselines are calculated by procedures. However, a market response report must rely on a model. For the purpose of this chapter, a model is defined as a correspondence between an empirical relational system (a restricted domain of the real world) and a logical relational system (usually a deductive branch of mathematics). (See Figure 8.2.) For example, in marketing,, each brand in a product category is often represented by an attractiveness number. A brand's market share is modeled as the ratio of its overall attractiveness to category attractiveness. Computing attractiveness ratios is the essence of the multinomial logit model. In this model, real-world objects (brands) and empirical relationships among these objects (their respective physical movement from store shelf to household shelves) are represented by hypothetical constructs (attractiveness numbers) and logical relations among these constructs (attractiveness ratios).

The critical difference between a model and a procedure is that a model must have both internal (deductive) consistency and external (inductive) relevance, whereas a procedure requires only a crude form of internal consistency. That is, if certain steps are permuted or omitted, a procedure will fail to produce the desired result. Further, a procedure is totally action-oriented: it must be executed to function, and is not conducive to reflective, deductive thinking. A model, on the other hand, is not executable. It is potential and not kinetic in nature; its symbols and syntax are parts of a metaphor that facilitates reasoning about the real world. Managers derive results, forecasts, and conclusions about the real world by following deductive thought chains in a model. But these conclusions may or may not hold once they are transported back across the inductive bridge between the empirical and logical relational systems. Good models yield deductive conclusions that travel well.

This distinction between models and procedures is without doubt the most important one discussed in this chapter, because it strikes directly at the degree and type of artificial intelligence possessed by a system's report production facility.[9] Even unintelligent research system reports can answer fact-based questions. Model-based systems not only answer if-then questions, but they also generate a series of assertions, each of which is either true or false. These assertions stimulate management inquiries and facilitate a manager's understanding of marketplace activities.

For example, a testable hypothesis is formed from the completion of the following sentence: "If we raise our price 10 percent, our sales will . . . *decrease by 4,000 units.*" Since managers will base important decisions on the model

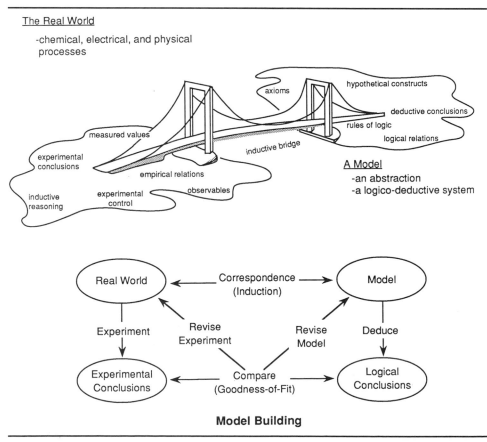

FIGURE 8.2. Modeling and Model Building

that produced this assertion, the model's accuracy should be constantly tested. Each model-generated statement affords such a test, and evidence for or against a model accumulates over time. Although discussion would lead into unnecessary technical detail, formal methods exist for using the accumulated evidence to revise a model's parameter estimates, so that the model "learns" as it performs.[10]

In their sales presentations, research suppliers often use selected evidence from test cases to illustrate how well a model has performed. Would-be clients should examine this evidence carefully. If managers realize that the models driving a system, rather than a few successful predictions, determine the system's true competence, they will ask the most demanding and telling questions of system's designers. Fancy graphs, fast turnaround, and high-tech report delivery methods are not enough if the system lacks a sound model or model base for a given product category, industry, or trade area. Chapter 18 discusses specific criteria for evaluating a model, criticizes certain types of models commonly used with scanner data, and offers an alternative approach.

THE ROUTINIZATION OF REPORTS

The final distinction considered in this chapter is that between standard reports and custom reports. The clearest way to apply this criterion is to examine a report's client base and the means by which the report is produced. Standard reports, such as those shown in Figure 8.1, serve a wide client base and are produced by an automated process. "Automated" means that both context and focal-analytic variables are identical from one client to the next. The supplier creates a single computer program that can produce an instance of the report from a client-specific data set. Client A's report differs from client B's only in the outcomes or realized values of report variables.

Standard reports are typically delivered at preassigned, regular intervals (for example, once per week, once every four weeks, or once per quarter), and they are usually delivered on hard copy. They are often less costly than custom reports, they are typically based on procedures rather than models, and they are usually market status rather than market response reports.

In contrast, custom reports are prepared at a client's request and to client specifications, through consultation between a supplier support team and the client. The support team reviews the client's business problem and then suggests one or more reports that would be of use. These are generated and delivered to the client, usually as part of a package that also includes an oral presentation, one-on-one interpretive sessions, and follow-up assistance.

Custom reports are often prepared for unique rather than ongoing activities—for example, new product tests, product launches, ad campaign launches, product repositionings, and packaging or distribution changes. Because these events occur sporadically, custom reports are delivered on an irregular schedule. They are more costly than standard reports and may be based on either a market response model or a procedure.

For example, an IRI Assessor Report uses a trial-repeat model to forecast a new product's ultimate sales peak and the time trend of its sales. The response model factors test-market sales into a trial component and several additional layers, each corresponding to a different "depth of repeat."[11] The forecast for overall response is built from separate forecasts for each of these components. The separate models are calibrated from IRI's extensive experience with previously introduced brands in similar categories.

The distinction between a standard and a custom report is not clear-cut and may depend on whether one assumes the supplier's or the client's point of view. A client may view its problem as unique; perhaps the firm is involved in its first new product launch in several years. The supplier, on the other hand, may see the problem as commonplace and may have a standard computer program ready to produce what appears to the client to be a highly customized set of reports. The framework described in this chapter assumes the client view in order to avoid overdependence on inferences about the supplier's strategies and modus operandi. Thus the custom reports listed in Table 8.1 generally are produced with substantial client support and tend to differ in content and context from one client to another.

AN EXAMPLE
OF THE EIGHT-FOLD CLASSIFICATION

This section illustrates the report possibilities generated based on the distinctions (status/response) × (procedure/model) × (standard/custom). There are actually only six outcomes, since two of the eight (2^3) cells are logically impossible: One cannot use a procedure to produce a market response report, whether standard or customized.

The example concerns reports that might be delivered to the manager of a typical gasoline service station. This uncomplicated setting is used in order to focus on the meaning of the framework rather than on superfluous details.[12] How can reports of various types help the manager with his or her responsibilities? Each of the six possibilities is shown in Table 8.3.

1. *Station close-out report.* This report is issued regularly at closing (10 p.m.) and summarizes the number of gallons of fuel pumped that day *by fuel type.* The station close-out report is a *standard* report because it is issued regularly, it is a *market status* report because it summarizes historical information (what happened that day), and it is based on a set of *procedures,* basically arithmetic operators.

2. *Fuel-type share-of-revenue report.* This report summarizes the proportion of total dollar revenue accounted for by each fuel type for a given day. Note that this report is also a *market status* report and is based on a set of *procedures.* However, it is a custom report because it is not issued regularly and because a technically qualified person—the manager—must intervene to produce parts of it.

TABLE 8.3.   Six Logical Report Types

	Market Status Reports	
	Standard	**Custom**
Procedure	1. Station Close-out report	2. Fuel-type share-of-revenue report
Model	3. Time-till-tanks-empty report	4. Early-attendant-release report

	Market Response Reports	
	Standard	**Custom**
Procedure	Not possible	Not possible
Model	5. Early-closing projected-revenue report	6. Island reconfiguration report

3. *Time-till-tanks-empty report.* This report is issued regularly at closing each night and estimates the time until each underground fuel storage tank is empty. It is a *standard, market status* report, but it is based on a *model* that integrates empirical data about past usage rates, fuel tank dimensions, and customer arrivals to forecast future usage rates.

4. *Early-attendant-release report.* This report answers the question: "What would the station's sales revenues have been last Tuesday if the manager had allowed one (of two) attendants to go home early?" This report must be based both on historical results and on a *model* that accounts for the possibility of lost sales due to the inability of a single attendant to keep up with demand. It is not a market response report in the sense that term is used here because it "projects" to an alternative past, not to an unknown future. Thus it is a *status* report prepared on a *custom* basis, since it is not standard output from the reporting system.

5. *Early-closing projected-revenue report.* This report is issued regularly each night at 8 p.m. and answers the question: "If we close at 9 p.m. tonight, what will our revenues be?" It is a *standard* report, based on a *model* of market *response.*

6. *Island reconfiguration report.* This report is issued at the district manager's request and answers the question: "If we change island 2 from self-service to full service, what will our monthly revenues be?" This is also a market *response* report based on a *model,* but it is prepared on a *custom* basis for the district manager.

Note that reports 1 and 2 can be generated by relying on a series of empirical measurements from tank-level sensors and clocks, coupled with tank volume data. These measurements need only be manipulated arithmetically to produce report content. As reports 1 and 2 show, empirical measurements are historical data (empirical facts) and indicate "what is," or more precisely, "what was." That is, they indicate a system's status in either the immediate or distant past.

Reports 3, 4, 5, and 6 all rely on models. These models might involve variables such as customer arrivals per time period, customer expenditures per stop, and fuel prices—both this station's and trade-area competitors' prices. Models describe the way things work in general, not what is or what has happened. Thus reports based on models are less time-specific than those based on procedures.

SINGLE-SOURCE REPORTS

With these definitions as background, we can categorize some of the reports currently available from A. C. Nielsen and IRI. (See Table 8.4) Over 20 report types are fit into the framework, and each report type is itself a bundle of individual reports. For example, there are eight reports in Nielsen's Retail Accounts series. There are dozens of individual reports produced by SCAN*Pro Modeler, by Assessor, and by Apollo. No attempt is made here to illustrate the content of any of these reports; this task is left for Chapters 9 through 11. However, a few comments about Table 8.4 are in order.

First, the easiest reports to classify are those that are clearly based on a model. For example, IRI's Assessor series uses a combination of a brand preference model and a trial-and-repeat model to predict a brand's equilibrium long-run market share, to estimate the sources of this share (for example, cannibalization versus draw), to produce diagnostic information to help management in strategy selection (for example, should the company reposition on a certain attribute?), and to do low-cost screening of elements of alternative marketing plans.[13] In brief, whenever a report makes projections to future time periods, new products, new trade areas, or new customer classes, that report is based on a model.

It is often difficult, however, to decide in what cases procedures alone are at work. For example, even though SAMI's TradeMaster (not shown in Table 8.4) offers a high-tech solution (an interactive user interface delivered on CD-ROM technology), TradeMaster and its companion report generators DecisionMaster and SalesMaster are primarily ensembles of data retrieval and data formatting techniques, all of which are procedures.

In many cases, a report could fit into any of several cells in Table 8.4. Certain features might suggest that a report be classified as one type, while other features suggest a different classification. For example, the PC-based systems offered by Nielsen (pc-SCANTRACK) and by IRI (pcInfoScan) are primarily data retrieval systems; many of their functions are driven by procedures. However, both systems produce certain reports that are based on elementary models. In these mixed cases, a report is given the higher designation; hence these systems have been classified as model-based.

TABLE 8.4. Available Single-Source Reports Classified by Report Type

	Market Status Reports	
	Standard Reports	**Custom Reports**
Based on procedure(s)	IRI • Apollo: National Product Library A. C. Nielsen • Retail Accounts • GEMINI Market Service • Cooperator (food, Rx, mass merch.)	A. C. Nielsen • ADPRO
Based on model(s)	IRI • PromotionScan • pc InfoScan • Apollo: Vivid & Total Store • CoverStory • SalesPartner A. C. Nielsen • SCAN∗Pro Modeler • pc-SCANTRACK	IRI • Apollo: Vivid & Total Store

	Market Response Reports	
	Standard Reports	**Custom Reports**
Based on model(s)	IRI • Apollo: Vivid & Total Store A. C. Nielsen • SCAN∗Pro Monitor • SCAN∗Pro Planner	IRI • Assessor • Apollo: Total Store • CPG-DSS Reports • Custom Project Group A. C. Nielsen • SCAN∗Pro Modeler

The Role of Computer Technology

It is not surprising that most reports produced by today's single-source systems are procedure-based. Computer science has progressed from an obsession with data and data processing to other forms of decision support, especially model-based support. Konsynski and Sprague[14] outline this progression as follows: First, *basic data processing* processed transactions for stand-alone EDP jobs, with each program having its own files. Next, *file management* integrated EDP jobs for related functions, sometimes sharing files. Then *database management* arrived with software systems that separated data from the programs that used those data. When *query and report generation* facilities were added to these systems, English-like query languages facilitated ad hoc requests for special reports. Models, sophisticated ways of manipulating data, were embedded in the data-processing system for some well-structured problems (for example, inventory), but modeling was generally considered a separate type of application.

Thus the main accomplishments of database management systems have been to manage large amounts of data, to establish independence between data and programs, and to provide a logical structure for the data. Single-source systems (and geodemographic systems as well) must employ the technology available from computer science. Since no generally acceptable basis for managing models exists, reports based on models tend to be customized.[15] These reports are produced on an ad hoc rather than a routine basis. However, developments in model management systems are expected to have a considerable impact on the implementation of marketing research systems, especially on a system's reporting capabilities and its use of models.

SUMMARY AND CONCLUSIONS

This chapter has presented a framework for classifying reports. The framework was used to generate a series of hypothetical reports, one of each type, and to classify existing single-source reports.

The framework consists of four characteristics, each with two levels: report content (focus/context), report time perspective (status/response), report operating premise (procedure/model), and report preparation (standard/custom). Analyzing a proposed report within this framework indicates what problems a report designer may encounter, how costly the report may be, and what data and design requirements will be critical. The framework does not provide a detailed blueprint for report design but does suggest some important design considerations.

The framework can be used to analyze existing reports from a marketing research system as well as to design new reports. As we have seen, however, the criteria are not entirely unambiguous. For example, the distinction between a standard and a custom report is often blurry because it is partly in the "eye of the beholder"—either the supplier or the client.

The most important distinction in the framework is that between a report based on a model and one based on a procedure. Model-based reports are far more difficult to construct: They require special expertise, specialized data processing, and special user interfaces. They are also more costly, but their cost is an indication that model-based reports are potentially more powerful than procedure-based reports. Models and the propositions that they furnish stimulate a manager's thinking by offering forecasts, alternative points of view, and proposals for action.

Notes

1. Although this chapter uses single-source reports as examples, the framework is general. It can be used to characterize reports generated by any type of research or management information system.

2. A *report* and a *report instance* are defined differently, with the former being the more general term. A *report* contains variables such as brand and market share. An *instance* of a report fixes these variables (or, in computer jargon, "instantiates" them) at certain levels, such as brand = Coke and market share = 38 percent.

3. The author first encountered the term *context variable* in John McCann, Bill Lahti, and Justin Hill, "The Marketing Gate," working paper, Duke University, Marketing Workbench Institute (September 1988). The idea has been used implicitly, though, in statistical and database software, for a long time.

4. Ibid., p. 14.

5. See John D. C. Little, "Decision Support Systems for Marketing Managers," *Journal of Marketing* 43 (Summer 1979), pp. 9-26.

6. Nearly all geodemographic system reports are also market status reports. In fact, single-source firms supply their clients with far more market response reports than do geodemographic firms.

7. A. C. Nielsen, *SCAN*Pro Promotion Analysis Services*, Brochure, p. 7.

8. Little, op. cit., p. 22.

9. Keeney and colleagues discuss this distinction as it influences the design of advanced support systems: "First of all 'intelligence' is essentially identified with the ability to model the world of reality (or interesting parts or subworlds) and to draw relevant conclusions from these models via appropriate inference mechanisms (operators). Relevance of the conclusions (and thus implicitly of the models) may ultimately be traced back to the evolutionary principle of 'relative fitness' or 'survival.' Consequently, the range and quality of models available to a system is what will basically determine its competence." See R. L. Keeney, R. H. Möhring, H. Otway, F. J. Radermacher, and M. M. Richter, "Design Aspects of Advanced Decision Support Systems," *Decision Support Systems* 4 (December 1988), p. 384.

10. An excellent example of such a method is discussed in Judea Pearl, "Fusion, Propagation, and Structuring in Belief Networks," *Artificial Intelligence* 29, (3) (September 1986), pp. 241–288.

11. "Depth of repeat" means that in a given time period some households will not buy the brand, some will buy it once, some will buy it twice, and so on. Those who buy it twice are one-time repeaters, and those who buy it n times are

$n-1$–time repeaters. The foundation for IRI's model can be found in Gerald J. Eskin, "Dynamic Forecasts of New Products Using a Depth of Repeat Model," *Journal of Marketing Research* 10 (2) (May 1973), pp. 115–129.

12. This setting also provides an example of a commonly encountered procedure: (1) Push the cash or credit button. (2) Remove nozzle from hook. (3) Turn handle to "on". (4) Dispense fuel into tank. (5) Return nozzle to hook. This is an excellent illustration of a procedure where the desired result is achieved only if the steps are not permuted.

13. For the original published article about Assessor, see Alvin J. Silk and Glen L. Urban, "Pretest Market Evaluation of New Packaged Goods: A Model and Measurement Methodology," *Journal of Market Research* 15(2) (May 1978), pp. 171–191. For a summary of the model's parts and functions, see Glen Urban and John Hauser, *Design and Marketing of New Productions*, Englewood Cliffs, NJ: Prentice-Hall, 1980, pp. 397–401. Assessor has undergone repeated validation since 1978, and various aspects have been improved as a consequence.

14. See Benn Konsynski and Ralph Sprague, Jr., "Future Research Direction in Model Management," *Decision Support Systems* 2(1) (March 1986), pp. 103–109.

15. The idea that an ensemble of models might also be managed in a model management system (MMS) is new. A MMS tries to do for models what DBMSs did for data. That is, they try to build a "meta-model" of logical relationships between model types, to separate the physical and logical storage of models, and to provide a "manager-friendly" language to manipulate models for decision-making purposes.

APPENDIX 8A:
LINKING MARKETING RESEARCH REPORTS
AND AUTOMATIC CONTROL THEORY

> Marketing research links the consumer, customer, and public to the market-er through information—information used to identify and define market-ing opportunities and problems; generate, refine, and evaluate marketing actions; monitor marketing performance; and improve understanding of marketing as a process.[1]

The main text of this chapter presented a framework for classifying reports and il-lustrated important distinctions between report types. This appendix shows how certain elements of the report framework are special cases of automatic control theory. Control theory is particularly relevant in marketing since a brand's sales or market share can be managed in real time by adjusting the brand's price, advertising intensity, and in-store merchandising activities. Real-time decision making may be a way of transforming scanner data from a relatively low-value commodity into a valuable information advantage according to Blair Peters, group research manager for Kraft's marketing information department.[2] This appendix outlines some of the issues that must be considered in order to realize this vision. Precise resolutions to most of these issues are presented in Chapter 18.

The Control Principle

In marketing's dominant paradigm, decision making is defined as the resolution of a choice dilemma. According to this view, a manager makes a decision by outlining a series of alternatives, evaluating these, and then choosing one. In the control framework, decision making is finding a means to achieve a desired state of affairs.[3]

The central problem with the traditional approach is that it ignores the dy-namic aspects of the decision environment. For example, a manager who wishes to control a brand's market share (the process variable) may decide to manip-ulate the brand's price and feature activity (the instrumental variables). But clearly, the problem will not be solved by a one-time price change or a one-time feature. Even in the absence of competitive reactions, the brand's share may first increase and later decrease due to consumer stockpiling, forward can-nibalization, and brand switching. These effects and others reveal themselves at different points in time. That is, the effects are inherently related through time dependence, not cross-sectional dependence.

In control theory, the problem structure takes system dynamics explicitly into account. Dynamics emanate from laws of supply and demand, from system responses to changes in instrumental variables, and from environmental shocks. A more complete view of the manager's problem must consider these "laws of motion," must weigh the cost of manipulating instrumental variables with the benefits to be gained, and must explicitly trade off present costs and gains with those expected in the future.

To date, marketing applications of control theory have been largely conceptual due to the absence of mathematically precise natural laws governing the system to be controlled.[4] Unlike their engineering counterparts, marketing scientists cannot take recourse in laws of mechanics ($F = mA$), laws of physics ($e = mc^2$), or laws of thermodynamics ($Pv = Kt$).[5] However, recent developments linking control theory and econometrics now place marketing scientists in a position to seriously consider real-time control of certain variables such as sales and market share.

The following sections match the real-world context of marketing management with various aspects of mathematical control theory. This correspondence considers a number of important questions, including: Which variables can and should be controlled? What are the most appropriate instrumental variables? What manner of control—feedback or feedforward—is most effective in a given decision environment? We turn now to these issues.

Feedback or Feedforward Control?

The main text of this chapter drew a clear distinction between market status and market response reports. These ideas can be reframed in the context of control theory. Specifically, market status reports are produced by feedback control systems, whereas market response reports are produced by feedforward control systems—a distinction often ignored by single-source system developers but critical to productive decision support.

A manager who must achieve certain objectives can use either feedback or feedforward control. Like the speedometer on a car, market status reports provide feedback on the current state of a system. Like a trip-planning calculator, which can project a fuel stop from the current fuel consumption rate, market response reports provide feedforward on future states.

Figure 8.3 illustrates these differences. In the feedback system, on the left, a manager sets the desired level of a strategic variable, such as market share. The set point must balance psychologic and economic considerations. Once established, the set point is implemented via the control engine, that is, the programs designed to accomplish the objective. Results are then measured by collecting data from the environment, and adjustments are made to counteract deviations from the set point.

A commonplace feedback system, thermostatic control of room temperature, provides a useful analogy. Consider the problems present in such a system and their single-source counterparts. First, there is the problem of sampling error. To control room temperature, the thermostat must be located in an appropriate position in the room. Better yet, have several thermostats located in strategic places; having multiple measurement points increases the effective sample size and makes the sampling process more representative. The room's temperature would then be tracked by the network average. In a modern single-source system, sampling in various metro-markets throughout the country offers a comparable disaggregated view of the process variable (sales).

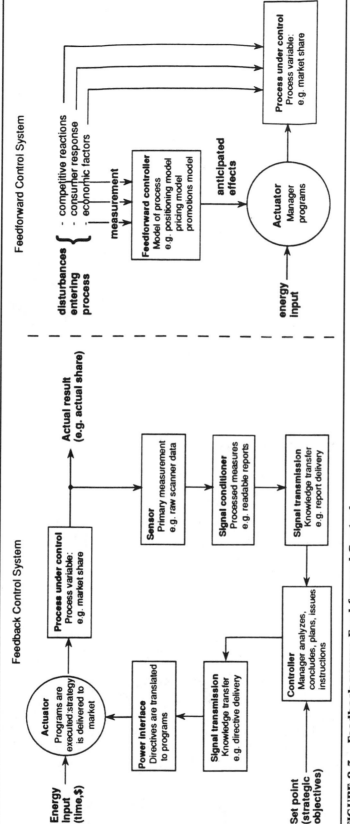

FIGURE 8.3. Feedback versus Feed forward Control

Source: Based on Figures 1-4 and 5-9 in J. Michael Jacob, *Industrial Control Electronics*, Englewood Cliffs, N.J.: Prentice-Hall, 1988.

Second, there is the problem of measurement error; is the thermostat mechanically accurate? Although scanning is more accurate than surveying, it still suffers from a variety of measurement errors. For example, inaccurate data may enter a system due to high-cone scanning errors, missing prices, misaligned data, and duplicate data.[6]

Finally, there are problems in both systems due to time delays. For example, once the thermostat detects a deviation from the set point, it takes time for the heating or air-conditioning unit to click on, and even more time for it to alter the room's temperature. In addition to the front-end response delay, there is the back-end problem of overshooting the set point once the unit clicks off. It should be emphasized that although single-source systems provide fast feedback, they do not shorten the back-end delay involving strategy formation and implementation.

This analogy suggests that successful feedback control depends on accurate measurement of the process variable and on the ability to direct it up or down. In other words, feedback control relies exclusively on market status reports combined with a very rudimentary control engine. In a feedback system, there is no need to forecast values of the process variable. Feedforward control, however, depends on market response reports and therefore requires precise forecasts. With feedforward control, a manager tentatively sets control parameters and then forecasts the response using a model of the process. The forecast is used to reset control parameters until the anticipated response matches management's target. This is pure, iterated if-then reasoning, as the right side of Figure 8.3 shows.

The trade-off between feedback and feedforward boils down to this: Feedforward is only as good as the response model it employs, and feedback is only as good as the data about the present state of the system. The choices are (1) between risky prediction and accurate measurement, and (2) between a reactionary stance (feedback) and a strategic stance (feedforward).

As an example, consider the differences between setting prices by feedforward versus feedback. A feedforward system measures the loads and disturbances going into the system and uses them to calculate the signal to be delivered to the program actuator so that the potential impact of these disturbances can be canceled before they affect the process variable. Therefore, for feedforward pricing a manager needs (1) current prices and current demand for all relevant competitors, (2) a model of consumer response to price changes by brand, (3) a model of competitive response by competitor, and (4) a model of the influence of macroeconomic factors that interact with price to influence primary demand. So equipped, a manager can play enough if-then games to set prices.

In a feedback system, the manager need only observe whether the state of affairs improves or deteriorates when price is changed. This incrementalist approach achieves suboptimal control since it uses no model of the system, but suboptimal control may be good enough. In principle, if feedback is fast and if prices can be reset faster than competitors can respond, the manager will win the game.

Feedback Delays in Marketing

Although feedback control is simpler, feedforward control is necessary in marketing management because feedback delays are usually too long. As Brehmer remarks, "To control a [delay-prone] system a feedforward strategy is needed. Such a strategy uses a model to predict the state of the system from available information, and uses these predictions to decide upon suitable control actions."[7]

Feedback delays are common in marketing information systems. One might even characterize research systems as evolving in the direction of monitoring the market more accurately and more frequently.[8] Furthermore, feedback delay is just one of the delays in the system. Delays also occur at other nodes in the feedback loop, as Figure 8.3 illustrates. Delays occur in the transmission of signals from management (program directives), at the power interface (program implementation), and in the transmission of reports (knowledge dissemination). Some of these delays have been shortened by developments in other fields, but important delays remain, many related directly to a firm's marketing function.[9]

What Do Managers Want?

Feedforward systems need complex forecasting models and therefore need a human controller who can perform complex cognitive processing. These stringent requirements are summarized by Jacob: "If all variables are taken into consideration and measured accurately, and if the feedforward equation is correct and performed accurately by the controller, the process variable will track the set point."[10] A feedback strategy, however, imposes fewer cognitive requirements: It models only the control action's effect on the system, and this model need not be particularly precise. If it simply but surely points in the right direction, further feedback will indicate how it can be adjusted. However, a feedback strategy results in optimal control only when feedback delays are insignificant in relation to the time necessary for control inputs to work.

The central point of the argument is that product managers prefer to use feedback control because it is cognitively less demanding, but systems designers typically prefer feedforward (if-then) management. Designers want to avoid the long delays inherent in traditional research systems and, equally important, they like models. This tension between what is better and what is easier creates a thorny but potentially fertile environment for single-source suppliers and their report delivery specialists. However both positions have merit, and, as illustrated shortly, marketing mix variables sort themselves naturally into the two control camps.

How Fast Is Fast?

One must not be confused by the time dimension in this framework. Time runs as fast or as slow as a system permits. In other words, each system has its own clock that depends on the events, players, and technology in the system. As an illustration, brochures distributed by pony express are no less effective than brochures distributed by direct mail, as long as production, distribution, demand, and other relevant features of the system also unfold at a preindustrial pace. From the competitive viewpoint, what is critical is a firm's relative, not absolute, advantage.

Implications for Single-Source Reporting

Areas Susceptible to Control

Currently, market status reports measure sales (or market share), price, and promotions (features, displays, and couponing). Why the focus in these areas? Because they are relatively unaffected by delays in feedback, transmission, and implementation. In other words, among marketing mix variables, management can change price and promotion most easily and quickly. Changes in the physical product or its packaging involve design and manufacturing delays, changes in physical distribution involve lengthy contractual negotiations, and changes in advertising require periods of creativity and implementation. Table 8.5 summarizes the delays that affect various control strategies.

The columns in the table indicate various elements of the management process and the rows are arranged from the area least problematic to the area most problematic. For example, a manager can easily gain feedback about the current store-by-store price levels of his or her brands. This manager can also issue a directive—by electronic mail, telephone, fax, or satellite—to change prices. The price change can be implemented within a few hours, since resetting prices in a UPC-scanner environment means issuing a computer command and perhaps changing shelf tags. The manager can then track—in real time—the effect of the price change on sales volume.

Attempts at Feedback Control

To this point it has been argued that managers prefer a feedback approach that relies on market status reports, but that long system delays necessitate using feedforward. Attempts to implement the feedback philosophy in today's data-rich environment also encounter other setbacks. As McCann, Lahti and Hill note, "Marketing managers in charge of the brands have more opportunities than they do time and other resources to capture them."[11]

One solution to the information overload problem is market exception reporting. This approach will be briefly discussed in order to focus on certain aspects that need more attention.

CoverStory from IRI is a good example of a market exception report. CoverStory automatically writes memos that summarize important trends in a category—by brand, by region, and by key account. CoverStory and its counterparts, such as SalesPartner, rely on a combination of database query, statistical, heuristical, and expert system techniques to automate every stage of the exception-reporting process, including data collection, data analysis, and report writing. Of course, the decision of what constitutes an exception requires judicious use of inferential statistics, a level of technical detail that is often unpalatable to the line manager.

There are two critical dimensions to the exception reporting process: (1) establishing normative standards and (2) designing efficient procedures that

TABLE 8.5. Delay Considerations in Designing a Marketing Control System

		Major Source of Delay				
	Strategy Tool	Information Feedback	Management Directives	Program Implemenation	Tracking	Knowledge Dissemination
Feedback control	Price strategy (information)	Minor	Minor	Minor	Minor	Moderate
	Promotion strategy (information, coupons, features, and displays)	Minor	Minor	Moderate	Moderate	Moderate
Feedback and/or feedforward control	Advertising strategy (creativity, contracts)	Moderate	Moderate	Moderate	Minor	Moderate
	Physical distribution (contracts)	Minor	Moderate	Major	Moderate	Minor
Feedforward control	Packaging (creativity, manufacturing, contracts)	Minor	Moderate	Moderate	Minor	Moderate
	Product strategy (creativity, manufacturing, contracts)	Minor	Major	Major	Moderate	Moderate

detect deviations from the norm. Since point 1 entails the entire field of normative model building, a thorough discussion is beyond the scope of this appendix. Suffice it to say that the process of baselining sales and other variables is still in its infancy.

With regard to point 2, it is interesting to illustrate the problem with a real example. Figure 8.4 shows a Shewhart chart for four years of data for a nationally distributed consumer packaged good.[12] This brand's share was in a steady state at 4 percent prior to 1986. However, as the CUSUM chart on the right indicates, the process shifted downward in January 1986 to a new steady state of about 3.2 percent.[13]

For feedback control, both charts are critical. The Shewhart chart alone is insufficient for determining whether the process is in or out of control since random error distorts the underlying information. Put another way, today's managers make both type I and type II errors when monitoring market share, but they are more likely to make a type I error; that is, they believe share has changed when in fact the observed change is due to chance.

The CUSUM chart filters noise out of the data, making a process shift easier to detect. Such changes are easily overlooked with a Shewhart chart. For example, if the process mean shifts one standard deviation (1σ), the average run length (that is, the expected number of observations before an "out-of-control" signal is received) is 44 based on a $\pm 3\sigma$ Shewhart chart. This means that even with weekly scanner data, nearly a year would pass before management was alerted to a possible problem![14]

In summary, in those areas susceptible to feedback control, managers need formalized criteria built into an exception report for two important reasons. First, the increased periodicity of scanner data exerts considerable pressure on product managers to use short-term tactics rather than longer-term strategy. Fifteen years ago share estimates were available sporadically. Despite the inconvenience, managers of that era were less likely to fall prey to a "fire extinguisher" mentality. Today scanner data and their associated market status reports represent a major psychological barrier to strategic thinking.

Second, scanner data are subject to considerable sampling error, especially in certain product categories and when viewed at disaggregate levels, for example, in a metro-market as opposed to the nation as a whole. Managers must guard against overreacting, because marketing programs that attempt to realign sales with a sales target can be costly. Discussions with brand managers at Procter & Gamble, General Mills, Kraft, and other packaged goods firms suggest that they often react to share changes far below one or two standard errors of the process. Balancing this is a need for accurate calibration of normative standards and highly sensitive statistical techniques that detect process changes soon after they occur.

Conclusion

Practicing managers tend to view their job mainly in control theory terms, a viewpoint that has clear advantages over the more traditional decision-theoretic view. However, it is only in the last few years that marketing research technol-

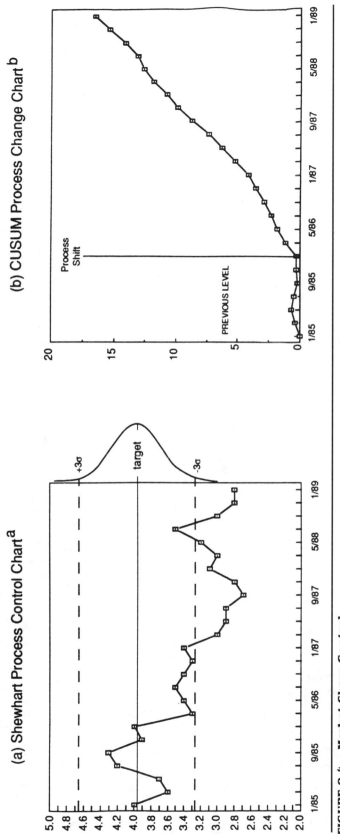

FIGURE 8.4. Market Share Control

[a] A Shewhart chart plots data versus time.
[b] A CUSUM chart plots the cumulative sum of data minus target. (See note 13.)

125

ogy has made it possible to apply control principles to product management problems.[15]

This appendix has outlined key issues for marketing's application of control theory. The argument is that feedback control relies on market status reports whereas feedforward control relies on market response reports. Managers would rather use feedback because it is simpler, but feedback is applicable only in cases where delays are very short.

The appendix identified two types of instrumental variables that meet the "short delay" criterion: packaged goods prices and in-store promotions. However, incorporating these variables in a feedback system suffers from two major limitations. First, establishing normative standards is difficult; current baselining models leave much to be desired.[16] Second, even given reasonable baselines, the problem remains of accurately and quickly detecting deviations from the norm.

The most satisfactory answer appears to be feedforward systems that simultaneously model the market's response to management decisions and capture marketplace dynamics. Chapter 18 reviews such a system, which is based on a combination of econometric modeling (Bayesian vector autoregression) and dynamic control theory. It differs from current approaches by emphasizing multivariate dynamics that lead to realistic baselines and very quick (one-week) response times to deviations from the baseline.

Notes

1. Lawrence D. Gibson, "What is Marketing Research?" *Marketing Research* (March 1989) pp. 2–3.

2. See Blair Peters, "The Brave New World of Single-Source Information," *Marketing Research* (December 1990), pp. 13–21.

3. See Berndt Brehmer, "Strategies in Real-Time Dynamic Decision Making," Uppsala University (Sweden) Psychological Report prepared for the Conference in Memorium to Hillel Einhorn (June 1988), University of Chicago.

4. See, for example Bernard J. Jaworski, "Toward a Theory of Marketing Control: Environment Context, Control Types, and Consequences," *Journal of Marketing* 52 (July 1988), pp. 23–39; and Kenneth A. Merchant, "Progressing Toward a Theory of Marketing Control: A Comment," *Journal of Marketing* (July 1988), pp. 40–44.

5. Stated in words, these three natural laws are: (1) Force equals mass times acceleration. (2) The (potential) energy contained in a mass of magnitude m is equal to m times the speed of light squared. (3) The pressure P exerted on the walls of a container of volume v is equal to a constant K that depends on the mass of the gas and t, its absolute temperature.

6. See Appendix 7A and also Gerald Eskin, Mitchel Kriss, and Magid Abraham, "Retail Scanner-Data Problems and How Infoscan Defeats Them," Information Resources, Inc. (ca. 1990).

7. Brehmer, op. cit.

8. See Appendix 6A, which reviews the progression from periodic surveys to written diaries to scanner panels.

9. For example, computer-aided design (CAD), computer-aided manufacturing (CAM), and computer-integrated manufacturing (CIM) have reduced the delay between project initiation and steady-state manufacturing.

10. J. Michael Jacob. *Industrial Control Electronics*, Englewood Cliffs, NJ: Prentice-Hall, 1988, p. 319.

11. See John McCann, Bill Lahti, and Justin Hill, "The Marketing Gate," Working Paper, Duke University, Marketing Workbench Institute (September 1988).

12. Data were supplied by Procter & Gamble Co. with the stipulation that brand identifiers be removed.

13. A CUSUM chart plots CUSUM $= \Sigma_t(ms_o - ms_t)$, where the set value ms_o is management's target market share, and ms_t is the brand's market share in time period t. If the process is in control, then $ms_t = (ms_o + \tilde{\epsilon}_t)$, where $\tilde{\epsilon}_t$ is an independent identically distributed random variable. In this case, CUSUM is a random walk with mean 0. However, if the process experiences a shift of size δ so that the new steady-state level is $ms_0 + \delta$, then CUSUM will grow rapidly, since each period a factor of $|\delta|$ accumulates.

14. See Robert V. Hogg and Johannes Ledolter (1987), *Engineering Statistics,* New York: Macmillan, Chapter 8.

15. The technology is catching up to long-standing proposals to use control theory in marketing. For example, as long ago as 1966, Little suggested using an adaptive control approach to promotional spending. See John D. C. Little, "A Model of Adaptive Control of Promotional Spending," *Operations Research* 14 (November–December 1966), pp. 1075–1097.

16. See Robert C. Blattberg, Byung-Do Kim, and Jianming Ye, "Defining Baseline Sales in a Competitive Environment," Working Paper (March 1992), Kellogg Graduate School of Management, Northwestern University, pp. 1–35.

9 SINGLE-SOURCE REPORTS FOR MANUFACTURERS

INTRODUCTION

This chapter has two primary purposes: (1) to review the standard single-source reports designed for packaged goods manufacturers and (2) to illustrate applications of these reports to brand management problems. The review provides references for users of single-source systems and offers report prototypes for system designers.

To help brand managers monitor the business environment and track their brands' performance, standard reports highlight problem areas and efficiently summarize current events. When management action rather than tracking is called for, several reports are used in unison, often supplemented by expert counsel. The chapter presents case examples to illustrate the process of linking single-source reports to solve complex, multistep management problems. The examples deal with the appropriate balance between advertising and promotion, the shift of power between manufacturers and retailers, and the process of regional marketing planning.

With respect to channel power, the examples emphasize how manufacturers can use trade support to elicit desired responses from retailers. A manufacturer seeks better shelf positioning for its brand, more feature activity, and better price deals. Retailers who accept a manufacturer's proposal are indicating a willingness to accept lower margins or to otherwise share in program cost. Securing these concessions requires that manufacturers take detailed, imaginative approaches.[1]

The case histories presented here suggest that brand managers tend to shun complex modeling and prefer standard reports that transform raw scanner data into summary tables. As Douglas Haley and Kenneth Kranz of Nestlé Foods indicate:

> The Holy Grail of marketing modeling is a total "Market Response Model." This starts with the "main effects" of spending for each brand within a defined market and set time period.... It also estimates the interactions between effects. Frankly, we're not there yet.[2]

Despite this gap between theory and practice, Haley and Krantz suggest that "single source data can be used now—without complex modeling and using available aggregate measures—to make spending allocation decisions."

Single-source suppliers such as A. C. Nielsen and IRI would probably disagree that current applications rely too heavily on empirical analyses rather than on sound theory. The criticism may be overstated; sophisticated modeling is used to partition a brand's sales into a base component and an incremental component due to promotion activity.[3] This partition links—using a complicated time series model—incremental sales in a given time period to the promotion events that took place during that time period. Furthermore, both suppliers offer "what-if" analyses based on models that forecast what would happen if a current promotional program were applied in a new market area.

Despite these advances, single-source data represent a vast, largely untapped reservoir for improved market modeling. Suggestions for stronger theoretical foundations are presented in Chapter 18.

This chapter focuses solely on applications for manufacturers. Chapter 10 concentrates on applications for retailers, and Chapter 11 addresses applications for the media. These three industry segments represent the primary users of single-source data. Applications in industries outside packaged goods are beginning to appear (for example, Equifax markets ELCAP, a single-source system for major appliances), but systems outside packaged goods do not yet constitute a client base large enough to warrant specific attention.

MARKETING MANAGEMENT FROM A MANUFACTURER'S VIEWPOINT

Strategic Considerations

A manufacturer typically produces and sells several brands competing in the same product category and has entries in several categories. (See Table 9.1.) From the perspective of overall performance and strategy, between-category problems dominate. Macroanalytic tools such as product portfolio analysis and broad financial planning are the basis for strategic decision making.[4]

However, most packaged goods companies are still organized from a bottom-up perspective, and brand management reigns supreme. From this perspective, a manager and his or her staff are responsible for the financial well-being of one

TABLE 9.1. Management from the Manufacturer's Viewpoint

Aspect	Manufacturer Concerns
Business setting	• Managing multiple lines that span several categories • Focusing on competition nationally but also regionally, in metro-markets, and by key account • Managing multiple production sites • Transacting with many retailers
Key strategic considerations	• Optimizing the marketing mix • Planning in all submarkets • Allocating funds for in-store promotions • Tailoring promotions to local conditions

Objectives	• Effective marketing
	  —Primarily to retailers as clients
	  —Secondarily to the ultimate consumer
	• Increased sales
	  —Increased market share
	  —Increased market penetration
	  —Increased merchandising support

Controllable variables	• Price (suggested list price)
	• Promotion
	  —Trade vs. consumer
	  —National vs. local
	• Channel selection
	• New product development, design, and packaging

or several brands competing in a given product category. Fortunately, the highly disaggregate data in a single-source system can be compiled layer by layer (UPC–SKU–variety–brand–category–product line) to allow management to zoom back and forth between the macro and micro perspectives.

Demand/Supply-Side Issues

In addition to managing demand, manufacturers must manage supply-side problems, including operations at multiple production sites and transactions with multiple vendors. A key supply-side issue is the availability of a sound internal accounting system, one that can decompose total costs into factor costs (parts, material, labor) and marketing costs (both fixed and variable). Marketing costs, especially the variable costs associated with specific programs or promotional events, are difficult to assess and are often unrecorded or poorly kept, according to John Totten.[5]

Currently, single-source suppliers rely on a client firm's cost accounting system for this information. However, single-source systems could monitor promotion costs and develop cost standards within and across product categories. These possibilities are discussed in more detail in Chapter 11, where Nielsen's ADPRO database product is reviewed.

Level-of-Analysis Considerations

The objectives of a manufacturer are to increase profitable sales and market share. To do so requires careful analysis and manipulation of marketing mix variables nationwide as well as by market. Regional marketing planning has substantially improved the efficiency of marketing programs while increasing the workload of marketing managers. Examples in this chapter illustrate why: Single-source systems permit a level of detail unheard of a decade ago, including neighborhood, household, and individual-level analyses, and advances in geodemography permit pinpointed delivery of strategy to these microtargets. The computational and managerial burdens associated with micro-marketing weigh heavily on the modern brand manager. We will see how systems such as Metaphor, InfoScan, and SCAN*Pro shift part of this burden to automated systems.

Appropriate Client Considerations

Table 9.1 suggests that manufacturers market primarily to retailers, not to ultimate consumers. Although this has long been the case, a new wrinkle was added in the 1980s: The balance of channel power swung away from the manufacturer to the retailer. IRI's 1988 annual report alludes to the impact of this power shift: "Annual new product introductions have nearly doubled in the past five years—from under 6,000 in 1983 to over 11,000 in 1988. But a minimal increase in grocery store shelf space, the increasing data sophistication of retailers, and the shorter time given a new product to prove itself have made it very difficult to introduce a new product successfully in today's environment."[6]

Today each manufacturer in a given category must present a range of price, feature, and display "bids" to a retailer, who evaluates the bids received from all manufacturers in the category. It is the fortunate manufacturer whose bid is selected. Later examples show how single-source data help manufacturers demonstrate the value of their brands to retailers so that their proposed programs will be selected.

TRADE PROMOTION REPORTS FOR MANUFACTURERS

Packaged goods manufacturers invest more than $20 billion annually in trade promotions designed to influence the behavior of both retailers and ultimate consumers. The major single-source suppliers have each designed a series of reports to assist manufacturers in planning promotion events. Examples of these services include InfoScan reports offered by IRI and SCAN*Pro reports offered by A. C. Nielsen.[7] Although these services differ with respect to their theoretical foundations, report formatting, delivery methods, and associated client support, their objectives are similar. Here we discuss trade promotion services at a generic level in order to convey key points. Examples from specific services are used as illustrations.

Description

Trade promotion systems produce reports by item (UPC), by brand, by market, and by retail account. In these reports a brand's total sales in a given time period are partitioned into a baseline level and an incremental sales component. Incremental sales are those beyond a brand's nominal or baseline sales level, and are attributed to the promotion activities in effect during the time period in question. Suppliers such as IRI and Nielsen use proprietary models to partition total sales. In each case the basic idea is to fit a time series model to a brand's sales levels in nonpromotion weeks and calculate incremental sales by comparing the weekly volume for the promoted item to that item's baseline.[8]

Trade promotion systems use data from a supplier firm's single-source database. As outlined in Chapter 7, InfoScan reports use data from the 2,400 stores in its 66 projectable InfoScan markets. These data are supplemented by consumer panel data—including about 60,000 households—and by data from IRI's BehaviorScan cities. Key account data are also incorporated, including approximately 125 key accounts in the top 20 IRI markets.

Nielsen's competing approach, SCAN*Pro, uses SCANTRACK data supplemented by panel data from the NPD/Nielsen joint venture. Store data are collected from 2,700 stores and projected to both the $2 million and $4 million scanner universes. These stores are located in 50 major markets and represent 128 retail chains. Household data are collected from 41,500 households (15,000 national and 26,500 local), with the national panel dispersed among the 2,700 SCANTRACK stores.[9]

Reports and Delivery

Promotion-tracking services offer both standard and custom reports delivered in hard copy and on-line. A report is generated for a specific UPC, brand, or category selling in a specific market area in certain stores during a fixed time period. The focal-analytic variables in these reports include:

- A brand's market share and sales, in both units and dollars
- The percentage of volume sold with any merchandising[10]
- The average number of weeks a brand was on feature, on display, on feature and display, or price-reduced
- The average price of the item promoted and nonpromoted
- The average percentage of price reduction
- The percentage of volume sold on discount, on feature, on display, or on feature and display

IRI Reports for Manufacturers

IRI offers five standard hard-copy reports, delivered every four weeks and including as many as 13 measures. These are Category Topline Report, Category Trended Report, Volume and Merchandising (Key Account Report), Feature and Display Report (Key Account Report), and Consumer Report (Panel Data).[11,12]

A Category Topline Report for frozen breakfast foods is shown in Figure 9.1. Note that this report is a standard market status report.[13] The contextual variables are shown in the title section and the focal-analytic variables in the main body. For example, during this four-week period, Eggo waffles sold 1.457 million units of large packages of regular waffles at an average price of $1.58. These sales represent an 8.67 percent share of the traditional frozen breakfast foods category. During the period 25.4 percent of Eggo large-package waffle volume was sold in stores merchandising the brand, and 36.2 percent of the ACV for these stores involved merchandised sales.

IRI's other hard-copy reports for manufacturers are discussed more thoroughly in the appendix to this chapter. These reports are also delivered in PC versions via pcExpress, pcInfoScan, and InfoScan Data Server. Custom client services are available for brand managers who want to probe more deeply.

Nielsen Reports for Manufacturers

Nielsen's SCAN*Pro series consists of three components:

> SCAN*Pro Monitor, which delivers a custom database to monitor in-store promotion execution and the sales associated with each retail event
>
> SCAN*Pro Modeler, which provides custom application of promotion modeling to address specific promotion issues
>
> SCAN*Pro Planner, which is a PC-based support tool that simulates the sales and financial impact of planned promotion alternatives to help a manufacturer optimize promotion spending

Monitor analyzes the effects of in-store displays, price reductions, and newspaper advertising by retailers. It calculates a level of baseline sales for each UPC item and then links incremental sales to the various merchandising conditions. Clients receive the output on a personal computer and are instructed in a simple procedural language so that they can navigate through weekly sales by product, by store, and by market.

SCAN*Pro Modeler is a customized version of Monitor. Modeler is designed for manufacturers who want their promotions systematically analyzed by Nielsen consultants. With this service, the key issues are discussed with the brand manager, but the analytical work is performed by Nielsen technical staff. Table 9.2 shows a SCAN*Pro Monitor profit report for sparkling water sales in four West Coast cities.

Both IRI and Nielsen can provide "what if" market response analyses with their respective systems. Typically these analyses show what would happen if a promotion event conducted in one market were executed in another market.

These are the 13 client-selected measures. The same set of measures is reported each period.

The four-week period covered in this report.

COMPANY: Company A (Client)
CATEGORY: Frozen Breakfast Foods (Name of Category)
REGION AREA: Total U.S. (Market, region covered on report)
VOLUME MEASURE: Units (Unit of measure/volume equivalency used on report)

InfoScan
CATEGORY TOPLINE REPORT

TIME PERIODS: 10/12/87 - 11/08/87
IRI WEEKS: 424 - 427

	Volume Sales	Type Volume Share	Dollar Sales	Type Dollar Share	ACV WTED Distr.	Avg$ Per Unit	%Vol Any Merch	%ACV W/Any March	%ACV W/Dsp Only	%ACV W/Fea Only	%ACV W/Dsp & Feat	Avg$ D Only (Unit)	Avg$ F Only (Unit)
CATEGORY-FRZN BREAKFAST FOODS	31,226M	100.00	56,220M	100.00	100.00	1.34	21.5	98.3	33.6	91.2	26.9	1.16	1.20
TRADITIONAL FROZEN BREAKFASTS	15,465M	100.00	24,985M	100.00	100.00	1.22	24.3	94.3	19.8	81.6	17.3	1.04	1.07
WAFFLES	11,529M	74.55	17,854M	71.46	100.00	1.16	25.3	92.7	16.3	77.3	15.0	1.00	1.03
EGGO	5,197M	133.61	8,616M	34.49	100.00	1.27	18.2	72.1	3.7	42.5	4.8	1.04	1.19
REGULAR	4,252M	27.50	6,709M	26.85	99.8	1.23	19.1	62.5	3.2	36.6	4.4	1.01	1.18
SMALL	2,794M	18.07	4,542M	18.18	99.5	1.12	15.8	37.2	2.3	18.1	2.5	0.95	0.98
LARGE	1,457M	9.43	2,167M	8.67	90.3	1.58	25.4	36.2	1.0	20.4	2.2	1.46	1.46
NUTRI-GRAIN	944,977	6.11	1,906M	7.63	92.6	1.39	14.6	34.8	0.7	12.2	0.7	1.28	1.23
SMALL	944,977	6.11	1,906M	7.63	92.6	1.39	14.6	34.8	0.7	12.2	0.7	1.28	1.23
ROMAN MEAL	245,927	1.59	387,995	1.55	55.0	1.18	29.2	21.2	1.0	10.4	0.5	1.27	0.91
REGULAR	245,927	1.59	387,995	1.55	55.0	1.18	29.2	21.2	1.0	10.4	0.5	1.27	0.91
SMALL	245,927	1.59	387,995	1.55	55.0	1.18	29.2	21.2	1.0	10.4	0.5	1.27	0.91
FROSTY ACRES	4,941	0.03	5,619	0.02	0.6	0.53	0.0	0.0	0.0	0.0	0.0	0.0	0.0
REGULAR	4,941	0.03	5,619	0.02	0.6	0.53	0.0	0.0	0.0	0.0	0.0	0.0	0.0
SMALL	4,941	0.03	5,619	0.02	0.6	0.53	0.0	0.0	0.0	0.0	0.0	0.0	0.0
ALMAC	1,864	0.01	1,312	0.01	0.1	0.22	74.9	0.1	0.0	0.0	0.0	0.0	0.0
REGULAR	1,864	0.01	1,312	0.01	0.1	0.22	74.9	0.1	0.0	0.0	0.0	0.0	0.0
SMALL	1,864	0.01	1,312	0.01	0.1	0.22	74.9	0.1	0.0	0.0	0.0	0.0	0.0
CHEF AMERICA	266,690	1.72	1,095M	4.38	85.9	2.31	35.9	51.4	1.8	39.7	1.0	2.20	2.09
BELGIAN	266,690	1.72	1,095M	4.38	85.9	2.31	35.9	51.4	1.8	39.7	1.0	2.20	2.09
SMALL	266,690	1.72	1,095M	4.38	85.9	2.31	35.9	51.4	1.8	39.7	1.0	2.20	2.09
VAN'S BELGIE	6,255	0.04	33,522	0.13	9.0	1.68	27.5	2.6	0.2	0.0	0.0	1.72	0.0
BELGIAN	6,255	0.04	33,522	0.13	9.0	1.68	27.5	2.6	0.2	0.0	0.0	1.72	0.0
SMALL	6,255	0.04	33,522	0.13	9.0	1.68	27.5	2.6	0.2	0.0	0.0	1.72	0.0
OLD BRUSSELS	228	0.00	456	0.00	0.6	0.80	0.0	0.0	0.0	0.0	0.0	0.0	0.0
BELGIAN	228	0.00	456	0.00	0.6	0.80	0.0	0.0	0.0	0.0	0.0	0.0	0.0
SMALL	228	0.00	456	0.00	0.6	0.80	0.0	0.0	0.0	0.0	0.0	0.0	0.0
EMPIRE KOSHER	341	0.00	456	0.00	0.6	1.95	22.3	0.1	0.1	0.0	0.0	1.99	0.0
BELGIAN	341	0.00	456	0.00	0.6	1.95	22.3	0.1	0.1	0.0	0.0	1.99	0.0
SMALL	341	0.00	456	0.00	0.6	1.95	22.3	0.1	0.1	0.0	0.0	1.99	0.0

Custom Product Hierarchy -- This is the order in which items and aggregations of items appear on your InfoScan reports.

During this four-week period, Eggo Large Waffles sold 1,457M units of large packages of regular waffles at an average price of $1.58. This was an 8.67 share of traditional frozen breakfast sales. During the period, 25.4% of Eggo large package waffle volume was sold in stores with any merchandising while 36.2% of the ACV had any merchandising activity.

FIGURE 9.1. A Category Topline Report
Source: IRI.

TABLE 9.2. SCAN∗Pro Monitor Profit Report

From Week Ending 02/28/87
Through Week Ending 07/25/87

For Sparkling Water

	LA	SF	SEA	POR	Total
Total volume	40,126	9,617	683	0	50,426
Promoted volume	26,892	4,902	403	0	32,197
Percent promoted volume	67.0	51.0	59.0	∗	63.8
Baseline volume	34,219	8,230	518	0	42,967
Incremental volume	5,907	1,387	165	0	7,459
Incremental gross return	15,063	3,259	380	0	18,702
Promotion spending ($)	15,000	3,000	4,000	1,000	23,000
Incremental profit	63	259	(3,621)	(1,000)	(4,298)
Return on promotion (%)	0.4	8.6	(90.5)	(100.0)	(18.7)

Key to markets listed in the report:
LA   Los Angeles
SF   San Francisco
SEA   Seattle
POR   Portland
Source: A. C. Nielsen Co.

(Several examples are provided in subsequent case studies.) The brand manager can perform the "what if" analyses on his or her personal computer or can shift the work to representatives of the supplying firm.

Summary

Trade promotion services help a brand manager determine the key factors that drive his or her brand's sales and market share. In brief, these systems:

- Track how much promotional activity is taking place by brand, by market, by retail account, and by time period
- Show how an item is being priced at retail, with and without price discounts
- Relate a brand's pricing policy to the competition at different levels of promotion activity
- Analyze when and where sales volumes fell short of expected levels
- Calculate how much incremental sales, share, and profit resulted from a specific promotion event
- Forecast the relative effectiveness of the same promotion event in different markets

We turn now to three case studies that illustrate how single-source data can help solve real brand management problems. These cases involve problems with a Nestlé beverage product and a frozen dinner entree.

CASE 1:
REALLOCATING TRADE SUPPORT BY MARKET[14]

Nestlé Corporation has been using single-source data—primarily from A. C. Nielsen's SCANTRACK system—since 1985. This example shows how Nestlé management analyzed the effectiveness of retail trade support for one of its beverage products and how trade support was effectively reallocated.

Trade support consists of special efforts by a retailer to display and feature a given brand. Surprisingly, prior to single-source systems, many manufacturers could monitor support only indirectly, often with annoying delays and considerable measurement error.

Step 1: Promotion Support by Market

Using SCANTRACK data and the Metaphor system, a Nestlé manager produced the chart shown in Figure 9.2, which shows the brand's promotion support expressed as the percentage of stores in each market providing trade support in a given week.[15] (The analyses shown here were accomplished in less than one week.) Two promotion events, one in March and the other in September 1988, are shown. In Boston, for example, the product received support accounting for 16 percent of the ACV during the March event.

Step 2: Promotion Response by Market

Single-source data provide enough detail so that the impact of an event's support can be disaggregated by market. For example, in Kansas City total volume in March was 68,688 pounds. SCANTRACK analyses indicated that 5,049 pounds (7.9 percent of the total) were due the promotional event. (See Figure 9.3.)

Figure 9.4 shows which elements of the program generated the incremental volume. Feature ads provided 68 percent of the support and 81 percent of that market's incremental volume. The ads were 2.38 times more effective than the displays, a fact suggesting that a revised allocation might be more effective.

Clearly, the analysis in Figure 9.4 is simplistic, since it ignores both decreasing returns to scale in each promotion vehicle and possible feature-display interactions. However, the SCANTRACK system offers a model that accounts for interactions between features and displays and uses nonlinear marginal response functions. "What if" analyses were run using this model to determine what the incremental volume might have been if all Kansas City stores promoting the Nestlé brand had featured it. The projected sales are shown in Figure 9.5 and compared to the actual sales. Results suggest an additional 5 percent in sales, increasing the volume from 68,688 to 72,208 pounds. Nestlé management conducted similar analyses across other markets to suggest more effective allocation of trade support funds for this brand.

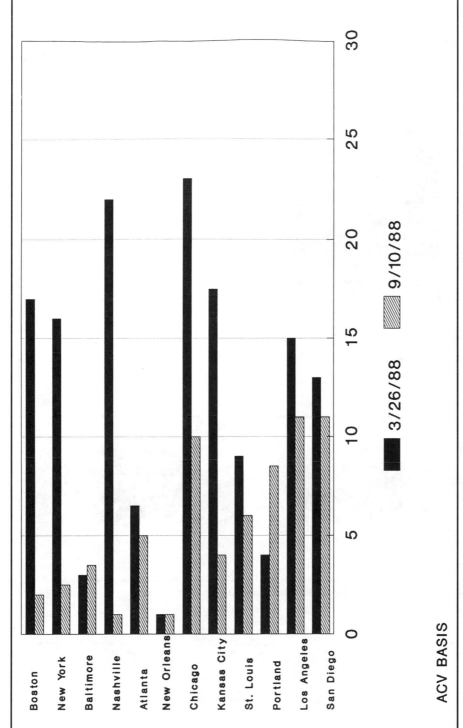

ACV BASIS

 3/26/88   9/10/88

FIGURE 9.2.   Promotion Support by Market (Percent of Store Weeks Supporting)
Source: Advertising Research Foundation (Haley and Kranz, 1989).

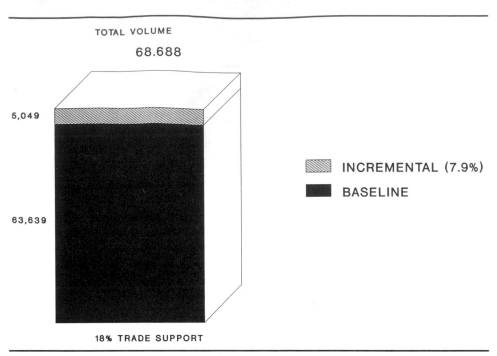

FIGURE 9.3.   Kansas City Promotion Response (Beverage Brand A)
Source: Advertising Research Foundation (Haley and Kranz, 1989).

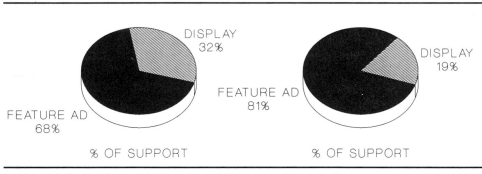

FIGURE 9.4.   Value of Promotional Support, Kansas City
Source: Advertising Research Foundation (Haley and Kranz, 1989).

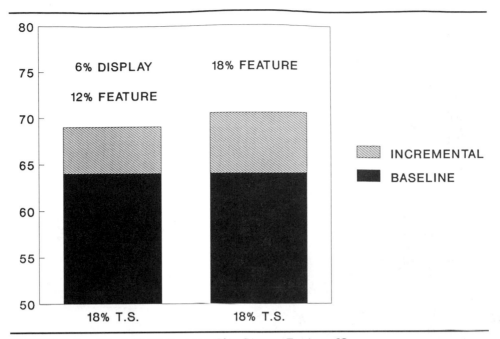

FIGURE 9.5. What If All Kansas City Stores Featured?

Source: Advertising Research Foundation (Haley and Kranz, 1989).

CASE 2:
MANUFACTURER-RETAILER NEGOTIATIONS

This example focuses on how a brand manager might induce retailers to feature his or her company's brand(s). Here the brand is a Nestlé beverage that competes in a highly seasonal category. In 1989 support ranged from a high of 86 percent in Denver to a low of 30 percent in Jacksonville, Florida, as Figure 9.6 shows. The wide variation in trade support suggested that Nestlé seek ways to induce retailers in low-support markets to increase their support. However, this goal could be accomplished only if Nestlé could provide clear evidence that the retailer stood to gain in the process.

Analyses were carried out market by market. In Washington, D.C., for example, the support at the time (49 percent) generated an incremental volume of 12.2 percent. (See Figure 9.7.)

The majority of support and volume came from displays, but the greatest opportunity for Nestlé was a display/feature combination. As Figure 9.8 shows, 6.6 percent support generated a 12.1 percent response. This ratio (12.1/6.6 = 1.83) was considerably higher than the corresponding ratio for features alone (0.74) or for displays alone (0.97).

The magnitude of this opportunity is clearly illustrated in Figure 9.9, which was generated by two different "what if" analyses using SCANTRACK models. The bar on the left shows the nominal (no change) analysis. The bar in the middle shows that maintaining total support at 49 percent but reallocating this support to the feature-display combination would result in an incremental volume that

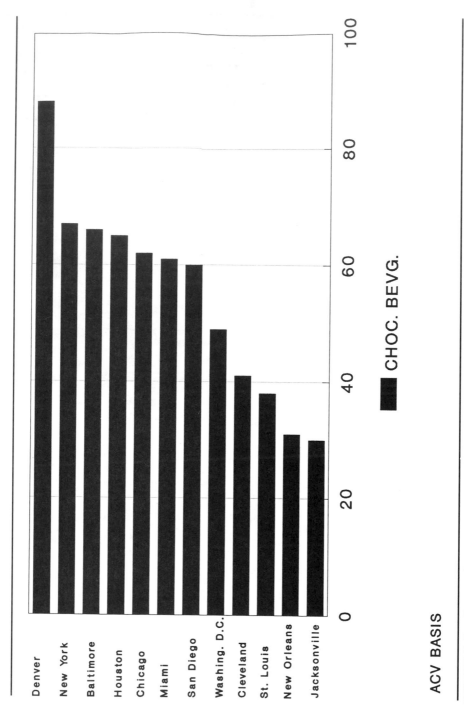

CHOC. BEVG.

ACV BASIS

FIGURE 9.6. Promotion Support by Market (Percent of Store Weeks Supporting)
Source: Advertising Research Foundation (Haley and Kranz, 1989).

140

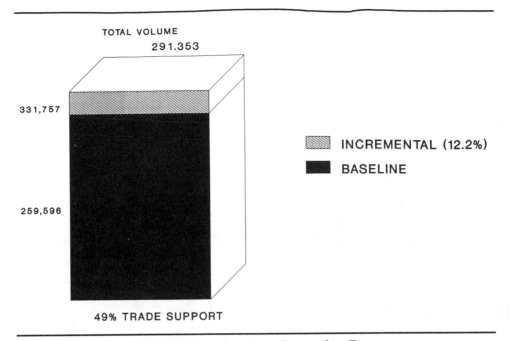

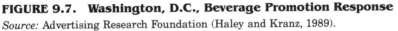

FIGURE 9.7. Washington, D.C., Beverage Promotion Response
Source: Advertising Research Foundation (Haley and Kranz, 1989).

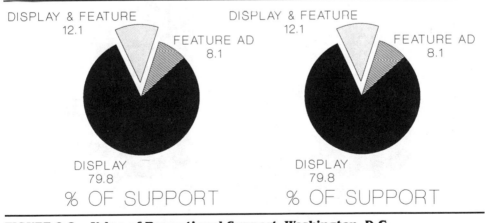

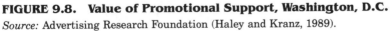

FIGURE 9.8. Value of Promotional Support, Washington, D.C.
Source: Advertising Research Foundation (Haley and Kranz, 1989).

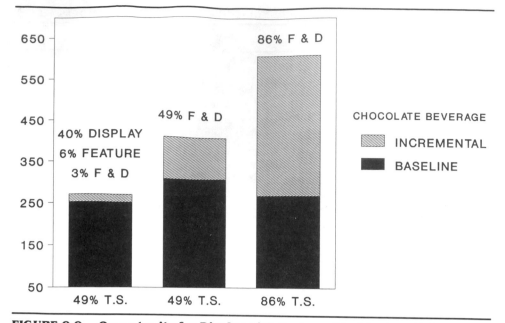

FIGURE 9.9. Opportunity for Display with Feature, Washington, D.C.
Source: Advertising Research Foundation (Haley and Kranz, 1989).

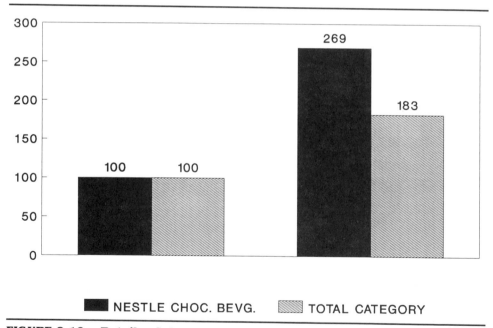

FIGURE 9.10. Retailer Sales Story: Benefits to Nestlé and Retailer
Source: Advertising Research Foundation (Haley and Kranz, 1989).

142

more than paid for the extra cost associated with a feature-display program. The bar on the right shows that if total support in Washington, D.C., were increased to 86 percent to match Denver's support, the expected incremental volume would be 334,998 pounds, a 115 percent increase over the nominal level at the time.

These figures promised outstanding results for Nestlé if the company could convince D.C. area retailers to cooperate. Convincing evidence was generated in the form of Figure 9.10 which shows how increased support was expected to affect the Nestlé brand and the category as a whole: Nestlé would move 2.7 times more product, and category volume would in turn increase by 83 percent. Nestlé management used this chart to demonstrate to retailers that using a feature-display combination to promote its brand would be a win-win situation. Not only would the retailer benefit from increased Nestlé sales, but category sales would not be damaged. Competing brands might even benefit due to the increased attention focused on the category.

CASE 3: BDI/CDI PITFALLS

Brand managers traditionally have analyzed promotion effectiveness by comparing—in a given market—a brand's development index (BDI) with the corresponding category development index (CDI). If a category sells well but a brand does not, then the brand has a problem.

Figure 9.11 shows, for 21 regional markets, the BDI and CDI levels for a frozen entree for the 52 weeks ending June 12, 1988. In Seattle and Minneapolis the category is highly demanded, but the brand enjoys only average sales levels.

The BDI/CDI approach is an improvement over focusing exclusively on a brand's volume and ignoring differences in population between markets and in taste between brands. As industry expert Jan Gollins notes, however, this approach still suffers from two important problems. First, the BDI/CDI approach[16] ignores differences in the actual levels of trade promotion in different markets— that is, differences in a brand's *promotion support factor.* Second, the approach ignores differences in the potential impact of trade promotion in different markets—that is, differences in a brand's *promotion response factor.*

A more general model that considers both these factors is shown in Figure 9.12. In this model, all four BDI/CDI conditions are crossed with the four possible combinations of promotion support and promotion response. The resulting 16 cells are then grouped by strategic action. For example, "opportunity markets" are those that exhibit a low BDI/CDI ratio and that could or do respond well to support.

Response to trade support is measured by comparing base to incremental volumes for past promotion events. By arranging the 21 markets into this new strategic framework, the manager found that Atlanta, Cleveland, Denver, Boston, Miami, Tampa, Minneapolis, and Dallas were all high-opportunity markets, and that the last two markets were especially promising. (See Figure 9.13.) This conclusion differs substantially from the conclusion (based on Figure 9.11) that only Seattle and Minneapolis could be developed. Further, a review of previous

BDI - RedBud Lean Wt. Brand

CDI - Entree Category	High - - - 111+	Average - - - - - - 90 - 110	Low - - - < 90
High - - - 111+	Cleveland New York Los Angeles Detroit Philadelphia Boston San Francisco Denver San Diego	Seattle Minneapolis	
Average - - - - - 90 - 110	Miami Tampa Atlanta Chicago	Dallas	Houston Kansas City St. Louis
Low - - - < 90			Memphis Birmingham

(52 weeks ending 6/12/88)
IRI InfoScan

FIGURE 9.11. CDI/BDI Analysis

Source: Advertising Research Foundation (Gollins, 1989).

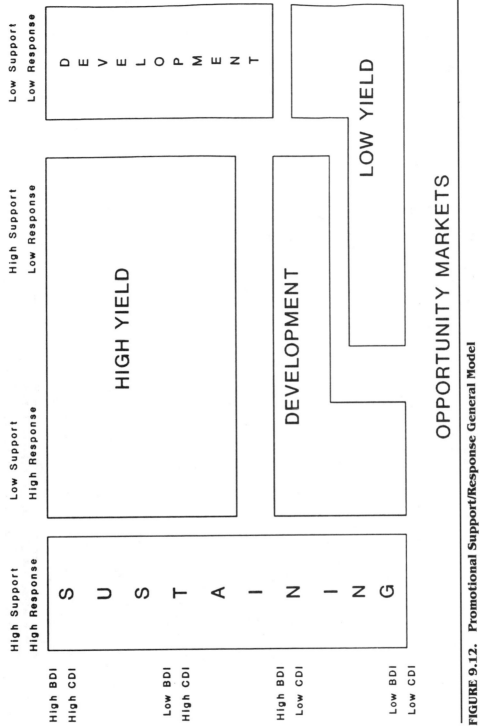

FIGURE 9.12. Promotional Support/Response General Model

Source: Advertising Research Foundation (Gollins, 1989).

RedBud Lean Wt. Brand

	High Support High Response	Low Support High Response	High Support Low Response	Low Support Low Response
High BDI High CDI	Los Angeles Seattle New York San Diego Chicago San Francisco Philadelphia		Atlanta Cleveland Denver Miami Boston Tampa	Detroit
Low BDI High CDI	St. Louis		Minneapolis Dallas	Kansas City
High BDI Low CDI		Memphis		
Low BDI Low CDI				Houston Birmingham

FIGURE 9.13. Promotion Support/Response

Source: Advertising Research Foundation (Gollins, 1989).

promotion revealed that in all of these markets more than 50 percent of the merchandising effort had been in one form only: price reductions. Little or no use had been made of features and displays. Computer simulations with InfoScan models revealed that, with proper merchandising, volumes could be increased by 8 to 11 percent in these cities.

Linking the Analysis to Geodemographics

The manufacture also wanted to communicate with retailers in these markets to offer them merchandising suggestions. To do this, IRI linked scanner data with PRIZM geodemographic data to pinpoint household consumption differences. These differences were then matched to a retail store's neighborhood profile, and different types of merchandising programs were prepared to fit each store's local shopper environment.

Figure 9.14 shows remarkable differences in the top five PRIZM segments between "premium" and "regular" dinners for each brand:[17]

TV Dinner	Entree
Middle America	Money and Brains
Small Town	Pools and Patios
God's Country	Urban Gold Coast
Suburbia	Suburbia
Shotguns and Pickups	Rank and File

The two brands clearly attract vastly different consumer types; only one segment—Suburbia—overlaps in the top five. A store surrounded primarily by the neighborhood types listed on the left not only prefers to carry the lower-priced TV dinner but chooses different promotional devices to support it. Although this analysis is not designed to influence the national advertising campaigns for these two brands, it clearly shows that different media and different messages should be emphasized to accommodate the taste and income differences in the consumers of each product.

SUMMARY AND CONCLUSION

This chapter has reviewed the standard reports that single-source suppliers offer to manufacturers of packaged goods. These reports permit a manufacturer to track a brand's sales and market share over time by category, by consumer segment, by region, and by store. Standard reports also permit the identification of the level and types of promotions an item receives and the impact of these promotions on that item's incremental sales.

Price levels, distribution intensity, out-of-stock problems, and consumer response to various types of promotion events are also tracked, summarized,

148

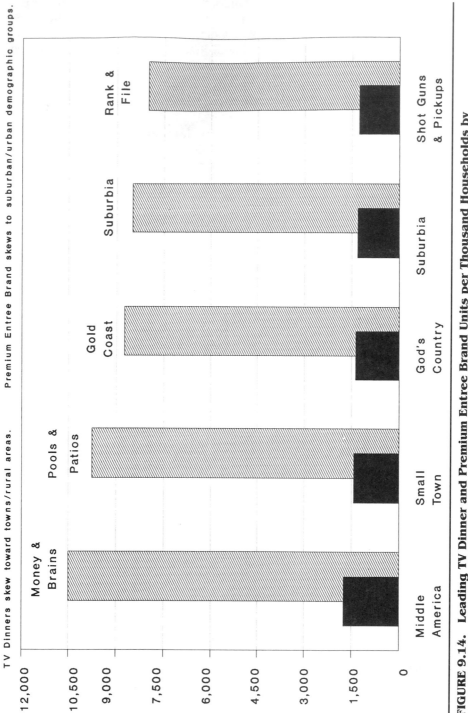

FIGURE 9.14. Leading TV Dinner and Premium Entree Brand Units per Thousand Households by Geodemographic Group

Source: Based on Gollins, 1989.

and analyzed in standard single-source reports. The reports permit a manufacturer to develop annual plans; prepare trade reviews; set sales and market share objectives; evaluate the effectiveness of features, displays, and price discounts; and determine the positioning of its brand(s) relative to competitors in the same category.

Although standard reports are useful, they are typically supplemented by a wide range of special client services. By confining attention to hard-copy reports, this chapter has only scratched the surface of the client support available in the business information services industry.

The chapter also provided three illustrations of actual applications of standard reports for manufacturers. These applications demonstrate how multiple reports can be brought to bear on a single problem in order to investigate fully that problem's strategic implications. The cases reviewed here focus on manufacturer-retailer relations, the trade-off between advertising and promotion, and regional market planning. In each case, single-source data combined with powerful report delivery allowed a manager to engage in a penetrating, thorough analysis and to propose sound solutions.

Notes

1. Chapter 17 pursues manufacturer sales programs in more depth.

2. See Douglas F. Haley and Kenneth E. Krantz, "How to Use Single Source Data to Increase Sales Effectiveness: Case Histories," in *Fulfilling the Promise of Single Source Data,* Transcript Proceedings, ARF Conference, New York (June 22, 1989), pp. 37–51.

3. For details on IRI's partitioning methods, see Magid M. Abraham and Leonard M. Lodish, "PromotionScan: A System for Improving Promotion Productivity for Retailers and Manufacturers Using Scanner Data and Household Panel Data," Working Paper, Information Resources, Inc. (February 1990).

4. Ibid., pp. 1–3.

5. Totten was IRI's director of new products. His close contacts with hundreds of IRI clients provides a comprehensive personal view of internal cost accounting in packaged goods firms. (Personal communication 2/5/90.)

6. Information Resources, Inc., *1988 Annual Report*, p. 9.

7. For detailed distinctions between these services, the reader is advised to contact client representatives at the respective firms.

8. For details on IRI's methodology, see Abraham and Lodish, op. cit., pp. 11–20.

9. See "SCANTRACK Services: Fact Sheet" as well as "Nielsen SCANTRACK Household Services," both published by A. C. Nielsen Co. (January 1990).

10. Each store is either merchandising the item or is not. Stores are weighted by all-commodity volume (ACV).

11. IRI's panel database was formerly known as the Marketing Fact Book. The database provides access to individual consumer purchase records from InfoScan

households in IRI's metro sampling pods and minimarkets. Clients can analyze store and brand loyalty patterns, trial and repeat purchases, demographic patterns, responses to promotion events, and many other issues of interest.

12. IRI's Consumer Report is produced on a quarterly basis. The others are produced every four weeks.

13. See Chapter 8 for details on the report classification system employed in this book.

14. Cases 1 and 2 are based on Haley and Krantz, op. cit.

15. Each week, each store in a given trade area is placed into one of two conditions: a promotion condition or a nonpromotion condition. The "percent of store weeks supporting" is defined as the ratio of "total stores by weeks promoting" to "total stores by weeks." This measure is then weighted by each store's ACV to account for differences in store volumes.

16. This example is based on an application of InfoScan data as originally reported in Jan Gollins, "Why Market Share Is Not Enough," in *Fulfilling the Promise of Single Source Data,* Transcript Proceedings, ARF conference, New York (June 22, 1989) pp. 103–118.

17. PRIZM's geodemographic segments are described in detail in Chapters 12 through 15.

APPENDIX 9A:
DETAILS ON OTHER STANDARD REPORTS
FROM INFORMATION RESOURCES, INC.

IRI supplies five standard hard-copy reports for manufacturers through its InfoScan report series. Details of these five are reviewed in this appendix, and illustrations of several of these reports are provided. The five include IRI's Category Topline Report, Category Trended Report, Volume and Merchandising Report, Feature and Display Report, and Consumer Report.

Category Topline Report

Delivered every four weeks, the Category Topline Report provides a snapshot of store data in the total United States for the most recent four-week period. For each line in a manufacturer's product hierarchy—excluding UPCs—the values for up to 13 selected measures are reported. (See the main text of this chapter for further detail.)

Category Trended Report

Delivered every four weeks, the Category Trended Report provides information on store data in the total United States as well as in individual markets. Up to 13 column headings marking time periods appear across the top of the page, as shown in Figure 9.15. These typically include weekly, 4-week, and 12-week reporting periods, as well as comparisons from a year ago or from more recent periods.

The Category Trended Report contains a block of data for each item and level in the product hierarchy. In each block, the values for each selected measure are reported for each time period. With this report a manufacturer can:

- Track the distribution growth or decline for all brands in a selected category
- Track sales and share by category, segment, UPC, or other dimension over time
- Identify the level and type of promotions his or her products receive
- Evaluate the volume associated with retail promotions, by brand or by item
- Analyze average prices to determine whether trade allowances have been passed through to the consumer
- Develop annual plans and prepare trade reviews

Volume and Merchandising Report

The Volume and Merchandising Report is a key account report that integrates volume and merchandising data on all items detailed in a manufacturer's product hierarchy for individual retail chains or accounts within a market. This report is available only for certain cooperating retail chains.

Custom Client Hierarchy -- This is the order in which items and aggregations of items appear on your InfoScan reports.

There are client-specified time periods for the data in each column. Comparisons to prior periods of year-ago periods may also appear in up to 3 of these columns.

The entire time period covered in this report.

COMPANY: Company A *(Client)*
CATEGORY: Frozen Breakfast Foods *(Name of Category)*
REGION AREA: Total U.S. *(Market, region covered on report)*
VOLUME MEASURE: Ounces *(Unit of measure/volume equivalency used on report)*

TIME PERIODS: 06/22/87 - 10/11/87
IRI WEEKS: 408- 423

InfoScan
CATEGORY TRENDED REPORT

CATEGORY-FRZN BREAKFAST FOODS	1-Week Ending 09/20	1-Week Ending 09/27	1-Week Ending 10/04	1-Week Ending 10/11	1-Week Ending 10/18	1-Week Ending 10/25	1-Week Ending 11/01	1-Week Ending 11/08	4-Week Ending 10/11	4-Week Ending 11/08	12-Week Ending 11/08	44-Week Ending 11/08
VOLUME SALES	7,511m	71,452m	7,901m	7,717m	7,715m	7,785m	7,666m	8,060m	30,580m	31,226m	89,968m	318,604m
TYPE VOLUME SHARE	100.00	100.00	100.00	100.00	100.00	100.00	100.00	100.00	100.00	100.00	100.00	100.00
DOLLAR SALES	13.239m	13,363m	14,153m	13,766m	13,912m	13,969m	13,942m	14,298m	54,520m	56,220m	159,630m	548,490m
TYPE DOLLAR SHARE	100.00	100.00	100.00	100.00	100.00	100.00	100.00	100.00	100.00	100.00	100.00	100.00
ACV WEIGHED DST	100.0	100.0	100.0	100.0	100.0	100.0	100.0	100.0	100.0	100.0	100.0	*
AVG PRICE PER UNIT	1.32	1.32	1.31	1.31	1.33	1.33	1.35	1.34	1.32	1.34	1.33	1.32
%VOL W ANY MERCH	22.0	23.8	24.9	23.8	21.2	21.0	18.6	25.0	23.6	21.5	21.5	20.6
%ACV W ANY MERCH	90.3	91.4	91.4	91.0	91.3	92.1	91.6	91.7	93.4	98.1	98.3	*
%ACV W DISP ONLY	19.3	19.2	17.7	16.4	18.1	18.2	18.3	16.7	34.9	33.6	51.4	*
%ACV W FEAT ONLY	57.4	63.4	62.5	70.5	73.8	64.7	63.1	69.1	91.2	91.2	95.7	*
%ACV W DISP & FEAT	6.8	8.0	4.3	12.3	10.0	9.2	5.3	10.0	22.1	26.9	30.0	*
AVG$ DISP ONLY (UNIT)	1.10	1.08	1.16	1.03	1.15	1.12	1.21	1.15	1.09	1.16	1.13	1.10
AVG$ FEAT ONLY (UNIT)	1.06	1.02	1.09	1.10	1.15	1.17	1.26	1.22	1.07	1.20	1.14	1.11
TRADITIONAL FROZEN BREAKFASTS												
VOLUME SALES	3,832m	3,676m	3,916	3,824m	3,759m	3,804m	3,808m	4,091m	15,250m	15,365m	44,979m	160,353m
TYPE VOLUME SHARE	100.00	100.00	100.00	100.00	100.00	100.00	100.00	100.00	100.00	100.00	100.00	100.00
DOLLAR SALES	5,982m	5,778m	6,235m	6,088m	6,095m	6,214m	6,219m	6,546m	24,084m	24,984m	71,653m	252,272m
TYPE DOLLAR SHARE	100.00	100.00	100.00	100.00	100.00	100.00	100.00	100.00	100.00	100.00	100.00	100.0
ACV WEIGHTED DIST	100.0	100.0	100.0	100.0	100.0	100.0	100.0	100.0	100.0	100.0	100.0	*
AVG PRICE PER UNIT	1.17	1.17	1.18	1.19	1.21	1.21	1.23	1.22	1.18	1.22	1.29	1.18
%VOL W ANY MERCH	28.0	27.4	26.6	24.7	21.9	22.8	21.3	30.5	26.7	24.3	25.1	24.6
%AVC W ANY MERCH	82.3	81.7	83.0	82.9	80.1	75.4	80.5	83.8	95.0	94.3	98.0	*
%ACV W DISP ONLY	11.1	9.8	9.1	9.1	9.3	9.2	8.2	8.2	21.7	19.8	36.0	*
%ACV W FEAT ONLY	39.0	46.2	45.9	55.4	53.0	43.0	47.9	58.5	81.6	81.6	90.1	*
%ACV W DISP & FEAT	2.1	3.8	3.1	8.9	6.3	2.1	2.2	3.2	12.7	17.3	12.0	*
AVG$ DISP ONLY (UNIT)	0.98	0.88	0.98	0.85	1.02	1.02	1.10	1.01	0.93	1.04	1.00	0.96
AVG$ FEAT ONLY (UNIT)	0.89	0.83	0.93	0.99	1.00	0.99	1.07	1.18	0.91	1.07	0.99	0.97
WAFFLES												
VOLUME SALES	2,903m	2,754m	2,907m	2,855m	2,806m	2,861m	2,839m	3,022m	11,420m	11,529m	33,792m	120,485m
TYPE VOLUME SHARE	75.76	74.92	74.24	74.66	74.63	75.21	74.55	73.87	74.89	74.55	75.13	75.14
DOLLAR SALES	4,322m	4,130m	4,438m	4,345m	4,356m	4,404m	4,468m	4,625m	17,235m	17,854m	51,536m	181,620m
TYPE DOLLAR SHARE	72.24	71.47	71.18	71.37	71.48	71.92	71.84	70.65	71.56	71.46	71.92	71.99
ACV WEIGHTED DIST	100.0	100.0	100.0	100.0	100.0	100.0	100.0	100.0	100.0	100.0	100.0	100.0
AVG PRICE PER UNIT	1.11	1.10	1.13	1.13	1.16	1.15	1.18	1.17	1.12	1.16	1.14	1.13
%VOL W ANY MERCH	29.0	28.1	26.5	24.8	23.2	25.1	22.7	29.8	27.1	25.3	26.0	25.8
%ACV W ANY MERCH	74.4	75.6	76.1	74.3	71.7	69.9	73.8	77.3	93.2	92.7	97.0	*
%ACV W DISP ONLY	8.5	7.9	7.7	6.6	6.7	7.2	6.8	6.8	18.1	16.3	31.6	*
%ACV W FEAT ONLY	36.3	39.3	37.1	46.7	44.4	35.3	40.0	49.6	75.3	77.3	88.1	*
%ACV W DISP & FEAT	2.0	2.0	2.5	6.3	5.2	1.3	1.2	1.0	10.3	15.0	11.0	*
AVG$ DISP ONLY (UNIT)	0.93	0.82	0.93	0.76	0.94	0.98	1.09	0.99	0.86	1.00	.95	0.92
AVG$ FEAT ONLY (UNIT)	0.83	0.75	0.86	0.94	0.97	0.94	1.04	1.15	0.84	1.03	.93	0.91

These are the 13 client-selected measures. They are reported in a block for each line of the product hierarchy.

FIGURE 9.15. A Category Trended Report
Source: IRI

The format for this report is identical to that of the Category Trended Report. This report is an excellent tool for managing the sales force and for business reviews with the retail trade. With it a manufacturer can:

- Track distribution of possible out-of-stock problems by account
- Track sales and share by category, segment, UPC, or other dimension across time within an account

- Determine the level and type of merchandising a retailer used for the manufacturer's products and for competitive products
- Determine the volume associated with a retailer's merchandising for the manufacturer's products and for competitive products
- Track average prices to determine whether the retailer is passing trade allowances through to the consumer
- Compare a specific retailer to the total market in terms of volume, share, merchandising, price, and distribution
- Set goals and evaluate results on the basis of volume, share, displays, features, and other relevant criteria

Feature and Display Report

The Feature and Display report is delivered every four weeks and is similar to the Volume and Merchandising Report except that sales volume and volume-related measures are not included. This report provides information on features, displays, and price reductions for all items in a manufacturer's product hierarchy for retail chains in each market. (A manufacturer is limited to 10 selected variables for the Feature and Display Report.) With this report a manufacturer can:

- Track distribution or possible out-of-stock problems by account
- Determine the level and type of merchandising a retailer used for the manufacturer's products and for competitive products
- Track average prices to determine whether the retailer is passing trade allowances on to consumers
- Set goals and evaluate results on the basis of features, displays, and prices

Consumer Report

Delivered quarterly, the InfoScan Consumer Report provides purchase information collected from the InfoScan household panel. Clients receive consumer purchase information projected to the total United States. In addition, clients can choose between four standard region summaries or data on 6 of the 21 metropolitan markets. This report is an excellent top-line tool for brand or product managers who wish to develop marketing plans. Sales management can use the information to plan trade ads, brochures, and business reviews.

The Consumer Report uses the same product hierarchy as the other reports in the InfoScan series, as shown in Figure 9.16. All measures are reported with quarterly data points, and many are also reported at four-week intervals. Depending on the measures selected, a manufacturer can:

- Determine penetration, buying rate, and purchase frequency for the category or segments of its products as well as for competitive products

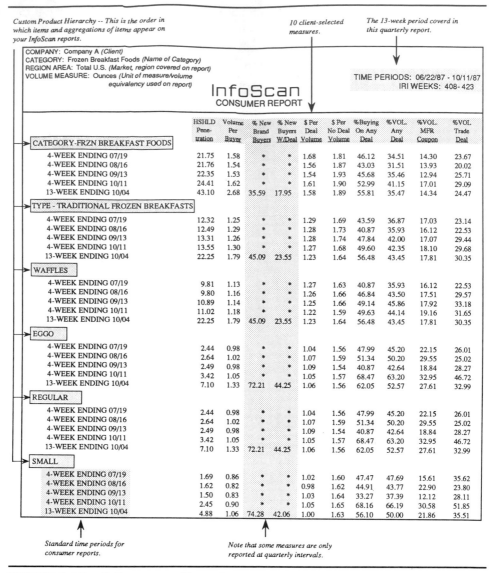

Custom Product Hierarchy -- This is the order in which items and aggregations of items appear on your InfoScan reports.

10 client-selected measures.

The 13-week period coverd in this quarterly report.

COMPANY: Company A *(Client)*
CATEGORY: Frozen Breakfast Foods *(Name of Category)*
REGION AREA: Total U.S. *(Market, region covered on report)*
VOLUME MEASURE: Ounces *(Unit of measure/volume equivalency used on report)*

TIME PERIODS: 06/22/87 - 10/11/87
IRI WEEKS: 408- 423

InfoScan
CONSUMER REPORT

	HSHLD Penetration	Volume Per Buyer	% New Brand Buyers	% New Buyers W/Deal	$ Per Deal Volume	$ Per No Deal Volume	%Buying On Any Deal	%VOL. Any Deal	%VOL. MFR Coupon	%VOL. Trade Deal
CATEGORY-FRZN BREAKFAST FOODS										
4-WEEK ENDING 07/19	21.75	1.58	*	*	1.68	1.81	46.12	34.51	14.30	23.67
4-WEEK ENDING 08/16	21.76	1.54	*	*	1.56	1.87	43.03	31.51	13.93	20.02
4-WEEK ENDING 09/13	22.35	1.53	*	*	1.54	1.93	45.68	35.46	12.94	25.71
4-WEEK ENDING 10/11	24.41	1.62	*	*	1.61	1.90	52.99	41.15	17.01	29.09
13-WEEK ENDING 10/04	43.10	2.68	35.59	17.95	1.58	1.89	55.81	35.47	14.34	24.47
TYPE - TRADITIONAL FROZEN BREAKFASTS										
4-WEEK ENDING 07/19	12.32	1.25	*	*	1.29	1.69	43.59	36.87	17.03	23.14
4-WEEK ENDING 08/16	12.49	1.29	*	*	1.28	1.73	40.87	35.93	16.12	22.53
4-WEEK ENDING 09/13	13.31	1.26	*	*	1.28	1.74	47.84	42.00	17.07	29.44
4-WEEK ENDING 10/11	13.55	1.30	*	*	1.27	1.68	49.60	42.35	18.10	29.68
13-WEEK ENDING 10/04	22.25	1.79	45.09	23.55	1.23	1.64	56.48	43.45	17.81	30.35
WAFFLES										
4-WEEK ENDING 07/19	9.81	1.13	*	*	1.27	1.63	40.87	35.93	16.12	22.53
4-WEEK ENDING 08/16	9.80	1.16	*	*	1.26	1.66	46.84	43.50	17.51	29.57
4-WEEK ENDING 09/13	10.89	1.14	*	*	1.25	1.66	49.14	45.86	17.92	33.18
4-WEEK ENDING 10/11	11.02	1.18	*	*	1.22	1.59	49.63	44.14	19.16	31.65
13-WEEK ENDING 10/04	22.25	1.79	45.09	23.55	1.23	1.64	56.48	43.45	17.81	30.35
EGGO										
4-WEEK ENDING 07/19	2.44	0.98	*	*	1.04	1.56	47.99	45.20	22.15	26.01
4-WEEK ENDING 08/16	2.64	1.02	*	*	1.07	1.59	51.34	50.20	29.55	25.02
4-WEEK ENDING 09/13	2.49	0.98	*	*	1.09	1.54	40.87	42.64	18.84	28.27
4-WEEK ENDING 10/11	3.42	1.05	*	*	1.05	1.57	68.47	63.20	32.95	46.72
13-WEEK ENDING 10/04	7.10	1.33	72.21	44.25	1.06	1.56	62.05	52.57	27.61	32.99
REGULAR										
4-WEEK ENDING 07/19	2.44	0.98	*	*	1.04	1.56	47.99	45.20	22.15	26.01
4-WEEK ENDING 08/16	2.64	1.02	*	*	1.07	1.59	51.34	50.20	29.55	25.02
4-WEEK ENDING 09/13	2.49	0.98	*	*	1.09	1.54	40.87	42.64	18.84	28.27
4-WEEK ENDING 10/11	3.42	1.05	*	*	1.05	1.57	68.47	63.20	32.95	46.72
13-WEEK ENDING 10/04	7.10	1.33	72.21	44.25	1.06	1.56	62.05	52.57	27.61	32.99
SMALL										
4-WEEK ENDING 07/19	1.69	0.86	*	*	1.02	1.60	47.47	47.69	15.61	35.62
4-WEEK ENDING 08/16	1.62	0.82	*	*	0.98	1.62	44.91	43.77	22.90	23.80
4-WEEK ENDING 09/13	1.50	0.83	*	*	1.03	1.64	33.27	37.39	12.12	28.11
4-WEEK ENDING 10/11	2.45	0.90	*	*	1.05	1.65	68.16	66.19	30.58	51.85
13-WEEK ENDING 10/04	4.88	1.06	74.28	42.06	1.00	1.63	56.10	50.00	21.86	35.51

Standard time periods for consumer reports.

Note that some measures are only reported at quarterly intervals.

FIGURE 9.16. A Consumer Report
Source: IRI

- Determine consumer loyalty among different segments for different products in the category
- Examine weekly grocery expenditures by the manufacturer's consumers versus consumers of competitive products
- Determine the extent to which consumers are using manufacturer coupons or purchasing with retailer incentives

- Determine if promotions or deals were effective in generating volume from buyers who had not purchased the brand before

InfoScan consumer panel data are also available for ad hoc analyses using IRI's on-line system called PROMPT. With PROMPT a manufacturer can reserve on-line access to the subscribed category or categories for all historical panel data collected during the term of subscription.

10 SINGLE-SOURCE REPORTS FOR RETAILERS

Today's marketplace requires retailers to know their customers better than ever. With the emergence of niche marketing, more than 10,000 new product introductions each year and limited shelf space, retailers are looking for ways to know just who their customers are, and how best to meet their needs. It's more than understanding what is selling, it's being able to identify who buys what so that you can retain not only your existing customers, but also attract new ones. This is a tall order.

Nielsen ClusterPLUS/SCANTRACK brochure

INTRODUCTION

Single-source systems originally focused on data-gathering technology and on applications for manufacturers, who are interested in their brands' performance in geographically dispersed markets. Retailers, who are almost exclusively interested in category sales in their immediate trading areas, did not benefit much from these systems; nor did retail chains, who need analyses of competition at multiple sites.

This chapter shows how single-source systems have changed to accommodate packaged goods retailing problems. The chapter begins by contrasting the business settings, strategic considerations, and objectives of retail management and brand management. Next, it overviews the U.S. retail environment in packaged goods, focusing on forces that encouraged system development. Subsequently, the text reviews retail reports offered by the main data suppliers, including space management reports, new item analysis reports, item deletion reports, and others. The final section outlines developments that may make it possible to accurately model particularly vexing retail issues, such as cross-category sales within an outlet. Such models require detailed, store-level data that were unavailable before the introduction of single-source technology.

RETAIL VERSUS BRAND MANAGEMENT

Table 10.1 contrasts the retail and manufacturer situations in four areas: business setting, strategic considerations, objectives, and controllable variables. Because retailers differ from manufacturers in their business orientation, they also have different strategic considerations. Manufacturers seek to optimize the marketing mix; they must plan for regional markets and support a national sales program by allocating funds to local markets. Retailers, on the other hand, must decide where to locate during periods of expansion and how to design new stores that will attract consumers and facilitate stocking and inventory control. Once a store is designed, space management becomes the most pressing problem; each year as many as 10,000 new items compete for available supermarket shelf space. Retailers must also conduct promotions and assess profitability for each of the more than 26,000 items in a typical supermarket.

Strategic considerations enter directly into a retailer's day-to-day and week-by-week objectives. The primary retail objective is effective merchandising. Margins in the packaged goods industry are thin, averaging only 3 to 4 percent. Retailers want to increase both store traffic and sales per shopper while minimizing holding costs and other costs of goods sold. They accomplish these goals by controlling only a few elements—space, prices, facings, promotions, and sources—in a rapidly changing, intensely competitive environment.

THE U.S. RETAIL ENVIRONMENT
IN PACKAGED GOODS

Size

Although competition among retailers is intense, the stakes are dazzling. For example, total U.S. retail sales in 1988 were $1.629 trillion, up 7 percent over 1987 and up more than 19 percent over 1985.[1] Of this total, packaged goods accounted for $304.4 billion. In other words, on average each of the 90.3 million U.S. households spends $3,300 annually on food and other grocery items.

TABLE 10.1.   Management from the Retailer's Viewpoint

Aspect	Retailer concerns	Manufacturer Concerns
Business setting	*Store:* • Managing 26,000+ items • Focusing on category, not brand sales • Focusing on trading-area and local competition *Chain:* • Managing multiple store formats • Transacting with multiple vendors	• Managing multiple lines that span several categories • Focusing on competition nationally but also regionally, in metro-markets, and by key account • Managing multiple production sites • Transacting with many retailers
Key strategic considerations	• Site location, chain expansion • Store design • Space management and product assortments • Direct product profitability • Promotion analysis	• Optimizing the marketing mix • Planning in all submarkets • Allocating funds for in-store promotions • Tailoring promotions to local conditions

Objectives	• Effective merchandising
	  —To increase store traffic
	  —To increase sales per shopper
	• Effective space utilization
	  —To allocate scarce display and feature resources
	  —To maximize the impact of newspaper ads
	• Efficient control
	  —To minimize holding costs
	  —To maximize sales velocity
		• Effective marketing
		  —Primarily to retailers as clients
		  —Secondarily to the ultimate consumer
		• Increased sales
		  —Increased market share
		  —Increased market penetration
		  —Increased merchandising support

Controllable variables	• Space management: format and layout
	• Price and price reductions
	• Promotion (in-store, trade-area)
	• Sourcing
	• Item analysis
		• Price (suggested list price)
		• Promotion
		  —Trade vs. consumer
		  —National vs. local
		• Channel selection
		• New product development, design, and packaging

Large chain stores (those with ACV above $2 million) account for about 65 percent of sales (see Figure 10.1). Meanwhile, the small, independent grocer, once well respected, has shown steady share declines during the last decade, down from 13.1 percent to 11.0 percent between 1985 and 1989 alone.

Scanner Technology and Store Competition

With changes in consumer demographics, altered lifestyles, inflation, and other forces, retail margins have become smaller and consumers' loyalty to specific stores weaker—a deadly combination for the small independent. Smaller retailers typically cannot afford sophisticated, cost-cutting technology such as UPC scanners to help manage supply-side problems. They have survived by depending on loyal neighborhood customers willing to pay higher prices. But weakened store loyalty has undermined the small retailer's customer base, making it increasingly difficult to compete against efficient retail giants.

For stores that can afford them, UPC scanners reduce costs and increase demand. Scanners are standard equipment today in the majority of retail food stores, as shown in Figure 10.2.[2] In 1981 only 4,568 food stores were scanner-equipped (21 percent of the 21,752 stores existing at that time). Today about 20,672 stores (68 percent of 30,400) are scanner-equipped.

Scanner penetration differs by market, ranging among all food stores from a low of 34.7 percent in Memphis, Tennessee, to a high of 79.2 percent in Denver, Colorado. (See Table 10.2.) If one tallies only large supermarkets, those with

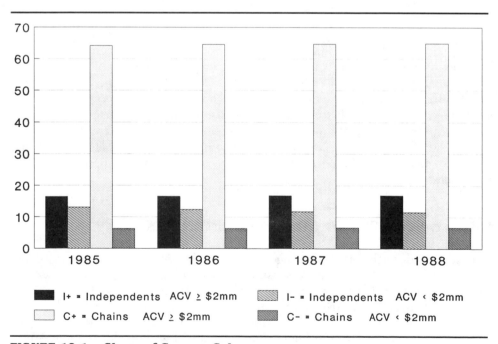

I+ ▪ Independents ACV ≥ $2mm
I− ▪ Independents ACV ‹ $2mm
C+ ▪ Chains ACV ≥ $2mm
C− ▪ Chains ACV ‹ $2mm

FIGURE 10.1. Share of Grocery Sales
Source: 1989 Nielsen Annual Review of Retail Grocery Store Trends, p. 4.

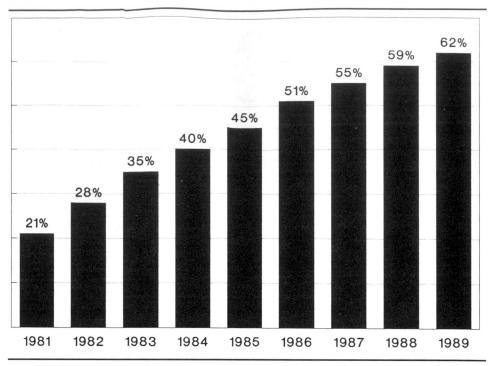

FIGURE 10.2. **Estimated Dollar ACV of Scanning Stores as a Percent of Total Grocery Business**
Source: 1989 Nielsen Annual Review of Retail Grocery Store Trends, p. 11.

annual sales of at least $4 million, scanner penetration ranges from 56.8 percent in Raleigh-Durham, North Carolina, to 91.7 percent in Denver.

As Chapters 6 and 7 point out, scanner technology is the basis for the development of the modern single-source research system. Reports discussed in subsequent sections of this chapter rely on the continued diffusion of scanner technology throughout the national markets shown in Table 10.2. Furthermore, the spread of scanners to mass merchandising and drug stores suggests that the complex software developed for packaged goods will soon be applied in many other industry sectors.

SINGLE-SOURCE REPORTS FOR RETAILERS

This section describes retail packaged goods applications of single-source data. Four specific report types are discussed: Apollo, a space management system from IRI; two specialized standard report series, from A. C. Nielsen and IRI; and TradeMaster, from Arbitron/SAMI. The review is representative but not exhaustive. For further detail on these and other retail reports, the reader is advised to contact each of the single-source firms reviewed in this section. Additional reports that combine scanner data and geodemographic data are discussed in Chapter 17.

TABLE 10.2. Scanner Penetration by Market

Market	Known Scanner-Equipped Stores	Percent of All Food Stores	Percent of Supermarkets over $4 Million	Market	Known Scanner-Equipped Stores	Percent of All Food Stores	Percent of Supermarkets over $4 Million
Albany	95	48.2	61.6	Miami	359	73.9	87.6
Atlanta	225	48.6	66.1	Milwaukee	121	59.5	68.0
Baltimore	119	57.1	67.1	Minneapolis	209	60.5	81.6
Birmingham	187	51.9	75.2	Nashville	132	45.9	80.5
Boston	337	62.6	77.4	New Orleans/Mobile	336	61.1	83.0
Buffalo/Rochester	123	60.1	72.9	New York	505	54.7	59.6
Charlotte	81	39.1	48.6	Oklahoma City/Tulsa	136	39.2	58.2
Chicago	436	75.5	87.1	Omaha	102	55.2	82.2
Cincinnati	164	61.5	75.9	Orlando	209	69.1	87.8
Cleveland	194	48.0	60.5	Philadelphia	289	49.5	59.2
Columbus	145	64.6	84.5	Phoenix	261	64.2	78.8
Dallas	388	60.5	77.8	Pittsburgh	227	52.5	70.3
Denver	235	79.2	91.7	Portland	270	65.2	84.6
Des Moines	75	54.6	77.5	Raleigh/Durham	150	38.7	56.8
Detroit	207	48.0	60.8	Richmond	172	43.6	64.8
Grand Rapids	129	53.9	72.6	Sacramento	114	54.7	68.2
Hartford/New Haven	122	56.8	67.5	Salt Lake City/Boise	204	60.9	83.9
Houston	329	66.7	86.3	San Antonio	137	51.2	70.4
Indianapolis	156	56.6	71.5	San Diego	116	71.3	79.7
Jacksonville	141	63.1	89.3	San Francisco	364	67.3	77.8
Kansas City	209	56.1	79.8	Seattle	333	71.5	84.0
Little Rock	114	47.0	78.8	St. Louis	249	70.0	89.4
Los Angeles	777	76.1	82.4	Syracuse	100	56.5	71.1
Louisville	139	49.1	77.8	Tampa	376	70.1	87.1
Memphis	105	34.7	65.9	Washington, D.C.	335	67.0	79.4

Source: 1989 Nielsen Annual Review of Retail Grocery Store Trends, p. 11.

Figure 10.3 summarizes the nature and extent of retail applications of single-source data by type. It shows that retailers use single-source reports to decide when to add or delete an item; to track an item's movement; to bargain with suppliers; to allocate shelf space; to forecast, promote, and advertise; and to control inventory. We begin by reviewing a system designed to solve the complex space management problems associated with adding or deleting items and with allocating shelf space.

Apollo, from Information Resources, Inc.

Apollo is a comprehensive space management system that assists retailers with store formatting, remerchandising, and inventory planning. Apollo focuses on all relevant store levels: the arrangement of items on a single shelf, the arrangement of shelves within a section, and the arrangement of sections within a store.

The system produces both visual and statistical reports. For example, using the VIVID option, a shelf section can be displayed on a CRT screen or in a color photograph as it would appear in the store. To accomplish this, VIVID accesses IRI's National Product Library database of stored video images and arranges "items" (that is, item images) on "shelves" (shelf images) to match a manager's specifications.

Other components of the system include Apollo Total Store and the Apollo New Product Introduction Service. Total Store moves from VIVID's section-by-section focus to the complete store environment. Management can trade space (on screen) between sections; identify problem areas that exhibit slow movement, low profit, or frequent out-of-stocks; and can reallocate space according to

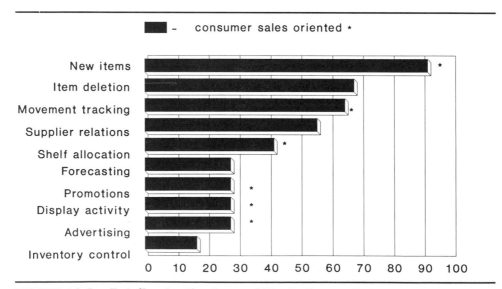

FIGURE 10.3.   Retailer Applications of Single-Source Data
Source: A. C. Nielsen, *The Trade,* brochure based on a retailer survey conducted in 1989.

one of several available criteria (such as profit-to-space ratios or direct product profitability).

The New Product Introduction Service, designed primarily to help manufacturers test or launch a new item, also assists retailers who are considering stocking the item. The item is displayed in a carefully selected sample of Apollo stores and merchandised according to a predetermined interstore experimental design. Sales and movement data are then tracked to determine the item's sales impact.

Table 10.3 summarizes the standard reports available from Apollo and indicates their functions. Apollo attacks one of the most important problems in retail management: optimal use of available space. As a subsequent section indicates, developments in the near future are likely to make this complex problem easier to solve.

Packaged Reports

IRI and A. C. Nielsen offer similar standard report packages for other facets of retail management. This discussion uses Nielsen's SCANTRACK reports to illustrate the concepts, with IRI's Insights series outlined as a point of contrast.[3]

SCANTRACK

In Nielsen's SCANTRACK system, weekly in-store scanner data are organized into seven major reports (see Figure 10.4), currently delivered via both hard copy and an electronic delivery system. Retailers can also request data and reports on tape or diskette for in-house use and consulting support from Nielsen's staff of experts.

Figure 10.4 shows how the various reports are designed for different applications. For example, using Nielsen's Market Sales Report, managers can compare dollar sales for 116 Nielsen-defined product groups accumulated into departmental totals. This report, issued every four weeks, supports supplier dialogues, market share analyses, and budgeting.

The bottom portion of the figure shows additional detail for Nielsen's Market Sales Report. In this sample, total sales dollars are reported by department for the Cincinnati market, and changes in these totals from one four-week period to another are shown. Sales are further divided by product category within department. The actual report is 10 pages long and shows these totals for all 116 product categories.

IRI Insights

IRI's Insight series is a standard package of retail reports designed to compete with Nielsen's SCANTRACK series. Insights contains four modules: Buyer Insights, Category Insights, Vendor Insights, and Executive Insights. Although the modules offer different perspectives, their cores are similar; for example, each contains a Market Share Overview, a Department Ranking Report, and an Items

TABLE 10.3. IRI's Apollo Reports

Report Name	Current Status			Planning		Tracking
	Echo Check on Current/Proposed Schematic[a]	Inventory Control/Space Use	Movement, Sales, and Profits by Items/Sections	Alternative Use of Existing Space	Current versus Proposed Schematic	Performance of Old versus New Schematic
Shelf Fact Sheet	By shelf					
Shelf Detail	By SKU					
Space Productivity		By item within shelf				
Ranking Report						
By unit			Totaled by section			
By dollar sales			Totaled by section			
By profit contribution			Totaled by section			
Space utilization				By cubic feet By item within shelf		
Section Comparison					By dollar sales By profit sales	
Remerchandising Impact						Items deleted, added, etc.

[a] A schematic is either a lifelike view or a blueprint depiction of how a store shelf or shelves and their facings (aisle fronts) are arranged.

164

SCANTRACK Major Markets
Trade Applications   Report Types

Uses	Market Sales Report	Item Sales Report	New Item Report	Items not Handled Report	Supplemental Detail Report	Department Ranking Report	Stores Handling Analyses
Supplier Dialog	▲	▲	▲				▲
Promotion Analysis	▲	▲			▲	▲	▲
Share of Market	▲	▲			▲	▲	▲
New Items		▲	▲	▲	▲		▲
Delistings		▲					
Plan-o-Gram/Resets		▲					
Localized Marketing					▲		▲
Brand Mix/Depth							▲
Seasonality					▲		
Product Group Review			▲				▲
Testing		▲		▲	▲		▲
Budgeting	▲	▲					

MARKET SALES REPORT

CURRENT: 4 WEEKS ENDING 01/31/87 (FROM WEEK ENDING 01/10/87)
PREVIOUS: 4 WEEKS ENDING 01/03/87 (FROM WEEK ENDING 12/13/86)
YEAR AGO FIGURES NOT AVAILABLE

	DOLLAR SALES.....		DOLLAR SALES PERCENT CHANGE		SHARE OF DOLLAR SALES......			OPERATOR SHARE OF MARKET DOLLAR SALES		
	CURR 4 WEEKS	PREV 4 WEEKS	CURR VS PREV	CURR VS Y/A	CURR 4 WEEKS	PREV 4 WEEKS	Y/A 4 WEEKS	CURR 4 WEEKS	PREV 4 WEEKS	Y/A 4 WEEKS
TOTAL SALES DOLLARS Cincinnati	139,495,196	143,648,046	-2.9	N/A	100.0	100.0	N/A			
DRY GROCERY ITEM TOTALS Cincinnati	69,995,713	72,272,180	-3.1	N/A	50.2	50.3	N/A			
BABY FOOD Cincinnati	1,062,378	1,013,537	4.8	N/A	.8	.7	N/A			
BAKING MIXES Cincinnati	1,159,368	1,136,647	2.0	N/A	.8	.8	N/A			

FIGURE 10.4. SCANTRACK Reports

Source: A. C. Nielsen.

165

Not Carried Report. The Vendor and Executive Insight series add a Vendor Overview Report to this core.

Like SCANTRACK, Insights reports provide a retailer with summaries of such performance measures as dollar sales, unit sales, and percentage of units sold during merchandising events. These measures are reported by store, by department, by vendor, and by other breakdowns for specific weeks and markets.

SCANTRACK and Insights are excellent examples of standard market status reports that permit retail management to gauge the effectiveness of past policy. They differ from the next product to be discussed, Trademaster, in their delivery mode: Trademaster reports are transmitted on CD-ROM rather than on hard copy.

TradeMaster from SAMI

TradeMaster is a highly flexible electronic report delivery system designed specifically for the retail trade. Two years of single-source data serve a software analysis package, all delivered on CD-ROM.[4] This delivery form yields important benefits: flexibility, immediate response, and local control.

Table 10.4 is a highly condensed overview. To execute a report, managers select from options presented in three menus; there is no programming language to learn. First managers select the report format(s), and then they select from four categories of focal-analytic variables. Finally, they activate TradeMaster's report generator to receive on-screen output that can be routed to a printer or elsewhere in the firm's electronic mail system.

TradeMaster's report formats cross four business aspects (growth, performance, trend, and planning) with three issue areas (market, performance, and product), as the box for step 1 indicates. The key to building a TradeMaster report, however, is step 2. First the user selects a growth period for analysis and a base period for comparison. The user then zeros in on a specific geography, selecting one or more trading zones, markets, or regions for analysis. Next the manager selects from a long list of analytics, including dollar measures, all-commodity volume, item counts, prices, product development indices, distribution sales indices, and others not shown in Table 10.4. Each analytic measure includes data on dollar or unit share at the market level, at the chain level, in a parent product category, or for a specific product type.

To conclude the format specification step, the manager selects the particular product unit to be analyzed among predefined options that represent the hierarchies of observation units commonly analyzed by retail management. For example, the manager can examine the category-brand-SKU hierarchy, the category-segment hierarchy, the entire manufacturer-universe division, or one of several others.

The last frame in the figure shows a sample report from TradeMaster, for cereal meal bars in the San Francisco Bay area. TradeMaster illustrates the power of electronic delivery: It can produce actionable reports on command, on desk, and on time that respond to management's need for historical tracking and analysis.

TABLE 10.4.   TradeMaster from SAMI

Step 1: Select Format

	Growth	Performance	Trend	Planning
Market	Mk-Growth	Mk-Perf.	Mk-Trend	Mk-Planning
Performance	Pf-Growth	Pf-Profile	Pf-Trend	Pf-Planning
Product	Pr-Growth	Pr-Perf.	Pr-Trend	Pr-Planning

Step 2: Select Variables

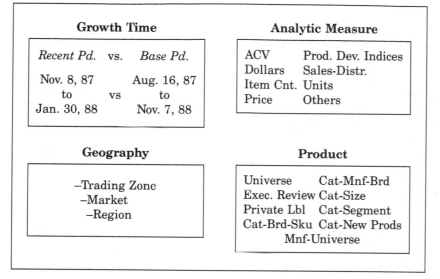

Growth Time			**Analytic Measure**	
Recent Pd.	vs.	*Base Pd.*	ACV	Prod. Dev. Indices
			Dollars	Sales-Distr.
Nov. 8, 87		Aug. 16, 87	Item Cnt.	Units
to	vs	to	Price	Others
Jan. 30, 88		Nov. 7, 88		

Geography	**Product**	
–Trading Zone	Universe	Cat-Mnf-Brd
–Market	Exec. Review	Cat-Size
–Region	Private Lbl	Cat-Segment
	Cat-Brd-Sku	Cat-New Prods
	Mnf-Universe	

Step 3: Generate Report

Total: Grand total
Type: Dry Grocery-Food
Parent: Cereal
Product: Cereal Meal Bars
Market: San Fran CA

Performance Growth
11/08/87 to 01/30/88
vs
08/16/87 to 11/07/88
Dollars in 10s

Measure	Recent	Base	Diff	Pct. Change
Dollars (Market)	24166	15114	9052	59.89
Dollars (Chain)	7265	4341	2925	67.38
Dollar Share of Market	30.06	28.72	1.34	4.68
Dollar Benchmark Index	95	95	0	−0.05

Source: SamScan database.

SYSTEM BREAKTHROUGHS FOR RETAILERS

This section of the chapter discusses three major developments in retailing, each a direct result of single-source data: the merging of single- source and geodemographic research systems; the development of integrated, localized systems; and the "market basket" model, an idea that may pave the way for integrated space management packages and retail management expert systems.

Single-Source and Geodemography

Four major geodemographic systems are currently available: ACORN, Cluster-PLUS, PRIZM, and MicroVision. Each system consists of about 45 segments (or clusters) of unique neighborhood types developed from U.S. Census data.[5] A geodemographic system permits management to know each segment's demographic, media, and product ownership profiles.

Geodemographic codes from any of these systems can be assigned to each member of a single-source panel to link packaged goods purchasing, response to marketing signals, and demographic geography. For example, rather than segmenting buyers of disposable diapers solely on the basis of "stage in family life cycle" or "arrival of a newborn," a geodemographic system can pinpoint specific geodemographic types that exhibit above-average consumption of this item.

Figure 10.5 illustrates a ClusterPLUS analysis based on this characteristic. Seven segments have buying indices above 120: segment 12 ("High Mobility Working Couples"), segment 23 ("Low Mobility Rural Families"), segment 27 ("Average Income Families in Single Units"), segment 33 ("Rural Blue Collar Workers"), segment 36 ("Middle Income Hispanics"), segment 43 ("Center City Blacks"), and segment 47 ("Lowest Income Black Female Headed Families.") Some of these segments, such as "High Mobility Working Couples," might be anticipated intuitively, but others may not be. Furthermore, a given store's trade area may have disproportionate numbers of one or more of these segments, a circumstance that will strongly influence the retailer's allocation of shelf space to disposable diapers and the brands (price lines) carried.[6]

Outside packaged goods, firms can use point-of-sale data linked to geodemographic data to expand both parts of their client base—their in-store and their nonstore customers. This link was successfully exploited by Banana Republic and Williams-Sonoma, who iterated a process of direct marketing, followed by retail expansion, followed by direct marketing, and so on by identifying who their customers are and where these people are concentrated geographically.

Single-source panels in the apparel, sporting goods, and cosmetic industries, among others, can thus close the in-store/nonstore marketing loop by permitting retailers to:

1. Coordinate in-store promotions with micro-media campaigns matched to the needs and locations of specialized target segments
2. Customize catalogs for different geodemographic segments
3. Choose new sites, using refined trade-area response elasticities[7]

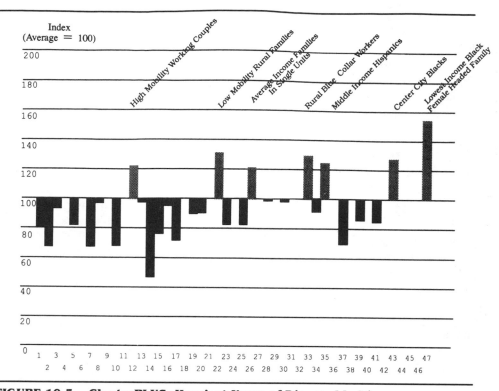

FIGURE 10.5.   ClusterPLUS: Heaviest Users of Disposable Diapers
Note: Only those segments with indices exceeding 120 are shown.
Source: Donnelley Marketing Information Services.

Integrated Localized Systems

Although single-source systems are powerful tracking and diagnostic tools, they are less potent when it comes to implementing micro-strategy. In other words, single-source systems allow information to flow from neighborhoods to management but do not now deliver management strategy back to targeted neighborhoods.

A localized database, however, performs this function. It provides the names, demographics, and buying habits of shoppers frequenting a single store. Examples include the Vision system (from Advanced Promotion Technologies) and the UKROPS experiment in Virginia.[8] With Vision, for example, customers cooperate by using a store card that gives them electronic coupon, check-cashing, and game-playing rights.[9] With these data, a retailer can create local trade-area programs based on lists of users and nonusers of each item in their store. For example, the retailer can issue a checkout coupon for Pepsi to a family buying Coke or can mail a diaper manufacturer's purchase coupon directly to neighborhood families with infants. As a consequence, the retailer's promotion money is leveraged, and merchandising efforts are precisely targeted.

Retail Expert Systems

Retail expert systems are likely to develop in three stages. In the first stage, they will use single-source data to construct market basket models.[10] In the second stage, market basket models will lead to a comprehensive space management package. In the third stage, space management will be integrated into a complete retail management platform.[11]

Stage 1: From Single-Source Data to Market Basket Models

Current applications of single-source data focus on how couponing and price deals affect the sales of a particular brand. This single-brand focus was designed with the manufacturer, not the retailer, in mind.

For retailers, understanding consumer demand means understanding direct and cross-elasticities among the array of items in a single outlet. A retailer must accurately model the total in-store environment if retail space is to be managed intelligently. In other words, a retailer can establish reasonable supply-side policies only if he or she has a thorough and realistic understanding of demand.

The market basket problem is extremely complex. One way to solve it is to apply a series of nested and interrelated market share–sales volume models. As Cooper and Nakanishi remark in the last few pages of their book,

> Extrapolating the approach in this book ..., we would divide the market basket into categories, model the total expenditures as we would a category-volume model, and model the shares among categories as we would a market-share model. Within each category we would have a nested pair of models for category volume and brand shares. This illustrates two levels of what might turn out to be a more articulately leveled scheme.[12]

Further articulation should be helpful. The store environment is composed of at least four layers of intertwined demand: demand within a set of shelf-keeping units (SKUs), demand among SKUs of the same variety, demand among categories, and demand among departments. Within each of these layers the choices facing consumers represent both direct and indirect trade-offs and, hence, direct and cross-elasticities of demand. A true market basket model must forecast not only how an item's sales respond to its own vector of characteristics but also how the item's sales respond to the vector of characteristics for every other item in the store. Further, this share analysis must be embedded in a series of absolute-volume models.

With single-source data available, the complicated microcosm of in-store demand can be understood better now than at any other time in the history of retailing. Both major suppliers of single-source data, and a number academic researchers, are bearing down on this challenging task.

Stage 2: Market Basket Models and Space Management

Researchers are developing market basket models because retailers need to manage store space intelligently. Space management models are the mirror image of market basket models; they are the supply-side view of retail demand.

Rudimentary space management models have been available since the late 1960s.[13] Most of these are based on rules of thumb; for example, they may allocate space in proportion to an item's sales volume, its revenue, its weighted gross margin, or its contribution to profit. These rules, however, are simplistic and are often difficult to implement. For example, how does the retailer allocate costs in order to calculate item-by-item profit contribution?

The trend is to adopt a demand framework incorporating direct and cross-elasticities in order to model share within and across logical product divisions as well as modeling overall volume.[14] This conceptually elegant framework has become feasible only with the availability of single-source data. Before, model builders were unwilling to invest effort in gloriously refined yet totally unestimable approaches. Now the promise of single-source data has energized the modelers, who seek deeper insight and are driven by the allure of financial rewards for a major conceptual breakthrough.

Stage 3: Expert Retail Systems

Although impressive, space management models cannot do the job alone. They will become one component of a comprehensive expert system for retail management. The reason is that key retail decisions involve adding new lines, deleting existing ones, and managing qualitative dimensions. And different retail environments demand different approaches. Furthermore, quantitative models require experiential knowledge if they are to be applied prudently.

Figure 10.6 provides an overview of some of the files, models, and facilities that might compose a retail expert system. Data files are separated from models to ensure that files can be easily updated and maintained.

Retailing is an area where experience and expertise pay tremendous dividends, but talent is scarce and experience varies widely in the pool of prospective managers. Thus a good system will be distinguished by its knowledge base and inference rules. General retailing knowledge, as well as knowledge specific to a particular chain, outlet type, or location, can be accumulated and used effectively. A good system will be able to conduct dialogues with the manager on such diverse topics as promotions planning, personnel scheduling, competitive tactics, and pricing.

CONCLUSION

This chapter has reviewed single-source reports for packaged goods retailers. To put these reports in context, the chapter contrasted problems faced by retail store

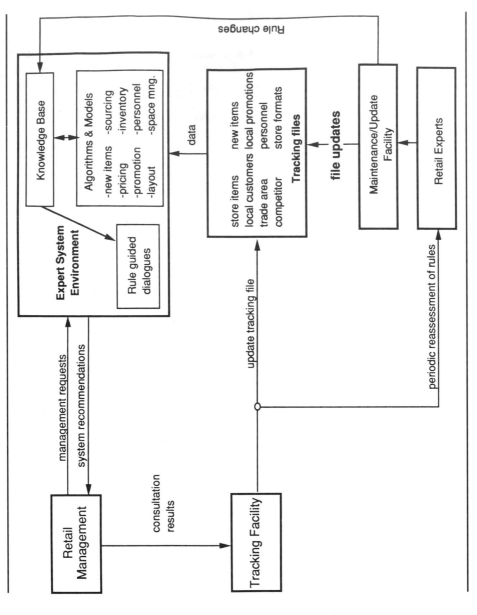

FIGURE 10.6. A Retail Expert System

172

managers with those faced by brand managers. It also discussed problems faced by the typical packaged goods retailer and listed single-source reporting services designed to solve some of these problems. These services include IRI's Apollo system for space management, Nielsen's SCANTRACK reports, IRI's Insights series, and SAMI's TradeMaster for operations review.

The final section described possible developments in retail packaged goods management. These include creative blends of single-source and geodemographic data, deeper modeling of cross-category sales, and management's use of retail expert systems.

This chapter represents only a modest introduction to integrated research systems for retail management. New systems appear frequently, and interested managers should review marketing and trade journals to keep abreast of developments. For example, innovations in micro-merchandising systems that link store data, scanner data, and geodemographic data in a unified package are described in Chapter 17. Packaged goods retail specialists are urged to read that chapter, as well as Chapters 12 through 16, which contain information pertinent for non–packaged goods retailers.

Notes

1. Figures are the latest available at the time of writing.

2. See the appendix to Chapter 6 for further detail regarding the introduction of scanners. See *Retailer Applications of Scanning Data,* published by the Food Marketing Institute (1985), for a summary of supply-side applications (such as inventory control) of in-store scanning data.

3. See A. C. Nielsen, *Nielsen SCANTRACK Reports for Retailers: Description and Usage,* 1989, pp. 1–23.

4. When SAMSCAN was discontinued in October 1990, SAMSCAN data were replaced by InfoScan data.

5. ACORN (44 clusters) is a product of CACI Inc.–Federal. ClusterPLUS (47 clusters), PRIZM (40 clusters), and MicroVision (with two versions, 50 clusters and 95 clusters) are products of R.R. Donnelley Marketing Information Services, Claritas Corporation, and Equifax: National Decision Systems, respectively. For a detailed exposition of geodemography, see Chapters 12 through 16 as well as Michael J. Weiss, *The Clustering of America,* New York: Harper & Row, 1988.

6. Chapter 17 shows how to link scanner data and geodemographic data such as those shown in Figure 10.5 with a store's trade area (household) composition.

7. A trade area elasticity takes the following form: A 1 percent increase in 13- to 17-year-olds means an x percent increase in trade-area potential for a given item, such as Levi 501 jeans. By partitioning a trade area into its geodemographic components, one can calculate refined elasticities of the type: A 1 percent increase in the number of *Blue Bloods Estates* households means an x percent increase in Levi 501 jean sales. Trade-area elasticities are crucial for store location decisions. Less obviously, they permit the efficient distribution of display and other promotion funds among stores in a retail chain because they match customer demographics with item-by-item demand.

8. See "Dahl's Offers Shoppers Vision," *Des Moines Register,* July 15, 1990, sec. G.

9. See Roy Schwedelson, "New Wave Database," *Direct Marketing* (March 1988), pp. 40–41, 58; and *Direct Marketing Newsletter,* 9, (September 1988).

10. A "market" or "shopping basket" model focuses on the array of items in a retail outlet to determine the interconnections—from shoppers' points of view—among these items. For example, how is demand for potato/stuffing side dishes linked to choices for margarine (versus butter), corn oil (versus olive oil), and canned (versus frozen) vegetables? More generally, a shopping basket model examines whether the demand for certain item arrays covaries directly or inversely with demand for other arrays.

11. These developments will take longer than the interlocks among single-source, geodemographic, and local databases. Interlocks are primarily contractual and only secondarily theoretical. In contrast, significant conceptual breakthroughs are necessary to develop the ideas discussed in this section.

12. Lee G. Cooper and Masao Nakanishi, *Market-Share Analysis: Evaluating Competitive Marketing Effectiveness,* Boston: Kluwer Academic, 1988, p. 264.

13. See for example, Alain Bultez and Phillipe Naert, "SH.A.R.P.: SHelf Allocation for Retailer's Profit," *Marketing Science* 7 (Summer 1988), pp. 211–231; and Naert, Bultez, Els Gijsbrechts, and Piet Vanden Abeele "Asymmetric Cannibalism in Retail Assortments," *Journal of Retailing* 65 (Summer 1989), pp. 153–192. These authors review PROGALI, OBM, CIFRINO, SLIM, COSMOS, and HOPE, all proprietary space management products.

14. See Cooper and Nakanishi, op. cit., and Bultez and Naert, op. cit.

11 SINGLE-SOURCE REPORTS FOR ADVERTISING AGENCIES: SCANNER-BASED AND ELECTRONIC RESEARCH SERVICES

At many ad agencies, marketing research remains the adversary to creativity.

Agencies are abdicating the (research) function to their clients, who are abdicating much of it to the big-time research houses. Some end users who practice the art or science don't even call it "research" anymore. Now it is "information" or, better yet, "intelligence."

> Howard Schlossberg,
> "Don't Toll the Bell Yet: Market Research Is
> Merely Evolving, Not Dying"

INTRODUCTION

There are three dominant supply-side forces in packaged goods marketing; manufacturers and retailers—the subjects of Chapters 9 and 10, respectively—and the media, including television, magazines, newspapers, and other vehicles through which advertising agencies deliver commercial messages. Manufacturers, retailers, and the media serve fundamentally different functions. Put simply, manufacturers produce, retailers distribute, and the media sells. Of course, retailers also sell using point-of-purchase promotions to encourage brand switching

175

and impulse buying. However, broadcast and print advertising fulfill strategic goals that cannot be accomplished at the point of purchase. These include providing product information, creating a brand's image, and maintaining brand equity.

The ensuing pages discuss scanner-based and electronic research services designed to support day-to-day media decisions as well as to improve understanding of how marketing communications work in general. The chapter begins with a brief review of the economic forces that gave rise to these new reporting services, concentrating on television, where most ad dollars are spent. Next, the new services are contrasted with traditional television ratings services. Deficiencies in traditional systems and their impact on the development of new systems such as Nielsen's ADPRO and Viewtel from ViewFacts, Inc. are reviewed in detail. The chapter concludes by previewing future developments in media research services.

A REVISED CLASSIFICATION
OF SINGLE-SOURCE SYSTEMS

Single-source systems can be classified into three basic types: promotion systems, television systems, and intermedia systems. InfoScan and SCANTRACK are promotion systems since, aside from sales volume, they concentrate on scanner facts about in-store promotions such as price deals, features, displays, and couponing.[1] As Chapter 6 details, promotion systems were developed in the mid-1980s and were designed first to support brand management and later to support retail management.

In the 1990s, single-source data suppliers are adding reports especially designed to meet the needs of advertising agencies. These reports come from the two new approaches: television systems and intermedia systems. Nielsen's ADPRO is currently the only working example of an integrated television advertising system. Likewise, Viewtel is unique as an intermedia system. These two systems represent the industry's response to competitive, technological, and environmental forces. These forces are reviewed next in order to provide a clearer understanding of emerging decision support needs.

Competitive Forces

The 1970s and 1980s were marked by new product innovations spurred by rapidly growing consumer markets. Today, growth has stagnated, provoking a climate of me-too-ism in which product imitations far outnumber true innovations.[2] To combat product plagiarism, companies now try to roll out their new products in roughly half the time that they used to take.[3] Increased time pressures require foreshortened planning horizons that place tremendous stress on managers and their research support staffs. For example, Don Packard, director of research at Frankel & Co., a Chicago-based marketing services firm, says, "Today, people want your marketing research plan at the end of the meeting."[4]

Intense competitive pressures require more efficient management structures and fewer layers of management personnel.[5] The personnel that remain must be close to the data summarizing marketplace activities. Although products can be copied, efficient internal organizations and technically sophisticated managers cannot be cloned; nor can accurate, prompt research results, often the trump card in the high-stakes game of category dominance. Sound research permits a firm to win against both domestic and foreign competitors, even those who are sophisticated users of the "new television," the second major change agent.

The New Television

As little as 15 years ago, novel media research services seemed unnecessary given the stable television environment. Three major networks, whose programming was similar and predictable, monopolized the airwaves. But during the 1980s, changes in the number of TV stations, programming techniques, and daypart use traumatized the industry. Cable TV emerged in full force;[6] satellite TV reached the remotest points on the planet; and sports, news, weather, comedy, and music television filled unused time slots and reached precisely targeted niches. In other words, previously sporadic coverage of geographic space, temporal space, and topic space changed to virtually saturated coverage of each of these dimensions.

Effective use of the new television requires adequate understanding of its impact. As argued shortly, traditional ratings services were unable to assess this impact, whereas the new services based on single-source data can.

Advertising Effectiveness

A third development in the late 1980s—research using scanner data—called into question the impact of television advertising and its cost-effectiveness relative to sales promotion. These studies revealed the large, immediate impact of store promotions on sales volume and concluded "that advertising is not the strongest determinant of purchase behavior. The other marketing variables, especially price, are also (along with brand loyalty) *more* effective than advertising."[7] Members of the television advertising community were understandably dismayed when this conclusion was published. It strongly suggests that television advertising is wasteful and that its effects on sales are minimal.

Subsequent research calmed some of these fears, and reflection about the functions of advertising versus those of sales promotion forced managers to reevaluate the role of each tool. For example, despite the dramatic sales spikes induced by in-store promotions, IRI reported in 1989 that "payout statistics on promotions are dismal. Roughly 16% of trade promotions are profitable. Furthermore, promotions' effects are often purely short-term except for new products."[8]

Why the dismal results? Promotions often cannibalize an item's own future sales, both at retail, and at the trade level. At retail for example, consumers may switch to a promoted brand to gain the price discount but not repeat-buy the item at its regular price. At the trade level, retailers typically forward-buy during a manufacturer's promotion; they stock up at the reduced price and sell this stock after the promotion period ends. Furthermore, retailers may pass only a fraction of the deal through to consumers. For example, in 54 percent of the cases studied by Curhan and Kopp (1986), no savings were passed through at all.[9]

In contrast to promotion's sharp response blip, advertising effects on sales volume may not be felt for several weeks, and then are likely to be distributed over several time periods. Effects may last for as long as two years, even for packaged goods with short repurchase cycles. Further complicating matters is the fact that promotion and advertising interact to affect brand loyalty and price sensitivity. Because of this interaction, retailers are more likely to pass promotions through for brands with strong images.

The point is that retailer behavior during promotions is tied directly to a brand's equity built through advertising. This means that researchers are comparing apples and oranges when they compare promotion sales spikes to the much more subtle effects of television advertising. More often than not, the effectiveness and profitability of a promotion depend on cumulative advertising effects. As Simon Broadbent of Leo Burnett argues, "Without supporting marketing activity, base sales of a brand will often decline. Brand values are not permanent. . . . This base may be maintained or improved by both advertising and by deal promotion activity"[10]

These interactions are clearly difficult to unravel even with the best statistical techniques. IRI concluded that, at the very least, the death of advertising as a strategic tool had been greatly exaggerated:

> The current trend towards promotion spending is not sound from a marketing productivity standpoint. When the strategic disadvantages of promotions are included, that is, losing control to the trade and training consumers to buy only on deal, then the case is compelling for a reevaluation of current practices and the incentive systems responsible for this trend.[11]

Summary: The Emergence of New Report Types

These forces are both perplexing and disquieting to the practicing advertising manager who wants no-nonsense answers to pressing problems. But straight answers about the relative effectiveness of advertising versus sales promotion are hard to come by. Careful studies often reach opposite conclusions. For example, Tellis (1988) suggested that advertising does not induce new triers: "In other words, advertising has a small effect in winning new buyers but a relatively stronger effect in reinforcing intensity of preference."[12] Givon and Horsky (1990), on the other hand, concluded that it does: "The implications of our finding . . . [are that] advertising induces trial and after that the consumption experience takes over. Advertising which up to now was considered to have lagged effects may in fact in many product categories be similar to price deals in only having short-run trial inducing effects."[13]

This confusion represents an opportunity for single-source suppliers to offer new databases and new report types that address the pressing concerns of practicing managers. The next section reviews traditional ratings services to provide a point of contrast with the new single-source media reports, which will be discussed subsequently.

TRADITIONAL SYSTEMS

Traditional television ratings services—for example, those offered by A. C. Nielsen, and Arbitron—provide extensive breakdowns of the U.S. television viewing audience. Program ratings and shares are tabulated by TV market, by daypart, by demographic segment, and by station. These ratings are the basis for cost schedules and media buying plans.[14]

Traditional ratings services index program popularity. They are not designed to be full-line strategic marketing tools, a limitation that has become increasingly obvious given the competitive pressures outlined earlier. For example, traditional services do not link a specific television household to that household's purchase behavior; nor do they provide any expanded information about a program's content, the nature of competing ads running on the same show, or ads running for the same brand on different shows.

Data sources for media are likewise oriented toward media buying, not strategic planning. In other words, these services deal with advertising delivery, not consumer response. Focusing solely on delivery results in an overemphasis on (often meaningless) demographic splits; for example, a given medium may be directed at 18- to 26-year-olds when in fact age has little bearing on consumer purchase behavior. Further, traditional media data are derived from disparate sources, each of which is intended to do the best job of measuring just one medium. Therefore, when doing intermedia comparisons, one finds a lack of comparability on a number of dimensions, including samples, measurement goals, and target group definitions. Finally, traditional services fail to provide measures of the actual effects of the advertising. Hence the data needed for making intermedia trade-offs are missing.[15]

SINGLE-SOURCE SYSTEMS

As the foregoing overview suggests, traditional services leave many important questions unanswered: How does this time slot interact with program content and audience characteristics to influence sales? Is this the right creative approach for this program's audience? Which combination of daypart and program type maximizes sales impact in the over-50 audience in Los Angeles?

Single-source systems are able to respond to these and many similar questions. This section reviews two of these systems: ADPRO, from A. C. Nielsen, and Viewtel, from ViewFacts, Inc. ADPRO is a packaged goods television system, and Viewtel is an intermedia system that includes non-packaged goods as well as services. Each system's distinct advantages and disadvantages are highlighted in the discussion.

Nielsen's ADPRO

The design schema for the Ad Tracker database that supports ADPRO is shown in Figure 11.1. A schema shows the tables, data fields, and linking fields in a relational database. A review of a system's schema draws attention to the system's "fact bank" and the logical organization of these facts.

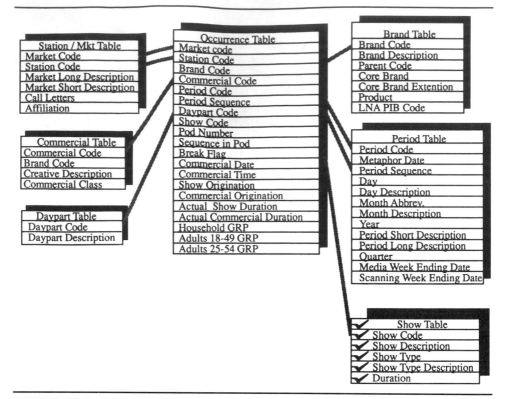

FIGURE 11.1   The Ad Tracker Schema
Source: A. C. Nielsen.

Ad Tracker is an occurrence database (see the middle table in Figure 11.1). This means that every time a spot runs on any channel, for any product, in any market, the details of that spot are recorded.[16] For example, if the same spot— "girl with violin" advertising a headache remedy—runs four times in a single day in a given metro-market, all four occurrences are recorded. One can elaborate on a given occurrence by moving to a different point in the schema to expand on the spot's theme (commercial table), on market demographics (occurrence table), on product characteristics (brand table), on show characteristics (show table), and on audience characteristics (occurrence table).

Each show's audience—and, by aggregation, a brand's audience—is identified so that viewing behavior and purchase behavior can be linked. Further, using the principles of geodemography described in Chapters 12 through 16, the system can target audiences far more precisely than is possible with traditional demographics.

Several aspects of the Ad Tracker database warrant further discussion. First, notice the detail available in the brand table. This table contains information about not only the item in question, but also about its parent brand and core brand. For example, the field labeled "brand code" is filled by a particular brand name such as Sanka. The parent code for this brand is the Maxwell House Coffee Division of General Foods. Sanka is also Maxwell House's core brand in the instant coffee category. One of its extensions is Brim.[17]

As the brand table illustrates, ADPRO uses a "product line" design that fully supports category management, not just brand management. Traditional ratings systems do not permit users to generate reports that capture the effects of product line marketing or the effects of coordinated campaigns.

Traditional systems also rarely store information about ad content and, as a result, cannot address important questions regarding qualitative dimensions of advertising's effectiveness. As Tellis remarked when discussing the limitations of his study, "the content of the advertising is not considered. Including such information would revolutionize our testing of advertising effects and is probably the most promising research direction."[18]

To address this void, ADPRO's commercial table describes each ad's creative content, including its primary message and mode of conveying that message—information that can be used to test hypotheses about the causal effects of ad content on brand awareness, attitude change, and purchase behavior. For example, creative content may interact positively or negatively with program content and style. Therefore ADPRO stores information about each show on which an ad airs, as shown in the show table. This information can be used to determine whether a specific creative approach, such as Claymation, is more effective in the context of a news program or in other programming formats, such as MTV.

The next section reviews three specific reports available from ADPRO in order to illustrate system output. Remember that ADPRO is a commercial system designed to produce easy-to-use reports for practicing managers. The reports illustrated here reflect this commercial intent, not the research goals of the academic community.

Report Examples

Show type summary

Advertising managers need to be aware of the types of programs on which their products' ads air. However, a traditional ratings system does not provide this information. Generating the answer by reviewing corporate records is tedious, inefficient, and inaccurate. The problem is even more complex if the information must be reported only for specific markets, which is typically the case with today's emphasis on regional marketing management.

Table 11.1 shows a sample show type summary for a one-week period aggregated across all Procter & Gamble ads airing in the Los Angeles market. In all, 986 commercials were aired, lasting a total of 27,900 seconds (or 7.75 hours). Most of these commercials were aired during situation comedies (21.3 percent), daytime dramas (14.9 percent), and during feature films (12.5 percent). An advertising manager who needs additional information about the specific programs—such as their air time, other brands advertised, or creative themes used—can have these reports on desk or on screen in a matter of seconds.

TABLE 11.1. Show Type Summary: Week Ending Jan. 01, 1989, through Week Ending Mar. 26, 1989

Parent: Procter & Gamble Co.
DMA: Los Angeles

Show Type	Number of Commercials	Total Duration	Duration Share
Adventure	43	1,275	4.6
Audience participation	19	405	1.5
Award ceremonies, pageants	3	90	0.3
Child–day–animation	3	90	0.3
Comedy variety	3	90	0.3
Conversations, colloquies	64	1,860	6.7
Daytime drama	160	4,155	14.9
Documentary, general	2	60	0.2
Documentary, news	2	60	0.2
Feature film	119	3,480	12.5
General drama	25	690	2.5
General variety	23	660	2.4
Instructions, advice	9	210	0.8
News	65	1,950	7.0
Official police	4	105	0.4
Participation variety	7	180	0.6
Popular music–contemporary	5	150	0.5
Private detective	26	780	2.8
Quiz-giveaway	90	2,595	9.3
Quiz-panel	11	240	0.9
Science fiction	40	1,020	3.7
Situation comedy	203	5,955	21.3
Sports anthology	18	540	1.9
Sports commentary	1	30	0.1
Sports event	27	810	2.9
Suspense, mystery	5	150	0.5
Unclassified	9	270	1.0
Total	986	27,900	100.0

Source: Nielsen Media Research.

Brand share-of-voice analysis

A manager who oversees the marketing of a cold remedy, for example, may want to know the potential impact of selected ads reaching various market segments. Gross ratings points (GRP) and share of voice (SOV) summarize this potential for a four-week period, as shown in Table 11.2.[19] The report indicates that in Los Angeles, among adults 50 years and older watching weekday-afternoon television, Alka-Seltzer-Plus ads aired on programs averaging 28 GRP and a 20 SOV. These averages exceed those for competitive products in this market. Further analyses of sales response among this segment combined with the cost of generating these sales would provide critical insights for future campaign decisions.[20]

TABLE 11.2. Brand Share-of-Voice Analysis

DMA: Los Angeles
Demo: Adults 50+
Daypart: M–F Afternoon
Report Period: March 1989

	Week Ending									
	Mar. 4, 1989		Mar. 11, 1989		Mar. 18, 1989		Mar. 25, 1989		Total	
	GRP	SOV	GRP	SOV	GRP	SOV	GRP	SOV	GRP	SOV
Alka-Seltzer Plus cold remedies	17.3	12.0	19.5	12.4	33.2	20.1	42.2	44.8	112.2	20.0
Comtrex cold remedies multisymptom	0.0	0.0	24.1	15.4	20.9	12.7	0.0	0.0	45.0	8.0
Contac cold remedies max-str/12-hr/caps	20.2	14.0	27.4	17.5	7.2	4.4	0.0	0.0	54.8	9.8
Cotylenol cold remedies children's/chwble/tabs	31.3	21.7	9.7	6.2	8.3	5.0	7.4	7.9	56.8	10.1
Pedia Care cold remedies syrup	17.6	12.2	4.5	2.9	8.1	4.9	2.8	3.0	33.0	5.9
Thera Flu cold remedies powder	0.0	0.0	24.9	15.9	16.6	10.0	0.0	0.0	41.5	7.4
Triaminic cold remedies syrup	0.0	0.0	18.9	12.1	39.9	24.1	3.4	3.6	62.2	11.1
Triaminic Nite Light cold remedies syrup	28.2	19.5	2.9	1.8	10.8	6.5	5.7	6.1	47.5	8.5
Tylenol Cold cold remedies multisymptom/caps	12.3	8.5	7.3	4.7	11.2	6.8	7.4	7.9	38.2	6.8
Tylenol cold remedies children's/chwble/tabs	7.4	5.1	16.1	10.3	1.9	1.1	3.3	3.6	28.7	5.1
Vicks Nyquil cold remedies	6.8	4.7	1.3	0.8	3.4	2.0	4.4	4.7	15.9	2.8
Vicks Nyquil cold remedies cherry	3.1	2.1	0.0	0.0	3.8	2.3	10.4	11.1	17.3	3.1
Vicks Nyquil cold remedies children's/cherry	0.0	0.0	0.0	0.0	0.0	0.0	6.9	7.4	6.9	1.2

Source: Nielsen Media Research

Creative description review

As a final example of an ADPRO report, Table 11.3 summarizes the creative contents of Procter and Gamble cold remedy ads airing in Los Angeles on shows whose primary audience consists of adults 18 to 49. Of the seven themes used, the three dominant ones are (a) "a couple sneezing in bed," (b) "a man sitting by a grandfather clock", and (c) "a woman sneezing while her husband sleeps comfortably."

The report reveals that although the first theme (a) aired in more local commercials than theme (c), its show garnered gross ratings points only marginally better. This fact may suggest a need to revise the program schedule assuming cost constraints are not violated.

The creative review raises another issue: whether or not theme (b), "man sits by grandfather clock", is effective. This commercial is the most used, as its 30.5 (overall) share of voice indicates. Does the ad generate profitable sales among this audience? If not, perhaps the theme is inappropriate. If so, perhaps this theme should replace those that are less effective.

A report such as the one shown in Table 11.3 can help an advertising executive match themes to precisely targeted geodemographic markets; can assist in the evaluation of themes offered by different advertising agencies; and, if used imaginatively, can trim wasted advertising dollars from the firm's strategic plan.

Limitations of and Future Research with ADPRO

ADPRO currently produces only market status reports that summarize what happened rather than predicting what will happen. On the plus side, these summaries are much more detailed than those available from traditional systems. Additional experience with ADPRO should enable designers to produce more sophisticated reports based on market response models. ADPRO's database, especially if linked with an intermedia system, can also support a variety of academic studies that may lead to a reasonably complete theory of advertising's effects on consumer behavior.

INTERMEDIA SYSTEMS

Single-source systems were earlier classified into three types: promotion systems, television systems, and intermedia systems. InfoScan and SCANTRACK are promotion systems, and ADPRO is a television advertising system. This section illustrates a system of the third type: Viewtel, from ViewFacts, Inc.

Both ADPRO and Viewtel are responses to certain deficiencies encountered with the older promotion systems. Three key problems can be identified.[21] First, a firm's marketing communications are delivered through a variety of vehicles, of which in-store promotions are only a part. Depending on the brand,

TABLE 11.3.   Creative Description Review:
Week Ending Jan 01, 1989
through Week Ending Mar 26, 1989

Parent: Procter & Gamble Co.
DMA: Los Angeles
Demo: Adults 18–49

	Local			
	Number of Commercials	GRP	Total Duration	SOV
Couple sneezing in bed	201	896.4	6,030	27.4
Little boy cannot sleep	9	55.0	135	1.7
Little boy cannot sleep/wakes mom	1	5.4	30	0.2
Man sits by grandfather clock	254	1,138.7	7,620	34.8
The cold you worry most about	23	159.3	690	4.9
Woman refusing to take medicine	24	159.0	360	4.9
Woman sneezing/man sleeping	189	857.2	5,670	26.2
Total Procter & Gamble Co.	701	3,271.1	20,535	100.0

	Network			
	Number of Commercials	GRP	Total Duration	SOV
Couple sneezing in bed	32	250.0	960	16.3
Little boy cannot sleep	59	190.8	885	12.4
Little boy cannot sleep/wakes mom	NA	NA	NA	NA
Man sits by grandfather clock	40	327.7	1,200	21.3
The cold you worry most about	111	351.6	3,330	22.9
Woman refusing to take medicine	20	235.0	300	15.3
Woman sneezing/man sleeping	23	181.4	690	11.8
Total Procter & Gamble Co.	285	1,536.5	7,365	100.0

	Total			
	Number of Commercials	GRP	Total Duration	SOV
Couple sneezing in bed	233	1,146.5	6,990	23.8
Little boy cannot sleep	68	245.9	1,020	5.1
Little boy cannot sleep/wakes mom	1	5.4	30	0.1
Man sits by grandfather clock	294	1,466.3	8,820	30.5
The cold you worry most about	134	510.9	4,020	10.6
Woman refusing to take medicine	44	394.1	660	8.2
Woman sneezing/man sleeping	212	1,038.6	6,360	21.6
Total Procter & Gamble Co.	986	4,807	27,900	100.0

Source: Nielsen Media Services

other media such as magazines, outdoor advertising, and radio may play a major role, as Table 11.4 illustrates. Second, delivered communications affect more than just sales. Although increased sales may be the ultimate goal, marketing communications also generate awareness, change attitudes, engender preferences, and stimulate repurchases. Promotion systems measure only sales. ADPRO supplements sales measures by monitoring the amount of message delivered that is, share of voice and gross rating points. However, neither approach explicitly measures awareness or any of the other intervening variables just mentioned. Finally, neither promotion systems nor television systems try to decompose consumers' overall response to a commercial into responses to the creative elements that make up that commercial.

In summary, single-source systems designed to measure the impact of marketing communications have different objectives than single-source systems designed to measure the impact of promotion or television advertising. An alternative system would measure consumer exposure to all media, consumer media use, and consumer attitudes. A comprehensive system would also include services and non-UPC goods in its domain of inquiry as well as packaged goods. Viewtel accomplishes many of these objectives.

The Viewtel System

Viewtel is an electronic consumer panel in which surveys are downloaded and results are uploaded through a household's telephone. Surveys are displayed on a household's television set, and a respondent keys in responses using a wireless remote hand unit. All panelists report regularly on their television viewing, radio listening, and newspaper and magazine readership for a selected group of products and services. Subsets of the panel also respond to custom surveys targeted at individuals who exhibit specific product, purchase, or media behaviors.

Viewtel was pilot-tested in 1989–1990 using 1,000 Chicago area households. About 35 percent of the households that were asked accepted the Viewtel installation. Among installed households, survey response rates exceeded 85 percent. Expansion of the electronic panel concept is pending the outcome of a joint-venture negotiation with a leading marketing research firm.[22]

Case Study

To clarify Viewtel applications, the following discussion reviews a case study designed to solve a brand-positioning problem for Colgate toothpaste. The analysis consists of the following phases: First, Viewtel panel data are analyzed to assess brand loyalty and brand switching among Colgate and Crest buyers. (Crest and Colgate occupy rival positions in the Chicago market.) The analysis suggests targeting brand switchers with a focused message about Colgate quality. Next, broad media types—television, magazines, and newspapers—are then selected for their ability to deliver messages to the target segment. Finally, specific vehicles within each media class are selected.

TABLE 11.4 Intermedia Trade-offs for Selected Brands

Category	Advertisers/ Brands	Parent	Mag	Smag	News	Out	Net TV	Spot TV	Syn TV	Catv	Net Rad	Spot Rad	1989 Totals (000)
Beer	Budweiser	Anheuser-Busch	2.9	—	4.8	1.4	40.0	27.5	2.3	7.0	4.6	10.6	113,133.6
	Michelob Dry	Anheuser-Busch	1.3	—	—	0.9	41.4	4.7	4.4	4.1	1.0	0.7	57,663.5
	Busch	Anheuser-Busch	—	—	—	0.2	17.3	7.3	—	2.4	—	19.9	29,632.5
Soft Drinks	Coca-Cola Classic	Coca-Cola Co.	0.3	—	2.1	0.2	35.1	23.3	7.5	1.6	0.2	3.6	74,006.6
	Pepsi-Cola	Pepsico Inc.	0.6	—	1.2	1.1	20.4	33.6	1.1	1.1	—	6.6	66,097.8
	7UP	Dr. Pepper/ Seven Up Co.	—	—	—	—	17.8	0.8	4.6	4.6	1.4	—	26,085.4
Pain Relievers	Advil	American Home Products Corp.	4.0	0.1	0.1	—	33.9	1.7	1.4	1.8	—	—	43,068.6
	Tylenol	Johnson & Johnson	—	—	—	—	28.2	1.1	4.5	1.3	—	—	35,415.1
	Nuprin	Bristol-Myers Squibb Co.	0.6	—	—	—	19.9	2.1	3.8	1.8	—	—	28,109.9
Cereals	Frosted Flakes	Kellogg Co.	—	—	—	—	20.5	6.0	—	0.5	—	—	30,669.1
	Cheerios	General Mills Inc.	4.2	—	—	—	9.1	15.2	0.4	1.6	—	—	30,459.2
	Total	General Mills Inc.	0.2	—	—	—	14.7	5.5	0.5	0.8	1.8	—	23,518.0
Cigarettes	Marlboro Filter	Philip Morris	2.4	—	—	26.6	—	—	—	—	—	—	28,953.4
	Newport Menthol	Lorillard Inc.	—	—	0.3	27.4	—	—	—	—	—	—	27,667.4
	Alpine Menthol	Philip Morris	15.2	1.9	1.1	9.0	—	—	—	—	—	—	27,263.0

Key:
Mag: Magazines
Smag: Sunday magazines
News: Newspapers
Out: Outdoor
Net TV: Network TV
Spot TV: Spot TV
Syn TV: Syndicated TV
Catv: Cable TV
Net rad: Network radio
Spot rad: Spot radio

Source: "The Top 200 Brands," *Marketing and Media Decisions* (July 1990), pp. 36–38.

Situation analysis

Although Crest and Colgate are the top two sellers, Crest's market share in the Chicago market is nearly double that of Colgate. Preliminary analyses revealed that Crest's volume comes from one-time buyers (16 percent), loyal users (38 percent), and brand switchers (46 percent) whereas Colgate's volume is heavily dependent on switchers (68 percent), with loyals accounting for 21 percent and one-time buyers the remaining 11 percent.[23] Colgate's heavy dependence on switchers raises the cost of maintaining the brand's market share, as brand switching is typically deal-induced. In Chicago, Colgate's problem is compounded since Colgate switchers are more likely to buy on deal than are Crest switchers (43 percent to 28 percent, respectively). (see Figure 11.2.)

The key question generated by the situation analysis is why does Colgate have more switchers than Crest and why are they more likely to buy on deal? The answer revealed by Viewtel data is that although almost all Crest switchers (93 percent) agree that Crest is a quality product, only 84 percent of Colgate switchers feel similarly about Colgate. Thus people are switching to Colgate to take advantage of a deal, not because they feel that product benefits justify the switch. Even more telling is the result that Colgate switchers are more likely to agree that Crest rather than Colgate is a quality product.[24]

Communications objectives

The results of the analysis suggest the following objectives for Colgate's marketing communications. First, messages should improve consumers' perception of Colgate quality. The messages' primary target group is people switching to Colgate. Second, the attitudes of the target group should be tracked, and changes should be related to the level of message delivery.

Broad media strategy

The next step involved a comparison of the respective potential of magazines, television, and newspapers to reach Colgate switchers. Analyses reveal that heavy magazine readers account for 42 percent of Colgate switcher volume compared to just 25 percent for heavy television users. Although magazines are clearly the first medium of choice, they leave 31 percent of switcher volume unreached. To address this problem, light, medium, and heavy magazine users were cross-tabulated with both television and newspaper users to see if either medium might complement magazines.

Results show that to reach Colgate switchers, television is not a good complement to magazines. However, among Colgate switchers, nearly half of the light magazine users are also heavy newspaper readers; that is, for this target group, magazines and newspapers are complementary. Further, heavy magazine readers agree most with each of the following statements: "Colgate is not a quality product," "Colgate is less satisfactory than Crest," and that "I buy Colgate only on deal." Thus magazines complemented by newspapers deliver Colgate's message directly to those individuals who need it most.

Selecting specific vehicles

The next step is to select specific communication vehicles. This analysis can be carried out for individual titles, but here the discussion is limited to broad types.

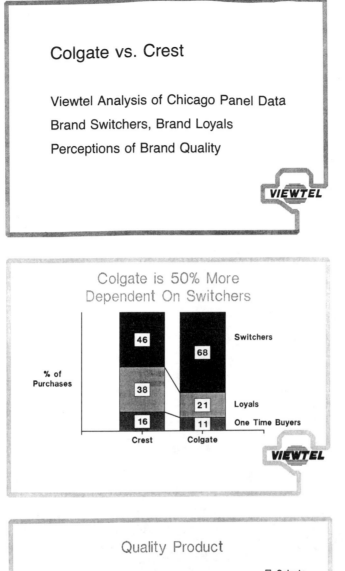

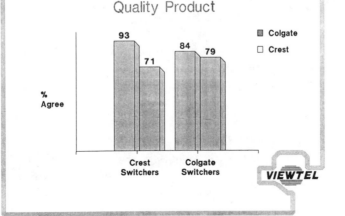

FIGURE 11.2 Steps in a Situation Analysis
Source: Viewfacts Inc.

(*Continued*)

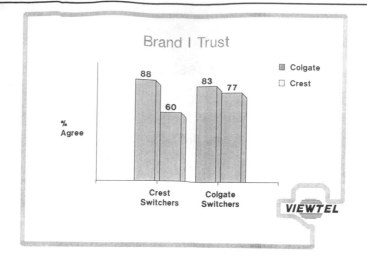

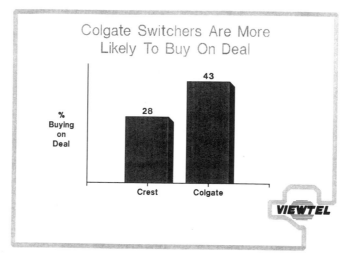

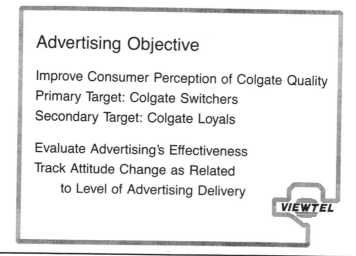

FIGURE 11.2   (*Continued*)

190

In particular, delivery indices were calculated for various types of magazines, newspapers, and television shows. The best choices are business magazines and national weekday newspapers.

Tracking the campaign's impact

The final step in this solution is to track the effects of the communications program. This step is particularly difficult to implement with traditional survey research methods, but it can be routinely implemented with Viewtel. Colgate switchers, already identified in the Viewtel panel, receive periodic follow-up surveys regarding their evaluation of Colgate quality. Scores on the resulting index are regressed against the number of exposures—from all media—that a panelist has to the new campaign; these data are collected directly by the Viewtel system. Using these techniques, Viewtel tracks attitude changes over time as a function of exposure among the targeted group. Tracking tells the manager whether or not the advertising works and what exposure levels are required to trigger the necessary attitudinal response.

Limitations of Viewtel

Viewtel offers several advantages over promotion and television systems. The most notable advantage is its ability to clarify the role of intervening variables as they contribute to advertising's bottom line effects. Thus Viewtel addresses an important problem in communications management. Of course, the system is not without limitations; some of these may be corrected in future generations, and others are more or less inherent to the approach.

For example, the validity of Viewtel conclusions depends on the panel design. The panel must be large enough to minimize problems of statistical inference; panel approaches are often handicapped by small sample sizes, especially when they focus on particular target groups such as Colgate switchers. In other words, the panel must be large enough that subsample sizes remain sufficiently representative.

Viewtel methods are also relatively obtrusive. Obtrusiveness may be unavoidable in systems designed to illuminate the effects of awareness, preference, and other cognitive states leading up to the purchase decision; such systems require frequent data collection using a question/response format. Of course, obtrusive measures invariably suffer from problems of cooperation. In the present case, cooperation problems are coupled with a "choice of respondent" problem: Which family member responds to a given survey, the one who is most cooperative or the "right one"? Clearly, different household members are exposed to different media, and each family member influences the household's purchase decisions differently.

To extract the most from survey information, individual surveys must also be carefully designed. For example, using a within-subjects design—that is, periodic questioning of the same people—to track the effects of an ad campaign could lead to biased results as respondents become sensitized to a survey's purpose and less cooperative under repeated questioning.

Finally, it would seem that the most productive use of Viewtel is in conjunction with volumetric data for each panelist; some link with either SCANTRACK or InfoScan is needed to model advertising's effects on sales, not just its effects on intervening variables.[25]

Despite these criticisms, Viewtel offers important decision support for advertising managers. Its hard benefits include fast turnaround, deep understandability of why an ad works or does not work, and precise estimates of consumer response to advertising exposures.

CONCLUSION

This chapter has discussed scanner and electronic-based reports produced by modern media systems. Media systems are classified into three types: (1) promotion systems, such as InfoScan and SCANTRACK; (2) television systems, such as Ad Tracker, and (3) intermedia systems, such as Viewtel.

Two sets of forces conspired during the 1980s to undermine confidence in traditional media systems. First, technological breakthroughs enabled widespread use of cable television, satellite television, database marketing, and other forms of high-tech micro-marketing. Thus today's media environment is highly fragmented. Second, empirical studies in the late 1980s sparked widespread acceptance of retail promotions as the prime generator of profitable sales. Although the validity of this approach is suspect, today's marketing managers are heavy users of promotion, encouraged in part by the precise targeting capabilities of the new systems.

Unlike traditional systems, which are driven by media buying (supply-side) needs, newer systems monitor demand-side forces. In particular, Ad Tracker brings together in one comprehensive database audience characteristics, show characteristics, and show environments to determine how these factors interact to influence retail sales. Intermedia systems such as Viewtel attempt a similar linkage of print and electronic media.

Of the three areas—manufacturer, retailer, and media—the media has been least affected by the single-source concept. Thus in the years to come, important changes in the systems discussed in this chapter, as well as the emergence of newer systems, can be expected.

Notes

1. Neither IRI nor A. C. Nielsen integrates print, outdoor, or radio advertising into its databases. As discussed later in the chapter, Nielsen integrates television advertising into SCANTRACK via its ADPRO service.

2. See James C. Schroer, "Ad Spending: Growing Market Share," *Harvard Business Review* 68(1) (January–February 1990), pp. 44–48.

3. This is according to George Day, former director of the Marketing Science Institute. (Quoted in Howard Schlossberger, "Don't Toll the Bell Yet: Market Research Is Merely Evolving, Not Dying" *Marketing News* 24(1) (January 8, 1990), pp. 1–2,13).

4. Ibid.

5. See Arthur Shapiro, "Downsizing and Its Effect on Corporate Marketing Research," *Marketing Research* 2(4) (December 1990), pp. 56–59.

6. The Cable Television Advertising Bureau reports that in 1990 cable penetration reached 59 percent of U.S. households and projects it to reach 65 percent by 1994. Basic cable's share of both total day (42 percent) and prime time (37 percent) exceeds that of any of the three networks (20 percent maximum). In 1990 the percentage of the public tuning in to cable increased by 12 percent over 1989, while viewing decreased 2–9 percent among the networks.

7. This quote is from the study that arguably received the most attention: Gerard J. Tellis, "Advertising Exposure, Loyalty, and Brand Purchase: A Two-Stage Model of Choice," *Journal of Marketing Research* 25 (May 1988), pp. 134–144.

8. See Magid Abraham and Leonard Lodish, "Advertising Works," Information Resources, Inc., 1989, pp. 1–10; and Magid Abraham, "Fact-Based Designs to Improve Advertising and Promotion Productivity," paper presented to the Advertising and Promotion Workshop, New York Hilton (February 22–23, 1990).

9. For more detail see, Robert C. Blattberg and Scott A. Neslin, *Sales Promotion: Concept, Methods and Strategies*, Englewood Cliffs, NJ: Prentice-Hall, 1990, especially Chapters 11 and 12.

10. See Simon Broadbent "Modeling Beyond the Blip," *Journal of the Market Research Society* 32(1) (January 1990), pp. 61–102.

11. Abraham and Lodish, op. cit. IRI's study was based on over 360 BehaviorScan tests (1984–88) where the effect of an increase in media weight on sales was tested. These tests were analyzed to discern the impact of advertising on sales and to separate it from effects due to other marketing variables or due to chance.

12. Tellis, op. cit.

13. See Moshe Givon and Dan Horsky, "Untangling the Effects of Purchase Reinforcement and Advertising Carryover," *Marketing Science* 9 (Spring 1990), pp. 171–187.

14. See Kent Lancaster and Helen Katz, *Strategic Media Planning*, Chicago: National Textbook, 1988.

15. For further discussion of these points, see Jim Spaeth and Mike Hess, "Single-Source Data: The Missing Pieces," 1989 and Mike Hess and Jim Spaeth, "Toward Intermedia Measurement: An Early Look at the Potential of the VIEWTEL Database," 1989, both working papers prepared for the Advertising Research Foundation.

16. Ad Tracker is currently monitoring television advertising in 23 metromarkets. Nielsen has completely automated information capture from a spot. The company uses a pattern recognition device that decodes a commercial, frame by frame, in order to identify it. Human intervention is not required.

17. See the appendix to this chapter for definitions and examples regarding the Ad Tracker schema.

18. Tellis, op. cit., p. 193.

19. GRP is the product of the reach of a medium and the mean audience exposure to the medium. A brand's share of voice is its share of the total value of the main media exposure in the product category.

194 Single-Source Systems

20. For further perspectives on the influence of SOV and GRP on market share, see James C. Schroer, "Ad Spending: Growing Market Share," *Harvard Business Review* (January–February 1990), pp. 44–49. For example, Schroer concludes that ad spending can increase a brand's market share, but a firm must spend at least double the amount spent by its major rival and continue this spending level for at least three years.

21. Hess and Spaeth, op. cit.; and Spaeth and Hess, op cit.

22. Viewtel also operates a split-cable advertising testing service called Scan Canada. The service is similiar to BehaviorScan and operates from a medium-sized Canadian town located in the Vancouver area.

23. A Colgate switcher is defined as someone buying Colgate this purchase occasion who bought another brand on the last purchase occasion.

24. Seventy-one percent of Crest switchers agree that Colgate is a quality product, whereas 79 percent of Colgate switchers agree that Crest is a quality product. Reinforcing these findings are those indicating that 60 percent of Crest switchers "trust" Crest.

25. For a discussion of why systems such as Viewtel should be linked to volumetric data, see Verne B. Churchill, "The Role of Ad Hoc Research in a Single-Source World," and Gale D. Metzger, "Single-Source: Yes and No (The Backward View)," both in *Marketing Research* (4) (December 1990), pp. 22–26 and 27–33, respectively.

APPENDIX 11A
CODES IN THE AD TRACKER SCHEMA

Occurrence Table

Ad Tracker is an "occurrence database." This means that every time a spot runs on any channel, for any product, in any market, the details of that spot are recorded. For example, if the same spot—"girl with violin" advertising a headache remedy—runs four times in a single day in a given market, all four occurrences are recorded. One can elaborate on a given occurrence by moving to a different point in the schema to expand upon the theme, the market, the product, and the audience watching.

The GRPs for a particular spot are recorded in the occurrence table, where spot = (market + time + show + channel).

Brand Table

Brand code:	A brand name, such as Sanka
Brand description:	An identification code that combines brand + core + parent
Parent code:	Maxwell House Coffee Division
Parent description:	Long version of parent code
Core brand:	Sanka (same as the brand in this case)
Core brand extension:	Brim
Product:	Ground coffee, instant coffee, decaffeinated coffee, etc.
LNA PIB code:	An internal code used by Nielsen for ordering data tapes, designed to summarize all of the preceding information

Dayparts

Daypart code:	An alphanumeric code for dayparts
Daypart description:	M–F early morning
	early fringe
	late morning
	prime time
	late night
	⋮
	Sat. morning
	⋮
	Sun. morning

Station/Market Table

Market code:	23 Nielsen designated market areas, or DMAs (similar to Arbitron's ADIs, or "areas of dominant influence," both of which refer to geographic areas that fall under the broadcast umbrella or signal reach of a particular television station; neither DMAs nor ADIs are in a 1-to-1 correspondence with Nielsen scanner markets)
Market long and short descriptions:	Descriptions that provide more or less detail on a market
Station code:	Station identification code
Call letters:	Station call letters (e.g., WKRP in Cincinnati)
Affiliation:	ABC, NBC, CBS, TNT, Fox, etc.

Commercial Table

Commercial code:	A code that identifies each spot (name, creative content, etc.)
Creative description:	Cold remedies: • Couple sneezing in bed • Little boy can't sleep • Man sits by grandfather clock • The cold you worry most about • Woman refuses to take medicine • Woman sneezing/man sleeping

Period Table

Period code (key):	Day, sequence number (Jan. 3, run 2)
Metaphor date:	Internal code to link ADPRO data to the Metaphor system
Day:	1,2,3...
Day description:	Monday, Tuesday...
Period long description:	APR 09, 1989
Period short description:	YY MM DD (year, month, day format)
Media week:	Ends on Sunday (used for data aggregation purposes)
Scanning week:	Ends on Saturday (used for data aggregation purposes)

PART THREE

GEODEMOGRAPHIC SYSTEMS

12 THE GEODEMOGRAPHIC CONCEPT

Geodemographics is based on two simple principles. The first is that two people who live in the same neighborhood . . . are more likely to have similar characteristics than are two people chosen at random. The second is that neighborhoods can be categorized in terms of the characteristics of the population which they contain, and that two neighborhoods can be placed in the same category, i.e., can contain similar types of people, even though they are widely separated.

James Rothman,
Journal of the Market Research Society,
special issue on geodemographics

INTRODUCTION

A geodemographic research system contains aggregate demographic information about households nested within geographic units—such as census block groups—in order to transfer knowledge about these households to corporate executives responsible for developing marketing strategy. The geographic units in the system are clustered so that those with similar demographic profiles are collected in a single cluster called a geodemographic market segment. Typically between 40 and 50 such segments/clusters are formed.

Geodemographic research systems are used in direct marketing for list qualification, media analysis, and lifestyle profiling. They are used strategically to locate retail outlets, to reposition products, to profile trade areas, to analyze market potential, and to plan market entries. These systems are used in virtually every branch of marketing. "Nowhere are the advances in information services more clearly illustrated than in relation to geodemography. With applications that range from sample selection to the linking of disparate research databases, from direct marketing to branch location strategy, geodemographics provides the researcher with major opportunities."[1] Figure 12.1 shows how geodemography is applied in a variety of marketing application areas.

Four prominent geodemographic systems currently exist in the United States: ACORN, by CACI Inc.–Federal; ClusterPLUS, by Donnelley Market-

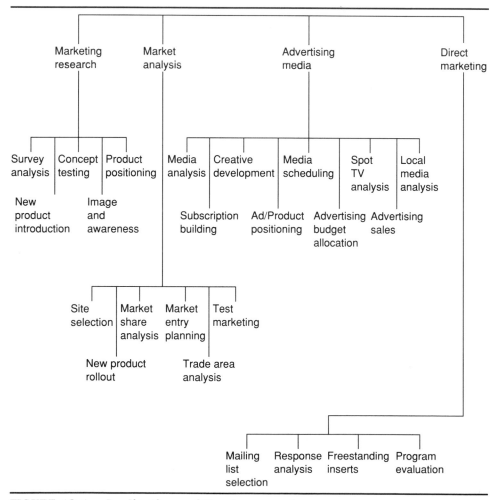

FIGURE 12.1.   Applications of Geodemography

ing Information Services; PRIZM, by Claritas Corporation; and MicroVision, by Equifax: National Decision Systems. This chapter describes how these systems are constructed and how they work. It provides a framework to give the applications discussed in subsequent chapters a firmly grounded conceptual basis. Chapter 13 compares the four United States-based systems with respect to certain key characteristics. Chapter 14 delves more deeply into application details and discusses trends and forthcoming developments in the United States. Chapter 15 concentrates on desktop geodemographic systems, and Chapter 16 discusses geodemographic systems available outside the United States. Appendices to these chapters provide additional detail about related topics, including the raw material for these systems, United States census data, and cluster analysis, the statistical methodology used to create them.

GEODEMOGRAPHIC SYSTEMS

A Qualitative Overview

Although geodemographic systems involve the application of multivariate statistical procedures and high-tech data processing, they have an intuitive foundation: the assumption that people share demographic characteristics, tastes, values, and purchasing habits with their closest neighbors. As a result, relatively homogeneous collections of households can be located indirectly—not by clustering people (which would require data that are largely unavailable), but by clustering neighborhoods. Data to complete this task are readily available from the U.S. Bureau of the Census.

Geodemographic (GD) clustering was originally designed to support firms in the direct marketing industry. The idea is based on three sound principles of market segmentation: Good segments should be sizable, profitable, and reachable. The last criterion, reachability, was largely unattainable with pre-1970 methods. GD systems, which first came on-line in the early 1970s, supplied the missing link—the postal ZIP code—to connect demographic and geographic market potential.

Every geographic unit defined by the U.S. Bureau of the Census, such as a census tract, a census block group, a county, or an enumeration district, is associated with either a single ZIP code or a unique collection of ZIP codes. (See Appendix 12A for an overview of U.S. census data.) Fortunately, any geographic unit relevant to marketing strategy can also be analyzed or profiled at the ZIP code level. This includes single-family dwellings and other places of residence, but also larger geographic units pertinent to marketing decisions, such as Nielsen's designated market areas (DMAs), Arbitron's areas of dominant influence (ADIs), a magazine's readership list, or a retailer's trade zones (for example, Kroger marketing areas, or KMAs). As will be illustrated shortly, GD market segmentation thus uses geography to link (databased) information about otherwise diverse objects such as people, places, and media.

Early Applications

L.L. Bean, Spiegel, and other direct marketers were among the early users of GD systems. Managers at a company such as L.L. Bean know that their potential customers are scattered throughout the country. But rather than mail expensive catalogs to every address, a more cost-effective method is to locate geographic concentrations of "L.L. Bean types." Marketing strategy should be delivered directly and precisely to these concentrations using a "marketing bullet" rather than the shotgun strategy of earlier eras.

Repeated validation studies conducted in the mid-1970s using PRIZM—the original GD system—suggested that the idea had considerable merit. Not only did various geodemographic segments respond differently to different product offerings, but PRIZM consultants were able to show management at L.L. Bean and elsewhere how to link information about their target segments to other marketing services to form a composite network of information about purchase behavior, media viewing habits, and product ownership. By using a geodemographic research system, management at L.L. Bean and many other direct marketing firms could track not only where its clients lived, but also what magazines they read, what television shows they watched, and what other products they owned.

By the late 1970s it was clear that the geodemographic approach was a success. Although the concept is now more than 15 years old, some of its implications are just beginning to be recognized. To appreciate these, we need a more detailed understanding of the idea.

A DETAILED LOOK

The Raw Material: U.S. Census Data

The starting point for creating a geodemographic system is U.S. census data arranged for analysis in a large data matrix, as shown in Figure 12.2. The rows (observations) in this matrix are census block groups. The columns are measures of each block group.

In its decennial census, the U.S. government collects information from each household for about 150 different variables.[2] These include the marital status of individuals in a household, ages, genders, educational levels, national background, years of residence at that location, income, employment, and many others.

To ensure privacy, the census bureau does not report these measures on a household-by-household basis. In fact, the smallest unit for which complete statistics are available is the census block group (CBG). A block group usually contains about 300 households.[3] For example, income for a particular block group is reported in terms of the block group's percent of households with incomes in the bureau's predefined categories.

These aggregate measures form the columns in the geodemographic data matrix. Each block group is uniquely characterized by its vector of scores across

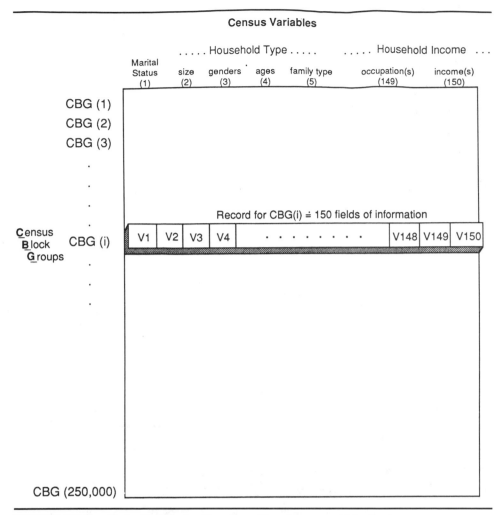

FIGURE 12.2. Data Matrix to Create a Geodemographic System

all variables. As shown in Figure 12.2, block group i is a vector of 150 numbers. Although this vector is unique, there are others very similar to it scattered throughout the matrix. The objective is to identify and cluster census block groups with similar score profiles. People living in similar block groups share a large number of important socioeconomic and demographic characteristics. As a consequence, their buying habits, media preferences, and product choices are often similar.

Statistical Analyses

Although the data matrix for this problem is extremely large, modern high-speed computers can sift through it easily to locate similar CBGs. The exact routine differs by supplier, but the basic concept is the same in all four cases.

The search involves two steps. The first is to remove any unnecessary redundancy in the variable space. In other words, certain variables may be measuring the same latent construct, such as "socioeconomic status." If so, this redundancy should be removed before the second step, which consists of clustering block groups.

Step 1: Factor Analysis of Variables

An an example of redundancy, suppose the census bureau reported household income in both dollars and thousands of dollars. If so, then "household income" would be measured twice, and this variable's effective impact on the subsequent cluster analysis would be double its correct impact.

This problem is fairly easily rectified. In the hypothetical case, the two measures—income in dollars and income in thousands of dollars—would be correlated perfectly, that is, $r = 1.00$. Hence the redundancy could be identified through an analysis of product-moment correlations, and one or the other measure could be eliminated.

A multivariate technique that examines the correlations between variables and removes redundancies is factor analysis. Although details would take this discussion too far afield, the result of factor-analyzing a data matrix is illustrated as the horizontal condensation shown in Figure 12.3. The original data matrix is reduced from 150 fields in width to something much smaller—typically to between 25 and 35 "factors," where each factor represents a whole group of (highly intercorrelated) raw variables that measure the same thing. Each CBG then receives a score on each of these factors. Because mostly redundant information is removed by this process, the "trimmed" data matrix still contains almost all (usually upwards of 80 percent) of the valid or nonredundant information contained in the original matrix.

Step 2: Cluster Analysis of Block Groups

The second step is to use the factor score matrix (which is now 250,000 rows or CBGs by about 30 columns or factors) to find clusters of census block groups. Cluster analysis is a multivariate technique used to solve problems of this sort. The principal goal is to find block groups that have similar score profiles across all factors. The distance between every pair of block groups is computed, and block groups that are "close together" are placed in the same cluster. However, "close together" in this sense does not refer to physical distance but rather to distance in the space of variables defined by the factor analysis. The formula for the distance (d) between two block groups **x** and **y** is:

$$d(\mathbf{x}, \mathbf{y}) = \left[\sum_{i=1}^{n} (x_i - y_i)^2 \right]^{1/2}$$

where:

$$\mathbf{x} = (x_1, x_2, \ldots, x_n)$$
$$\mathbf{y} = (y_1, y_2, \ldots, y_n)$$

Census Variables

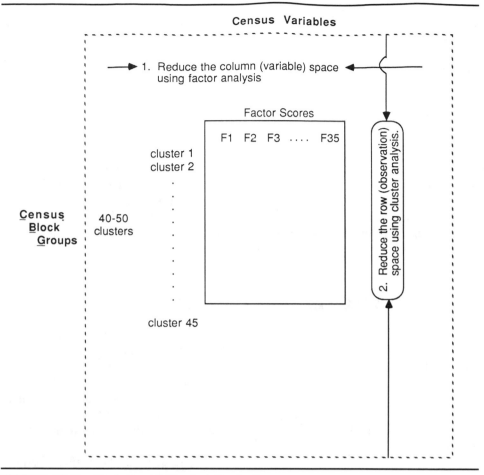

FIGURE 12.3. **Factor and Cluster Analysis**

x and **y** are the n-dimensional factor score vectors associated with two block groups, that is, two rows in the factor score matrix.

The formula produces a numerical index that measures the similarity between two block groups.[4] Block groups that are indexed as extremely similar are placed in the same cluster. As a consequence, block groups nested within the same cluster exhibit nearly the same scores across all factors.

Results

The result of this process is to divide the 250,000 census block groups into a much smaller number of clusters or geodemographic market segments. The four main suppliers have each decided that between 40 and 50 clusters is optimal.[5]

In a single cluster there are therefore an average of about 6,000 CBGs. The actual composition of each cluster varies, of course, and is determined by the computer alogorithm used by the GD firm, which in turn is guided by certain statistical criteria. (Details are given in Appendix 12B.) The critical point is that all 6,000 block groups in a single geodemographic segment are quite similar. They are much more similar to each other than they are to block groups in other clusters.[6] This brings us back to the point made in the chapter's opening quote: Two households from the same cluster are more likely to have similar characteristics than two households chosen at random.

The block groups in a single cluster are scattered throughout the country. Even though they are geographically dispersed, households in these block groups are likely to exhibit similar purchase habits because they share so many traits. For example, a high proportion may be interested in the L.L. Bean product line. In effect, the cluster analysis can locate all potential L.L. Bean clients regardless of whether they live in a neighborhood in Maine, a suburb of Chicago, or a section of Los Angeles.

PRESENTATION OF RESULTS TO CLIENTS

Each of the four major systems—ACORN, ClusterPLUS, PRIZM, and MicroVision—presents the results from this factor-then-cluster process slightly differently. The designers of each system also assign descriptive names to each segment. The complete lists of names and cluster descriptions are discussed in Chapter 13. Here a simple generic version of a geodemographic system is briefly described. Then an example from each system is used to illustrate how descriptive labels help clients to visualize the members of each segment, to see the people behind the numbers.

The generic system is presented in Figure 12.4. This illustration assumes that six clusters/segments (rather than 40 or 50) were identified using the factor-cluster process. The six segments are mutually exclusive (a given CBG belongs to one and only one of them) and collectively exhaustive (every CBG belongs to a segment; none is left unclassified). They form a perfect partition of all the CBGs in the United States and, hence, all U.S. households, since each household lives in one and only one CBG. For purposes of the example, these six segments are referred to as Circles, Triangles, Squares, Stars, Ovals, and Diamonds.

A closer examination of the composition of one segment will help clarify the geodemographic concept. The diamonds, for example, are a collection of highly similar census block groups that are geographically dispersed throughout the United States but demographically virtually identical. Similarly, CBGs in the other segments are also geographically separated but matched demographically. In fact, Diamond CBGs, Star CBGs, and the other groups are thoroughly mixed in the natural spatial environment. The process of creating the geodemographic system unmixes them, sorting all CBGs into six useful categories.

In real systems such as ACORN and PRIZM, the names given to the various neighborhood types are both clever and descriptive. Table 12.1 shows the name and vital characteristics of the wealthiest segment identified within each of the four U.S.-based systems. This segment is referred to as Old Money in the

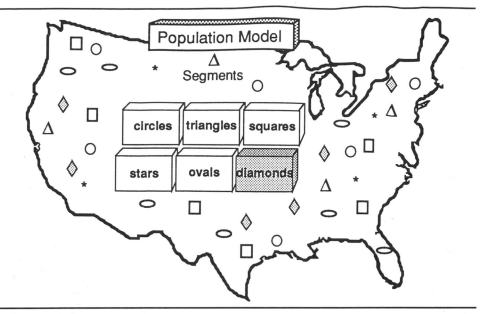

FIGURE 12.4. A Generic System

**TABLE 12.1. The Wealthiest Segment
in Each of the Four Geodemographic Systems**[a]

	ACORN	ClusterPLUS	PRIZM	MicroVision
Name	Old Money	Established Wealthy	Blue Blood Estates	Upper Crust
Size (households)	451,352	1,178,161	494,852	844,776
Median household income	na	$66,432	$41,094	na
Percent of incomes $50,000 or more	50–60 (est.)	95	38	50
Percent home owners	90	93	83	92
Percent professional and management	53	54	51	55

	U.S. Figures[b]		
	1980	**1988**	**1993**
Population	226,545,808	254,301,936	255,799,536
Households	80,398,672	90,836,160	97,234,024
Median household income	$16,886	$25,915	$27,880
Percent of incomes $50,000 or more	4.6	16.3	19.8

[a] Based on 1980 census figures and various brochures, fact sheets, and technical reports from each firm.
[b] From CACI Demographic & Income Forecast Report, CACI, Fairfax, VA, press date 3/2/88.

ACORN system, as Established Wealthy in ClusterPLUS, as Blue Blood Estates in the PRIZM system, and as Upper Crust in MicroVision.[7] Each supplier supplements these top-line descriptions with other information, also discussed in detail in the next chapter.

A BASIC APPLICATION: LIST QUALIFICATION

Figure 12.5 is included to foreshadow the applications discussed in Chapters 13, 14, and 15. Here two lists—a direct marketer's house list (its active clients) and a list of subscribers to *Cash Flow* magazine—have been sorted into the generic

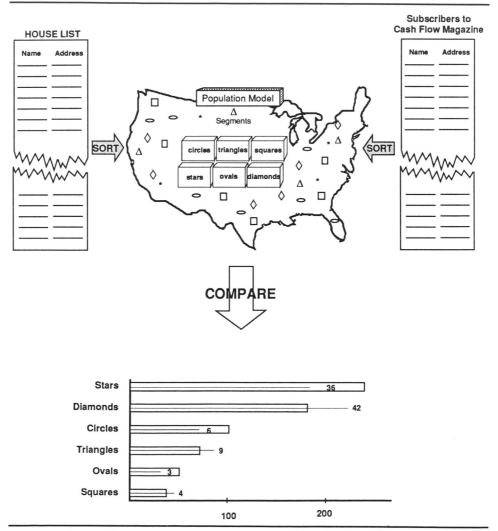

FIGURE 12.5. List Qualification

system. The graph at the bottom shows that relative to the U.S. population, Stars and Diamonds represent a disproportionate share of this direct marketer's customer base. For example, in the U.S. population 8 percent are Stars whereas among this direct marketer's clients 19 percent are Stars. The index formed by the ratio of these two numbers ($19/8 = 2.38 \times 100 = 238$), shown as the thick bar in the graph, provides an easy way to "profile" this direct marketer's customer base, matching it against the known response pattern among current customers.

The thin lines in the graph indicate that the list from *Cash Flow* magazine provides a good match for this direct marketer. The majority of its readers are Diamonds (42 percent) and Stars (36 percent), so these two segments appear to be ideal targets if past client behavior is an accurate guide. The direct marketer will want to buy names from the list broker handling *Cash Flow* magazine. This list should be sorted by ZIP code, and only those ZIP codes associated with Diamonds and Stars should be used.

CONCLUSION

This chapter has explained the geodemographic concept, outlined marketing applications of commerical GD systems, and reviewed the statistical procedures—factor and cluster analysis—used to create such systems. Factor analysis removes unwanted redundancy from the census data used to characterize census block groups. Cluster analysis then sorts all U.S. census block groups into a set of mutually exclusive, collectively exhaustive market segments. A commercial system such as ACORN, ClusterPLUS, PRIZM, and MicroVision comprises anywhere from 40 to 50 such segments.

The fundamental precept of geodemography is that households living in the same neighborhood tend to share buying habits, product preferences, and other elements of consumer behavior (such as media use patterns). Geodemography does not claim that patterns match exactly among neighborhood families, only that neighbors tend to be more alike than families picked at random from the general population. In other words, knowledge of a household's GD segment membership adds critical information that permits management to better predict that household's behavior.[8]

Evidence abounds supporting the claim that GD segmentation is helpful. For example, when a firm's client list is sorted into a GD system, most of the dollar volume (for a given item) is accounted for by a handful of GD segments; that is, 80 percent (or more) of the firm's business is accounted for by 20 percent (or less) of the general population. Management typically chooses the top three to five GD segments as targets and uses the GD system to accurately profile members of each target—by demography, media use habits, place of residence, and many other characteristics.

Finally, a GD system forms a valuable link—via its emphasis on physical location—between various decision support databases. The elegance and efficiency of this link relative to other possibilities is discussed in subsequent chapters. Suffice it to say here that alternative approaches to segmentation have certain weaknesses not inherent in geodemography. For example, links using individual person IDs, such as Social Security numbers, are illegal. Segments based on unobservable characteristics, such as a person's "preference for (something)" or "political persuasion," are unreachable. And systems that use a specific purchase behavior, such as "bought Coke on the last store visit," are really promotion tools rather than segmentation schemes.[9]

Notes

1. Peter Sleight and Barry Leventhal, "Applications of Geodemographics to Research and Marketing," *Journal of the Market Research Society* 31 (January 1989), pp. 75–101.

2. In 1990 about one out of every six households responded to the full questionaire, and the remaining households responded to an abbreviated form with fewer than 150 data fields.

3. A census block group includes the households in an area four to six city blocks square. A precise definition is given in Appendix 12A. Analyses could be done with other census units, such as census tracts or countries; however, the census block group is the smallest unit for which complete data are available. There are approximately 250,000 CBGs or equivalents in the United States. Results for larger units can be obtained by upward aggregation.

4. This formula generates the Euclidean or straight-line distance between two block groups. Other distance formulas exist, but this one is the most commonly used.

5. To be exact, ACORN uses 44 clusters, ClusterPLUS 47, and PRIZM 40; MicroVision comes in 50-cluster and 95-cluster versions.

6. Although the *average* cluster contains about 6,000 CBGs, any particular cluster might contain substantially more or fewer CBGs. The size varies as a function of the number of CBGs that share certain characteristics; one cluster might naturally consist of only 2,500 CBGs, and another might naturally consist of more than 8,000.

7. The specific census block groups that compose each of these four systems differ because they are based on the unique statistical methods of each supplier. The phrase "This segment is referred to . . ." means that the wealthiest segment in each system is shown, not that different suppliers have assigned different names to the same segment.

8. The value of geodemographic information in any given application can be calculated using principles from decision analysis and probability theory. For example, given the prior (or unconditional) marginal probability that a household chosen at random from the U.S. population will buy item X, then Bayes' theorem permits the calculation of the posterior probability that H will buy X given information about the household's GD membership. If appropriate costs and payoffs are available, then posterior probabilities can be integrated over all GD segments to quantify the value of the GD system for that application.

9. A thorough debate about the value of "event-defined" niche marketing versus geodemography would take this presentation too far afield. However, events (household buys Coke, baby arrives in household) require unique data collection techniques, may or may not have persistent effects on other household behaviors, and do not lead to segments that are easily profiled or analyzed via standard techniques— thus their characterization as promotion tools rather than segmentation systems.

APPENDIX 12A:
OVERVIEW OF U.S. CENSUS DATA

Introduction

The Census Bureau tabulates data for geographic areas that range from entire states to small villages to city blocks. This massive amount of data is computerized so that bureau and other users can produce geocoded files, reference maps, maps for field operations, and thematic maps for publication. The Census Bureau also defines the geographic framework used to present data in nearly all statistical summaries and reports produced by the U.S. government.

Table 12.2 provides a brief description of each geographic area used by the Census Bureau. These are arranged in their natural hierarchical structure in Figure 12.6A and 12.6B; counts for each type for both 1980 and 1990 are provided in Table 12.3. These areas include four national regions, nine divisions, the states within these regions, and various other categories, both political and statistical. For example, in 48 states the first order division is the county.[1]

The Census Bureau makes a distinction between political areas and statistical areas, though both of these are geographical units. Political areas are

TABLE 12.2.   Census Area Definitions

Political Areas

United States: The 50 states and the District of Columbia; data are also collected for Puerto Rico, the Virgin Islands of the United States, Guam, American Samoa, the Northern Mariana Islands, and the other Pacific territories for which the U.S. Census Bureau assists in the census-taking process.

States: The 50 states.

Counties, Parishes, Statistically Equivalent Areas: The first order divisions of each state, the District of Columbia, Puerto Rico, and the outlying areas; counties for 48 states; parishes for Louisiana, boroughs and census areas for Alaska; also, independent cities in Maryland, Missouri, Nevada, and Virginia; municipios in Puerto Rico.

Minor Civil Divisions (MCDs): Minor civil divisions are legally defined subcounty areas such as towns and townships. For the 1990 census, these are found in 28 states, Puerto Rico (barrios), and several of the outlying areas.

Incorporated Areas: Political units incorporated as a city, town (excluding the New England states, New York, and Wisconsin), borough (excluding Alaska and New York), or village.

American Indian Reservations: Areas with boundaries established by treaty, statute, and/or executive or court order.

Alaska Native Regional Corporations (ANRCs): Business and nonprofit corporate entities set up by the Alaska Native Claims Settlement Act (P.L. 92-203) to carry out the business operations established by and for Native Alaskans under the act. Twelve ANRCs have specific boundaries and cover the State of Alaska except for the Annette Islands Reserve.

Statistical Areas

Alaska Native Village Statistical Areas (ANVSAs): A 1990 census statistical area that delineates the settled area of each Alaska Native Village (ANV). Officials of Alaska Native Regional Corporations (ANRCs) or other appropriate officials delineated the ANVSAs for the Census Bureau for the sole purpose of presenting census data.

represented in the U.S. political system by elected officials. These areas include states, counties, minor civil divisions (for example, townships), special areas (such as Indian reservations), congressional districts, voting districts, and school districts. Statistical areas constitute the bases for statistical counts but are not part of the political-electoral structure of the nation. These areas include regions, divisions, metropolitan areas, urbanized areas, census county divisions, census tracts, and other special units such as tribal jurisdiction statistical areas and Alaska native village statistical areas.

The census block group is a statistical, rather than political, unit. Since it plays such an important role in geodemographic systems, a full description is given below.

A Census Block Group (CBG) is a small, usually compact area, bounded by streets and other prominent physical features as well as by certain legal boundaries. In urbanized areas, CBGs usually cover 4–6 city blocks on a side but may be as large as several square miles in less urbanized areas.[2]

TABLE 12.2. (*Continued*)

Tribal Designated Statistical Areas (TDSAs): Geographic areas delineated by tribal officials of recognized tribes that do not have a recognized land area for 1990 census tabulation purposes.

Tribal Jurisdiction Statistical Areas (TJSAs): Geographic areas delineated by tribal officials in Oklahoma for 1990 census tabulation purposes.

Census County Divisions (CCDs): Areas defined by the Census Bureau in cooperation with state and local officials in states where MCDs do not exist or are not adequate for reporting subcounty statistics.

Unorganized Territories (UTs): Areas defined by the Census Bureau for those portions of a state with MCD's where MCDs do not exist or are not adequate for reporting subcounty statistics.

Census Designated Places (CDPs): Densely settled population centers without legally defined corporate limits or corporate powers defined in cooperation with state officials or local data users.

Census Tracts: Small, locally defined statistical areas within selected counties, generally having stable boundaries, and, when first established, designed to have relatively homogeneous demographic characteristics.

Block Numbering Areas (BNAs): Areas defined for the purpose of grouping and numbering blocks in counties without census tracts.

Block Groups: A collection of census blocks sharing the same first digit in their identifying number within census tracts or BNAs.

Census Blocks: Small, usually compact areas, bounded by streets and other prominent physical features as well as certain legal boundaries. In some areas, they may be as large as several square miles. Blocks do not cross BNAs, census tracts, or county boundaries. There are two types of block-numbers: *collection* block number (3-digit) and *tabulation* block number (3-digit with a suffix). A tabulation boundary, such as a political boundary, can split (subdivide) a collection block. Once the 1990 census tabulation boundaries are final, the Census Bureau will assign an alphabetic suffix to a block split by a tabulation boundary, but the three-digit collection block number will remain unchanged. For example, collection block 101, split by a 1990 political (tabulation) boundary, will become tabulation blocks 101A and 101B.

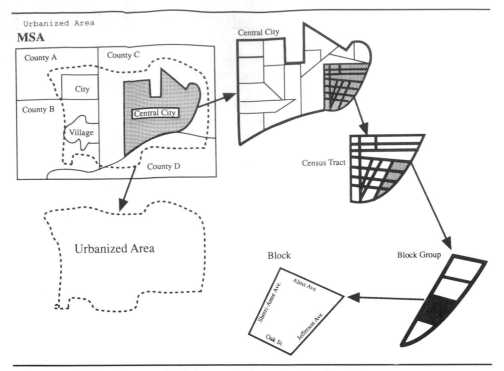

FIGURE 12.6A. Census Divisions within an Urbanized Area
Source: U.S. Bureau of the Census.

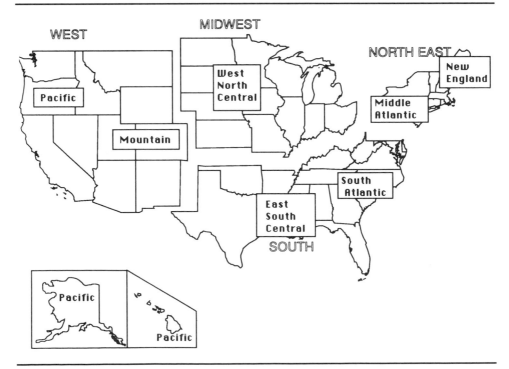

FIGURE 12.6B. Census Divisions: U.S. as a Whole
Source: U.S. Bureau of the Census.

TABLE 12.3. Census Geographic Units[a]

	1980	1990 (est.)
Political Areas		
United States		
Regions	4	4
Divisions	9	9
States	50	50
District of Columbia	1	1
Outlying areas	6	5
Counties, parishes, and other statistically equivalent areas	3,231	3,231
Minor Civil Divisions	30,429	30,300
Incorporated Places	19,176	19,500
American Indian Reservations	275	300
Alaska Native Villages	209	—
Alaska Native Regional Corporations	12	12
Statistical Areas		
Alaska Native Village Statistical Areas	—	215
Tribal Designated Statistical Areas	—	50
Tribal Jurisdiction Statistical Areas	—	15
Census County Divisions	5,276	5,300
Unorganized Territories	62	60
Other statistically equivalent areas	274	300
Census Designated Places	3,733	4,000
Census Tracts	43,383	48,200
Block Numbering Areas	3,404	11,200
Block Groups[b]	156,163	190,000
Blocks	2,473,679	8,500,000

[a] *Source:* "Tiger/Line Prototype Files, 1990," U.S. Department of Commerce, Bureau of Census Technical Documentation (1989), p. 29.

[b] The text refers to "250,000 census block groups" as the unit of analysis for a geodemographic system. Although there are fewer CBGs than this, the matrix analyzed to create a GD system contains nearly 250,000 rows. The analysts include other statistical units (CBG equivalents) in non-urban areas where CBGs are undefined. These include Minor Civil Divisions, Incorporated Places, and Census Designated Places.

The Census Bureau

The U.S. Bureau of Census has a number of major administrative divisions, including the Geography Divison and the Data User Services Division (DUSD). The DUSD is particularly important to marketing scientists since it supplies census data to commercial and private clients. Its primary concern is to make the data resources of the Census Bureau more accessible to and useful for the nation's urban planners, social scientists, businesses, and other data users. To help these parties acquire, understand, and apply Census Bureau products, the DUSD holds seminars and workshops at Census Bureau headquarters in

Washington, D.C., and in locations around the country. The DUSD also prepares catalogs, guides, indices, case studies, procedural histories of major programs, and other reference aids. Most important for the developers of marketing research systems, the DUSD sells computer-readable products, microfiche, and reports; it promotes these products through such channels as newsletters, conferences, exhibits, and direct mailings.

History

The U.S. Bureau of Census has maintained a distinguished record of innovation in data collection and processing techniques since the first census was conducted in 1790. These innovations include the first use of maps to portray U.S. statistical areas in 1890; the first use of a mechanical tallying machine, the Seaton Device, in 1872; the introduction of electronic machine tabulation, the Hollerith Machine, in 1890; the introduction of scientific sampling techniques in census-taking in 1940; the first major use in census-taking of a computer, UNIVAC-1, in 1951; development of the first optical sensing device for computer input, FOSDIC, in 1953; development in 1968 or the GBF/DIME System for assigning addresses to geographic locations; and the application of computer graphics for the Census Bureau's map presentations in 1975.

Census Methodology

For censuses before 1951, the Bureau's data collection methodology relied on enumerators visiting every household and business in the United States. Using Census Bureau maps, they matched each residence with its census geography and recorded information about both the physical dwelling and its occupants. By 1960, this process had become prohibitively expensive and time-consuming. Instead of having enumerators deliver 1960 census data questionnaires, the Census Bureau asked the U.S. Post Office to deliver some of the forms. Enumerators then collected the completed form from each household and used personal interviews to handle long-form questionnaires. Geographically, the 1960 process remained unchanged; enumerators still assigned each living quarter to its geographic location based on personal observation.

The success of the post office delivery technique led to the adoption of the mail census—mailout/mailback—technique. Since enumerators no longer visited every household, in the mid-1960s the bureau initiated major changes in its approach to the preparation of geographic products. The new approach resulted in the development of address coding guides (ACGs). These ACGs provided computer-based information that allowed the Census Bureau to link addresses to streets and other features shown on existing and updated Census Bureau maps. The bureau used these ACGs and an enhanced file structure, the Geographic Base File/Dual Independent Map Encoding (GBF/DIME), to process the workplace responses from the 1970 census. In simple terms, the GBF/DIME technique enhanced ACG files by encoding more features and providing powerful new file-editing capabilities.

All the geographic products from past censuses—including the maps, the ACGs, the GBF/DIMEs, and the geographic reference files—suffer from divergent ways of describing the earth's surface. Conflicting definitions eventually caused problems; that is, each product had to be prepared separately, a process that required complex clerical operations and literally thousands of person-hours. Errors accumulated and inconsistencies were introduced when these products were brought together.[3]

In order to alleviate these problems and to take advantage of important advances in information processing, the Census Bureau developed a new system called TIGER. Prior to its use for the 1990 census, TIGER was in development and underwent extensive tests for more than eight years. The first commerical versions of TIGER were made available in late 1991. This systems marks a new era of geodemography.

The TIGER System

The Topologically Integrated Geographic Encoding and Referencing System (TIGER) automated the mapping and related geographic activities for the 1990 decennial census and provides a foundation for continued automation of the Census Bureau's geographic operations. TIGER represents important new opportunities for developers of marketing research systems because of its scope and detail.

In simple terms, the TIGER file consolidates the separately prepared maps and other geographic products of the past into one seamless, nationwide database capable of providing the products and services necessary for the 1990 census. To avoid duplicating geographic automation work done by others, the Census Bureau entered into a major cooperative agreement with the U.S. Geological Survey (USGS). This project refined the automated processes developed to convert USGS 1:1,000,000–scale maps into computer-readable files that meet the mission responsibilities of both agencies.[4]

The TIGER System is rich in possibilities for products produced by the Census Bureau: full-color maps that bring detailed data to life, microcomputer-based geographic information systems, maps for the entire country (down to the CBG) on a single CD-ROM disc, direct access to Census Bureau data tabulations through a "map" displayed on a graphics terminal, and so on.

Some of these products will be developed by the bureau, but many more will be developed by corporations. For-profit companies often transform census files into products and services that have commerical value for various industries, applications, and market segments. These commercial ventures include the four geodemographic firms discussed in Chapters 12 to 16 as well as many others, such as National Planning Data Corporation, a supplier of refined census data to the major geodemographers.

The Census Bureau will limit its own output of products to those shown in Table 12.4. The bureau's policy is not to compete head-on with private enterprise, partly due to limited resources, but also to avoid being distracted from its primary responsibility by tasks that can be better fulfilled by for-profit firms.

Table 12.4 is arranged into three major sections: maps, reports, and computer files. The maps break down into two primary subgroups: (1) maps showing information on the geographic structure tabulated in the 1990 census and (2) maps providing displays of data in appropriate geographic distributions. The reports available from TIGER are limited to street index guides, but a variety of

TABLE 12.4.   TIGER Products[a]

TIGER System Maps

Map	Description
1990 Census Block-Numbered Maps	Large-scale, most detailed maps by tabulation block. Shows block ID-code, boundaries, and other details and features.
1990 Census County Block Maps	County maps produced at the maximum practical scale on a reasonable number of map sheets; 1–4 sheets, 32" × 32".
Summary Reference Maps (Outline Series)	Include County Subdivisions Voting District, State MSA, County, Congressional Districts, Native American Areas, and Urbanized Areas maps. These outline maps vary in content and scale but mainly show area names and boundaries with some features.
Statistical Thematic Maps	Depict statistical topics published as multi-colored single-sheet wall maps and page-sized maps. Themes include population density.

TIGER Reports

Report	Description
Street Index Guides	Small-scale maps that index streets in a particular geographic unit; e.g., city block groups, counties, etc.

TIGER Computer Files
(expected availability date in parentheses)

File	Description
TIGER/BOUNDARY (1991)	Contains coordinate data for several specific boundary sets; e.g., counties, tracts, block groups, etc.

computer-readable files supplement the bureau's "hard-copy" output. For further detail about these products, see U.S. Bureau of the Census, *FACTFINDER for the Nation: Census Bureau Programs and Products*, CFF No. 18 (rev.) May 1990, pp. 1–24.

Notes

1. Counties are replaced by parishes in Louisiana; boroughs and census areas in Alaska; independent cities in Maryland, Missouri, Nevada, and Virginia; and municipos in Puerto Rico.

TABLE 12.4. (*Continued*)

TIGER Computer Files
(expected availability date in parentheses)

File	Description
TIGER/LINE (1991)	Provides digital data for all features displayed on 1990 census maps and the associated geographic area codes on either side of every mapped feature—released for units such as states, counties, and census blocks.
TIGER/DATA BASE (1991)	Contains digital data for all points, lines, and areas displayed on 1990 census maps in a standard digital cartographic interchange format.
TIGER/AREA (1992)	Equates specific subsets of census geographic areas to program-defined areas. Any area (trade area, area of dominant influence, etc.) can be defined, and all blocks in the area can be aggregated, analyzed, and summarized.
TIGER/COMPARABILITY (1991)	Contains data that provide comparability information for the same geographic unit in 1980 and 1990. Provided only for Census Tracts.

[a] *Source:* Robert A. LaMacchia, Silla G. Tomasi, and Sheldon K. Piepenburg, "The TIGER File Proposed Products," delivered at the National Conference of State Legislators, Hartford, CT (November, 1987).

   2. For a more formal but less descriptive definition, see the *1990 Census of Population and Housing,* Tabulation and Publication Program, U.S. Department of Commerce, Bureau of the Census, July 1989.

   3. For example, miscoded digits in a geographic identifier (such as coding 8885 instead of 8855) or omission of a block number resulted in mismatches that affected other Census Bureau products, often with disastrous results.

   4. A description of this entire process can be obtained from Robert W. Marx, Chief, Geography Division, Bureau of the Census, Washington, D.C. 20233.

APPENDIX 12B:
CLUSTER ANALYSIS FOR GEODEMOGRAPHIC
MARKETING RESEARCH SYSTEMS: AN OVERVIEW

All four geodemographic systems were developed using the statistical method known as cluster analysis. Appendix 12B summarizes some key points about this technique. A simple illustration is used to convey the essentials and to show how cluster analysis is applied to geodemographic problems. Following the explanation, some strengths and weaknesses of centroid clustering, the approach used by the major suppliers, are discussed. Additional technical detail is available in a number of texts and monographs.[1]

Cluster Analysis in Geodemographic Systems

The objective of geodemographic cluster analysis is to find census block groups (or even smaller geographic units such as ZIP+4 postcode areas) that are similar to one another across all census variables.[2] The working principle is that two block groups with similar score profiles will contain similar types of families living in roughly parallel environments. Clustering block groups is, therefore, an indirect way of finding households that look, live, and respond alike.

Cluster analysis is analogous to sorting any collection of things—marbles, coins, silverware, or dogs—into homogeneous subgroups. The sorting process is based on criteria such as color, denomination, function, or breed, respectively. Sorting partitions a collection or set into smaller groups or subsets. Within a group, members are similar with respect to the chosen criteria, but between groups there are clear distinctions. For example, sorting a collection of dogs by breed yields several groups. Within any one breed, such as Golden Retriever, the dogs look alike, although subtle individual differences are apparent. Despite each animal's unique characteristics, a specific golden retriever still looks much more like other golden retrievers than it looks like members of another breed such as Great Dane or Boxer.

When sorting dogs by breed, an amateur can rely on visual cues and informal judgment. Experts are able to refine the partitioning process because they rely on more cues and can accurately assess each dog's "scores" on each cue.[3]

The cues in a geodemographic system are census variables, and each census block group (CBG) has a unique profile of scores across cues. Because similarity of CBGs can not be determined visually, the clustering process must be formalized; the vagaries of human judgment must be replaced by the precision of mathematics. The net result, however, is analogous to that obtained in any sorting process. The 250,000 CBGs are partitioned into 40 or 50 clusters. Within a single cluster, members are very similar, though individual differences remain. As a collective, each group is quite different from any of the other groups that have been recovered by the analysis.

Consider a case where there are only 10 CBGs, each scored on two variables, as shown in Table 12.5. In this example the scores for each variable range from zero to ten. Although in practice score ranges are not this orderly, raw scores are typically standarized to avoid improper effects due to differences in measurement units.[4] A scan of the data matrix in Table 12.5 provides a rough

TABLE 12.5. Scores for 10CBGs

Points (Census Block Groups)	V1	V2
a	4	2
b	5	3
c	5	2
d	7	1
e	8	1
f	8	2
g	2	7
h	1	8
i	4	8
j	3	10

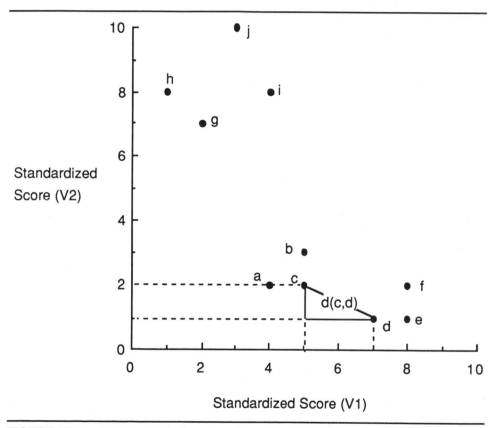

FIGURE 12.7. CBGs Plotted on Two Census Variables

idea of which CBGs are similar to one another. For example, a, b, and c have score profiles that are nearly the same.

If each census block group is plotted in a two-dimensional space using the variables as axes, then their similarity or dissimilarity becomes more apparent. A plot is shown in Figure 12.7. Even a cursory glance at Figure 12.7 suggests that there are natural clusters of census block groups. Of course, it is not clear how many clusters exist. The answer depends on how finely one wants to partition these data. If only two clusters are required, then C1= {a,b,c,d,e,f} and C2 = {g,h,i,j} is a natural choice. However, the first cluster could be divided further into C1.1 = {a,b,c} and C1.2 = {d,e,f}. If greater refinement were desired, then one would split the second cluster into C2.1= {h,g} and C2.2= {i,j}. The selection of an appropriate number of clusters requires seasoned judgment, but it is also a function of a project's purpose, management's needs, and comprehensibility.

Switching from an algebraic (data matrix) approach to a visual/spatial approach eases the task of identifying natural groupings in this small example. In practice, with 250,000 CBGs and 150+ census variables, a plot like Figure 12.7 is infeasible. Therefore, the cluster analyst must find a way of "seeing" the natural groupings in a data set without being able to look.

The visual cue that suggests that natural groupings in Figure 12.7 is interpoint distance. Fortunately, the distance between any two points in space can be defined even if these points lie in 150 dimensions rather than in two dimensions. Clustering algorithms rely on interpoint distances to search for groups of points that are close together.

In two dimensions, the distance between two points is calculated by using the Pythagorean theorem. For example, the distance between points c and d in Figure 12.7 can be expressed algebraically in terms of each point's coordinates on the two dimensions as shown in equation (1).

$$d(\mathbf{c,d}) = [(5-7)^2 + (2-1)^2]^{1/2} = 2.23 \tag{1}$$

In words, the length of the hypotenuse (e.g., the side connecting points c and d) is obtained by squaring the length of the side parallel to axis V1, $(7-5)^2$ in this case, squaring the length of the side parallel to V2, $(2-1)^2$ in this example, adding these two quantities, and taking the square root of the sum.

Formula (1) generalizes to any number of dimensions as shown in formula (2). The only change needed is to sum over all n dimensions rather than over just two.

$$d(\mathbf{x,y}) = \left[\sum_{i=1}^{n}(x_i - y_i)^2\right]^{1/2} \tag{2}$$

where

$\mathbf{x} = (x_1, x_2, \ldots, x_n)$ and
$\mathbf{y} = (y_1, y_2, \ldots, y_n)$ are vectors (points) in
n-dimensional space.

The next section explains in more detail how the 10 CBGs in Figure 12.7 would be partitioned in an actual application.

Centroid Clustering

The four major geodemographic systems are each based on a particular approach to cluster analysis called centroid clustering. A centroid clustering technique attempts to find high density regions of CBG points—ball-like clusters—in the multivariate space of census scores.

Several computer algorithms are available to perform centroid clustering. These include the KMEANS algorithm, the BC-TRY package, and FASTCLUS in SAS, to name a few. Two variations of centroid clustering have been applied to the geodemographic problem. The first, called the KMEANS approach, predefines the number of clusters sought and forms these clusters using an iterative procedure that minimizes an explicit objective function. The second method also iterates to a solution, but there is neither an explicit objective function nor a predefined number of clusters. With the second approach, descriptive summaries of the clusters formed at any given stage are used to help determine the appropriate number of clusters.

Commonalities Between the Two Approaches

Both these approaches are iterative. They begin with arbitrary starting points, form temporary clusters, add a new point to a cluster if the point is closest to that cluster's centroid, and continue to rearrange the points until no further changes are helpful.

The centroid of a cluster of points is a single point found by taking the mean score on each dimension across all points in the cluster. For example, in Figure 12.8, if $\{i,j\}$ were a cluster, then its centroid would have coordinates $(4 + 3)/2 = 3.5$ on dimension one and $(8 + 10)/2 = 9.0$ on dimension two; e.g., the centroid is the point (3.5, 9.0) indicated by the asterisk near points i and j. (If i and j are considered objects with equal weights, then their center of gravity or two-dimensional balance point is precisely at the point asterisk.) The distance from a point to a cluster is defined as the distance from the point to the cluster centroid. The distance between two clusters is defined as the distance between their centroids.

All centroid algorithms try to find tightly packed, ball-like clusters. In a ball-like scatter of points, the mean distance from all points to the cluster centroid is small. These algorithms, therefore, search for swarms of points where distances within the group are small while between-group distances are large.

KMEANS

The KMEANS algorithm formalizes this objective by trying to partition all the points into a fixed number of clusters in a way that minimizes total within-cluster error. Error in a single cluster is defined as the total squared distance from each member point to the cluster centroid.

With KMEANS clustering, the analyst fixes the number of desired clusters. The algorithm then selects a starting point (an initial set of centroids), and points

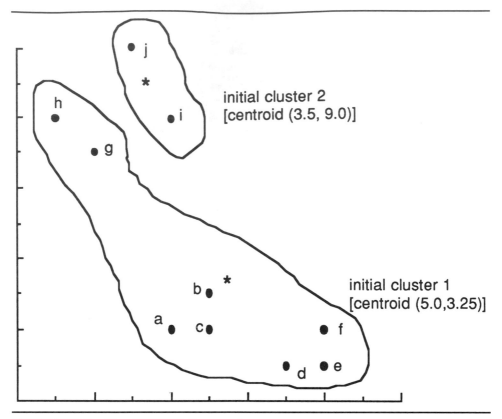

FIGURE 12.8. The KMEANS Approach

are assigned to the centroid to which they are closest. Once new points are added to a cluster, the cluster centroid shifts. Thus, in a subsequent step, points must be reassigned to their closest centroid; this is a process designed to minimize error. This process of assignment, centroid shift, and reassignment continues until a minimum error solution is found.

For example, in Figure 12.8, if two clusters are desired, KMEANS might start with the two most distinct points, e and j, as preliminary centroids. KMEANS would then apply a special intitialization criterion to generate a preliminary division of the points into two groups.[5] Applying this criterion results in the split shown in Figure 12.8 where {i, j} are in one preliminary group and all the other points are in the second preliminary group. The centroid for group 2 is also shown in the exhibit as an asterisk.

At this stage, points would be reassigned to their nearest centroid, resulting in the partition {a, b, c, d, e, f} and {g, h, i, j}. The centroids would shift, and in this case the process would terminate because further shifts cannot improve the two-group partition.

Problems with KMEANS

The primary problem with the KMEANS approach is that it is subject to *local minima*. This means that the algorithm can incorrectly "believe" that it has found the best (minimum error) solution when it has not. Local minima arise because the KMEANS approach is sensitive to the starting point. The algorithm's progress toward a global minimum is also hindered by trying to assign points one at a time. Given a particularly poor starting configuration, the algorithm can gain momentum and proceed down an algorithmic cul-de-sac.

Local minima can sometimes be avoided by rerunning a KMEANS analysis using different starting points. If the algorithm repeatedly converges to the same solution, then this solution is probably the best one (the global minimum error). It should be emphasized, however, that using multiple starting points in no way guarantees a (globally) minimal error for a predefined number of clusters.

Other Approaches

Other centroid algorithms, such as the BC-TRY system or SASs FASTCLUS, do not explicitly minimize an error function. They do, however, evaluate the efficiency of a solution at various stages. These algorithms start by slicing the space into a number of regions and counting the points in each region. Regions with high densities are chosen as core object types. The centroid in each core is computed, and points are clustered with their nearest centroid, just as in the KMEANS procedure. New centroids are then computed, and the process iterates until it stabilizes.

Because the number of clusters is not predetermined, an algorithm like BC-TRY reports cluster solutions for a series of levels; that is, for G groups, for G-1, G-2 and also for G+1, G+2 groups, and so forth. For example, in Figure 12.7, one must decide between the 2, 3, and 4 group solutions depending on how tightly packed (homogeneous) one wants the clusters to be.[6]

The distinction between these two approaches can be summarized by saying that the KMEANS algorithm fixes the number of clusters at G and seeks the best partition of the points subject to this constraint. Other centroid algorithms yield several solutions at different levels of coarseness/fineness and ask the analyst to decide after the fact how many clusters seems best. In commercial applications, the "best" number of clusters is determined by mixing purely scientific criteria (e.g., statistical tests of the null hypothesis of "no clusters") with managerial criteria such as interpretability and manageability.

CONCLUSION

Carefully performed analyses with either of these approaches will result in an appropriate and actionable partition of census block groups for application in a geodemographic research system. Competitive pressures and a need for easily interpreted results have forced the major suppliers to use 40 or 50 clusters rather than 400. Given the constraints of achieving a 40 to 50 group solution, prudent application of any of several available algorithms should result in the emergence of fairly similar groups.

The 1990 census presents an opportunity for each company to rethink its system. The micro-marketing philosophy has pushed certain suppliers to offer a finer partitioning of the national market. Counterbalancing the push toward refinement is the client need for continuity from one decade to another; that is, frequent users of a particular system become used to that system's standard segmentation model. Clients want to continue to use the same groups from previous versions of a system. Selected solutions to this tradeoff are discussed in Chapter 13.

Notes

1. For example, see William R. Dillon and Matthew Goldstein, *Multivariate Analysis: Methods and Applications,* Chapter 5, New York: Wiley, 1984; Paul E. Green and Donald S. Tull, *Research for Marketing Decisions,* 4th ed. Chapter 13, Englewood Cliffs, NJ: Prentice-Hall, 1978; Gilbert A. Churchill, Jr., *Marketing Research: Methodological Foundations,* 4th ed., Hinsdale, IL: Dryden Press, 1987, pp. 777–788; and a variety of monographs and brochures dedicated to one or several specific clustering algorithms.

2. Certain vendors supplement census data with their own proprietary data in order to cluster ZIP+4 areas. For example, National Decision Systems developed its geodemographic product MicroVision using the Equifax Consumer Marketing Database (ECMD). ECMD includes a variety of financial data about each household; that is, number of credit lines open, sum of high credit, and so on. Further detail is available in Chapter 13.

3. The word *cue* stands for a trait (a variable, a dimension, a characteristic) that can be used to describe all dogs. A particular animal's score on a given cue is an instantiation (level, degree) of the general concept. For example, each dog has a weight. A particular dog's weight is a specific level on the weight dimension.

4. Most cluster routines are preceded by a factor analysis of variables. Factor analysis eliminates redundancy among raw scores and controls the effects of different measurement units for different types of variables. Following a factor analysis, each CBG is assigned a series of factor scores, one per recovered factor. Unlike the original variables, factors are uncorrelated. For example, one of the factors in the PRIZM system is household income. This factor is a composite, or a weighted sum, of variables such as household member occupations, number of workers in a family, and their various wage levels. A second approach used by CACI eliminates the factor analysis step and works directly with census variables, 49 variables in CACI's case. The variables are standardized prior to the cluster analysis so that their measurement units are comparable; however, raw variables are not necessarily statistically independent (e.g., nonredundant).

5. Details of KMEANS' initialization algorithm are given in Dillon and Goldstein, pp. 187–188. There is no failsafe method for choosing the initial position of the G centroids where G is the predetermined number of groups. KMEANS specialists offer various suggestions, such as picking G points that are maximally dispersed or picking G points at random.

6. For further discussion of these points, see David J. Curry, "Some Statistical Considerations in Clustering with Binary Data," *Multivariate Behavioral Research* (April 1976), pp. 175–188.

13 GEODEMOGRAPHIC RESEARCH FIRMS: THE BIG FOUR

Here was a new way of looking at the nation—not as fifty states but rather [as] forty neighborhood types, each with distinct boundaries, values, consuming habits and political beliefs.

Michael J. Weiss,
The Clustering of America

INTRODUCTION

Chapter 12 gives a top-down explanation of the geodemographic concept but does not provide detail about existing commercial systems. This chapter reviews the four major U.S. GD systems (ACORN, ClusterPLUS, PRIZM, and MicroVision) in detail, highlighting the segments that comprise each system and profiling the companies that build and maintain them.

All four systems adhere to the generic model described in Chapter 12. However, important differences among the systems exist. System builders implement the factor and cluster analysis phases differently, sometimes supplement census data with proprietary data, and may include other observation units (such as postal ZIP codes) in the analysis.

Two statistical approaches for evaluating the results from a GD analysis—the Lorenz curve (or Gains Chart) and the chi-square discrimination test—are also outlined in this chapter. These methods permit a system user to decide whether geodemography can improve his or her firm's targeting relative to the standard baseline of targeting to the general population. The statistical tools are illustrated using two basic examples. Interested readers, especially technical specialists who need detail for writing computer programs to implement Lorenz curve analysis, should refer to the appendix of Chapter 15.

Chapters 13 and 14 explore many of the common features of competing geodemographic systems. For example, each firm offers various types of indices that assist a client interested in profiling customer lists, sales accounts, retail trade areas, or media. Each company also offers (in their mainframe systems and the desktop systems, which will be discussed in Chapter 15) specialized mapping and site location analyses. Arguably, the most important differences among GD suppliers are their unique approaches to problem-solving, pricing, and customer relations. Readers are advised to contact corporate representatives in order to become better informed about the competitive advantages offered by each system.

THE BIG FOUR U.S. SYSTEMS

Table 13.1 shows the name, size, founding year, and sponsoring firm for each system. The systems range in size from a minimum of 40 clusters to a maximum of 50. Of the four, PRIZM is the oldest, although both PRIZM and ACORN are second-generation systems. PRIZM was originally developed with 1970 census data using ZIP codes as the observation unit. PRIZM's second generation, based on the 1980 census, replaced the ZIP code with the census block group. Although it is based on 1980 census data in the United States, ACORN is a second-generation system because it imported statistical methods to the United States from a British counterpart developed during the mid-1970s. ClusterPLUS and VISION (MicroVision's predecessor) were both developed in the United States using 1980 census data. With the completion of the 1990 census each of these systems is now in a second generation.

TABLE 13.1. The Four U.S. Geodemographic Systems

Name	Number of Segments	Date Created (U.S.)	Company Name	Year Founded
ACORN	44	1981	CACI–Federal	1962
ClusterPLUS	47	1982	Donnelley Marketing Information Services	1917
PRIZM	40	1974	Claritas	1971
MicroVision	50 (95)	1983	Equifax: National Decision Systems	1901 (1979)

CACI: THE ACORN SYSTEM

Company Background[1]

ACORN is an acronym for A Classification of Residential Neighborhoods. The system was created by CACI, a high-technology and professional services corporation founded in 1962, with annual sales in 1987 of approximately $135 million worldwide. ACORN is produced by CACI's Advanced Marketing Systems Group; other divisions include systems engineering, logistics sciences, proprietary analytical software products, and market analysis consultancies groups. CACI's markets include defense, aerospace, communications, financial, real estate, retailing, and other sectors of public and private enterprise.

According to company literature, the ACORN system "draws vivid social, financial, housing, and lifestyle portraits through the use of a precise customer profiling system." As with each GD system, CACI's demographers examined the characteristics of the roughly 250,000 CBGs using U.S. census data as described in Chapter 12. The result was 44 distinct market segments, each containing households with a unique propensity to purchase specific products and to use certain media.

In addition to the United States, the ACORN system is also marketed in the United Kingdom, Canada, Finland, France, Germany, Norway, Sweden, Italy, and Australia. In each country it is based on the appropriate census unit for that market. (For example, the British equivalent of a CBG is an enumeration district of which there are approximately 130,000.)[2]

ACORN Segments

Table 13.2 shows the 44 ACORN segments, the descriptive name assigned to each segment, and their sizes relative to the U.S. population. Table 13.2 also shows how the basic ACORN segments have been grouped. For example, the three wealthiest segments—Old Money, Conspicuous Consumers, and Cosmopolitans—comprise ACORN's A Group. Each GD firm presents its segments in this two-tier fashion. Segments in a single "supergroup" share a number of characteristics and offer a broader but often more convenient breakdown of the market. Supergroups are discussed in more detail on page 238–239.

DONNELLEY MARKETING INFORMATION SERVICES: THE CLUSTERPLUS SYSTEM[3]

Company Background

Donnelley Marketing Information Services was formed in 1882 as a branch of R. R. Donnelley and Sons, a Chicago-based printing firm. The company specialized in preparing telephone directories for publication. In 1922, it began to compile mailing lists of automobile and truck owners, renting these lists to automotive parts manufacturers interested in selling through the mail. In 1961, the operation was acquired by the Dun and Bradstreet Corporation and in 1976, as

TABLE 13.2. The ACORN Market Groups and Segments

ACORN Segment	Description	1987 households (hundreds)	Percent
A Group	Wealthy Metropolitan Communities	3,564,811	4.0
A1	Old Money	451,352	0.5
A2	Conspicuous Consumers	922,885	1.0
A3	Cosmopolitan Wealth	2,190,574	2.4
B Group	Trend-setting, Suburban Neighborhoods	16,687,141	18.6
B4	Upper Middle Income Families	2,449,714	2.7
B5	Empty Nesters	2,269,223	2.5
B6	Baby Boomers with Families	3,189,811	3.5
B7	Middle Americans in New Homes	4,766,129	5.3
B8	Skilled Craft and Office Workers	4,012,264	4.5
C Group	Apartment House and College Communities	9,027,364	10.0
C9	Condominium Dwellers	1,791,874	2.0
C10	Fast-Track Young Adults	5,329,368	5.9
C11	College Undergraduates	291,272	0.3
C12	Older Students and Professionals	1,614,850	1.8
D Group	Big City Urban Neighborhoods	2,632,285	2.9
D13	Urbanites in High Rises	1,092,782	1.2
D14	Big City Working Class	1,539,503	1.7
E Group	Hispanic and Multiracial Neighborhoods	6,679,236	7.4
E15	Mainstream Hispanic-American	2,084,862	2.3
E16	Large Hispanic Families	1,376,915	1.5
E17	Working-Class Single Families	1,322,383	1.5
E18	Families in Pre-War Rentals	988,885	1.1
E19	Third World Melting Pot	896,191	1.0
F Group	Black Neighborhoods	5,287,730	5.9
F20	Mainstream Family Homeowners	2,800,466	3.1
F21	Trend-Conscious Families	1,711,474	1.9
F22	Low-Income Families	775,790	0.9
G Group	Young Middle-Class Families	7,547,408	8.4
G23	Settled Families	3,083,219	3.4
G24	Start-up Families	4,464,189	5.0

part of a corporate identity program, the marketing division of Donnelley became known as Donnelley Marketing Information Services, one of the five companies in the parent corporation's Marketing Services Group.[4]

Besides maintaining its National List Service, Donnelley has a Field Marketing Services Group that performs person-to-person product sampling and couponing in high traffic areas. The company is also known for its consumer direct marketing and sales promotion programs, including the Carol Wright cooperative mailing program, which delivers cents-off coupons and product samples

TABLE 13.2. *(Continued)*

ACORN Segment	Description	1987 households (hundreds)	Percent
	Blue-Collar		
H Group	Families in Small Towns	10,197,072	11.3
H25	Family Sports and Leisure Lovers	1,871,137	2.1
H26	Secure Factory and Farm Workers	1,844,301	2.1
H27	Family Centered Blue-Collar	2,864,162	3.2
H28	Minimum Wage White Families	3,617,472	4.0
	Mature Adults		
I Group	in Stable Neighborhoods	19,278,939	21.4
I29	Golden Years Retirees	2,212,030	2.5
I30	Adults in Pre-War Housing	4,625,729	5.1
I31	Small-Town Families	5,616,421	6.2
I32	Nostalgic Retirees and Adults	915,838	1.0
I33	Home-Oriented Senior Citizens	1,808,360	2.0
I34	Old Families in Pre-War Homes	4,100,561	4.6
	Seasonal and		
J Group	Mobile Home Communities	1,891,753	2.1
J35	Resort Vacationers and Locals	755,265	0.8
J36	Mobile Home Dwellers	1,136,488	1.3
	Agriculturally		
K Group	Oriented Communities	854,733	1.0
K37	Farm Families	574,487	0.6
K38	Young, Active Country Families	280,246	0.3
	Older, Depressed		
L Group	Rural Towns	5,754,606	6.4
L39	Low-Income Retirees and Youth	2,838,200	3.2
L40	Rural Displaced Workers	79,508	0.1
L41	Factory Worker Families	2,438,956	2.7
L42	Poor Young Families	397,942	0.4
M Group	Special Population	530,618	0.6
M43	Military Base Families	456,357	0.5
M44	Institutions: Residents and Staff	74,261	0.1
	U.S. Total	89,933,696	100.0

to more than 30 million "heavy user" households; the Carol Wright Hispanic coupon and sampling program, which reaches 2.2 million Hispanic families; and the New Age cooperative coupon and sampling program, which reaches 12.2 million "50-and-over" households.

ClusterPLUS

ClusterPLUS was originally created in 1982 by an extensive analysis of 1980 census data. Donnelley analysts isolated 64 key census variables via their version of the factor analysis stage in the creation of a geodemographic system. Cluster analysis was then applied to produce the 47-cluster scheme known as ClusterPLUS.

In 1986 and in each year since, Donnelley has evaluated the Cluster-PLUS typologies against current year data using its DQI^2 index.[5] DQI^2 contains about 200 demographic and behavioral variables on 78 million households; it is in effect a miniature U.S. census and can track changes in ethnic composition, areas of new development, and changes in household affluence. With DQI^2 Donnelley keeps track of how neighborhoods are changing by evaluating data for individual households within the CBGs that make up a cluster type. If the two are significantly different, then the CBG is reassigned to its appropriate segment. The complete list of ClusterPLUS segments is shown in Table 13.3.

TABLE 13.3. The ClusterPLUS Market Groups and Segments

ClusterPlus Segment	Description	Percent of U.S. Population	Percent of U.S. Households
Group 1	Highly Educated, High-Income, Suburban Professionals	10.3%	8.5%
S01	Established Wealthy	1.5	1.3
S02	Mobile Wealthy with Children	2.2	1.1
S03	Young Affluents with Children	2.2	2.1
S04	Suburban Families with Teens	1.7	1.5
S05	Established Affluents	2.7	2.5
Group 2	Urban, Mobile, Professionals above Average Income	5.5%	6.2%
S07	Affluent Urban Singles	2.9	3.3
S10	Young Professionals	1.4	1.5
S14	Urban Retirees and Professionals	1.2	1.4
Group 3	Above Average Income, Homeowners, White-Collar Families	10.2%	9.4%
S09	Nonurban Working Couples with Children	4.2	4.0
S11	Small-Town Families	2.9	2.6
S16	Urban Working Families	3.1	2.8
Group 4	Above Average Income, Older White-Collar Workers	6.7%	6.6%
S08	Older Mobile Well-Educated	2.0	2.0
S13	Older Small-Town Households	2.1	2.0
S15	Older Nonmobile Urban Households	2.6	2.6
Group 5	Younger, Highly Mobile, Above Average Income	10.4%	10.1%
S06	Highly Mobile Young Families	3.1	3.0
S12	Highly Mobile Working Couples	3.8	3.8
S18	Working Couples with Children	1.4	1.3
S19	Young Ex-Urban Families	2.1	2.0

TABLE 13.3. *(Continued)*

ClusterPlus Segment	Description	Percent of U.S. Population	Percent of U.S. Households
Group 6	Younger, Mobile, Below Average Income, Fewer Children	10.5%	11.2%
S17	Young Urban Educated Singles	2.2	2.6
S20	Group Quarters	1.3	0.7
S24	Young Urban Ethnics	2.6	3.1
S25	Young Mobile Apartment Dwellers	2.6	2.8
S35	Small-Town Apartment Dwellers	1.8	2.0
Group 7	Average Income, Blue-Collar Families, Primarily Rural	14.7%	14.3%
S21	Rural Families with Children	3.9	3.8
S23	Low Mobility Rural Families	1.8	1.7
S27	Average Income Families in Single Units	2.0	2.0
S28	Mobile Less-Educated Families	3.7	3.6
S36	Middle Income Hispanics	1.7	1.6
S37	Average Income Blue-Collar Families	1.6	1.6
Group 8	Below Average Income, Older, Few Children	13.2%	13.7%
S22	Older Below Average Income Homeowners	1.6	1.7
S26	Old Rural Retirees	2.1	2.2
S29	Older Urban Ethnics	2.2	2.2
S31	Older Low Income Couples	1.8	1.9
S32	Lower Income Single Retirees	1.3	1.4
S33	Stable Blue-Collar Workers	1.9	1.9
S39	Low Income Blue-Collar Workers	2.3	2.4
Group 9	Less Educated, Low Income Rural, Blue-Collar Workers	11.1%	10.9%
S30	Low Income Farmers	2.0	2.0
S34	Rural Blue-Collar Workers	1.3	1.3
S41	Rural Manufacturing Workers	2.2	2.1
S42	Southern Low Income Workers	2.9	2.9
S43	Low Income Black Families	2.7	2.6
Group 10	Very Low Income, Urban Blacks, Apartment Dwellers	8.5%	9.1%
S38	Lowest Income Urban Retirees	1.2	1.5
S40	Lowest Income Retirees—Old Homes	1.1	1.2
S44	Center City Blacks	1.6	1.8
S45	Lowest Income Urban Blacks	1.3	1.4
S46	Lowest Income Hispanics	2.0	2.0
S47	Lowest Income Black Female-Headed Families	1.3	1.2

CLARITAS: THE PRIZM SYSTEM
Company Background

In 1974 Jonathan Robbin, a computer scientist turned entrepreneur, introduced the first generation of PRIZM (Potential Rating Index for Zip Markets) using 1970 census data. Based in Alexandria, Virginia, Robbin's company Claritas (Latin for "clarity") had been launched earlier in 1971.[6] Before settling on a 40-cluster solution, Claritas analysts tested more than three dozen models, some with as many as 100 clusters. However, the 40-cluster version was an excellent compromise between manageability and discriminating power. In discussions with Michael Weiss, author of *The Clustering of America*, Robbins explains that "There's a greater latitude for error when the cookie cutter is so small and the number of unclassifiable types becomes quite large. With more clusters you could pinpoint a monastery or a prison, but that's hardly meaningful in a marketing sense."[7]

When the cluster system was launched in 1974[8] magazines such as *Time*, *Newsweek*, and *McCall's* were among the first clients, sorting their subscription lists by cluster to publish upscale editions featuring ads promoting luxury cars and furs to residents of Blue Blood Estates and Money and Brains. As Weiss notes, "We leave a lengthy paper trail on how we behave, through subscription lists, mail orders, and warranty cards—records that can be converted into clustered addresses. In the neighborhoods where people read *The New Republic*, for instance, they tend to eat croissants rather than white bread."[9]

In addition to PRIZM, the company now offers Affluent Markets (a system for reaching very high income households), Name Scoring Models (a PRIZM-based multivariate procedure for selecting the most responsive names from a mailing list), REZIDE (an encyclopedia of ZIP code demographics), and QBase (a database of the most useful demographic data items geocoded by block group, census tract, market, and other census units).[10]

PRIZM

The PRIZM lifestyle segmentation system is the key to the successful integration of these and other Claritas products. PRIZM consists of 40 clusters divided into 12 supergroups as shown in Table 13.4. The names of many PRIZM clusters—

TABLE 13.4. The PRIZM Market Groups and Segments

PRIZM Segment	Description	Percent of U.S. Population	Percent of U.S. Households
Group S1			
S28	Blue Blood Estates	0.62	0.66
S08	Money and Brains	1.11	1.00
S05	Furs and Station Wagons	2.23	2.47
Group S2			
S07	Pools and Patios	3.33	3.18
S25	Two More Rungs	1.06	0.94
S20	Young Influentials	2.95	2.61

TABLE 13.4. *(Continued)*

PRIZM Segment	Description	Percent of U.S. Population	Percent of U.S. Households
Group S3			
S24	Young Suburbia	5.30	5.80
S30	Blue-Chip Blues	5.17	5.68
Group U1			
U21	Urban Gold Coast	0.47	0.28
U37	Bohemian Mix	0.83	0.60
U31	Black Enterprise	1.30	1.37
U23	New Beginners	4.80	4.29
Group T1			
T01	God's Country	2.71	2.81
T17	New Homesteaders	4.77	4.93
T12	Towns and Gowns	2.16	2.29
Group S4			
S27	Levittown, USA	4.65	4.53
S39	Gray Power	2.02	1.60
S02	Rank and File	1.15	1.11
Group T2			
T40	Blue-Collar Nursery	1.67	1.86
T16	Middle America	4.92	4.94
T29	Coalburg and Corntown	2.61	2.66
Group U2			
U03	New Melting Pot	1.37	1.16
U36	Old Yankee Rows	1.92	1.82
U14	Emergent Minorities	2.21	2.29
U26	Single City Blues	2.20	1.95
Group R1			
R19	Shotguns and Pickups	2.53	2.69
R34	Agri-Business	4.12	4.17
R35	Grain Belt	1.48	1.52
Group T3			
T33	Golden Ponds	2.96	2.81
T22	Mines and Mills	1.87	1.90
T13	Norma Rae-Ville	2.99	3.21
T18	Old Brick Factories	2.00	1.87
Group R2			
R10	Back-Country Folks	4.24	4.34
R38	Sharecroppers	3.66	3.83
R15	Tobacco Roads	1.01	1.12
R06	Hard Scrabble	1.03	1.11
Group U3			
U04	Heavy Industry	2.09	2.00
U11	Downtown Dixie-Style	2.41	2.39
U09	Hispanic Mix	1.60	1.70
U32	Public Assistance	2.48	2.51

Blue Blood Estates, Shotguns and Pickups, Tobacco Roads—are instantly recognized by frequent users of geodemography. Robbins and his associates deserve credit for starting the tradition of using vividly descriptive, colorful segment labels to animate system applications of geodemography.

NATIONAL DECISION SYSTEMS: THE MICROVISION SYSTEM

Company Background[11]

National Decision Systems was formed in 1979 by H. Michael Stansbury and Thomas Gay as a spinoff of MIS, Inc., a San Diego–based marketing research company founded by Stansbury in 1971. Before its purchase by Equifax in July 1988, NDS was one of America's fastest growing privately held corporations. In 1986 and again in 1987, the company was recognized by *INC.* magazine as a member of their 500 fastest growing companies, with sales of $18 million just prior to signing the Equifax agreement. As part of Equifax's Marketing Services Division, NDS employs approximately 250 people and includes McDonalds, Sears, Citicorp, and Aetna among its clients.

In addition to MicroVision, NDS offers a variety of other products, including INFOMARK, a fully integrated desktop decision support system that allows users to produce site-specific and market-area maps in-house; FutureVISION, an advanced geodemographic segmentation tool that tracks "feeder and depositor" clusters to each cluster in the MicroVision system; TeleVISION Targeting System, a tool for purchasing spot TV based on MicroVision; and Equis, a direct response segmentation and targeting system based on individual specific information rather than on census or household level data.

MicroVision

MicroVision is National Decision System's entry in the geodemographic systems category. MicroVision combines 112 census variables with proprietary data on individuals aggregated to the ZIP+4 level. (Aggregation protects each individual's right to privacy.) The proprietary data (30 variables) focuses primarily on financial characteristics such as an individual's average installment credit, minimum bank balance, and aggregated debt burden.

Using ZIP+4 geography permits NDS to dynamically update all major facets of the MicroVision system. Specifically, ZIP+4s are first clustered to a 95-subcluster solution. Then the 95 subclusters are aggregated one more level to form MicroVision 50. Changes at the ZIP+4 level are logically transferred up through this nested scheme by regularly updating the (values of) variables in the cluster algorithm, altering (if need be) the defining variables in the cluster structure, and updating consumption detail at the household level (which in turn updates these levels for the ZIP+4 neighborhood). Thus, NDS updates all cluster variables at the ZIP+4 level without changing the (normalized) cluster definitions. ZIP+4s are simply reassigned based on their revised levels on cluster-defining factors. The result is that marketers do not have to relearn a new system or experience any disruption in the way they apply MicroVision segmentation. Forty-eight active and two residual segments were identified in this way as shown in Table 13.5.

TABLE 13.5. The MicroVision Market Groups and Segments

Segment No.	Segment Name	Group No.	Percent of U.S. Households
1	Upper Crust	01	0.93
2	Lap of Luxury	01	1.85
3	Established Wealth	01	2.68
4	Mid-Life Success	01	0.67
5	Prosperous Ethnic Mix	01	2.75
6	Good Family Life	01	1.53
7	Comfortable Times	01	0.85
8	Movers and Shakers	04	2.41
9	Building a Home Life	03	0.54
10	Home Sweet Home	02	5.41
11	Family Ties	02	4.40
12	A Good Step Forward	04	2.15
13	Successful Singles	09	0.66
14	Middle Years	01	0.12
15	Great Beginnings	04	3.68
16	Country Home Families	02	5.34
17	Stars and Stripes	02	1.83
18	White Picket Fence	02	5.91
19	Young and Carefree	03	0.53
20	Social Security	06	2.02
21	Sunset Years	06	0.61
22	Aging America	02	2.92
23	Settled In	02	4.95
24	Metro Minority Families	08	1.85
25	Bedrock America	03	2.98
26	Mature Years	07	1.64
27	Middle of the Road	05	0.47
28	Building a Family	03	1.55
29	Establishing Roots	05	0.47
30	Retirement Age	06	0.98
31	Golden Times	06	0.79
32	Metro Singles	04	2.48
33	Living Off The Land	07	2.58
34	Books and New Recruits	04	0.91
35	Late-Life Laborers	02	4.56
36	Metro Ethnic Mix	09	1.60
37	Moving Ahead Minorities	09	0.61
38	Back Country	02	5.79
39	On Their Own	04	3.54
40	Trying Metro Times	04	3.04
41	South Of The Border	08	0.78

(continued)

TABLE 13.5. *(Continued)*

Segment No.	Segment Name	Group No.	Percent of U.S. Households
42	Hanging On	08	2.17
43	Low-Income Blues	08	0.31
44	Hard Years	08	0.41
45	Struggling Minority Mix	09	1.30
46	Difficult Times	08	2.56
47	University USA	09	0.71
48	Inner City Singles	09	0.92
49	Anomalies	10	0.13
50	Unclassified	11	0.13
			100.00

Source: MicroVision: *Marketing Guide Descriptions and Analytical Tables,* Equifax: *National Decision Systems,* Equifax Marketing Decision Systems (EMDS), pp. 7–8.

STANDARD GEODEMOGRAPHIC PRODUCT LINES

Each GD firm provides many products and services beyond sorting a client's customer list into a geodemographic system.[12] Four standard products round out each firm's product line:

1. Hierarchical groupings of the segments into "supergroups"
2. Buying power or market penetration indices
3. Full color maps that illustrate where members of a particular segment reside
4. Other graphical products that describe a client's target market segments

These standard products are discussed briefly in this section.[13]

Supergroups

Most clustering algorithms link clusters in a hierarchical tree. An analyst examines this tree to determine at what point to "cut it;" that is, to determine how many clusters to retain. These trees naturally index the similarities among the 40 to 50 segments in a GD system and are used to create clusters of clusters, or *supergroups*. Supergroups simplify discussions with clients and facilitate particular applications.

For example, in the ACORN system, the supergroup called Group A consists of the segments labeled Old Money, Conspicuous Consumers, and Cosmopolitan Wealth. Although these are three separate segments in the ACORN system, households in these clusters share important characteristics, as outlined in a company brochure: "ACORN Group A neighborhoods are the most affluent in the U.S. The three market segments in Group A include professionals, business managers, and older families. Group A households are characterized by very high incomes and home values and high levels of educational achievement."[14]

In all, ACORN has identified 13 supergroups. The creators of ClusterPLUS, PRIZM, and MicroVision also identify supergroups for their systems. For example, there are 10 "Enhanced Cluster Descriptions" in ClusterPLUS, as shown in Table 13.3. In PRIZM 12 supergroups have been identified, as shown in Table 13.4 and in MicroVision 11 supergroups have been formed, as shown in Table 13.5.

Supergroups allow marketing strategists to focus very quickly on key segments and their associated media habits, shopping styles, and shopping baskets. For example, ACORN's Group A members tend to share high demand for imported wine, imported beer, and yogurt. Their tastes are in sharp contrast to members of Group H, Blue Collar Families in Small Towns, who exhibit low demand for all three of these product lines.

Buying Power, Market Penetration, and Affluence Indices

Various indices provided by each supplier measure the buying power or affluence of each geodemographic segment, a product's penetration into a segment, or other facets of the segment's behavior. For example, PRIZM's Zip Quality (ZQ) Index is "a weighted composite of education and affluence variables that permits clusters to be ranked and grouped according to recognized socio-economic levels."[15] PRIZM's ZQ index is standardized so that the grand average across all segments is 50, as shown in Table 13.6 for three PRIZM supergroups. In the exhibit, members of Blue Blood estates score 92 (42 points above the national average), while members of the segment called Hard Scrabble are far below average and relatively poor, as their score of 34 indicates. Standardization is common practice among the four GD suppliers because it permits report users to easily recognize deviations from the mean.

Other indices are baselined to a client's product. For example, in the MicroVision system a client's total customer base or a sample of this base is first classified into the 48 MicroVision segments. MicroVision then produces a Customer File Report that contains a variety of fields, including an index that measures the likelihood that a household in a certain MicroVision segment would be a customer of this client.

Table 13.7 demonstrates this for several MicroVision segments, including Movers and Shakers. *Base* is the universe from which a client's customers are drawn. There are 192,329 Movers and Shakers (MS) households in this client's base area, and 13,125 are customers of this client. The penetration rate is $(13,125 \div 192.329) = 68.2$ per 1,000. MS households account for 9.6 percent of this firm's customer list but only 3.1 percent of the households in the base area. Therefore, MS households are 3.09 $(9.6 \div 3.1)$ times more likely to be this client's customer than is the average household in the base area.

TABLE 13.6.   Zip Quality Scores in Three PRIZM Supergroups

		Percent of U.S. Households	Percent of U.S. Population	ZQ Score
S1	Educated, Affluent Executives and Professionals in Elite Metro Suburbs	4.13%	3.96%	78
28	Blue Blood Estates	.66	.62	92
8	Money and Brains	1.00	1.11	77
5	Furs and Station Wagons	2.47	2.23	74
S4	Middle-Class, Post-Child Families in Aging Suburbs and Retirement Areas	7.24%	7.82%	53
27	Levittown, USA	4.53	4.65	54
39	Gray Power	1.60	2.02	53
2	Rank and File	1.11	1.15	49
R2	Mixed Whites, Blacks, Spanish, and Indians in Poor Rural Towns and Farms	10.40%	9.94%	39
10	Back-Country Folks	4.34	4.24	42
38	Sharecroppers	3.83	3.66	39
15	Tobacco Roads	1.12	1.01	36
6	Hard Scrabble	1.11	1.03	34

TABLE 13.7.   MicroVision: Movers and Shakers

Group Number	Segment	Customers Number	Customers Percent	Base households Number	Base households Percent	Penetration per thousand	Index
SU1	Upper Crust	11,347	8.3	161,306	2.6	70.3	319
SU2	Lap of Luxury	2,871	2.1	43,429	0.7	66.1	300
SU3	Established Wealth	22,011	16.1	1,197,400	19.3	18.4	83
UU4	White Picket Fence	5,742	4.2	378,453	6.1	15.2	69
UU5	Movers and Shakers	13,125	9.6	192,329	3.1	68.2	309

Source: National Decision Systems

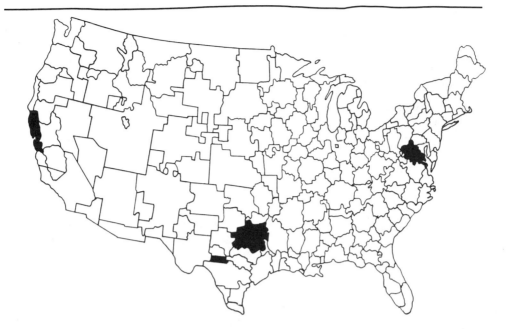

Key Demographic Indicators

Occupations	% Composition U.S.	Cluster	Index	Age Distribution	% Composition U.S.	Cluster	Index
Professional/Managerial	22.7	46.5	205	Under 18 Years	28.1	21.3	76
All Other White-Collar	30.3	34.6	114	18 - 34 Years	29.6	27.0	91
Blue-Collar	31.2	9.9	32	35 -54 Years	21.4	25.9	121
Service	12.9	8.3	64	55 - 64 Years	9.6	12.1	126
Farming/Forestry/Fishing	2.9	0.7	23	65+ Years	11.3	13.7	121
Household Income	13.2	5.6	42	Household Size	22.7	27.0	119
Less than $5,000	31.2	18.1	58	One Person	31.3	35.2	112
$5,000 - $14,999	26.6	19.9	75	Two Persons	32.8	28.9	88
$15,000 - $24,999	15.7	16.8	107	Three or Four Persons	13.2	8.9	67
$25,000 - $34,999	8.7	16.8	194	Five or More Persons			
$35,000 - $49,999	4.6	22.8	497				
$50,000+							

Base Population Counts - 1980 Census

Educational Levels	33.5	10.2	30		Count	% of U.S.
Some High School or Less	34.6	22.3	65	Households	888,040	1.1
4 Years High School	15.7	21.9	140	Population	2,273,041	1.0
1 - 3 Years College	16.2	45.6	281	Adults	1,789,153	1.1
4+ Years College				Adult Males	829,698	1.1
				Adult Females	959,455	1.1
				Median Household Income	$28,462	n/a
				Median Home Value	$94,543	n/a

FIGURE 13.1. Money & Brains: Heaviest Concentration by TV Market Areas

Source: Claritas Corporation.

Full-Color Maps

Geodemographic systems use maps to describe where members of various segments live and to facilitate a variety of applications in trade area analysis. For
example, Figure 13.1 is a simplified version of the map for PRIZM's Money and
Brains segment. (The map uses Arbitron's TV/radio markets (ADIs) as the geographic observation unit.)[16] The map shows that the heaviest concentrations of

Money and Brains households are in the San Francisco Bay area, in Dallas–Fort Worth, and in and around Washington, D.C. Maps like this provide an easily grasped overview of the geographic dispersion of households in a particular segment and facilitate client understanding of media selection, new product introduction, and physical distribution. For example, advertising for any product that appeals primarily to Blue Blood Estate households, such as a luxury car or expensive stereo equipment, should be concentrated in the ADIs shown in Figure 13.1.

Site-location software is also available to analyze geographic areas as well as to describe them. For example, National Decision System's Map Generating programs present full-color maps keyed from a client's choice of geographic unit. Its Shopping Center Analysis Package shows all shopping centers and major U.S. highways in a selected area, household trends in that area, market potential statistics, and shopping center profiles. These maps, illustrated in Chapter 15, are available by ZIP code, census tract, county, state, ADI, DMA, MSA, or other geographic units.[17]

TARGETING AND DISCRIMINATORY POWER OF GEODEMOGRAPHIC SYSTEMS

Given the common statistical basis for GD systems, a pertinent question is whether one system is demonstrably superior to the others. This section shows how to (partially) address this question using two basic statistical tools: the Gains chart and discriminatory chi-square analysis. These tools are subsequently used in Chapter 16 as yardsticks to assess four systems available in Great Britain. Although no U.S. comparisons are yet available, gains charts and chi-square tests are useful tools that should be part of the arsenal of any would-be user of geodemography.[18]

Gains Charts or Lorenz Curves

A Gains chart or Lorenz curve is the percentage of total sales accounted for by those 100p% (e.g., percentiles) of GD segments with the highest levels of per-member sales. Although this is a technical definition, its meaning is clarified by examining Figure 13.2. The first step is to select a specific target group, such as "owners of VCRs." Next, the analyst ranks the GD segments from highest to lowest by their percentage of VCR owners. Finally, the analyst plots the proportion of the general population—with and without a GD system—needed to reach a certain proportion of the target.

For example, the top three GD segments might account for 10 percent of the base population but 60 percent of VCR sales. (The plots shown in Figure 13.2 use cumulative percent of the base population as the x-axis and cumulative percent VCR owners as the y-axis.) An ineffective system offers no gain over a random selection of population members. Put another way, selecting members of the population at random produces a nominal baseline against which a particular GD system can be compared, as shown in Figure 13.2a. Figure 13.2b shows that

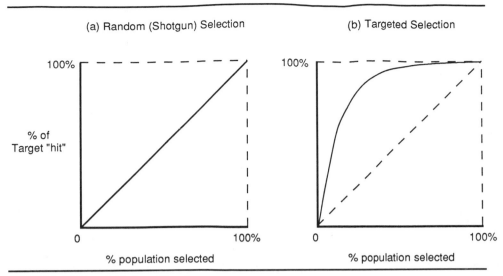

FIGURE 13.2. A Gains Chart

an effective system will reach target members at a rate exceeding the nominal baseline. The gain lines of different systems can be compared to index each system's effectiveness for reaching a common target.

Discriminatory Chi-Square

A second method for comparing systems or for benchmarking a single system against chance is to use a chi-square test. The reasoning is as follows: Suppose we want to determine if a GD system will help identify VCR owners. The system will be helpful if and only if the proportion of VCR owners varies widely across the segments in the system. In other words, if VCR ownership is very high among certain GD segments but low among others, then a geodemographic analysis can identify the high potential segments. Conversely, if VCR ownership is proportionately the same across all segments in a GD system, then the system offers no marginal improvement over a "shotgun" system that targets households at random.

For example, System A, shown in Table 13.8 has three segments—a1, a2, and a3. In this simplified case, 20 percent of the population (a set of 200 households) is in segment a1, 30 percent in a2, and 50 percent in a3. Exactly 220 people, or 22 percent the population, own a VCR. System A is nondiscriminating because 22 percent of the households in each segment also own VCRs. The resulting potential indices are perfectly flat, each equalling the population benchmark of 100. Thus, knowing that a household is in segment a1, for example, provides no additional information about that household's VCR ownership.[19]

The chi-square test can be used to determine whether a GD system offers improved discrimination over a baseline system. Higher values of chi-square

TABLE 13.8. A Nondiscriminating vs. a Discriminating GD System

| Segment | Proportion of Population | | Owners of VCRs | | Index |
	Number	Percent	Number	Percent	
System A: A Nondiscriminating GD System					
a1	200	20%	44	22%	100
a2	300	30%	66	22%	100
a3	500	50%	110	22%	100
Population	1000	100%	220	22%	100
System B: A Discriminating GD System					
b1	200	20%	5	2.5%	11
b2	300	30%	200	66.7%	305
b3	500	50%	15	3.0%	14
Population	1000	100%	220	22%	100

Note: χ^2 = 388.7 $(p \leq .001 \quad df = 2)$

imply more discrimination. The computational formula is shown below:

$$\chi^2 = \sum \left[\frac{(S_i - E_i)}{E_i} \right]^2$$

where

S_i = the number of households exhibiting the target behavior in segment i

E_i = the expected number of households in segment i (based on the national average) exhibiting the target behavior

$\sum$ = a summation taken over all segments

The chi-square statistic sums (normalized) deviations of observed versus expected behavior. Large χ^2 values indicate that the various segments in a given GD system exhibit unique behavior patterns and that the system is a useful targeting tool for the particular product or service under study. For example, System B, shown in Table 13.8, is highly discriminating. Its chi-square value is 388.7, compared to the value of 0 for System A.

Two other points about the chi-square technique: First, absolute levels of chi-square are meaningful even though population size, the number of segments, and the targeted behavior are specific to a particular context.[20] This is because chi-square levels can be compared to tabled values that account for different contexts; that is, the value 388.7 has a probability of less than 1/1000 of occurring by chance.

Though the absolute level of chi-square can be meaningfully compared to a nominal chance level in a given context, the generalization stops there. A comparison of two systems in one context cannot be generalized to any other context. For example, in the hypothetical VCR targeting problem, System B performs best, but the outcome might be different if we target "toilet tissue users" or "regular users of Crest toothpaste." In either case, a given system might not discriminate well because the particular behavior is common throughout the general population. These caveats explain why neither Gains charts nor chi-square tests can be used as a basis for generalized statements about the value of various systems. One system might perform best for a specific target group but not for others.[21]

Summary

Gains charts and chi-square tests are two useful but context-specific ways of comparing GD systems. Gains charts provide a visual summary of system performance as more and more "marginal" segments are employed. They help answer questions about the appropriate "depth" or "stopping point" for catalog mailings, media insertions, or other types of direct client contact because they indicate the point at which a system ceases to be effective. Chi-square tests quantify a system's ability to beat chance. They can also be used to compare the discriminatory power of competing systems for a specific application. Neither tool determines that one system is generally better than another.

CONCLUSION

The four major U.S. geodemographic systems—ACORN, ClusterPLUS, PRIZM, and MicroVision—are each based on census data analyzed via the "factor then cluster" model described in Chapter 12. This chapter reviews operational differences among these systems. The differences arise because development experts base their decisions on a unique selection of census variables possibly combined with proprietary data, a unique application of statistical methods, and varying criteria for factor and cluster retention. Despite these differences, the bare bones statistical systems that underpin each service are similar. More important variations are found in client services and in product delivery techniques.

Three principal types of client services were discussed in this chapter: supergroups, indices, and maps. These features were exemplified using information supplied by all four companies. The supergroups for each system were listed, and excerpts from ACORN and PRIZM brochures were used to describe the characteristics of certain supergroups. Examples of indices and maps from all four systems provided an enhanced understanding of these concepts.

Two techniques for comparing systems either to one another or to an absolute standard are the Gains chart and the discriminatory chi-square test. The chapter reviewed each method and illustrated how each is applied in theory.

Chapter 14 will examine a variety of marketing applications of geodemography and discuss additional features of each system. The most important of these, linkages to other marketing research databases, creates the real power of geodemography: an ability to locate, profile, and assess each segment in a particular system.

Notes

1. Background material for this section abstracted from brochures and fact sheets provide by CACI–Market Analysis Division: the Advanced Marketing Systems Group, Fairfax, VA.

2. See Chapter 16 for more detail about European geodemographic systems.

3. The information for this section is abstracted from "Donnelley Marketing History," a technical paper provided by Donnelley Marketing Information Services, a company of the Dun and Bradstreet Corporation.

4. The name Reuben R. Donnelley has since been appropriated by a separate Dun and Bradstreet company specializing in the sale and production of telephone directories and Yellow Pages advertising.

5. DQI stands for Direct Quality Index. DQI is a list selection tool first developed using 1960 census data. It was revised and renamed DQI^2 following the 1980 census.

6. Claritas is an independent firm but with a partnership interest now held by VNU, a $500 million Dutch communications firm. VNU provides financial backing for major new ventures. See *Claritas: Corporate Overview* (December 1985).

7. See Michael J. Weiss, *The Clustering of America*, New York: Harper & Row, 1988, p. 12.

8. The complete PRIZM service was officially launched in 1978. It includes links to media, product, and opinion surveys in addition to the cluster system. These links are discussed in Chapter 14.

9. Weiss, op. cit., p. 14.

10. Many of the functions performed by these mainframe products are now integrated in Claritas's desktop system called COMPASS. Chapter 15 is devoted exclusively to desktop systems. It reviews their properties and illustrates applications.

11. Material in this section was compiled from the "Corporate Fact Sheet" (Spring 1989) and other reference material provided by National Decision Systems, Encinitas, CA.

12. The process of sorting a list of names and addresses into a GD system is called *geocoding*. Geocoding is, in fact, a relatively minor aspect of the total product/service package offered by a GD firm; many smaller, specialist firms also perform geocoding.

13. The examples cited in this section are chosen so that each company receives approximately equal treatment. For any specific product offered by one firm, the other companies usually have a very similar product. Space limitations preclude a complete inventory of products offered by all four firms.

14. CACI, *The ACORN Market Segmentation System: User's Guide*, 1988.

15. See the PRIZM brochure entitled *The Marketer's Handbook: Book 1*, Claritas Corporation, 1984, p. 10.

16. Ibid., pp. 20–21. There are approximately 220 ADIs nationwide.

17. *MicroVision: Marketing Guide,* Encinitas, CA: National Decision Systems, 1985, p. 5. DMA: (Nielsen) Designated Market Area; MSA (Census Bureau) Metropolitan Statistical Area.

18. A truly comprehensive comparison of any two systems could be carried out. The details for such an experiment are discussed in a paper available from the author. Such a comparison would be costly and, to the author's knowledge, no such program of research has been or is being conducted.

19. More formally, the marginal probability of VCR ownership (in the general population) and the conditional probabilities of VCR ownership (by GD segment) are identical; that is, PROB (VCR) = PROB (VCR|aj),   [j = 1,2,3].

20. Context refers to the unique combination of {product $\oplus$ geographic market $\oplus$ GD system} that obtains in a particular application.

21. As Clive Humby remarks, "An overwhelming conclusion, based on analysis of over 100 product fields in this way is that there is no best system, indeed, the choice of system is in many ways academic. By their very nature the various neighborhood classifications can be seen as generic and each offer similar power." Clive R. Humby, "New Developments in Demographic Targeting—the Implications of 1991," *The Journal of The Market Research Society* 31 (January 1989), p. 52–73.

14 THE POWER OF GEODEMOGRAPHIC SYSTEMS

INTRODUCTION

Chapter 13 touched on the ability of geodemography to link diverse databases, an idea central to understanding the power of geodemography and one that will be developed in this chapter. The first section is a detailed follow-up to the example on list qualification outlined in Chapter 12. List qualification, an especially important activity for direct marketers, has now become part of the overall marketing strategy for most consumer products and services. The example shows how to qualify a particular list and how to support the resulting mail campaign with an efficient package of supplementary media.

The second section uses additional examples to illustrate the range of geodemographic applications for both products and services. Three particular examples are emphasized: product repositioning, catalog distribution, and site location. The data in each case are real, although proprietary details are excluded at the request of study sponsors.

The third section more fully describes the commercial databases that are linked by existing geodemographic systems. To aid intuition, 40 databases are classified into four categories. Databases containing UPC scanner data, media use data, and credit use data are classified as consumer behavior databases. Those in the cognitive category include VALs (values and lifestyles), the National Family Opinion poll, and the Gallup poll. Political databases linked by geodemography contain data on congressional districts, school districts, and townships. A fourth location-related category stores information about specialized observational units such as retail store trade areas, radio station signal "footprints," and magazine regional editions. The chapter describes in detail three databases—National Family Opinion, Simmons, and VALS—that are linked to all four of these major classes.

The chapter concludes by outlining some weaknesses of GD systems and indicating where improvements can be expected. Most current systems do not distinguish between individual, household, and neighborhood targets. Current systems cluster neighborhoods, thereby obtaining the advantage of using geography as the fundamental unit of analysis. However, disadvantages arise when data on consumer behavior are pooled over individuals and households in the same neighborhood. Supplemental analyses—some available with existing systems, others under development—can extract valuable information from individual-level data to better manage household-to-household variability within neighborhoods. We turn now to a more disciplined study of the building blocks of list qualification.

LIST QUALIFICATION

Figure 14.1 is a detailed follow-up to the list qualification example given at the end of Chapter 12. Using list qualification, direct marketers can assess a mailing list's overall value (i.e., the likely response from list members) and can select the particular ZIP codes to which to mail. In the lower right corner of Figure 14.1 is a new list: It could be a list of subscribers to *Cash Flow* magazine, a list of Visa Gold Card holders, or a list of individuals who recently flew Delta airlines to Europe. Intuition may suggest that the list contains valuable prospects, but their actual response characteristics are unknown. The direct marketer wants to quantify the value of the list, since buying names from such lists is costly and literally thousands of lists are available for purchase.[1]

Three other parts of Figure 14.1 must be explained before they can be integrated to solve the direct marketer's problem. (Each part of Figure 14.1 is also called a table to suggest that it could be printed out in a "flatfile" form as a single but rather lengthy table of data.) The center part, labeled Table b, consists of the master list of U.S. census block groups and the ZIP codes associated with each one. Each CBG comprises a particular set of ZIP codes, as the notation suggests. Once it is sorted into a geodemographic system, the central table provides the logical connection between the left and right parts of the figure.

The section of Figure 14.1 labeled Table a shows the geodemographic clusters (labeled A,B,C,...X) that compose the geodemographic system selected by the direct marketer. The section of Figure 14.1 labeled Table c shows the direct marketer's house list containing (possibly millions of) names and purchasing levels for its customers. Each customer's ZIP code facilitates the link to the GD system; that is, [ZIP code→CBG→GD cluster]. Various response levels are indicated by the number of plus signs in the response column. For example, individuals one and two are high responders, individual three has not responded in the last year, and individual four is a modest responder.

The census block group and ZIP code composition of each GD segment is also shown on the far left in Table a. This is a nested scheme; ZIP codes are (partially) nested within CBGs, which are nested within the GD segments. For example, segment A consists of a particular collection of CBGs that are

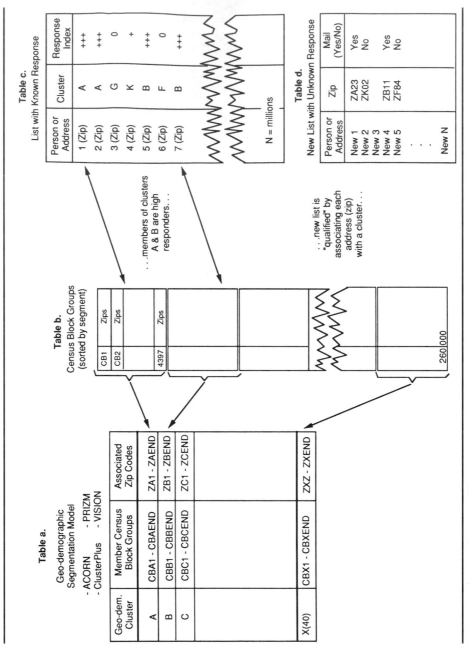

FIGURE 14.1. List Qualification

250

labeled CBA1 through CBAEND to denote both their association with segment A and the fact that, although there are thousands of such CBGs, the list ends somewhere. The ZIP codes associated with the CBGs in cluster A are labeled ZA1–ZAEND. Parallel notation is used for clusters B, C, and so on to the last GD cluster.[2]

Solution

These ingredients make a solution to the list qualification problem possible. First, the marketer uses the ZIP codes on the "known response" list to place each individual in his or her correct cluster, simply by using Table a to find where a given ZIP code from Table c fits in the segmentation scheme. In other words, the GD system acts as a mechanism to re-sort the entries in Table c. Results reveal which clusters contain disproportionate numbers of high responders. The example shows that households in segments A and B respond very positively. Members of clusters A and B become the target for this direct marketer. Households in other A and B neighborhoods are likely to be positively predisposed toward the marketer's product because these households share so many characteristics with the high responders.

The list under consideration (Table d) can now be searched to determine what proportion of it consists of members of the target segments. Lists with high incidences of A and B types will be good values, while lists with few of these types should be rejected. If the new list is accepted, the mailing can be further refined by selecting from it only those ZIP codes representing A and B neighborhoods. A critical point: the ZIP codes selected from Table d are not the same ZIP codes identified as having a high response rate in Table c. Both the target ZIP codes from Table d and the high response ZIP codes in Table c belong to the same geodemographic cluster within the segmentation model.

Supporting Media

The geodemographic system also allows the direct marketer to profile members of the target segments he or she selects and to support the scheduled mailing with ads in media that pinpoint these targets. It is likely that the direct marketer's internal records include only each customer's name, address, and purchase history. The GD system links the direct marketer's internal records with commercially available databases about media habits, product ownership patterns, credit card use, and other important information. The system can then produce a profile of the target segment that will help the marketer plan the overall marketing program. Two types of links are required, one based on a demographic analysis of the A and B targets (because media are often sold by demographic splits), the other based on media favored by the A and B targets. Both requirements are fulfilled by geodemography.

Demographic measurement of clusters A and B comes directly from the original census variables used to form the GD system. The process is an inverse procedure that traces cluster members scores back to the raw census variables.

For example, first locate the centroids of A and B in the factor score space. Second, note the scores of each centroid on each factor. Next, unravel the factors into their census variable constituents. (Recall that each factor is a linear combination of raw census variables.) Last, profile Clusters A and B on these constituents. For example, if Factor 1 is a measure of socio-economic well-being and Cluster A scores 140 on Factor 1, then the neighborhoods in Cluster A represent households with considerable wealth. Since Factor 1 is a combination of variables such as household income, profession, and home value, Cluster A can be profiled directly on these raw census variables if need be.

The link to media habits is facilitated as follows. The viewing, reading, or listening audience of any given advertising medium such as *Cash Flow* magazine can be sorted into the GD system. Various GD segments will be disproportionately represented in this audience; for example, most of *Cash Flow* magazine's audience may be from segments P and Q. To profile its clients, the direct marketer again uses an inverse procedure, seeking media whose audience primarily consists of A and B types. Since most national media have already sorted their audience into one or several GD systems, the direct marketer need only ask media representatives for profiling results. Appropriate media—those with disproportionately high incidences of A and B neighborhoods—are selected in this way.

A Concrete Example

Table 14.1 shows how the list qualification process works in practice. Here a manufacturer selling a consumer durable has asked ACORN to sort the manufacturer's client list into the ACORN system. The client asked that its identity be withheld, but ACORN's list profiling report clearly indicates that five clusters are particularly high responders. These five—Urbanites in High Rises, Old Money, Big City Working Class, Conspicuous Consumers, and Cosmopolitan Wealth—account for 52 percent of the current customer base but only 6.89 percent of all U.S. households. Their response indices range from 1509 to 379, averaging 757 on a size-weighted basis. These five clusters (and possibly the next four) constitute the targets for this product. Using the procedure described earlier, the manufacturer can now select media, profile members, and support a direct marketing campaign to these targets. Further, the ACORN system clearly indicates the product's nationwide market potential (since the number of households in the target segments can be combined with known average response rates per household). Results also help marketers select a retail distribution plan for the product; that is, to select stores in neighborhoods where members of the five targets are most heavily concentrated.

APPLICATIONS OF GEODEMOGRAPHIC RESEARCH SYSTEMS

Table 14.2 provides a synopsis of some other applications of geodemographic research systems. These include product positioning, repositioning, fund-raising,

TABLE 14.1. ACORN Market Segmentation Analysis
Prepared For: Your Product [28-July-1988]
Rank Ordered Acorn Market Segmentation Report with Statistical Test and Index

Segment Description	Current Number	Percent	Index Acorn	Index Stat.[a]	Statistical Test
D13 Urbanites in high rises	3862	18.33	1509	1509	************************************+
A 1 Old Money	1347	6.39	1274	1274	**********************************+
D14 Big city working class	2448	11.62	679	679	***************************
A 2 Conspicuous consumers	1384	6.57	640	640	**************************
A 3 Cosmopolitan wealth	1944	9.23	379	379	***************
B 5 Empty nesters	1151	5.46	217	217	*********
C11 College undergraduates	143	0.68	210	210	*********
C 9 Condominium dwellers	738	3.50	176	176	*******
B 4 Upper middle income families	931	4.42	162	162	******
M44 Institutions: residents and staff	25	0.12	144	100	****
I32 Nostalgic retirees and adults	187	0.89	87	100	****
E17 Working-class single adults	300	1.42	97	100	****
I30 Adults in pre-war housing	1137	5.40	105	100	****
C12 Older students and professionals	416	1.97	110	100	****
E19 Third world melting pot	178	0.85	85	85	***
C10 Fast-track young adults	757	3.59	61	61	**
I29 Golden Years Retirees	305	1.45	59	59	**
B 7 Middle Americans in new homes	627	2.98	56	56	**
E18 Families in pre-war rentals	112	0.53	48	48	*
B 6 Baby boomers with families	355	1.69	48	48	*
G23 Settled families	333	1.58	46	46	*
F21 Trend-conscious families	181	0.86	45	45	*

TABLE 14.1. (Continued)

Segment Description	Current Number	Percent	Index						
			Acorn	Stat.[a]	200	400	600	800	
B 8 Skilled craft and office workers	419	1.99	45	45	*				
I34 Old families in pre-war homes	368	1.75	38	38	*				
J35 Resort vacationers and locals	64	0.30	36	36	*				
F20 Mainstream family homeowners	180	0.85	27	27	*				
I31 Small-town families	283	1.34	22	22					
H27 Family centered blue-collar	133	0.63	20	20					
F22 Low-income families	36	0.17	20	20					
G24 Start-up families	193	0.92	18	18					
H26 Secure factory and farm workers	78	0.37	18	18					
L40 Rural displaced workers	3	0.01	16	16					
J36 Mobile home dwellers	42	0.20	16	16					
M43 Military base families	16	0.08	15	15					
I33 Home-oriented senior citizens	56	0.27	13	13					
K37 Farm families	16	0.08	12	12					
E15 Mainstream Hispanic Americans	54	0.26	11	11					
H25 Family sports and leisure lovers	46	0.22	10	10					
H28 Minimum wage white families	85	0.40	10	10					
L39 Low-income retirees and youth	60	0.28	9	9					
E16 Large Hispanic families	27	0.13	8	8					
L42 Poor young families	7	0.03	8	8					
K38 Young, active country families	4	0.02	6	6					
L41 Factory worker families	33	0.16	6	6					
TOTAL	21064	100.00	100	100					* = 25

Source: CACI-Federal.

TABLE 14.2. Applications of Geodemography

Application	Description
Repositioning	A geodemographic system was used to determine if changing the title of a national magazine from *Apartment Life* to *Metropolitan Home* along with upscaling its format would induce a shift in readership. Subscriptions before and after the change were classified by geodemographic segment to track subscriber trends.
Recruiting	Branches of the U.S. Armed Forces classify their recruits by geodemographic segment in order to determine where to locate recruiting centers and to decide what media and appeals work well to attract young men and women into the military.
Locating	A national chain of boutiques analyzed its clientele by geodemographic segment in order to determine the type of shopping center in which to locate to maximize store traffic. Supplemental analyses were used to select within-center locations and a store format.
Linking Research and Strategy	A household appliance manufacturer interested in coordinating distribution and media coverage for a new product linked each positive response from a national telephone survey to the respondent's geodemographic segment. Program results focused the manufacturer's new product roll-out, media selection, and distribution decisions.
Qualifying Lists	Direct marketers classify current clientele by geodemographic segment. A marketer then identifies segments that contain particularly high concentrations of those clients exhibiting superior purchase volumes. The marketer then identifies new lists that target these geodemographic segments.
Fund-Raising	Organizations seeking funds to support medical research, literacy programs, or other causes classify previous givers by geodemographic segment. Mailing lists and telephone contact lists with high concentrations of sympathetic segments are used to expand the program's donor base.

military recruiting, new product introduction, direct mail campaign monitoring, and retail location analysis. This section reviews several of these applications for readers who are considering using a GD system. The illustrations show that geodemography can be used in a variety of contexts by manufacturers, retailers, and service providers.

Magazine Repositioning

In their *Marketer's Handbook*,[3] Claritas Corporation shows how PRIZM was used to reposition a magazine originally entitled *Apartment Life*. The publishers of *Apartment Life* hoped to improve advertising revenues by changing their magazine's image and redirecting subscriptions to a more affluent and more urban readership. The publishers revised the magazine's format, changed its article mix, and renamed it *Metropolitan Home* to reflect the desired urban focus.

Although there are well-developed methodologies for product repositioning such as conjoint analysis and perceptual mapping, most of these concentrate on the "front end" of the problem: deciding on the new position and developing the positioning strategy. They give little attention to the measurement and validation of results, and so the outcomes of the repositioning strategies go untested. Managers often assume that the implemented strategies are effective or monitor them only loosely by performance criteria that may not be tied closely to the strategy or its anticipated effects. Tightly controlled before/after designs are rarely employed.

The publishers of *Metropolitan Home* wanted a precise before/after summary of how the repositioning strategy affected audience characteristics. Precision was necessary not only to decide whether the strategy had worked but also to convince a fresh group of would-be advertisers that their ads, if placed in *Metropolitan Home,* would reach the intended audience.

The PRIZM system was used to classify *Apartment Life's* subscribers (the "before" measure) and then to classify new subscribers to *Metropolitan Home* (the "after" measure.) Figure 14.2 shows the changes in four PRIZM segments. These changes reflect the trends seen in other segments of the PRIZM system as well.

Affluent segments such as Blue Blood Estates and Money and Brains showed dramatic upswings in their subscription rates to *Metropolitan Home.* For example, the concentration of "before" subscribers among Blue Blood Estates was high, about 2.5 times the national average, yet following the repositioning this concentration soared to nearly five times the national average—a doubling of penetration. A similar doubling occurred in Money and Brains. Overall, subscription rates among affluent, urbanized segments increased as planned.

At the other end of the spectrum, the few subscribers in less affluent segments such as Emergent Minorities and Gray Power tended to diminish following the repositioning. Although this aspect of the change was less important, it reflected a shift in readership commensurate with the plan.

Accurate and detailed data on audience characteristics are vital for the success of magazines, radio and television shows, and other mass media. Geodemographic systems provide a means for formulating and testing the strategies that purport to influence these characteristics. As this example illustrates, they also provide a convenient, easily understood way to summarize results and to convey their impact to buyers of media space and time.

Direct Marketing

Direct marketers like L.L. Bean want to formulate strategy and track campaign results. Table 14.3 shows part of a standard report for a catalog clothing marketer following the mailing of 589,649 catalogs.[4] The results are presented by PRIZM

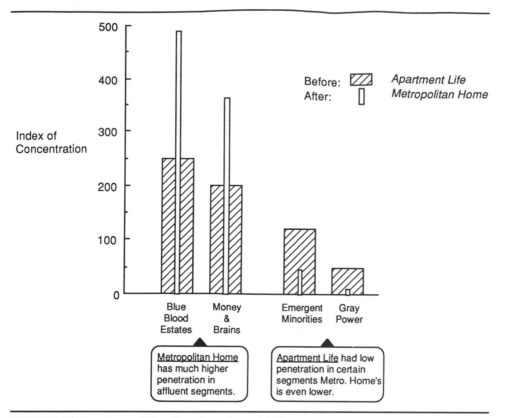

Index of Concentration

Before: Apartment Life
After: Metropolitan Home

Blue Blood Estates
Money & Brains
Emergent Minorities
Gray Power

Metropolitan Home has much higher penetration in affluent segments.

Apartment Life had low penetration in certain segments Metro. Home's is even lower.

FIGURE 14.2.   Repositioning *Apartment Life*

segment, a format selected to illustrate how a standard report can be used by marketing management.

In the first group are three segments that responded very positively to the catalog. For example, the nearly 17,000 catalogs sent to Blue Blood Estates households generated 461 orders (a 2.76 percent response rate) for total sales of nearly $25,000 and an average order of $54.00. Other segments that responded positively—Bohemian Mix and Black Enterprise—do not come from the same PRIZM supergroup as Blue Blood Estates. It is unlikely that these positive response rates could have been predicted purely from management judgment. The campaign results clearly point to considerable potential in three diverse segments.

Another telling aspect of this report, though, is that some segments which generated sizeable orders were much less profitable. For example, households in segment 32, Public Assistance, and those in segment 3, New Melting Pot, generated average orders of $54.23 and $60.68 respectively. But the costs associated with servicing these orders diminished much of their value. These costs, due primarily to returns and bad debts, lowered the net income per order to nearly half of its value in the top three segments.

TABLE 14.3. Profiling a Catalog Client File

Geodemographic Segment	Promos (Catalogs Mailed)	Orders	Percent Response	Dollar Sales	Average Order Size	Gross Income per Promo	Net Income per Order	Net Income per Promo
28 Blue Blood Estates	16,693	461	2.76	$24,895	$54.00	$1.49	$4.78	.13
37 Bohemian Mix	8,750	239	2.73	12,465	52.15	1.42	4.03	.11
31 Black Enterprise	29,763	850	2.86	42,653	50.18	1.43	3.95	.11
6 Hard Scrabble	3,842	108	2.81	5,048	46.74	1.31	2.62	.07
32 Public Assistance	6,413	151	2.35	8,189	54.23	1.28	2.61	.06
3 New Melting Pot	4,420	90	2.04	5,461	60.68	1.24	2.34	.05
35 Grain Belt	7,686	101	1.31	4,698	46.51	.61	−12.05	−.16
4 Heavy Industry	1,730	25	1.45	781	31.24	.45	−14.60	−.21
Total	589,649	16,400	2.78	$674,273	41.11	1.14	.62	.02

Source: Claritas Corporation.

Further analysis of returns showed that in certain segments costs far outweighed revenues. Grain Belt and Heavy Industry households showed much smaller average orders coupled with unreasonably high costs, so that the company was losing more than $12.00 on each order generated.

Reports like this one can be prepared routinely using a geodemographic system. Management can quickly evaluate a direct marketing campaign in order to refine the selection of target markets, to determine which list will be brought for future mailings, to tune the product line, and to select media for advertising support in the direct marketing effort. These points explain why all four geodemographic systems have developed links to other databases. These links and their value in marketing strategy are discussed next.

LINKED SYSTEMS

Two systems are linked if their suppliers have signed a contractual arrangement to cooperate and, further, if a directory or relational mapping has been created to allow users of one database to locate corresponding records in the second database. For example, ClusterPLUS and the A.C. Nielsen Corporation have established a link between the 47 ClusterPLUS segments and Nielsen's Designated Market Areas (DMAs), which quantify TV audience data.

Using this link, a marketer can translate TV viewing behavior into the geodemographic mode and vice-versa, expanding the capabilities of both systems. For example, one packaged goods manufacturer used the ClusterPLUS-Nielsen connection to market an ingredient used in baking cakes from scratch. The goal was to buy TV commercials only for programs whose audiences had large proportions of consumers who regularly bake from scratch. First, by cross-referencing with data from Simmons Market Research Bureau, the marketer identified the most promising ClusterPLUS groups. The top-ranking cluster was Low Mobility Working Families in which 39 percent bake from scratch as opposed to the national average of 17 percent. This cluster and the nine next highest-ranking clusters were pooled as a target group. Next, the marketer used Nielsen data to find the TV programs most watched by the target clusters. These included mainstream shows such as "America's Funniest Home Videos" and "Cheers" but also shows that have narrower appeal, such as "Rescue 911," "Major Dad," and "In the Heat of the Night." The marketer leveraged its advertising dollar by running commercials only on these shows.[5]

System Links

Figure 14.3 provides a generic summary of linked systems as a framework for the following discussion of the links among four U.S.-based systems. These links constitute the true power of these systems: They expand our knowledge about a given cluster and relate this knowledge to other pieces of information. Links make a system "smart;" they take seemingly isolated facts and cross-reference them with others related to the same problem. Links are what make systems more than idiot savants, more than vast "telephone directories" of detached data items to be recalled but not understood.

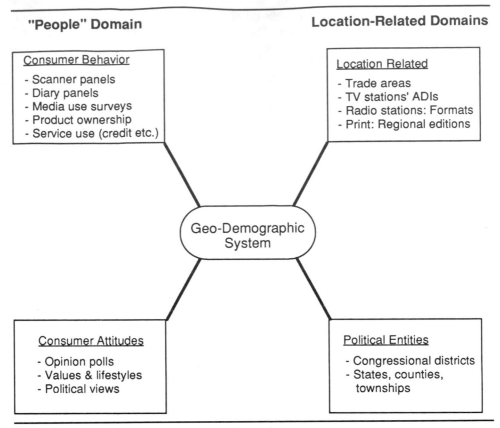

FIGURE 14.3.   Generic Summary of GD Links

Generically, there are four main types of connections available: connections to consumer behavior, to location-related entities, to consumer attitudes, and to political entities. For example, a GD system is linked to a scanner panel such as InfoScan once the 60,000 InfoScan panel households have been sorted into the GD system. This link connects food purchase records by household to cluster membership. It facilitates answers to such questions as, "Which three GD segments account for the highest purchase volume for bran cereals on a per-household basis?" To respond to this question, the system maps a segment into its purchase behavior. An inverse mapping answers a different question; "Among all households who bought beer on feature last week, what share is accounted for by each GD segment?"

Table 14.4 expands Figure 14.3, listing more than 40 suppliers of research data that have linked arrangements with one or more of the four GD firms. These include standing national panels of households, such as National Family Opinion's 300,000 U.S. families, National Panel Diary's consumer purchase panels, and many others. It also includes the suppliers of national mailing lists such as R.L. Polk and MetroMail, suppliers of TV and radio audience data such as Arbitron,

TABLE 14.4. System Links

Database or Service	Geodemographic System			
	ACORN	ClusterPLUS	PRIZM	MicroVision
Links Common to all 4 GD firms			Tier 1	
National Family Opinion (mail panel)	x	x	x	x
SIMMONS Marketing Research (media survey)	x	x	x	x
Stanford Research Institute VALs	x	x	x	x
Links Common to 3 of the 4 GD firms			Tier 2	
MRI: Mediamark Research	x		x	x
National Panel Diary		x	x	x
Scarborough (National and Major Markets)	x	x	x	
Gallup	x		x	x
Links Common to 2 of the 4 GD firms			Tier 3	
R.L. Polk (new car sales: the X1 list)	x		x	
MetroMail (National list and text file)	x		x	
Market Facts	x		x	
TELMAR	x		x	
IMS: Interactive Marketing Systems	x		x	
Accountline	x			x
A.C. Nielsen		x	x	
Links Unique to a single GD firm			Tier 4	
ACORN				
Demographic Systems, Inc.	x			
AT & T	x			
Media Market Research	x			
FMI	x			
TRW Information File	x			
CDS: Computer Data Services	x			
Hooper-Homes Credit Analysis System	x			
ClusterPLUS				
MRCA: Market Research Corporation of America		x		
CFD: Financial Services		x		
Arbitron		x		
PRIZM				
Birch Radio (audience interviews)			x	
Windsor			x	
Blair (ADVO, network mail inserts)			x	
Monroe Mendelsohn (study of affluence)			x	
Audited Advertising (door-to-door promos)			x	
Information Resources, Inc.			x	
Roper Associates (attitudes and opinions)			x	
MicroVision				
CCM (bankcard data)				x
DATAMAN (home mortgage data)				x
EPRI (major and minor appliance data)				x
ServeQuest (electric utility satisfaction data)				x

Source: This exhibit is based on data supplied by each geodemographic firm. The links shown here are subject to change. The reader is urged to contact each supplier for current information about that supplier's contractual relationships with a particular database or service.

broad-based information companies like AT&T and TRW, and specialized firms such as Audited Advertising, which monitors door-to-door promotions.

Table 14.4 is arranged in four tiers. The top tier shows those databases that are linked to all four geodemographic systems. Subsequent tiers show databases linked to three of the four systems, then those linked to two, and finally those linked to just one of the four GD suppliers.

Table 14.4 can be scanned by rows to reveal which geodemographic systems are linked to a specific database or service, and it can be scanned by columns to reveal the particular databases to which a specific GD firm is linked. For example, MetroMail can select its lists by either ACORN or PRIZM clusters but not by ClusterPLUS or MicroVision clusters. Scanning down the last column shows that MicroVision is linked to 11 of the databases listed and to others not listed on the exhibit.

A discussion of each link would take us too far afield. However, a brief summary of the first three databases—NFO, Simmons, and VALS—will clarify the benefits of these linkages.

National Family Opinion Research

NFO maintains an active panel of 300,000 U.S. households, each of whom has agreed to respond accurately and promptly to periodic surveys. To avoid "panel burnout," NFO selects its active panel from an even larger group of 700,000 participating households. Each active household has been assigned a cluster code that places it into the cluster model of a given supplier. For example, ClusterPLUS knows the cluster to which any particular NFO panel household belongs.

This combination of databases permits the analysis by cluster of specific industries: women's tailored apparel, beverages, home furnishings, or video games. Household marketplace activity relative to these industries is supplied by both NFO's syndicated services division and its Multi-Client service group.

Simmons Market Research Bureau

Simmons compiles research data on consumer media and product use habits, including their annually updated *Study of Media and Markets*. This study is based on interviews with a national probability sample of 19,000 households. Members of each household discuss their media use (including magazines, television, radio, newspaper, cable TV, outdoor media, and yellow pages) as well as their use of brands in 800 categories of products and services. Extensive demographic data are also available for each respondent.

Cluster codes have been appended to each household in the Simmons database. To enhance the reliability of this link, Simmons has agreed to classify two consecutive years of its survey so that 38,000 households are classified at any single moment.

The Simmons link makes it possible for clients of any of the geodemographic research systems to determine whether there are significant cluster-to-cluster variations in the incidence of product, brand, or media use among households in the Simmons study. Clients of a geodemographic research firm can identify new market opportunities very precisely by geographic unit. The links with other databases such as Nielsen and Arbitron (for ClusterPLUS and PRIZM) permit a product manager not only to know which segments use their product most frequently but also how to reach similar households effectively via print and broadcast media.

VALS: Value, Attitudes, and Lifestyle Typology

Stanford Research International developed a typology of people based on values, attitudes, and lifestyles. A large representative sample of the U.S. population was originally segmented into the nine VALs types. (The updated version of VALs has fewer types.) All four GD suppliers have taken the individuals in the VALs sample and classified them into their geodemographic model. In this way, a VALs profile of a client's current or projected customers can be established to quantify and locate attitudinal groups important to the client's business. This link can reveal unfulfilled needs for new products and lead to highly successful media and sales strategies. In essence, the VALS link allows GD clients to explore the psychological and lifestyle implications of their product designs and promotional appeals.

WEAKNESSES OF CURRENT SYSTEMS

GD systems have certain weaknesses. It is appropriate to discuss some of these in order to anticipate developments in this exciting branch of the marketing research industry. The greatest weakness of current systems is also their greatest strength: They focus on households rather than on individuals. This feature is a strength in some product categories and for certain strategic marketing variables. For example, in categories such as major appliances, minor appliances, and home furnishings, where the household is clearly the "consumer" of the product and where purchase decisions are likely to involve more than one household member, using the household as the observation unit is efficient and reasonable. Further, certain media tend to be used by a household as a unit. Messages in these media cannot be directed uniquely to an individual within the household. This is true for prime-time television ads and also for some print, package, and outdoor advertising.

Purchase behavior in selected product categories is also strongly driven by household rather than by individual characteristics. For example, a household's income influences each member's choice of ski equipment and ski area destination, even though each may have different tastes and preferences. Similar arguments can be made in other product categories where independence among household members is more illusory than real because of shared values, centralized buying, and household economic constraints.

Despite these arguments, in other product categories and for certain media the individual is far more important than the household. In these cases, most existing geodemographic systems are inefficient. For example, in product categories where personal tastes and product aesthetics are critical, the individual is the appropriate unit of analysis. This is true in cosmetics, music, and clothing. Although a marketer who uses a GD system can hope that his or her catalog is directed to the correct household member or that the buying individual is listening to the commercial, there is no guarantee. In many households nontargeted members may even prevent promotional messages from reaching a potential buyer in that household.

SUMMARY AND CONCLUSIONS

Geodemographic systems were developed to fill the needs of direct marketers and to overcome deficiencies in other methods, such as psychographic, benefit, or lifestyle segmentation. These earlier methods can identify homogeneous groups of individuals but cannot usually indicate how to reach these individuals efficiently through media, distribution channels, or direct sales. In contrast, GD systems link multiple databases containing supplemental information about household media habits, values, lifestyles, and product use. A GD model is, therefore, tied into a complex network of interlocking databases that are connected by common geographic, demographic, and temporal definitions.

Recent Developments

Geodemographic systems with the individual as the unit of analysis are under development, such as National Decision System's Equis System and Donnelley Marketing Information Service's DQI^2 database. Equis maintains a database of financial information for over 100 million Americans on more than 340 characteristics including age, marital status, move history, credit card activity, buying activity, credit relationships (by number and type), bankruptcies, and liens. This information is updated continuously at the rate of over 15 million changes per day.

Individualized databases like Equis are expensive to develop and maintain, and their effectiveness has yet to be demonstrated. However, the conceptual appeal of individualized systems is high. It is natural that these systems should emerge first in the financial community, where credit is granted primarily on an individual rather than on a household basis.

For this book, the link between GD and single-source systems is important. Both Nielsen and IRI cross-reference their household panels by geodemographic code, Nielsen with ClusterPLUS and PRIZM and IRI with PRIZM. These relational alliances are particularly critical for retailers who use them to move between packaged goods purchasing, response to marketing signals, and trade area analysis. For example, rather than simply segment canned soup buyers by family size or repurchase frequency, geodemographic links suggest unique buying, serving, and restocking propensities among GD market segments, especially the segments that make up the trade area of a given retail store. These tendencies can be tied directly to packaging, pricing, shelf management, and store choice decisions, as discussed in Chapter 17.

Outside packaged goods, the emergence of scanner technology and single-source consumer panels is influencing marketing strategy. Chapter 4 outlined how in-store sales and direct marketing can be coordinated to expand both parts of a firm's client base. Firms such as the Banana Republic and Williams Sonoma have iterated a process of direct marketing/retail expansion/direct marketing/retail expansion by identifying who their customers are and where these customers are concentrated. The advent of single-source panels in the apparel industry, in the sporting goods industry, and in other industries, will close the in-store/direct sales loop. Retail scanner data can be tied to extensive consumer demographics linked to a GD segmentation model. Since scanner data are collected at the individual level, retailers and direct marketers are beginning to customize their catalogs for different segments, choose new retail locations systematically, and coordinate in-store promotions with micromedia campaigns that are precisely matched to the needs and locations of the target segments.

Notes

1. A firm cannot literally purchase a list from a list vendor. The vendor sells a one-time use of the names and addresses on its list. The list resides in the vendor's computer, and in most cases the buyer receives only gummed labels or an invoice guaranteeing that pieces are mailed to designated addresses or address types.

2. A subscript could be used to emphasize the fact that a certain collection of ZIP codes is associated with CBG A_j. That is,

$$CBGA_j = \{ZAj_1, ZAj_2, ZAj_3, \dots ZAj_j\}$$

for $j = [1, \text{number of CBGs}]$. Note, however, that ZIP codes can cut across CBG boundaries. Hence, a given ZIP code could appear in more than one row of Table a. In other words, the CBG partition of ZIP codes is not mutually exclusive.

3. *PRIZM: The Marketer's Handbook (Book 1)*, Claritas Corporation, 1984. See also Weiss, *The Clustering of America*, pp. 41–43.

4. A nondisclosure agreement prohibits revealing the identity of the clothing marketer.

5. "Clusters Plus Nielsen Equals Efficient Marketing," *American Demographic Magazine* 12 (9) (September 1991), p. 16.

15 DESKTOP GEODEMOGRAPHIC SYSTEMS

Chapters 13 and 14 describe applications of the mainframe computer versions of geodemographic systems, versions that reside on a computer operated by technical staff in the firm that supplies the system. A client interested in applying mainframe geodemography contacts the vendor, selects a particular application such as site location analysis, then transfers relevant data to the vendor's computer, where it is geocoded. Geocoded data pass through the vendor's system, which generates standard reports relevant to the application.

In some cases, clients must transfer sensitive data to the vendor to accomplish the task. For example, to solve a site-location problem, the vendor would use corporate sales data broken down by current location so that current sales could be modeled as a function of trade area characteristics. Releasing corporate data is risky, even with a nondisclosure agreement from the GD vendor.

Security issues aside, to solve this problem out-of-house requires that the client meet repeatedly with the vendor to refine problem issues, examine preliminary results, and order follow-up analyses if partial results are inconclusive. If the client must solve other, similar problems, the marginal value of the vendor–client contact diminishes with repetition. For example, a client may have to locate dozens of new retail stores each year. In these cases, the client needs the productivity tools offered by geodemography but, after the first or second application, no longer needs consulting advice on how to apply these tools.

Integrated desktop systems place geodemographic tools at a manager's fingertips while reducing project costs, protecting sensitive data, and often improving the solution quality. This chapter defines a desktop geodemographic system, discusses the five competitive systems currently available, and illustrates their features with real but disguised applications. The examples demonstrate how desktop systems facilitate marketing strategies that coordinate competitive analyses, distribution, promotion planning, and site location.

Definition and Description

A desktop geodemographic system consists of a microcomputer (usually a 386 class machine with a minimum of 640K RAM and math-coprocessor), a full-color high resolution monitor, a hard-disc drive, a CD-ROM optical disc drive, a laser printer, and a color plotter. System software permits a business to integrate, manipulate, and analyze data from a variety of preloaded and business specific databases. Merged data are summarized in the form of reports, charts, and maps.[1]

Desktop systems come preloaded with U.S. census data (for people and for housing units), all levels of census geography or "cartographics" (in digitized map coordinate form), maps of major transportation routes (from USGS highway files), and U.S. postal divisions. Optional preloaded databases include location files for banks, shopping centers, and automobile dealers; data on individual households; Arbitron's Areas of Dominant Influence and Nielsen's Designated Market Areas (with digitized boundaries plus associated information for each ADI and DMA); and data on consumer expenditures in various product categories.

A desktop system also comes preloaded with the vendor's proprietary cluster model. For example Infomark, National Decision System's entrant in this category, comes preloaded with the MicroVision clusters and related information, while Market America (ACORN), COMPASS (PRIZM), and CONQUEST (ClusterPLUS) are also preloaded with their respective cluster systems. A fifth desktop system, Prime-Location (produced by National Planning Data Corporation), was discontinued in 1991 when National Planning Data Corporation merged with Claritas.

Power Combined with Privacy

The power of a desktop system derives from its ability to merge preloaded data with firm-specific data. For example, in 1987 The Toro Company digitized the boundaries of its sales territories and loaded this information into Infomark, along with proprietary data about each territory, including sales volume, market share, and information about the territory's sales representative. These firm-specific databases were supplemented by data on media availability and competitive data from commercially available databases.

Integrating preloaded data with sensitive internal accounting data was difficult before the desktop system. As Kirchner and Thomas remark, "With a desktop system, companies can now control the confidentiality of their projects because they no longer have to rely on data vendors to do the work, even though vendors still supply hardware, software, databases, and service." For companies in hotly competitive environments, confidentiality is of utmost importance. "We don't let anyone know what we are up to," says Bob Sullivan, director of McDonald's business analysis department. "Our desktop demographic workstation ensures the confidentiality of our marketing strategy."[2]

Leading Systems

Information about the five available systems is shown in Table 15.1. Entry-level lease arrangement range from about $10,000 to $15,000 per year. However,

TABLE 15.1.   Vendors of Desktop Systems

Desktop System	Vendor	Cluster System	Desktop Price
Market America	CACI Market Analysis 3040 Williams Drive Fairfax, VA 22031 phone: 703-218-4400 800-292-2224	ACORN	• $15,000 1 state • $1,500 each additional state • $30,400 all states • $54,000 3-year license
COMPASS	Claritas Corporation 201 North Union Street Alexandria, VA 22314 phone: 703-683-8300	PRIZM	• $20,000–$100,000 per year • delivered by market • regional systems available
CONQUEST	Donnelley Marketing Information Services 70 Seaview Avenue Stamford, CT 06904 phone: 203-353-7208 800-527-3657	ClusterPLUS	• state, regional, and national licenses available • multi-copy, multi-year options $9,500–$85,000+
Infomark	Equifax: National Decision Systems 539 Encinitas Blvd. Encinitas, CA 92024 phone: 619-942-7000 800-877-5560	MicroVision	• $11,000 1 state, 1 database • $17,800 national, 1 database • $20,000–$65,000+ with hardware
Prime-Location	National Planning Data Corporation P.O. Box 610 Ithaca, NY 14851-6010 phone: 607-273-8208	PRIZM	Now part of COMPASS

Source: Russell J. Kirchner and Richard K. Thomas, "Desktop Decisions," *American Demographics,* 11 (9) (August 1989), pp. 34–37.

once a system is fully loaded with optional but typically necessary databases, prices settle into the $30,000 per year range. Despite the cost, demand for these systems is steadily increasing. As of January 1990 there were over 500 desktop systems in place, generating between $10 to $20 million a year in revenues for their vendors. An estimated 600 systems were put in place by the end of 1991.[3]

Although much of this increase has come from new users of desktop systems, penetration among existing users is also increasing as clients decentralize their desktop operations. For example, Kelly Tritz, supervisor of marketing information for Toro's Outdoor Products Division, currently spends 10 to 20 percent of his time on Infomark, producing site-location, sales, and competitive analyses for his 53 district managers. Tritz says, "The managers love the reports, but I could easily devote 100 percent of my time to producing them."[4] Tritz is encouraging each district manager to acquire his or her own system and learn to produce reports now produced at the home office.

APPLICATIONS

It will prove instructive to trace a series of applications of desktop geodemography in the context of particular management problems, including the analysis of corporate sales by district and the location of new retail outlets. Sales analysis compares a firm's sales of a particular item to industry sales of the item, merging internal accounting data with industry data purchased from a trade association or commercial data supplier. Location analysis compares characteristics of potential sites and their surrounding trade areas. It merges data about competitive outlets already situated in a trade area, the concentration of "MicroVision core buyer types" in each trade area, the company's current sales penetration in an area, and an area's market potential.

Sales Analysis: Finding Untapped Potential in Certain Districts

The Toro Company's 53 sales districts are shown in Figure 15.1. For a particular product line, management compared Toro sales in a given district to industry shipments in the district. Better performance is indicated by higher ratios of these two numbers, called the sales rate. To determine which districts perform best during a given year, management loaded a digitized version of Figure 15.1 into Infomark and merged the geographic data with sales and market share information. Although the actual figures are proprietary,[5] Figure 15.1 shows the intersection between the rate of change in the sales rate and Toro market share. Management used these rates of change to evaluate district managers' performance in the two-year period of 1986 to 1987.

From a competitive point of view, regions that could support further development are those regions where industry growth is high but where Toro has a modest market share. District 530 in southern California and several districts

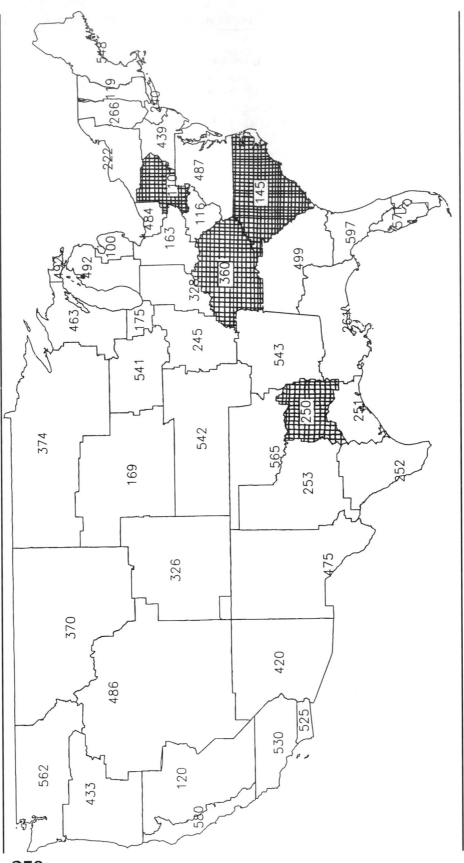

FIGURE 15.1. Toro Sales Districts: Districts with Untapped Potential

Source: Courtesy of the Toro Company.

in the southeast fit this description. These districts are cross-hatched in Figure 15.1.

A critical issue for Toro management is to avoid being misled by a low base rate problem with respect to sales growth. For example, district 530 in southern California may show high growth when 1986 and 1987 industry sales are compared simply because this district's industry sales were low in 1986.

Figure 15.2 indicates that this is not the case. Figure 15.2 uses a different partitioning of the United States than does Figure 15.1—one based on Arbitron's ADIs. It shows that in 1986 southern California had one of the highest sales rates in the nation. Armed with this information, management is assured that further marketing efforts are warranted to tap the considerable market potential of district 530.

In summary, the analysis outlined in this example had three steps. First, management loaded a digitized version of its sales territories into the GD system. Next, it loaded corporate sales and industry sales data by year and by territory. (Note that both changes in the sales rate and market share can be computed from these data.) Finally, management classified changes in the sales rate into various levels and displayed results on screen using cross-hatching and (in the original version) color-coding. The visual analysis was supplemented by a quantitative ranking of all territories according to their performance indices (change in sales rates from one year to the next).

Step one requires some time but is a fixed cost; once territories are loaded they serve as a basis for future applications. Steps two and three, the crux of the application, require only a few hours of a manager's time. If the database is updated regularly, subsequent analyses of this type are fully automated.

This application does not use small-area census geography or the Micro-Vision clusters resident on the Infomark system. The applications that we now examine use both these features.

Site-Location Analysis

Desktop systems can move back and forth quickly between perspectives that differ in scale, from the entire United States down to a single census block group. For example, the large-scale map in Figure 15.2 shows low industry shipments to the Upper Great Lakes region, an area in which Toro management was considering opening a distributorship.

Figure 15.3 shows a closer view, by county, of parts of Minnesota and Wisconsin bordering on Lake Superior. At this scale, areas too small to be seen on Figure 15.2 show high potential (wide vertical stripes). Toro market share was overlaid on this expanded view county by county to locate high-share counties (shown by wide horizontal stripes) as candidates for the new distributorship. (See counties numbered 27003, 27053, and 27307.)

Using this information, management proposed a location near Stillwater, Minnesota. Infomark provided detailed demographics for the population living within a certain radius of the proposed site (shown in Table 15.2). To project

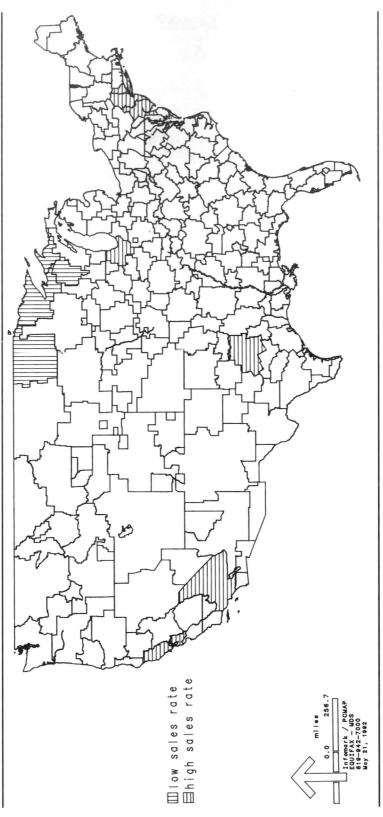

low sales rate
high sales rate

miles
0.0   256.7

Infomark / PCMAP
EQUIFAX - MDS
619-942-7000
May 21, 1992

FIGURE 15.2. Toro Base Rates Sales by ADI

Source: Courtesy of the Toro Company.

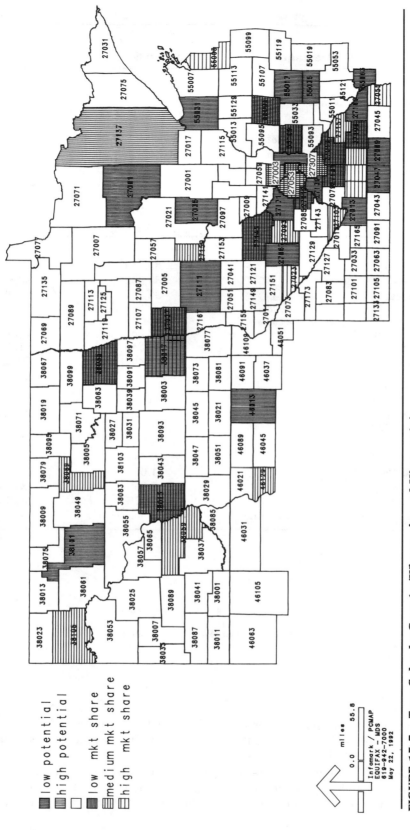

FIGURE 15.3. Toro Sales by County (Wisconsin and Minnesota)

Source: Courtesy of the Toro Company.

273

TABLE 15.2. Detailed Demographics for a Proposed Site

Context variables include the site name,
site number, and site location (latitude
and longitude).

↓

Pop-Facts: Full Data Report
by National Decision Systems

Hwy 36 and Manning   Site: 25
Stillwater, MN   coord: 45:02.20   92:51.99

Description	5.0 mile radius	10.0 mile radius
Population		
1993 Projection	35,816	212,229
1988 Estimate	33,622	198,807
1980 Census	30,252	177,082
Households		
1993 Projection	12,631	78,689
1988 Estimate	11,346	71,343
1980 Census	9,462	59,201
1988 Estimated		
Households by Income	11,346	71,343
$75,000 or more	14.11%	9.62%
$50,000 to $74,999	23.10%	21.94%
$35,000 to $49,999	23.34%	24.42%
$25,000 to $34,999	12.95%	15.21%
$15,000 to $24,999	11.65%	13.61%
$7,500 to $14,999	7.69%	8.53%
Under $7,500	7.17%	6.67%
1988 Estimated Average Household Income	$44,334	$40,731

This user asked for demographics
for a 5- and a 10-mile region
circumscribed about the site.

The report includes information on a variety of variables. In addition
to those shown here, the following are available:

Population	**Hispanic Population**	**Housing Units**	**Households**
by race	by race	by type	by type
by gender	by type	by occupants	by life cycle
by age		by value	by income
by marital status		by urban/rural	
by education level		by year built	

walking and riding lawnmower sales by census tract for the proposed site, MicroVision cross-referenced the ZIP+4 areas composing the proposed site's trade area with known high-demand ZIP+4 neighborhoods.[6]

This analysis, although easy to implement on the desktop system, is extremely sophisticated by modern business standards. It uses preloaded census data at the county level and combines these data with ZIP+4 detail generated

from MicroVision. High-potential ZIP+4 neighborhoods have already been identified from a sort of Toro's current customer list into the MicroVision system.
Furthermore, other potentially important geographic units, such as ADI radio
markets, can be linked by geodemography to the proposed site in Stillwater,
Minnesota. In this way, the system can easily identify the ADI radio market(s)
broadcasting to the homes in the outlet's surrounding trade area. Radio broad-
casts will support the outlet's grand opening and its subsequent week-by-week
sales activities.

MicroVision Core Buyer Types

One last example shows how a desktop system can perform even more detailed
analyses. Figure 15.4 codes five-digit ZIP codes in the Boston area according
to whether or not they are in a MicroVision core buyer segment. (The leading
zero on these ZIP codes has been dropped.) Recall, however, that ZIP codes
within a MicroVision cluster still vary in the actual incidence of a given firm's
clients. In other words, the mapping from a firm's best clients to a GD system
and back again to selected target segments is an inductive process; it involves
probabilistic, not deterministic, relationships. Thus, the following deterministic
reasoning is invalid: "Our top-ranked customers live in Cluster A ZIP codes;
therefore, all Cluster A ZIP codes contain top-ranked customers." Clearly, the
number of top prospects contained in a given A ZIP code may vary from 0
percent to 100 percent.

To avoid this anomaly and to ferret out the best census ZIP codes in a designated MicroVision segment, Infomark identifies the percentage of Toro core
buyer types in each ZIP code. ZIP codes with high percentages of these types
are shown by widely spaced horizontal lines in Figure 15.4 For example, ZIP
codes 1701 and 1776 both have high concentrations of type A (core) households.
However, this concentration is below 50 percent in ZIP code 1701 (no vertical
stripes) and above 80 percent in ZIP code 1776 (widely spaced vertical stripes).
These percentages may determine where a new outlet is located or how promotion dollars are allocated among an existing outlet's trade area neighborhoods.
Refined analyses such as this can be carried out quickly and conveniently on a
desktop system.

OTHER FEATURES OF DESKTOP SYSTEMS

The Toro example shows how a manufacturer of consumer durable products uses
a desktop geodemographic system for sales analysis, competitive analysis, and
site location. These systems have other features that facilitate applications by
marketing research firms, advertising agencies, newspapers, universities, service
organizations, and literally any business or government entity that engages in
consumer marketing. Our examples have emphasized trade area evaluation; that
is, creating custom geographic definitions of a firm's, store's, or service center's trade areas and linking this customized geography to the system's various
databases. All five geodemographic systems produce presentation-quality maps

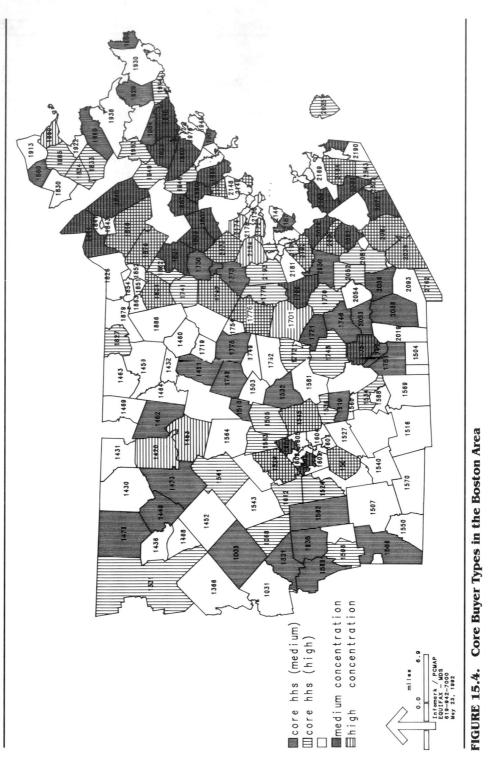

FIGURE 15.4. Core Buyer Types in the Boston Area

Source: Courtesy of the Toro Company.

on-screen or on a color plotter that permit coding of relevant data as part of the map. Thus, maps are linked with a system's databases to produce output that might be described as a geographic spreadsheet.

Each desktop vendor offers a system with certain unique capabilities not offered by other vendors. Space limitations preclude a comprehensive inventory of these features, but two examples may indicate the opportunities that special features offer for analysis. Prior to its acquisition by Claritas, National Planning Data Corporation used CD-ROM memory to store a library of high-resolution satellite photographs of the earth's surface. The system overlayed several of these photographs to produce a seamless composite of nearly any area in the United States, from Boston Harbor to a portion of San Francisco. When the satellite feature was invoked, a user saw an aerial view of the selected location and thereby gained firsthand knowledge of the location's infrastructure and physical features.

As a second example, the Compass system includes Yellow Pages directory (YPD) databases for all major U.S. cities. A Yellow Pages directory area is a unit of geography defined by a particular set of phone prefixes. As a unit of geography, a YPD area is analogous to an ADI, a county, or any other geographic unit; that is, the area has precise boundaries and a precise population of individuals and businesses that reside within those boundaries. A YPD system contains a demographic profile of each YPD area and details on the businesses in that area, usually arranged by Standard Industrial Classification (SIC) code.

Companies use this information to determine in which Yellow Pages directories to list. For example, Toro would cross-reference its new Stillwater location with the YPD databases to find the YPD areas within a 50-mile radius of the outlet. Toro might then link these directory areas with ZIP codes and ADIs to coordinate a direct mail and radio campaign before the new store's grand opening.

A Yellow Pages directory system also produces a variety of standard reports. Table 15.3, an excerpt from a report on consumer spending patterns available from Claritas, shows expenditures for personal items in Albertville, Alabama. The data on consumer spending are obtained from the diary portion of the consumer expenditure survey, which is conducted periodically by the Bureau of Labor Statistics with the assistance of the Census Bureau. The market index is the ratio of the weekly household expenditures in the study area to those in the nation as a whole. The report includes expenditures on food, tobacco, personal care services, household equipment, apparel, and entertainment. Households in Albertville have indices less than 1.00, indicating that they spend less than the national average in all categories shown, although their spending on tobacco products is relatively high.

The data in Table 15.3 are less current than, say, data from a scanner database. However, currency is not critical in many of these product categories since the purchase cycle is long. For example, households tend to replace their automatic dishwashers only once in a six-year period, a fact that makes annually updated data current enough for most marketing decisions. More important, these data can be linked with other databases in the system for a detailed picture of relevant product movement on an area-by-area basis. This feature makes desktop systems ideal tools for implementing micro marketing strategies for durable products.

TABLE 15.3. Sample Report from a Yellow Pages Directory System

1987 Consumer Spending Pattern (Directory 1010) Albertville (Weight: 100%)				Yellow Pages DataSystem 18 June, 87 AL BSA	
	Annual Expenditure				
	Aggregate (hundreds)	**Per Capita**	**Average Household**	**Weekly Average Household**	**Market Index**
Income					
(less average taxes)	384,507	7,419	19,417	373.40	0.69
Total expenditures	398,795	7,694	20,138	387.27	0.88
Food and Drink					
Food at home	54,696	1,055	2,762	53.12	0.90
Food away from home	18,423	355	930	17.89	0.84
Alcoholic beverages	6,560	127	331	6.37	0.87
Miscellaneous Personal Items					
Tobacco supplies	5,944	115	300	5.77	0.92
Personal care services	3,570	69	180	3.47	0.86
Household Equipment and Services					
Household textiles	1,251	24	63	1.21	0.79
Furniture	4,694	91	237	4.56	0.80
Floor coverings	647	12	33	.63	0.79
Major appliances	2,616	50	132	2.54	0.85
Small appliances	1,125	22	57	1.09	0.83
Domestic services	5,147	99	260	5.00	0.88
Apparel					
Women's apparel 16+	5,459	105	276	5.30	0.84
Men's apparel 16+	3,595	69	182	3.49	0.80

CONCLUSION

Desktop geodemographic systems put extensively preprocessed U.S. census data and a variety of other databases where they are most useful and most secure: on the manager's desk. This chapter reviews three specific applications—district sales analysis, site-location analysis, and core-buyer targeting—conducted by the Toro Company using Equifax's Infomark system. Each of these analyses takes only a few hours to complete, far less time than a traditional mainframe approach to the same problem. Such immediate feedback often suggests appropriate follow-up analyses that would otherwise be missed because of the long delays typical of a mainframe environment. Mainframe applications, which separate the manager from the data, also require an unrealistic amount of planning by the manager. When plans disintegrate, the result is usually wasted time and wasted money.

Several other report types are also illustrated in this chapter. The most notable is a Yellow Pages directory report from Claritas. Yellow Page reports reveal important marketing information both for households and for businesses in a geographic locale served by a single Yellow Pages phone directory. Each YPD area is cross-referenced with other geographic units such as MSAs, counties, ZIP codes, CBGs, ADIs, and DMAs. Users can also outline an arbitrary geometric area (a ring, a polygon, an irregularly shaped area) and profile the area according to the information stored in a YPD database. YPD areas are particularly useful for durable products and for other items with long purchase cycles. For packaged goods, pharmaceuticals, and items sold by mass merchandisers, single-source systems (as described in Chapters 6 to 11) are more appropriate.

Notes

1. See Russell J. Kirchner and Richard K. Thomas, "Desktop Decisions," *American Demographics*, 11 (9) (August 1989), pp. 34–37; and Richard K. Thomas and Russell J. Kirchner, *Desktop Marketing: Lessons from America's Best*, Ithaca, NY: American Demographic Books, 1991.

2. Kirchner and Thomas, op. cit.

3. Personal communication with George Moore, executive vice-president of Equifax (National Decision Systems), December 23, 1991.

4. Personal communication, February 22, 1990.

5. Data in this section have been altered in order to preserve confidentiality.

6. These data are not shown.

APPENDIX 15A:
LORENZ CURVES AND OTHER MEASURES
OF CUSTOMER CONCENTRATION

The examples in Chapters 12 to 15 suggest that a firm's clients are typically concentrated in relatively few geodemographic clusters, the top 3 to 8. This result is a variant of marketing's 80/20 principle: "Eighty percent of a firm's business comes from just 20 percent of its customers." Managers typically target future sales efforts toward these "heavy users" or "core buyers," allocating thousands of dollars for promotions, ads, and distribution plans for the purpose of reaching this select group.

This appendix examines the Lorenz curve, a mathematical-graphical tool, frequently used in geodemography, that quantifies the 80/20 principle. The appendix begins by defining a Lorenz curve and illustrating its graphic form. Next, the Lorenz curve is discussed more generally as one of several possible measures of customer concentration. Four abstract properties of these measures are outlined and illustrated. The properties are then used as a basis for evaluating the validity of the Lorenz curve approach. The Lorenz curve is shown to be misleading when used with cross-sectional data since it fails to account for stochastic elements in consumer behavior. In other words, if the technique is not applied judiciously, a firm may waste funds by directing them at inappropriate target segments. Finally, several alternative measures of customer concentration are discussed in light of these properties. One of these measures, the Gini index, requires special attention since it is a compact version of the Lorenz curve.

THE LORENZ CURVE:
A NONTECHNICAL DISCUSSION

Data for a Lorenz curve are given in Figure 15.5, which shows ten individuals ranked in ascending order of purchase volume. The top two buyers (numbers 9 and 10) account for 80 percent of the volume. Transforming these numbers to percentage terms and graphing them produces the graph shown in Figure 15.5. More formally, the Lorenz curve, which is denoted by $L(p)$, is the percentage of total sales accounted for by those $100p\%$ of individuals with the lowest levels of sales. The notation $100p\%$ stands for the pth-percentile. For example, if $p = 80$, then $100p\%$ refers to the bottom 80 percentile of the population. Thus, to draw Figure 15.5, first rank all individuals by their sales levels in a given time period.[1] Next, associate with each cumulative rank level a vertical point $L(p)$ of cumulative response. In Figure 15.5, for example, the vertical point associated with 80 percentile is $L(80) = 20$ percent of cumulative volume as indicated by the lines on the graph.

In geodemography, GD clusters replace individuals in this scheme. For example, in a 40-cluster GD system, a Lorenz curve ranks the clusters from worst to best in terms of the average (per individual) response rate. The graph then plots the cumulative percentage response rate. Table 14.1 provides an example of this process.[2]

Person	(x-axis) Purchasing Percentile	Purchase Volume	Cumulative Volume	(y-axis) Percent Cum. Vol.
1	lowest 10%	1	1	.1%
2	lowest 20%	5	6	.6%
3	30%	6	12	1.2%
4	40%	8	20	2.0%
5	50%	10	30	3.0%
6	60%	20	50	5.0%
7	70%	60	110	11.0%
8	80%	90	200	20.0%
9	90%	260	460	46.0%
10	100%	540	1,000	100.0%
	Total . . .	1,000		

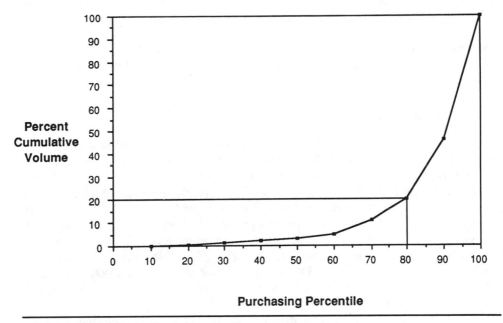

FIGURE 15.5. Data for a Lorenz Curve

SOME GENERAL CRITERIA

A Lorenz curve based on empirical observations is a powerful and often per-suasive tool. However, it has a number of shortcomings that are clear when the following general criteria for concentration indices are considered.

1. *Scale invariance:* A good concentration index should not depend on the scale used to measure sales.

2. *Partial transfers:* Transferring sales from an individual (or segment) with low sales to one with high sales should always increase the value of a concentration index.

3. *Time sampling:* A good concentration index should be invariant with respect to the length of the time period studied.

4. *Population instability:* A good concentration index should not depend on the number of customers (or segments) included. (In statistical terms, an observed value should be an unbiased estimate of the corresponding population value.)

It can be shown that the Lorenz curve satisfies the first two criteria (scale invariance and partial transfers) but that it fails to satisfy the last two criteria.[3]

Stochastic Elements of Consumer Behavior

The Lorenz curve fails to satisfy properties 3 and 4 because consumers do not make choices using fixed, deterministic, decision rules. In other words, there is a stochastic element, an element of unpredictability, in an individual's (or segment's) purchase patterns. The stochastic element requires managers who use geodemographic segmentation to guard against seeing differences where none exist.

Spurious Differences

To illustrate, suppose there is a list of 32,000 customers, each of whom decides on whether to buy product A or product B by flipping a fair coin. (The example is structured so that we know a priori that the relative market shares of A and B are determined purely by chance, not by any particular characteristic of the products or their marketing programs. This is admittedly an extreme case of stochastic behavior, but it clearly illustrates the problem.) Suppose further that in a given time period each customer has five purchase occasions. The laws of probability dictate that, on average, $(1/2)^5 \times (32,000)$, or 1,000 customers will buy product A on all five occasions. Of course, another segment of 1,000 customers will buy only product B, and the remaining 30,000 customers will have mixed sequences of A and B purchases.[4]

The manager of product A might label the types who purchased A all five times as *positive responders,* while he or she might label the types who purchased B all five times as *negative responders.* In other words, he or she might use these observed results to segment the client list into the best and worst prospect types. Clearly, however, there is a fundamental flaw in this segmentation plan because there are no true segments in this list of clients. The observed segments are illusory, due purely to the laws of chance.

This example also demonstrates that in some future time period the *positive responders* will regress toward the mean response, balancing their A and B purchases so that, in the long run, each *positive responder* will buy an equal proportion of A and B. To be precise, since *positive responders* are no different from other customers, very few—only about 32—will buy product A exclusively on the next five purchase occasions; that is, $(1/2)^5 \times (1,000) \cong 32$. The other 968 will distribute themselves over the other possible outcomes.

To summarize, though a given geodemographic segment may appear to consist of high response neighborhoods, these same neighborhoods (and a fortiori others in the same segment but not in the original list) may not buy as much of the product or may not buy it at all when given additional choice occasions. The buying behavior of these neighborhoods may regress toward the mean behavior, making their long-run market potential no better nor worse than the average.

THEORETICAL LORENZ CURVES

These considerations mean that, instead of basing important managerial decisions on observed Lorenz curves, a manager needs a theoretical Lorenz curve that is time-invariant. It must provide a measure that will be observed in the long run regardless of sampling variation. Such a measure is detailed by Schmittlein, Cooper, and Morrison using an approach based on a robust stochastic theory of consumer behavior.[5] Their approach is outlined below.

The NBD Model

The theory is based on the negative binomial distribution (NBD) model of consumer behavior, one of the most respected and most frequently verified models of stochastic choice. This model is based on three assumptions.[6]

1. Each individual has a fixed but unobservable long-run mean buying rate for the item in question.
2. Actual buying in any time period is the outcome of a random (Poisson) process with this fixed mean. In other words, even though an individual may buy an average of six cans of orange juice per month, in any one month this person's actual purchase level may differ from six.
3. Individuals differ with respect to their mean purchasing rates. In other words, some people simply buy more orange juice than others over the long run. These person-specific means, when viewed across individuals, are themselves outcomes of a random process that follows a gamma distribution.

These assumptions logically imply that for all individuals observed in any particular time period t, purchases follow a negative binomial distribution.[7] The manager can, therefore, use observed purchase rates in period t to rank individuals' volumes along a continuum from light to heavy and, based on these observed data, he or she can draw the corresponding Lorenz curve.

Spurious Segmentation Revisited

The key question posed by the stochastic view of buyer behavior is whether a Lorenz curve based on observed sales accurately represents customer concentration. This section shows that it does not. The reason: the true concentration of customers must be based on their real, long-run, buying rates, not on observed rates in a single-time period. However, the long-run rates are unobservable. Worse, without precautionary measures, an observed Lorenz curve always overestimates true concentration levels in high volume segments; that is, among so-called heavy users. Despite these problems, the correct Lorenz curve can still be accurately estimated. The solution is outlined here.

To show that observed Lorenz curves always overestimate the proportion of heavy users, consider the case where there are no differences in long-run buying rates, this time in a population of 100,000 people. When all individuals have the same long-run purchase rate, the NBD distribution reduces to a Poisson distribution. The mean of the Poisson, which we assume to be 1.68 units, governs the observed purchases of each customer in a given time period.

Table 15.4, in columns (a) and (b), shows how purchases would be distributed in a typical time period. Notice that some individuals—1,000 in this case—bought as many as six units in this particular period, even though their true long-run buying rate is the same as everyone else's.

Column (c) shows total sales broken down by units purchased. For example, the 15,000 people who each bought three units contributed 45,000 units, or 27 percent, to total sales.

The cumulative percent of total sales is shown in column (e). Column (e) contains the observed sales data that would normally be used to create a Lorenz curve. This column shows that 50 percent of the customers—those purchasing 0 or 1 unit only (the "light half")—accounted for only 18 percent of sales. The "heavy half" accounted for 82 percent of total sales.

TABLE 15.4. True vs. Observed Lorenz Curves

			Cumulative	
(a) Units Purchased	**(b)** Number of Persons	**(a) × (b) = c** Total Sales	**(d)** Percent of Persons	**(e)** Percent of Sales
0	19,000	0	19%	0%
1	31,000	31,000	50%	18%
2	26,000	52,000	76%	49%
3	15,000	45,000	91%	76%
4	6,000	24,000	97%	90%
5	2,000	10,000	99%	96%
6	1,000	6,000	100%	100%
Total	100,000	168,000		

mean
(units per person): 1.68

Source: Schmittlein, Cooper, and Morrison (1989).

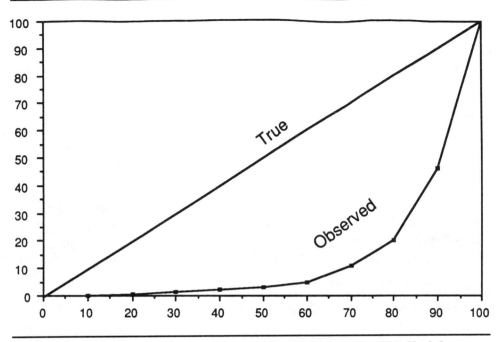

FIGURE 15.6. True vs. Observed Lorenz Curves Using the NBD Model

Management would be seriously misled if a Lorenz curve were drawn from these observed data. Figure 15.6 shows this curve, which suggests a considerable concentration of buying among heavy users. However, this curve is wrong because there are no true heavy users in this population. The true Lorenz curve is the 45° line shown in the Figure 15.6. The observed curve captures only the spurious concentration evident in this one period, a concentration due purely to random fluctuations in period-to-period buying.

Lorenz Curves and Length of Time Period

An accurate Lorenz curve must retain its shape regardless of the length of the buying period under study. In other words, true heavy users buy more of the product period after period than do true light users. The 1,000 individuals who bought six units are not true heavy users because next period they will distribute themselves proportionately over all seven categories. Thus, in periods of greater length the observed Lorenz curve will approach the 45° line. In general, Lorenz curves based on long periods are more accurate than those based on short periods.

Summary of Problem

In summary, consumer behavior is not deterministic. A stochastic or unpredictable element introduces noise into customer concentration measures such as the Lorenz curve. Unfortunately this noise always misleads management into believing that certain segments or certain types of individuals are heavier users than they really are. The example shows that even when there are no differences among customers—hence, no actionable volume-based segments— a Lorenz curve drawn with observed data will misleadingly suggest that core buyer types exist.

Solution to the Problem

The solution to this dilemma, outlined here, can be implemented by a competent statistician. The true Lorenz curve is a function of the percentile of interest, p, and the two parameters of the NBD distribution. To graph the true Lorenz curve, these parameters must be estimated.

Details of how to estimate the parameters of the NBD are given elsewhere; reviewing them here would derail the main line of argument.[8] However, using these estimates and the probability-generating formula for the NBD, one can sweep out the complete "true" Lorenz curve by letting p range from 0 to 1.[9]

GD Segmentation: Is It Worthwhile?

It should be emphasized that even though observed Lorenz curves overstate customer concentration, geodemographic approaches that target high responding segments are still worthwhile. The best estimate of response, based on one period's worth of data, is to order segments by their response per customer. However, a better approach is to track a sample of clients through two or three purchase cycles and to redo response indices based on multi-period rather than single-period purchase frequencies.

If this is impossible, perhaps because the product is purchased only once (such as life insurance), then follow-up studies on purchase rates among targeted segments are warranted to see whether these differ significantly from rates among nontargeted segments.

OTHER MEASURES OF CUSTOMER CONCENTRATION

A number of other measures of customer concentration have been suggested in the literature. Their names and properties are listed in Table 15.5. Because of its close association with the Lorenz curve, only one of these, the Gini index, is discussed here.

The Gini index provides a single number that summarizes the information contained in a Lorenz curve. Since greater concentration is indicated by Lorenz curves that are more bowed, the degree of "bowedness" is measured by the ratio of areas shown in Figure 15.7. Note the location of areas A and B: The Gini index is defined as a ratio of these two areas.

$$\text{Gini index} = \frac{\text{Area (A)}}{\text{Area (B)}}$$

TABLE 15.5. Measures of Customer Concentration

	Gini	Herfindahl	Entropy	K-Concentration
Scale Invariance	yes	yes	yes	yes
Partial Transfers	yes	yes	yes	no
Time Instability	no	yes	?	no
Population Instability	no	n.a.	n.a.	n.a.
Range of Index	(0,1)	([1/N], 1)	(0, log N)	(0,1)

Source: David C. Schmittlein, "Issues in Measuring Market Concentration among Firms, Suppliers, and Customers."

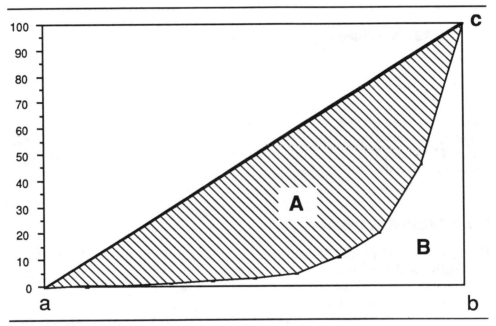

FIGURE 15.7. The Gini Index

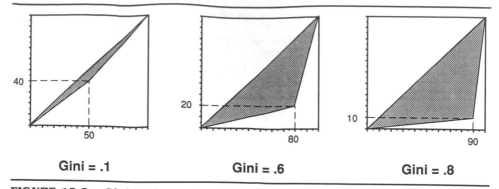

FIGURE 15.8.   Gini Indices Corresponding to Three Lorenz Curves

These three cases are simplified to convey the central idea. Each Lorenz curve is based on observed (discrete) data with one inflection point. A geometric argument can be used to find the shaded area in each figure.

When the axes are scaled in percentiles, as is usually the case, the right triangle *abc* (area B) has area 0.5. Thus, the Gini index may be rewritten as:

$$\text{Gini index} \;=\; 2 \;(\text{area A})$$

Figure 15.8 shows a few other examples that illustrate how the Gini index changes as a function of the bowedness in the corresponding Lorenz curve. Figure 15.8 shows that higher values of the Gini index are associated with more customer concentration.

CONCLUDING COMMENTS

This appendix defines and illustrates the Lorenz curve, a concentration measure frequently used to summarize the effectiveness of a given segmentation plan. Arguments show that a Lorenz curve based on observed counts always overestimates the amount of customer concentration. The appendix outlines a solution to this problem by fitting a stochastic model of buyer behavior to observed data and basing the Lorenz curve on the fitted model rather than on the observed data.

Other concentration measures are also reviewed briefly; one of these, the Gini index, is discussed in detail. The Gini index summarizes the information contained in a Lorenz curve. Management can use the Gini index to quickly diagnose the effectiveness of a proposed geodemographic segmentation plan. However, the Gini index and the Lorenz curve are subject to the same biases. Gini values reported to management should, therefore, be based on a fitted stochastic model to ensure their accuracy.

Notes

1. The response variable may be dollar revenues or unit revenues or some other relevant response measure.

2. Notice that this method skirts the issue of different absolute sizes among clusters. These sizes can be integrated into the analysis by reweighting the observed data—making a cluster's weight proportional to its size—and then projecting these reweighted values to the nation as a whole. Also note that sales might be ranked either in ascending or descending order. For example, Table 14.1 ranks clusters in ascending order. The resulting Lorenz curve is a mirror image of the one illustrated here.

3. See "Issues in Measuring Market Concentration among Firms, Suppliers, and Customers," David C. Schmittlein, working paper, the Department of Marketing, The Wharton School, University of Pennsylvania.

4. The expected distribution is:

5A		1,000
4A	1B	5,000
3A	2B	10,000
2A	3B	10,000
A	4B	5,000
	5H	1,000
Total		32,000

5. See David C. Schmittlein, Lee G. Cooper, and Donald G. Morrison, "Truth in Concentration in the Land of (80/20) Laws," working paper, University of Pennsylvania and UCLA, 1989.

6. See A. S. C. Ehrenberg *Repeat Buying*, Amsterdam: North Holland, 1972.

7. The term "logically imply" means that it is a mathematical fact that a gamma mixture of Poisson distributions is a negative binomial distribution. See Howard Raiffa and Robert Schlaifer *Applied Statistical Theory*, Cambridge, MA: Harvard University Press, 1961, especially Chapter 3.

8. See Ehrenberg (1972), op. cit.

9. The Lorenz curve at point p is denoted $L_\lambda(p)$. In terms of the gamma-mixing distribution of the NBD, it is written as follows:

$$L_\lambda(p) = \frac{1}{E(\lambda)} \int_0^{G(p)^{-1}} \lambda g(\lambda) d\lambda$$

where

$E(\lambda)$ is the mean of the gamma-mixing distribution.

$g(\lambda|r, \alpha)$ is the gamma-mixing distribution with parameters r and α, which are estimated via the NBD from a single period's worth of data.

$G(\lambda|r, \alpha)$ is the cumulative density function corresponding to the density function g.

16 EUROPE AND GEODEMOGRAPHY

All business surveys show that the 1992 message has been received.... The [Commission] intends to encourage businesses to anticipate the overall objective and to include a European dimension from now on in their strategic planning. Together with the general worldwide economic recovery, this business reaction to 1992 is the principal reason for the revival in investment in the Community.

Commission of the European Communities:
Fourth Progress Report of the Commission to
the Council and the European Parliament

INTRODUCTION

The marketing and technological elements that support geodemographic research systems are not unique to the United States. In fact, the ACORN system was introduced in Great Britain one year before the development of PRIZM in the United States. Today there are five major geodemographic systems competing in Britain, ACORN is available in other European countries,[1] and smaller competitors are emerging country by country.[2] The increased availability of GD systems is due to two important changes in the European market: the European Community's (EC) removal of internal trade barriers in 1992 and East-West unification.

This chapter reviews conditions supporting geodemography in Europe and provides information about existing European systems. The chapter is organized as follows: The first section outlines prerequisite conditions for the effective use of geodemography. The properties discussed provide a baseline against which given country environments can be assessed. Next, the chapter reviews direct and database marketing in Europe, Europe's regulatory environment beyond 1992, and European strategy delivery systems, including television and direct mail. Existing European systems are then reviewed and compared. The chapter concludes with remarks about developments that may shape European geodemography during the next decade.

COUNTRY FACTORS INFLUENCING THE USE OF GEODEMOGRAPHY

There are five macro-level prerequisites for the effective development and application of a GD system:

1. Existence of small area census geography
2. Existence of an efficient postal system linked to this geography
3. Diversity in the resident population
4. Well-developed media and communications systems
5. Existence of major client segments willing to purchase geodemographic information.

Although these prerequisites are met by nearly all EC countries, three aspects are particularly relevant: the diversity of the European population, the rapid development of new media, and the presence of both European and global marketing firms as potential clients.

THE EUROPEAN ENVIRONMENT

Population Size and Diversity

As Table 16.1 illustrates, the EC is 30 percent larger in population than the United States and nearly 300 percent larger than Japan. Population growth among the EC–12 is slower (1.6 percent per annum) than in the United States (5.5 percent) or Japan (4.0 percent). However, if the 12-member community expands to 15 and then to 18 members, as expected, the growth rates will change to 7.8 percent and 11.5 percent, respectively.[3]

The European population is more diverse demographically and culturally than the U.S. population. For example, Vandermerwe and L'Huillier suggest that Western Europe consists of six country clusters, as shown in Figure 16.1.[4] These clusters are suggested by language, economic, and cultural patterns.

Although differences in product use, shopping behavior, and preferences are culturally based, they are also linked to economic, education, and demographic factors that cut across cultural boundaries. For example, major metropoli-

TABLE 16.1. Basic Data for the EC

	EC	U.S.	Japan
Population			
EC-12 (1990)	325,011	248,855	123,599
EC-15 (1995)	347,744	256,324	126,084
EC-18 (2000)	362,381	262,458	128,591
	1.6%		
Growth Rate	7.8%	5.5%	4.0%
	11.5%		
Percent of Population (1990)			
Under 30	41%	47%	41%
Over 60	20%	17%	16%
GDP (billions, 1987)	$4,263.7	$4,436.2	$2,379.3
Per Capita (1987)	$13,208	$18,225	$19,510
Income Disparity	5.40	1.75	2.80
(Richest/Poorest)	Denmark/	Connecticut/	Tokyo/
	Portugal	West Virginia	Okinawa

Source: Sandra Vandermerwe and Marc-André L'Huillier, "Euro-Consumers in 1992," *Business Horizons* 32(1) (January–February 1989), pp. 34–40. Original source: *World Bank 1987–88 Population Report and World Projections.*

tan areas in all EC countries contain sophisticated urbanites much like "Money and Brains" from the U.S. PRIZM system or "Old Money" from the ACORN system. These people tend to have an international outlook; buy leading brands of durables, housewares, clothes, and automobiles; and exhibit less allegiance to cultural heritage than to high style. By being cognizant of the extremes of diversity and similarity, European GD systems support both within-country and cross-cultural segmentation.

Direct Marketing in Northern and Western Europe

One index of the need for GD systems is the extent of direct-marketing activity in a region, country, or country cluster. Although direct-marketing firms represent only about 10 percent of the GD-client base in the United States, a country's direct-marketing activity provides a good indicator of the availability of postal and census geography, the cornerstones of GD systems.

Table 16.2 shows mail-order and direct-marketing statistics for most EC countries and, by way of comparison, for Canada, Japan, Australia, and the United States. Variation among EC countries is evident, although some of this variation is due to regulatory constraints that will disappear after 1992. The table shows that direct marketing has gained an impressive foothold throughout Europe. For example, in Finland, France, the Netherlands, Sweden, Switzerland, the United Kingdom, and Germany, direct sales account for a higher proportion of retail sales than they do in the United States. Per capita sales in (West) Germany, Switzerland, Sweden, France, and Finland exceed per capita sales in Japan and approach the level found in Canada.[5] When the larger size of the European population is considered, its direct sales potential approaches that of the United States.

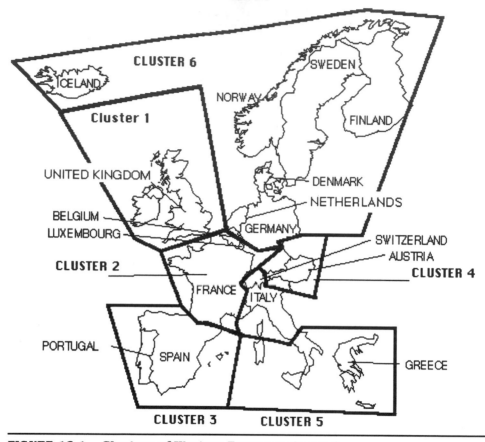

FIGURE 16.1.   Clusters of Western European Countries

Source: "Euro-Consumers in 1992." Sandra Vandermere and Marc-André L'Huillier, *Business Horizons,* Vol 32, No. 1. (Jan.-Feb., 1989), p. 34–40.

This potential has not gone unrecognized. Table 16.3 shows that the top three mail-order companies in the world are based in Western Europe. The German firms Otto Versand and Quelle are numbers one and two, followed by Great Universal Stores headquartered in the United Kingdom. U.S. firms occupy spots four through nine, with France's La Redoute at number ten. Part of the German dominance can be explained by the strength of the deutsche mark, allowing German firms to acquire leading U.S. mail-order companies. For example, Otto Versand owns Spiegel and Bertelsmann owns the Doubleday, Bantam, and Dell publishing companies.

Fishman suggests that European mail order has been handicapped by high postal rates, limited list media, low credit-card penetration, tighter regulations, and fragmented markets.[6] Against these odds, European firms have succeeded by innovative use of newspaper media, advances in interactive electronic marketing, attention to the quality of space and catalog graphics, and efficient use of agency-based catalog distribution. The regulatory unified Europe of 1992 promises even greater gains for direct-marketing firms that apply geodemographic techniques.

TABLE 16.2. International Mail-Order Direct-Marketing Statistics

	Sales (billions)	Year	Percent Retail Sales	Growth Rate Percent	Inflation Rate Percent	Population (millions)	Per Capita Sales
Europe							
Austria	$ 1.227	1990	3.9	7.5	3.3	7.6	161
Belgium	.736	1990	1.2	6.0	3.5	9.9	74
Denmark	.675	1990	2.8	-0.6	2.2	5.1	132
Finland	.584	1990	1.5	6.6	5.2	4.9	119
France	7.516	1990	2.5	4.4	3.4	56.0	134
Italy	1.419	1989	0.5	-1.7	6.5	57.0	25
Netherlands	1.042	1990	1.6	4.3	2.5	14.8	70
Sweden	1.351	1990	2.8	22.2	10.9	8.4	161
Switzerland	1.295	1990	2.6	5.2	5.4	6.6	196
United Kingdom	6.613	1990	2.8	0.8	9.3	57.0	116
West Germany	18.124	1990	4.2	16.9	2.7	61.8	293
Total Europe	41.563	—	—	—	—	332.4	100
Non-European Countries							
Canada	6.857	1990	—	10.0	5.0	25.9	265
Japan	11.230	1990	1.1	12.0	35.5	122.0	92
Australia	2.798	1989	5.0	25.0	8.4	16.1	174
Total Non-U.S	62.614	—	—	—	—	500.6	125
United States	151.614	1990	3.2	6.0	5.0	250.0	607

Source: Reprinted with permission of *Direct Marketing Magazine* (224 7th St., Garden City, NY 11530; October, 1991, p. 37.)

TABLE 16.3. The Ten Leading Global Mail Order Companies

Company Name	Country	Year of Data	Mail Order Sales (millions)	Type of Merchandise
Otto Versand	Germany	1990	7,415	General
Quelle	Germany	1990	6,350	General
Great Universal Stores	United Kingdom	1990	4,685	General
Sears, Roebuck & Co.	United States	1990	4,300	General, Insurance
United Automobile Association Services	United States	1990	4,291	Insurance
J.C. Penney	United States	1990	3,315	General, Insurance
Time Warner	United States	1990	2,784	Cable, Publishing
Telecommunications	United States	1990	2,602	Cable
Reader's Digest Association	United States	1990	1,757	Publishing
La Redoute	France	1989	1,642	General

Source: Direct Marketing (October 1991), p. 38.

EUROPE 1992 AND BEYOND

A single internal market consisting of almost 320 million consumers was officially dedicated December 31, 1992. The plan—set in motion by the Commission's 1985 white paper, "Completing the Internal Market"—significantly reduces the physical, technical, and fiscal barriers that have plagued postwar Europe. These restraints include varying national standards, time-consuming border controls, restrictions on the sale of banking services, laws limiting direct marketing, and state-owned television that severely restricted commercial messages. The plan is transforming the insular, protected national markets of postwar Europe to "an area without internal frontiers in which the free movement of goods, persons, services, and capital is ensured."[7]

Progress on this plan has been steady since the inception of the EC in 1951. However, since 1986, progress has been even more rapid due to changes in voting rule procedures within the European Council and increased trust on the part of member states. For example, the EC convened a special conference in December 1990 to start negotiations for the adoption of a single currency and to set up a system of central banks. A European currency, even if instituted only for commercial transactions, would facilitate the movement of goods and services throughout Europe. Manufacturing firms, for example, would be able to achieve previously infeasible economies of scale. Consumer goods manufacturers could mass market throughout Europe and would increase their use of large marketing research systems of the type found in the United States.

STRATEGY DELIVERY SYSTEMS IN NORTHERN AND WESTERN EUROPE

Geodemographic systems permit a firm to select target markets, but media must be available to deliver the firm's message to each target. Television and direct mail in particular are a GD system's natural partners. This section focuses on these two media and offers remarks about other developments that will impact the application of geodemographic systems in Europe.

Television[8]

To support a GD system, commercial television must be available, coupled with sufficient time for commercials. A wide variety of formats is needed to address targeted demographic profiles. Stations that serve well-defined local areas are also required to fulfill geographic targeting goals.

In the United States these requirements have permitted new formats to supplant network television as the prime strategy delivery tool. The two most formidable substitutes are cable and satellite direct television. In both cases, multiple channels permit precise targeting embedded in a consistent programming background of music, sports, news, comedy, or education.

In Europe the network television/direct television role reversal occurred even more rapidly than it did in the United States. The reason was that European executives had access to U.S.-proven technology and to pre-packaged programming in the form of U.S.-made movies, serials, game shows, mini-series, and sports shows. Two aspects deserve emphasis: the shift from public to private television and the shift from national to European television.

With regard to the first aspect, before 1980, Euro-TV consisted almost exclusively of state-owned channels subject to intense programming regulations. For example, in (*West*) Germany the two public stations could broadcast only 20 minutes of advertising per day and then only in blocks between 5:30 and 8:00 P.M. In France, as recently as 1983, there was only one privately owned station, Canal Plus.

Today, however, there are a variety of privately owned networks, many of which rely on direct satellite transmission; a technology that supports the shift to European television. European satellite television started in 1982 when the Australian media tycoon Rupert Murdock launched the satellite TV network Sky Channel. Since then no less than nine satellites have been launched:

Satellite	Country	Satellite	Country
TV-SAT1	Germany	Tele-X	Sweden
Olympus	European Space Agency[9]	BBS	United Kingdom
TDF1	France	Astra	Ireland
TV-SAT2	Germany	Eutelsat	P&T of European
TDF2	France		Communication

The first seven of these satellites broadcast signals that can be received directly by any household with a $500 parabolic receiving dish. The other two, Astra and Eutelsat, require the more expensive receiver used by cable companies who distribute the signal to their subscribers.[10]

European commercial television is now dominated by Murdock and three other media giants: Silvio Berlusconi, Robert Maxwell,[11] and Leo Kirch. Each of these entrepreneurs has mimicked Ted Turner's exploits in the United States. For example, in addition to Sky Channel, Murdock launched the BBS satellite in 1989 to create three new stations that serve the British market. Berlusconi controls the three commercial stations in Italy and is acquiring interests in French, German, and Spanish television. Maxwell's consortium owns part of TF1 (France's largest commercial station), controls MTV Europe, and owns shares of a German cable television company. It plans (though these plans have been jeopardized by the firm's financial problems) to launch its own satellite to start six new cable channels specializing in MTV, movies, sports, and children's shows. Kirch owns SAT1, the German cable network that will soon expand to reach at least half of (West) Germany's 24 million households.

In EC countries, further changes will be supported by the Commission's directive on "television without frontiers." As the Commission's fourth progress report states:

> The directive on television without frontiers, when adopted, will... guarantee the free circulation in the community of TV programs broadcast from any Member State and will also promote the production and distribution of audiovisual works of European origin.[12]

Experts fully expect that by 1996 certain parts of Europe will be served by more than 100 television channels.

Other Media

Other media such as newspapers, magazines, and outdoor displays are well-developed in EC countries. These are discussed thoroughly in other sources; detail that need not be repeated here.[13] However, videotex is more widely available in Europe than it is in the United States. The leading European videotex system is Minitel in France, with over 5.8 million terminals installed.[14] Other systems include one offered by British Telecom (initiated in 1980) with approximately 90,000 subscribers, and the German videotex system (started in 1983) with approximately 52,000 subscribers. Due to its prominence, we will briefly review Minitel and suggest the relevance of videotex for the development of marketing research systems.

Any French household served by telephone lines can subscribe to Minitel through the French telephone company. A subscription costs about 12 dollars per month and includes a keyboard/terminal with a 25 line by 40 character display in videotex mode and a 25 line by 80 character display in ASCII mode. With this terminal, the subscriber can access Minitel's on-line services, including a national phone directory, train schedules, stock prices, teleshopping services, and electronic mail. In addition to the fixed monthly charge, subscribers pay a variable charge per minute of connect time and may pay other charges depending on the service they are accessing.

Videotex and Marketing Research Systems

Marketing research data accumulate where transactions occur. Transaction points are often automated for reasons of operational control but their role in data collection is soon recognized, as in the cases of UPC scanner systems, credit cards, and bank cards. In the case of videotex-based sales, transaction data accumulate across a wide variety of product and service categories.

These data serve as ideal input to an integrated marketing research system. For example, one of Minitel's most important marketing activities is business-to-business catalog shopping. Office-supply companies, foodstuffs manufacturers, and others display their product and price listings on-screen. Businesses viewing this information can submit an order directly from their terminal. In this capacity, Minitel serves as a combination catalog and telephone number. The vendor accumulates a customer database directly from Minitel transactions. Catalog shopping on Minitel will likely spread to the consumer segment. If so, this database function will become extremely important to consumer goods marketers and their supporting research suppliers.

Transaction data flowing from the market to managers serves as a basis for strategy formulation. Minitel could also be used for the flip-side of this equation; that is, to deliver strategy back to the market via on-line sales promotions, price lists, and other forms of electronic direct mail. However, this capability is tightly controlled by French law. Companies are not allowed to use Minitel as an advertising or promotional medium, a policy designed to reduce consumer objections to adopting the system. The phone company reasoned correctly that to allow advertising would make subscribers feel as if they were paying for something that they did not want.

In theory, however, a videotex system can deliver messages and services to particular targets. These targets could be self-selected in the sense that each subscriber would be able to filter the source of incoming messages. With sophisticated electronic switching systems, a videotex system could be optimally controlled by both demand- and supply-side participants. Each firm would decide to which households to send their messages, and each household would decide from which firms they would be willing to receive messages.

EUROPEAN GEODEMOGRAPHIC SYSTEMS

European-based geodemography began in the United Kingdom when CACI launched the British version of ACORN in 1978.[15] Until 1985 ACORN was the sole European system, but since then competition has come primarily from four other U.K.-based suppliers. (See Table 16.4 for details.) These four—CCN Systems, Pinpoint Analysis Ltd., SPA Marketing Systems, and Credit and Data Marketing Services, Ltd. are expected, along with CACI, to be the dominant competitors in EC countries. For example, CACI has replicated its system in France, Germany, and in several other European countries, as will be discussed shortly. Because the EC plan calls for service as well as product-based economic unification, these firms and possibly others are developing systems on a country-by-country basis.[16]

The next section reviews the five British systems; the following section reviews the ACORN systems in Finland, France, Germany, Norway, and Sweden. Since the keenest competition exists in Great Britain, the British systems are discussed in more detail. (Research comparing the British systems, using Gains charts and chi-square tests, is discussed in Appendix B.) CACI's systems are summarized as a reference for the interested reader; details are relegated to Appendix C.

The British Systems[17]

The building block for British GD systems is the British Bureau of Census data collection unit known as the Enumeration District (ED). There are approximately 20 million households in Great Britain, which are sorted into about 130,000 EDs. Each ED contains on average 150 households, or about 400 people. Thus, the British ED, being the smallest census unit for which complete data are collected, is analogous to the U.S. system's CBG (census block group).

ACORN: A Classification of Residential Neighborhoods

The British version of ACORN is based on 40 census variables. The resulting system classifies every address in Great Britain into one (and only one) of 38 "neighborhood" types (segments). The system is supplemented by other services

TABLE 16.4. Geodemographic Systems in the United Kingdom

System	Number of Clusters	Census Base (launched)	Company	Other Products and Database Links
ACORN	38	1981 (1978)	CACI Market Analysis	Marketfile GB, Shopping Centre Planner, TGI, BMRC, NRS
MOSAIC	58	—	CCN Systems: Great Universal Stores	NRS, BMRC
PiN	60	1981 (1986)	Pinpoint Analysis, Ltd.	AGB, TCA, Attwood Panel databases, NRS
SET	26	—	SPA Marketing Systems	The Marketing Machine
SuperProfiles	150	1981	Credit and Data Marketing Services, Ltd.	NRS, TGI, the Electoral College Roll

of CACI, including Shopping Centre Planner and Marketfile GB, which CACI claims is Great Britain's largest marketing database. Marketfile GB contains all the company's demographic, economic, market research, retail, administration, and geographic data on a single, integrated computer system. Shopping Centre Planner is a spatial econometric model that can be calibrated to any particular retail activity. It involves the application of CACI's retail and population databases together with its model of the road network. The model can provide trade area statistics for 2,200 shopping centers together with measures of the attractiveness of each center. The system can also calibrate the effect of distance travelled on demand for a particular item.

MOSAIC: CCN Systems

CCN Systems is a subsidiary of Great Universal Stores. Its GD system, MO-SAIC, is based on financial and demographic information collected by CCN and Great Universal Stores. In this regard it differs from a pure GD system, one based solely on census data. MOSAIC contains 58 segments of residential addresses. These can be aggregated upwards to produce reports at three other levels of postal geography: by post code, by post code groupings, and by post code sectors. (These roughly correspond to ZIP codes, carrier routes, and districts in the United States.)

Like several other British systems MOSAIC is linked to the National Readership Survey (NRS), a continuous survey of newspaper and magazine readers divided into monthly studies, each weighted to reflect the current adult population of Great Britain.[18] Respondents to the Businessman Readership Survey (BSRS), which measures readership in the universe of managers and their technical advisors, are also coded into the MOSAIC System.

PiN: Pinpoint Analysis, Ltd.

Pinpoint, a strong rival to ACORN, was launched in 1986. The Pinpoint Identified Neighborhood System (PiN) uses 60 geodemographic segments based on the 1981 British census.

In 1988, Pinpoint formed a joint venture with another British research firm, AGB, to link the PiN System with AGB's TCA and Attwood panel databases. These links provide a way to monitor the consumer purchasing and retail shopping habits among a large sample from each of the PiN segments. They are analogous to links between single-source and geodemographic systems in the United States. The National Readership Survey has also been coded into the PiN system.

In addition to PiN, Pinpoint Analysis, Ltd., offers FiNPiN (Financial PiN), which adjusts the weights applied to the census variables by a segment's financial activity. FiNPiN is, therefore, a GD System specifically designed to reflect the financial characteristics of each PiN segment.

SET: SPA Marketing Systems

The SET System offered by Sales Performance Analysis is a social area classification system that is based on census data but which classifies postal sectors, rather than EDs, into 26 neighborhood types. The company also markets a computer software package, called The Marketing Machine, that performs a variety of geodemographic indexing, mapping, and reporting functions. The Marketing Machine is delivered on a desktop system that a client can use in-house.

SuperProfiles: Credit and Data Marketing Services, Ltd.

SuperProfiles is the largest of the GD systems in Great Britain, boasting 150 neighborhood types. The clusters are ranked on the basis of affluence and are regularly adjusted to reflect the latest government and commercial statistics.[19] Like several of the others, SuperProfiles is also linked to data from the National Readership Survey and to the British Market Research Bureau's Target Group Index (TGI). The TGI is an annual multi-product, multimedia survey conducted among a national sample of over 24,000 adults, ages 15 and up. It is analogous to the National Family Opinion poll conducted in the United States, a service described in more detail in Chapter 13.

Table 16.4 summarizes the number of clusters in each British system, the launch date, the parent company, and some of the other databases to which a system is linked.

ACORN Systems in Europe

CACI Federal has also calibrated the ACORN system in Finland, France, Germany, Norway, and Sweden. This section describes these systems. Keep in mind that each country's census geography is different. For example, the census hierarchy in France consists of commune, canton, district, department, and region, with 22 regions comprising the nation. In Finland the smallest unit is also called a commune—of which there are more than 500—but communes aggregate upward to provinces and then to 14 districts. In each case the ACORN system is based on that country's smallest unit for which complete census data are available.

The resulting systems vary considerably in size: Norway has 30 clusters, Germany has 53. The number of clusters is a function of the population of a country, its census geography, and the inherent ethnographic and socioeconomic diversity among households in the country. For example, a country with a homogeneous population would have fewer GD clusters than would a country with an ethnically diverse population, all other factors held constant.

Table 16.5 summarizes CACI's systems in the six European countries, with the U.S. system included as a baseline. Table 16.5 shows the databases and facilities maintained by CACI. In all cases, a standard ACORN GD segmentation system is available; the number of clusters is shown in parentheses. ACORN is supplemented by various ad hoc marketing research services as well as by other large databases that link it with retail locations, workplace statistics, and drivetime statistics.

Some of the principle services offered in other countries include standard market potential and segment profile reports, trade area analyses, and mapping studies to support site-location and competitive analyses. Contrary to the situation in the United States, credit analyses are not available in most other

TABLE 16.5. ACORN Systems in Europe

| Country | Census | ACORN | VALS | Available Databases[a] | | | | Facilities[a] | | | |
				Market Research	Retail Location	Workplace Statistics	Drive Times	Market Profiling Potential	Trade Area Analyses	Credit Analyses	Mapping Boundary Files
Finland	yes	yes (na)	—	yes	yes	—	—	yes	yes	—	yes
France	1982	yes (41)	—	yes	yes	—	yes	yes	yes	—	yes
Germany	1978	yes (53)	—	yes	—	—	—	yes	—	—	yes
Great Britain	1981	yes (38)	—	yes	yes	yes	yes	yes	yes	—	yes
Norway	yes	yes (30)	—	yes	—	—	—	yes	yes	—	yes
Sweden	yes	yes (29)	—	yes	yes	—	yes	yes	yes	—	yes
USA	1990	yes (44)	yes	yes	yes	—	—	yes	yes	yes	yes

[a] CACI offers other databases and facilities than those listed here.

countries due to tighter restrictions on corporate access to private records and stringent right-to-privacy laws.

CACI has standardized its reporting formats from one country to the next in order to ease the international manager's job of assimilating and using reported information. For example, Table 16.6 shows a product potential profile created by CACI in Great Britain for the manufacturer of Mumford Snack Bits.[20] In this case, some 40,000 British households with known consumption levels for this product were sorted into the 38 ACORN segments. The profile reveals that supergroup J, especially segments J34 and J35, contains the heaviest users, with indices of 161 and 176, respectively. Based on this report, the brand manager for Mumford Snack Bits would target retail outlets located in J34 (Spacious Inter-War Semis, Big Gardens) and J35 (Villages with Wealthy Older Commuter) neighborhoods. The retail distribution strategy would be coordinated with an intensified media campaign delivered to these neighborhoods, even if this meant decreasing funds to other areas, such as G25, with an index of 37.

DEVELOPMENTS IN EUROPEAN GEODEMOGRAPHY

The geodemographic environment is clearly more complex in Europe than it is in the United States. Differences in tastes and consumer behavior exist between EC nations due to differences in language, culture, and mores. However, as argued earlier, there are pockets of intense demographic and behavioral similarities in Europe that cut across national boundaries. Dr. Sandra Vandermerwe, a consultant affiliated with Geneva's International Management Institute, emphasizes this point when she says, "Think of clusters, not of countries. Manufacturers such as Benetton and Swatch can set up programs for these regional clusters. Others will require a second layer of regionalization that further recognizes pockets of Europe, a truly local strategy and message will be required for each area."[21]

Multilayered complexity is the raw material on which geodemography thrives. Because of it, a double-tiered matrix system is likely to be developed for the European market.

Two approaches to system development have been identified. The first is a bottom-up approach building from a series of individual country systems of the type developed by CACI. The individual systems will then be recast so that similar segments in different countries are identified. The second approach, a top-down system build, requires more initial planning and resources since it builds the system holistically, not incrementally, by country. This approach requires that census data be accumulated for all countries to be included in the system. These data are analyzed as a unit, treating the member countries much like member states are treated in a U.S. system.

A top-down approach is more likely to find segments that straddle country borders. For example, the Alsace region of France may end up in a French-German segment, whereas a country-by-country build would split the region along the national border.

Results from either approach will have to be fine-tuned to accommodate idiosyncracies. However, a double-tiered system will allow a client to plan marketing strategy at any appropriate level: within a single country, across several countries, or on a pan-European basis. The idea is illustrated in Table 16.7;

TABLE 16.6. ACORN Product Profile Great Britain (Mumford Snack Bits)

ACORN Group	Product (× 1000)	Percent	Base (× 1000)	Penet Percent	Percent	Index
A Agricultural Areas	185	4.0	1486	3.3	12.4	119
B Modern Family Housing, Higher Incomes	754	16.2	6452	14.5	11.7	112
C Older Housing of Intermediate Status	851	18.3	7944	17.8	10.7	103
D Older Terraced Housing	133	2.9	1996	4.5	6.7	64
E Council Estates—Category I	432	9.3	5294	11.9	8.2	78
F Council Estates—Category II	295	6.4	4311	9.7	6.8	66
G Council Estates—Category III	159	3.4	2946	6.6	5.4	52
H Mixed Inner Metropolitan Areas	146	3.1	1661	3.7	8.8	84
I High Status Non-family Areas	194	4.2	1631	3.7	11.9	114
J Affluent Suburban Housing	1103	23.8	7550	17.0	14.6	140
K Better-off Retirement Areas	222	4.8	1644	3.7	13.5	130

ACORN Type	Product (× 1000)	Percent	Base (× 1000)	Penet Percent	Percent	Index
A01 Agricultural villages	142	3.1	1089	2.4	13.1	126
A02 Areas of farms and small holdings	42	0.9	397	0.9	10.6	102
B03 Postwar functional private housing	173	3.7	1682	3.8	10.3	99
B04 Modern private housing, young families	120	2.6	1131	2.5	10.6	102
B05 Established private family housing	314	6.8	2424	5.4	12.9	124
B06 New detached houses, young families	139	3.0	1145	2.6	12.1	116
B07 Military bases	8	0.2	70	0.2	11.0	105
C08 Mixed owner-occupied and council estates	157	3.4	1571	3.5	10.0	96
C09 Small town centres and flats above shops	218	4.7	1837	4.1	11.8	114
C10 Villages with non-farm employment	261	5.6	1928	4.3	13.5	130
C11 Older private housing, skilled workers	216	4.6	2608	5.9	8.3	79

D12 Unmodernized terraces, older people	81	1.8	1196	2.7	6.8	65
D13 Older terraces, lower-income families	43	0.9	615	1.4	7.0	67
D14 Tenement flats lacking amenities	9	0.2	186	0.4	4.9	45
E15 Council estates, well-off older workers	132	2.9	1622	3.6	8.2	78
E16 Recent council estates	80	1.7	941	2.1	8.5	81
E17 Better council estates, younger workers	163	3.5	1850	4.2	8.8	85
E18 Small council houses, often Scottish	57	1.2	881	2.0	6.5	62
F19 Low-rise estates in industrial towns	139	3.0	2149	4.8	6.5	62
F20 Interwar council estates, older people	108	2.3	1487	3.3	7.3	70
F21 Council housing, elderly people	48	1.0	674	1.5	7.0	68
G22 New council estates in inner cities	55	1.2	901	2.0	6.1	58
G23 Overspill estates, higher unemployment	67	1.4	1200	2.7	5.6	53
G24 Council estates with some overcrowding	28	0.6	601	1.4	4.6	44
G25 Council estates with greatest hardship	9	0.2	243	0.5	3.9	37
H26 Multi-occupied older housing	15	0.3	104	0.3	14.7	141
H27 Cosmopolitan owner-occupied terraces	46	1.0	597	1.3	7.6	73
H28 Multi-let housing in cosmopolitan areas	13	0.3	188	0.4	7.0	67
H29 Better-off cosmopolitan areas	71	1.5	771	1.7	9.3	89
I30 High status non-family areas	89	1.9	789	1.8	11.3	109
I31 Multi-let big old houses and flats	85	1.8	607	1.4	13.9	134
I32 Furnished flats, mostly single people	20	0.4	234	0.5	8.6	83
J33 Interwar semis, white-collar workers	310	6.7	2849	6.4	10.9	104
J34 Spacious interwar semis, big gardens	406	8.7	2422	5.4	16.7	161
J35 Villages with wealthy older commuters	235	5.1	1282	2.9	18.3	176
J36 Detached houses, exclusive suburbs	153	3.3	997	2.2	15.3	147
K37 Private houses, well-off older residents	142	3.1	950	2.1	14.9	143
K38 Private flats, older single people	81	1.7	694	1.6	11.6	111
U39 Unclassified and unmatched respondents	167	3.6	1611	3.6	10.4	99
TOTALS	4641	100.0	44525	100.0	10.4	100

TABLE 16.7. A Double-Tiered Geodemographic System

European Supertype		Country				
		Belgium	Denmark	France	U.K.	
Geodemographic segment	1	√	√	√	√	yes
	2	√	√	√	√	.
	3	√	√	√	√	.
	4	√	√	√	√	.
	:	√	√	√	√	.
	k	√	√	√	√	yes
Common to all but one	k+1	√	√	√	No	partial
	:	√	√	No	√	.
	K	No	√	√	√	.
Common to all but two	l+1	√	√	No	No	.
	:	√	No	√	No	.
	L	No	No	√	√	partial
Unique types	M+1	√	No	No	No	unique
	:	No	√	No	No	.
	:	No	No	√	No	.
	M	No	No	No	√	unique

industry experts say that two companies, Equifax and CACI, are most likely to implement it.

CONCLUSION

The economic unification of Western Europe and democratization of Eastern Europe present new opportunities for consumer products manufacturers, service providers, and database marketers. Since the demand for marketing research systems is derived from activity in these economic sectors, we expect a rapid expansion of research suppliers in EC countries and eventually in Eastern Europe.

This chapter reviews factors that influence the use of geodemographic research systems and illustrates how these factors operate in the European Community. We concluded that the size, population diversity, and presence of prospective client firms can support geodemography throughout the continent. Further, other elements (such as satellite direct television, traditional media, and an efficient postal service) that support marketing strategy are present and increasing in sophistication in the European market.

Five competing GD systems based in Great Britain were compared: ACORN, Mosaic, PiN, SET, and SuperProfiles. ACORN systems in five other countries were also reviewed. The growth of GD systems in the United Kingdom suggests that geodemography will quickly diffuse throughout the European Community. This diffusion is likely to first occur on a country-by-country basis, with unified European systems emerging later.

Notes

1. Finland, France, Germany, Norway, and Sweden. See Table 16.5 for details.

2. For example, SARIN, an Italian firm, offers Microzone for Italy, a French firm, COREF, offers Les Lifestyles, and in Germany there is Demoskopie.

3. The EC consists of 12 members, the EC–12, but may expand to 15 by 1995 and later, around the year 2000, to 18. The EC–12 consists of Belgium, Denmark, France, Germany, Greece, Italy, Ireland, Luxembourg, the Netherlands, Portugal, Spain, and the United Kingdom. The EC–15 would add Austria, Norway, and Sweden; the EC–18 would also include Iceland, Finland, and Switzerland. See Sandra Vandermerwe and Marc-André L'Huillier, "Euro-Consumers 1992," *Business Horizons* 32(1) (January–February 1989), pp. 34–40. The appendix contains relevant statistics by country.

4. See Vandermerwe and L'Huillier, op. cit.

5. Figures cited for Germany largely reflect the situation in what was West Germany. Although direct marketing now exists in what was East Germany, its scale is small and statistics are not yet available.

6. See Arnold Fishman, "1986 International Mail Order Guide," *Direct Marketing* 50(4) (August 1987), pp. 168–171.

7. From the EC Commission's Single European Act, ratified July 1987.

8. Facts in this section are abstracted from "TV Moguls Battle for Europe," Fred V. Guterl, *Best of Business Quarterly* 10(4) (December 1988), pp. 76–82.

9. The European Space Agency (ESA) is a consortium of 13 West European countries.

10. See *The Audio-Visual Media in the Single European Market*, Periodical 4 (1988) published by the Office for Official Publications of the Communities, Brussels-Luxembourg.

11. Maxwell's death in November 1991 left his companies in a state of disarray, impeding their ability to sustain growth.

12. *Commission of the European Communities*, op. cit, p. 22.

13. See, for example, S. Jain, *International Marketing Management*, Columbus, OH: Merrill Publishing Co., 1990, and S. Onkvisit and J. Shaw, *International Marketing*, Columbus, OH: Merrill, 1989.

14. See George Nahon and Edith Pointeau, "Minitel Videotex in France: What We Have Learned," *Direct Marketing* 49(4) (January 1987), pp. 64–71, 125; and Anthony Ramirez, "'Baby Bells' Look Good to French," *New York Times*, October 10, 1991, p. D4.

15. Personal discussions with George Moore, one of the inventors (the others are Richard Webber and Kenneth Baker) of the ACORN system. Interestingly, both Webber and Moore later left CACI, Webber to develop MOSAIC for CCN in Great Britain and Moore to start National Decision Systems and VISION. See also J. R. Beaumont and K. Inglis, "Geodemographics in Practice: Developments in Britain and Europe," *Environment and Planning* 21 (A) (1989), pp. 587–604.

16. U.S. entrants in the European market and other developments, including double-tiered, EC-wide systems, are outlined in a later section of this chapter.

17. This section is based on Maureen Johnson, "The Application of Geo-Demographics to Retailing—Meeting the Needs of The Catchment," *Journal of the Market Research Society* 31 (January 1989), pp. 7–36.

18. In principle each month's study is based on 144 equal interviewer assignments but in practice, Scotland and certain areas in England and Wales are over-sampled in order to increase the unweighted numbers of readers of some important regional newspapers.

19. Each British firm updates its database on a regular basis.

20. The name of the product category is disguised to adhere to confidentiality guidelines imposed by the manufacturer.

21. Sandra Vandermerwe, "1992 and Promotion," *Adweek* 30(45) (November 6, 1989), pp. 6–9.

APPENDIX 16A:
THE EUROPEAN COMMUNITY

The European Community consists of 12 member nations, which are summarized in Table 16.8 on several economic dimensions. The four largest members are Italy, France, the United Kingdom, and the former West Germany, each having a population of about 60 million. The German economy has exhibited the most strength over the last decade, as its gross domestic product per capita suggests. (West) Germans enjoy a high standard of living, as evidenced by their ownership of cars (424 per 1,000 population) and telephones (621/1,000), although telephone penetration is even higher in Denmark (783/1,000). (Figures for East Germany are excluded from the table because accurate estimates were unavailable at the time of publication.)

Germany and France are arguably the key political and economic members of the European Community. These two countries have been willing to cooperate on most major elements of the unification program, such as a European central bank and a common currency. The United Kingdom, the third most powerful member, has been slower to approve many measures. However, the UK's separatist tendencies showed signs of diminishing in 1991 and 1992 as theories of unification became economic realities. For example, completion of the channel tunnel means that the UK is now more closely linked to the European continent than at any other time in its history. The tunnel facilitates the transport of goods and people between the United Kingdom and Europe and is expected to alter the distribution, labor, and investment practices of companies on both sides of the channel.

TABLE 16.8. Economic Data for EC Nations

	Units	Reference Period	Belgium	Denmark	France	Germany	Greece	Ireland
Population								
Total	Thousands	1985	9,857	5,113	55,162	61,015	9,950	3,562
Inhabitants per km^2	Number		323	119	101	245	75	51
Increase last 10 yrs	Percent		0.1	0.1	0.5	−0.1	1.0	1.2
Gross Domestic Product (GDP)								
At current rates	Billion US $	1985	79.1	57.9	510.3	625.0	32.8	18.2
Per capita	US $		8,022	11,319	9,251	10,243	3,294	5,123
Gross savings ratio	Percent GDP	1985	15.9	14.9	18.0	22.2	12.2	18.1
Government expenditures on goods and services	Percent GDP	1985	17.3	25.3	16.3	19.9	19.9	19.1
Standard of Living								
Private consumption	US $	1984	7,637	6,826	8,009	7,274	4,118	4,338
Cars/1,000 population	Number	1985	335	293	360	424	108	206
Telephones/1,000	Number	1985	414	783	541	621	336	235
Televisions/1,000	Number	1985	303	392	297	372	158	181

TABLE 16.8 *(Continued)*

	Units	Reference Period	Belgium	Denmark	France	Germany	Greece	Ireland
Population								
Total	Thousands	1985	57,128	366	14,484	10,230	38,602	56,618
Inhabitants per km²	Number		190	141	427	111	76	231
Increase last 10 yrs	Percent		0.3	0.1	0.6	0.6	0.8	0.1
Gross Domestic Product (GDP)								
At current rates	Billion US $	1985	358.7	3.6	125.0	20.7	164.2	449.7
Per capita	US $		6,278	9,745	8,628	2,032	4,253	7,943
Gross savings ratio	Percent GDP	1985	17.7	65.3	24.1	23.1	21.0	19.2
Government expenditures on goods and services	Percent GDP	1985	19.5	15.6	16.3	14.2	14.0	21.1
Standard of living								
Private consumption	US $	1984	6,254	8,540	7,270	3,076	5,456	6,535
Cars/1,000 population	Number	1985	355	414	341	135	240	312
Telephones/1,000	Number	1985	448	404	410	166	369	521
Televisions/1000	Number	1985	244	336	317	140	256	336

APPENDIX 16B:
STATISTICAL COMPARISONS
AMONG THE BRITISH SYSTEMS

Surprisingly, more comparative research has been completed for British GD systems than for those in the United States. Figure 16.2 shows cumulative Lorenz curves for four of the British systems: ACORN, MOSAIC, PiN, and FiNPiN.[1] For each system, the neighborhood types are arranged in decreasing order of discriminatory power, based on the ratio of customers in a given segment to British households overall. The cumulative percent of customers versus cumulative percent of British households is plotted for each system.

The results illustrate that, for this particular application, the PiN system works best, followd by ACORN, FiNPiN, and MOSAIC. For example, selecting 10 percent of the population using PiN yields a cumulative index of about 165. This means that 16.5 percent of the target population has been identitfied, a gain of 65 percent over a random (shotgun) procedure.

Chi-Square Tests

These four systems were also compared using the chi-square approach described in Chapter 13.[2] Recall that a GD system is helpful, say, for identifying VCR own-

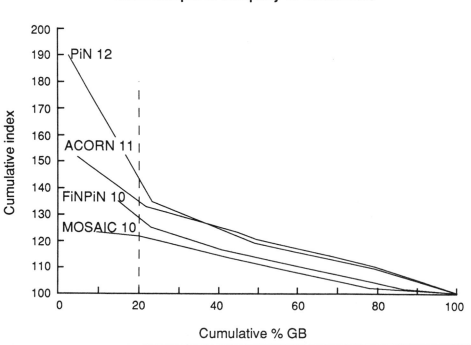

Data: sample of company 'A' customers

FIGURE 16.2.   Cumulative Lorenz Curves for Four British Systems

Source: Peter Sleight and Barry Leventhal, "Applications of Geodemographics to Research and Marketing" *Journal of the Market Research Society* 31 (1) (January 1989), pp. 75–101.

TABLE 16.9. **Chi-Square Tests for Four British Systems**[1]

System	Observed Chi-square[2]	Number of Segments
ACORN	491	11
MOSAIC	226	10
PiN	554	12
FiNPiN	305	10

[1] Abstracted from Table 3, p. 87, of Peter Sleight and Barry Leventhal, "Applications of Geodemographics to Research and Marketing," *Journal of the Market Research Society* 31 (1) (January 1989).

[2] Each of the observed chi-square values is significant at the $p = .001$ level (critical level $\approx$ 28, with 9 df).

ers, only if the proportion of VCR owners varies significantly between segments in the system.

Ten thousand customer postcodes were profiled in each system and used to target customers for a consumer durable. Although chi-square values were calculated at several levels, Table 16.9 shows a synopsis at the same levels used earlier in the Lorenz curves.

For this particular consumer durable, PiN and ACORN have the most descriminatory power. However, all four systems show significant variation; each exceeds the conservative chi-square cut-off by a considerable margin ($\chi^2 \geq 28$ has $p \leq .001$ with $df = 9$).

Summary

These two comparisons are context-specific. They should not be interpreted as general evidence favoring one British system over another. In fact, when other contexts are examined, results tend to balance out. According to James Rothman, "The general conclusion to be drawn from these comparisons would seem to be that differences are small and that the choice between systems varies according to the subject matter and the judgment and other needs of the user."[3]

Rothman also cites some comparisons of the actual overlap between systems. For example, Rothman found that when ACORN is compared directly to PiN by cross-classifying NRS respondents into both systems, 81 percent of those in ACORN Group A also live in PiN Type A. Since PiN Type A is larger, its profile consists not only of ACORN Type A (59 percent) but also of ACORN Types K (22 percent) and C (13 percent). Comparisons among other types also yield considerable overlap.

The would-be client in Great Britain, therefore, faces a situation similar to that faced by clients in the United States, and should select a company on the basis of its full range of services, not necessarily on the basis of claims about superior statistical results.

Notes

1. The appendix to Chapter 15 provides a review of the Lorenz Curve.

2. See Peter Sleight and Barry Leventhal, "Applications of Geodemographics to Research and Marketing," *Journal of the Market Research Society*, 31(1) (January 1989), pp. 74–101.

3. James Rothman, "Editorial," *Journal of the Market Research Society*, 31(1) (January 1989), pp. 1–5.

APPENDIX 16C:
ACORN SYSTEMS IN EUROPE

Tables 16.10–16.13 provide detail from CACI's ACORN systems in Britain, France, Norway, and Sweden. Each country's system is based on the census data unique to that country. The systems, therefore, differ in size and composition. For example, there are 39 ACORN segments in the British system, 41 in the French system, 30 in the Norwegian system, and 29 in the Swedish system. The tables show the size of each segment in absolute and percentage terms. Further detail can be obtained by contacting an ACORN representative.

TABLE 16.10. ACORN: Great Britain

	ACORN GROUPS	Current Population	Percent
A	Agricultural Areas	1,870,387	3.5
B	Modern Family Housing, Higher Incomes	9,240,962	17.1
C	Older Housing of Intermediate Status	9,622,087	17.8
D	Older Terraced Housing	2,309,623	4.3
E	Council Estates—Category I	7,046,273	13.0
F	Council Estates—Category II	4,844,799	9.0
G	Council Estates—Category III	3,867,644	7.2
H	Mixed Inner Metropolitan Areas	2,080,276	3.8
I	High Status Non-Family Areas	2,268,742	4.2
J	Affluent Suburban Housing	8,577,830	15.9
K	Better-Off Retirement Areas	2,064,291	3.8

	ACORN TYPES	Current Population	Percent
A01	Agricultural villages	1,431,922	2.6
A02	Areas of farms and small holdings	438,465	0.8
B03	Post war functional private housing	2,313,416	4.3
B04	Modern private housing, young families	1,870,727	3.5
B05	Establishing private family housing	3,206,083	5.9
B06	New detached houses, young families	1,511,279	2.8
B07	Military bases	339,457	0.6
C08	Mixed owner-occupied and council estates	1,885,816	3.5
C09	Small town centres and flats above shops	2,211,957	4.1
C10	Villages with non-farm employment	2,571,793	4.8
C11	Older private housing, skilled workers	2,952,521	5.5
D12	Unmodernized terraces, older people	1,353,182	2.5
D13	Older terraces, lower-income families	748,562	1.4
D14	Tenement flats lacking amenities	207,879	0.4
E15	Council estates, well-off older workers	1,868,836	3.5
E16	Recent council estates	1,487,727	2.8
E17	Better council estates, younger workers	2,661,338	4.9
E18	Small council houses, often Scottish	1,028,372	1.9
F19	Low-rise estates in industrial towns	2,485,760	4.6
F20	Interwar council estates, older people	1,586,035	2.9

TABLE 16.10. (*Continued*)

	ACORN TYPES	Current Population	Percent
F21	Council housing, elderly people	772,984	1.4
G22	New council estates in inner cities	1,073,155	2.0
G23	Overspill estates, higher unemployment	1,646,156	3.0
G24	Council estates with some overcrowding	821,826	1.5
G25	Council estates with greatest hardship	326,507	0.6
H26	Multi-occupied older housing	200,858	0.4
H27	Cosmopolitan owner-occupied terraces	572,936	1.1
H28	Multi-let housing in cosmopolitan areas	386,503	0.7
H29	Better-off cosmopolitan areas	919,979	1.7
I30	High status non-family areas	1,138,397	2.1
I31	Multi-let big old houses and flats	834,208	1.5
I32	Furnished flats, mostly single people	296,137	0.5
J33	Interwar semis, white-collar workers	3,072,990	5.7
J34	Spacious interwar semis, big gardens	2,684, 265	5.0
J35	Villages with wealthy older communites	1,582,134	2.9
J36	Detached houses, exclusive suburbs	1,238,441	2.3
K37	Private houses, well-off older residents	1,218,680	2.3
K38	Private flats, older single people	845,611	1.6
U39	Unclassified and unmatched respondents	293,884	0.5
	Area Total	54,086,798	100.0

Source: CACI Limited, London and Edinburgh.

TABLE 16.11. ACORN: France[1]

	ACORN GROUPS	1982 Population	Percent	Base Percent	Index
A	Retirement Areas and Areas of Old People	52373	5.9	6.4	92
B	Tourism and Tertiary Activities	732471	83.0	6.2	1334
C	The Heart of Rural France	3024	0.3	7.6	5
D	Small Agricultural Villages	379	0.0	8.2	1
E	Small Centres with Agriculture/Industry	10527	1.2	9.3	13
F	"Quiet" Cities in the Industrial Basin	19977	2.3	15.0	15
G	Rural Areas of Commuters	3918	0.4	6.2	7
H	Suburban Towns, Rapid Development	8461	1.0	7.8	12
I	Residential Suburbs	51368	5.8	6.4	90
J	Industrial and Commercial Towns	0	0.0	19.2	0
K	Metropolitan Areas (especially Paris)	0	0.0	4.8	0
L	Industrial Suburbs	0	0.0	2.8	0
	Area Total	882498	100.0	100.0	

	ACORN TYPES	1982 Population	Percent	Base Percent	Index
A01	Retirement by the sea and in the sun	12552	1.4	1.9	76
A02	Retirement in the countryside	16748	1.9	3.5	54
A03	Areas for family and sporting	23073	2.6	1.0	251

TABLE 16.11. *(Continued)*

ACORN TYPES	1982 Population	Percent	Base Percent	Index
holidays				
B04 The "classiest" resorts	320088	36.3	1.0	3685
B05 Metropolitan areas in the southeast	353885	40.1	1.0	3985
B06 Pleasant towns south of the Loire	58498	6.6	4.2	157
C07 Farming villages in the region of Centre	2952	0.3	1.7	19
C08 Towns and villages in the high valleys	0	0.0	1.0	0
C09 Hinterland of the Atlantic coast	0	0.0	2.8	0
C10 Agricultural areas in the North and West	72	0.0	2.0	0
D11 Villages in decline	118	0.0	2.6	1
D12 Poor towns, young active people	0	0.0	2.4	0
D13 Prosperous towns, young active people	140	0.0	1.5	1
D14 Old villages resisting decline	121	0.0	1.7	1
E15 Small centres, agricultural industry, in East	0	0.0	1.9	0
E16 Centres on Atlantic coast and in North	0	0.0	3.3	0
E17 Commuter areas, Parisian professional	10527	1.2	2.4	50
E18 Areas of young working people in West	0	0.0	1.7	0
F19 Industrial centres, development stopped	7311	0.8	2.8	29
F20 Modern cities with agriculture/industry	0	0.0	1.4	0
F21 "Working" towns in recession	3436	0.4	2.6	15
F22 Large, rural towns: commerce/tourism	9230	1.0	2.7	39
F23 Small towns with a mix of industries	0	0.0	3.8	0
F24 Poor villages: traditional industries	0	0.0	1.7	0
G25 Residential areas of young people	0	0.0	1.5	0
G26 Middle-class towns/areas	0	0.0	2.0	0
G27 Villages with professionals/commuters	3918	0.4	2.7	17
H28 New towns around Paris	0	0.0	0.8	0
H29 Poor, industrial suburbs	8461	1.0	2.0	48
H30 Tertiary suburbs of metropolitan areas	0	0.0	5.0	0
I31 Residential suburbs, middle-sized towns	51368	5.8	3.0	195
I32 Dormitory towns around large towns	0	0.0	3.5	0
J33 Young towns: industry and services	0	0.0	2.2	0
J34 Middle-sized towns, developing slowly	0	0.0	4.3	0
J35 Large, old towns, little development	0	0.0	1.8	0
J36 Small towns: industry and tourism	0	0.0	7.1	0
J37 Middle-sized towns, tradition of industry	0	0.0	3.9	0
K38 Chic areas and suburbs in West and South	0	0.0	3.0	0
K39 Business areas: East, Centre, and North	0	0.0	1.8	0
L40 Industrial suburbs of large towns	0	0.0	2.8	0
U41 Unclassified	0	0.0	0.0	0
Area Total	882498	100.0	100.0	

Source: Based on statistics provided by the French Census authorities. Base percent represents France as a whole.

TABLE 16.12. ACORN: Norway

	ACORN GROUPS	1980 Households	Percent	Base Percent	Index
A	Wealthy Family Areas, Young Suburban	5685	8.8	11.7	75
B	Wealthy Established Areas of Mixed Housing	1405	2.2	7.6	29
C	Well Established Suburbs and Towns	1408	2.2	6.0	36
D	Areas of Cheaper Family Housing	1452	2.2	9.7	23
E	Middle Norway	3055	4.7	8.4	56
F	Blue Collar/Working Areas	23771	36.7	27.3	134
G	Agricultural, Fishing, Forestry, and Hunting Areas	26889	41.5	20.6	202
H	Poor Inner City Areas	648	1.0	8.1	12
U	Unclassified	425	0.7	0.7	100

	ACORN TYPES	1980 Households	Percent	Base Percent	Index
A01	Exclusive family areas with teenagers	367	0.6	1.8	31
A02	Affluent areas, young families	2192	3.4	4.2	81
A03	Affluent, urban areas, young families	1409	2.2	2.2	99
A04	Younger families, more productive, less wealthy	1717	2.7	3.5	75
B05	Wealthy high status areas, few children	333	0.5	3.3	15
B06	Wealthy areas of town	1072	1.7	3.3	50
B07	Areas of public sector employees	0	0.0	0.9	0
C08	Older, well-established suburbs (Oslo)	304	0.5	3.1	15
C09	Older, established suburbs, towns (ex-Oslo)	1104	1.7	2.9	59
D10	Young families—first homes (not Oslo)	688	1.1	2.5	43
D11	Areas of young families in co-op flats	0	0.0	4.1	0
D12	Working areas—new co-op flats	764	1.2	3.1	38
E13	Middle Norway—towns throughout country	987	1.5	3.7	41
E14	Rural areas on outskirts of towns	2068	3.2	4.7	68
F15	Hydro areas	257	0.4	0.4	109
F16	Areas of traditional/heavy industry	1885	2.9	4.5	65
F17	Rural areas of mixed employment	7592	11.7	4.9	242
F18	Commuter areas—with families	4066	6.3	5.3	119
F19	Other commuter areas	4643	7.2	4.2	172
F20	Rural areas with mixed employment	3712	5.7	4.9	117
F21	Areas of production, young, quite wealthy	1616	2.5	3.3	76
G22	Areas of large farms	6919	10.7	5.0	216
G23	Fishing areas	387	0.6	2.9	21
G24	Areas of small holdings	8071	12.5	3.5	360
G25	Poorer areas of small holdings	6175	9.5	4.0	241
G26	Poor fishing areas	1130	1.7	2.0	89
G27	Traditional farming areas	4207	6.5	3.3	195
H28	Areas of pensioners, highly educated	648	1.0	6.7	15
H29	Immigrant areas	0	0.0	1.4	0
U30	Unclassified	425	0.7	0.7	100
	Area Total	64738	100.0	100.0	

Source: Based on statistics from Statistisk Sentralbyr. Base percent represents Norway as a whole.

TABLE 16.13. ACORN: Sweden

	ACORN GROUPS	1982 Households	Percent	Base Percent	Index
A	High Income Non-Family Areas	0	0.0	10.0	0
B	Poorer Non-Family Inner City Areas	2130	12.6	10.9	115
C	Higher Income Young Family Areas	6077	36.0	9.5	377
D	Very High Income Areas	273	1.6	4.8	33
E	Low Income Areas of Modern Co-operative Housing	2830	16.7	7.7	217
F	Rented Flats with Young Families	4	0.0	6.5	0
G	Mixed Housing Areas, often in Industrial Towns	1101	6.5	24.0	27
H	Old-fashioned Agricultural and Mining Communities	3449	20.4	7.9	257
I	Rural Areas with Some Industry	1032	6.1	18.6	33
U	Unclassified	0	0.0	0.0	0

	ACORN TYPES	1982 Households	Percent	Base Percent	Index
A01	Small but smart city flats	0	0.0	4.9	0
A02	Divided houses, young and old people	0	0.0	4.2	0
A03	Unmodernized old city houses	0	0.0	0.8	0
B04	Young urban couples in rented flats	0	0.0	5.7	0
B05	Co-ownership town centre flats	2130	12.6	5.3	239
C06	Better-off growing communities	868	5.1	5.3	97
C07	1960s and early 1970s housing, higher incomes	4837	28.6	3.4	854
C08	Spacious, modern, young executive suburbs	372	2.2	0.9	248
D09	Large, modern houses for the very well-off	0	0.0	1.7	0
D10	Established well-off suburbs	273	1.6	3.1	52
E11	Modern suburbs with high immigrant concentrations	0	0.0	1.1	0
E12	Student areas	1007	6.0	1.8	337
E13	Small modern flats for young families	0	0.0	2.4	0
E14	Small rented flats, young singles and pensioners	1823	10.8	2.4	442
F15	Modern co-ownership family housing	0	0.0	2.7	0
F16	Family homes with young children	4	0.0	1.3	2
F17	Postwar family suburbs	0	0.0	2.5	0
G18	Higher income centres	454	2.7	3.3	82
G19	Modern town-centres housing, older people	641	3.8	2.5	149
G20	Small industry centres	6	0.0	4.8	1
G21	1950s growth towns, some manufacturing	0	0.0	3.6	0
G22	Rural centres	0	0.0	9.8	0
H23	Mining areas	0	0.0	0.6	0
H24	Remote farming areas, poor housing	1061	6.3	2.5	247
H25	Traditional farming areas, poor housing	2388	14.1	4.8	292
I26	Prosperous rural areas, large households	998	5.9	4.2	141
I27	Villages with non-farm employment	0	0.0	8.2	0
I28	Farming and fishing areas (mostly Northern)	34	0.2	6.2	3
U29	Unclassified	0	0.0	0.0	0
	Area Total	16896	100.0	100.0	

Source: Based on statistics from Statistika Centralbyr. Base percent represents Sweden as a whole.

PART FOUR

ADVANCED TOPICS

17 MICROMERCHANDISING SYSTEMS

INTRODUCTION

Micromerchandising means tailoring the advertising, merchandising, and operating emphasis in a store to the shopping patterns of that store's customers. A micromerchandising system blends single-source data, geodemographic data, and trade area data in order to support precise retail practices at the store level while integrating business strategy across stores. For manufacturers a micromerchandising system facilitates fact-based selling, focused sales force execution, and store-specific merchandising. For retailers micromerchandising makes operations more efficient, helps target local marketing efforts, and coordinates these efforts with both the store's and the manufacturer's national campaigns.

This chapter explains the micromerchandising concept and presents two systems for implementing it. The chapter opens by reviewing arguments that establish the need for micromerchandising and contrast the properties of a micromerchandising system (MMS) with those of three traditional merchandising systems: trade area systems, geodemographic systems, and single-source systems. In each case, examples illustrate how the alternative approach works and why it may be less effective than micromerchandising.

Next, the text explores key assumptions of micromerchandising, especially the idea that it can support partnerships between manufacturers and retailers. Partnering runs counter to industry practice, where the separate interests of manufacturers and retailers are typically stressed. In fact, micromerchandising began as a manufacturer's tool to implement fact-based selling to improve a manufacturer's leverage with its retail accounts. However, the partnership view has encouraged system designers to try to balance the benefits received by both parties and to build systems that unify their efforts to manage consumer demand.

Three databases are used to build a micromerchandising system: a consumer purchases database (containing scanner data), a consumer characteristics database (containing geodemographic data), and a trade area database (that links a store to surrounding neighborhoods). The next section discusses the system-build process and illustrates it with concrete examples. Once built, a micromerchandising system produces forecasts of item potential on a store-by-store, as well as many other useful reports. Forecasting models disaggregate a trade area's overall population into segments with different buying habits, providing a detailed understanding of the interaction between shopper types, their location relative to the store, and their demand for different items sold there.

After system-build techniques have been explained, the chapter presents several applications. A mini-case stresses certain features while system reports illustrate others. The chapter closes by discussing limitations of existing systems and speculating about future developments.

TRADITIONAL MERCHANDISING APPROACHES

The innovations offered by a micromerchandising system are clearer if they are contrasted with features of three other approaches: trade-area–based systems, stand-alone geodemographic systems, and scanner-based systems. This section outlines the main features of these alternatives in order to point out one or two key flaws with each approach. An MMS unifies the distinct perspectives, thereby overcoming each flaw.

Trade Area Methods

Trade area merchandising systems define a store's trade area as a geographic polygon within which the store's shopper population lives. Census tracts surrounding the store are wholly or partly included in the store's trade area as a function of their size, their distance from the store, and their geographic orientation relative to the store. Directional gradients for this retail gravity model are based on population densities, competitor locations, physical barriers, and traffic patterns. Once a store's trade area is built, its demographic profile is fixed and defined as the composite profile of member census tracts.

The premier example of a trade-area–based merchandising system is General Food's Super Market Solutions.[1] Although Super Market Solutions can be used for a variety of brand management applications, three of its programs—Product Potential, Case Allocator, and Promotion Proposal Generator—illustrate the system's key application: to profile a product's existing customer base against households in store trade areas, indexing stores with respect to their potential to move the product.

Valid applications of the trade area method depend in large part on the system's definition of trade area, a definition that causes certain problems.[2] Most critically, a store's trade area is built top-down, using national averages to identify the size of its shopper population. This size estimate (for example, store S has 4500 shoppers per week) is linked only to the size of surrounding census tracts, not to their composition. The key flaw: a store's actual shopper population is not profiled by demography or by shopper groups that may prefer certain items over others. Simply put, a store's customers are not interviewed to determine where they live, who they are, or what they tend to buy, nor is this information gathered by non-interview techniques. Patronage is largely inferred on the basis of an implicit gravity model that connects a census tract's raw size and location to a store's location. As a result, trade-area–based systems do not identify specific types of shoppers as patrons of a given store.

Despite this weakness, trade area models have gained widespread acceptance because they offer marked advantages over older methods and because, unlike the approach reviewed next, they are specifically designed to solve packaged goods merchandising problems.[3]

Geodemographic Systems

Geodemographic systems have been adopted for merchandising applications, though these systems were originally built to solve direct-marketing problems, as reviewed in Chapters 12 to 14. Here we merely note their strengths and weaknesses as stand-alone retail merchandising systems.

One strength is that a GD system's perspective is the neighborhood, not the trade area. A neighborhood is considerably smaller and more homogeneous than a census tract. The idea of "neighborhood" is operationalized precisely in such systems using census block groups or postal ZIP+4 areas. For example, where a census tract might contain 4000 households, a census block group "neighborhood" contains only 300 households, and a ZIP+4 "neighborhood" contains only 10 to 15 households on average. Second, because they are linked to media databases, GD systems not only estimate sales potential as do trade area systems, but they also help a manufacturer or retailer capture a trade area's sales potential by coordinating national and local media efforts.

However, these advantages are counterbalanced by a lack of detailed data about stores and their customers. Specifically, a GD system does not contain volumetric data on consumer grocery buying patterns, nor does it contain information about item level sales. Because GD systems were not developed with packaged goods merchandising in mind, they do not provide a sales manager with precise recommendations about which stores to target or how many cases of an item to allocate to a given store. Therefore, although GD systems identify who lives in certain neighborhoods, they fail to link those neighborhoods to a given store's clientele or to that clientele's in-store shopping behavior.[4]

Scanner Systems

Knowledge of in-store shopping behavior is the forte of single-source systems such as InfoScan and SCANTRACK. As detailed in Chapters 9 and 10, both Nielsen and IRI have developed specific reporting services to support certain aspects of micromerchandising, such as fact-based selling. For example, IRI's PromotionScan brochure remarks:

> Retailers are becoming increasingly objective in their evaluation of in-store merchandising. Therefore, it's more important than ever to sell the volume and profit potential of your promotions to retailers. With PromotionScan

you can generate profit and loss statements for the retailer demonstrating the bottom line benefits of your programs.[5]

Despite voluminous data collected from both store and shopper panels, single-source systems do not explicitly link in-store behavior to neighborhood characteristics. In other words, a scanner system's brand-by-brand focus is too narrow for most merchandising applications. From the merchandising perspective, it would be better to have single-source data reported in a way that identifies the multiple store options facing a given family in order to account for store-switching behavior and to match trip type with store type.[6]

Rather than depend on single-source suppliers, a retailer could use its own scanner data to develop a custom-merchandising system. However, the retailer would have to be willing to devote the computer and analytic resources to perform complex analyses. Interested manufacturers could not provide help in this process since the needed data are proprietary to the retailer. Furthermore, the custom approach would not analyze all available products in a particular category because it focuses only on those products carried by the retailer. In other words, results would be biased (or non-existent) for new items and items not carried by the retail chain in question.

Figure 17.1 summarizes the foregoing discussion. It shows the three traditional perspectives and suggests that a more complete system would integrate all three.

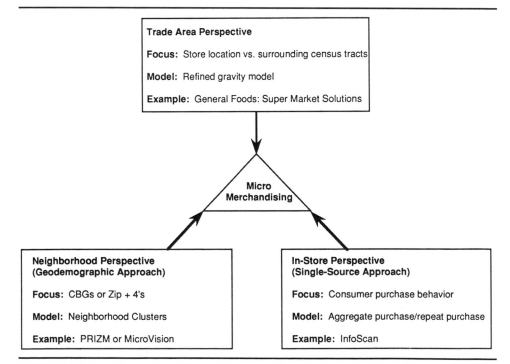

FIGURE 17.1.   Three Traditional Perspectives Integrated in a Micro-merchandising System

THE MICROMERCHANDISING CONCEPT

Traditional approaches compartmentalize the interests of a manufacturer and members of its retail distribution network, as Figure 17.2a illustrates. In the traditional view, the manufacturer focuses on sales to the trade and uses trade deals to stimulate retail orders. Once the retailer receives a product shipment, he or she assumes the primary responsibility for stimulating consumer take-away.[7] Thus, the traditional view vertically integrates demand, a process that, unfortunately, neutralizes a manufacturer's point-of-sale influence over consumer transactions and forces a retailer to make complex tradeoffs among merchandising strategies for items in the same category.

The micromerchandising concept fuses the interests of a manufacturer and its retailers and suggests that both parties share management of consumer take-away, as Figure 17.2b illustrates. In this revised view, manufacturers and retailers coordinate strategies as well as operational execution of these strategies. The result is mutual support to achieve manufacturer/retailer shared sales goals among a population of consuming households.

For the micromerchandising concept to work, channel partners must better understand consumers in each store's trade area yet maintain strategic coordination among trade areas. Micromerchandising helps position each store clearly in the minds of local-area consumers, an important goal given today's complex array of store images. Micromerchandising recognizes that distinct consumer segments respond differently to various pricing, assortment, and store layout plans. It facilitates precisely targeted marketing efforts that combine the retailer's local power with the manufacturer's national reach. This approach might better be

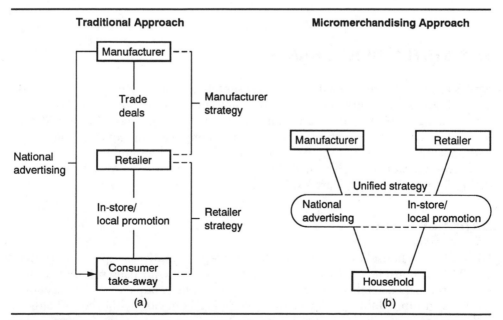

FIGURE 17.2. Merchandising Strategies

called "vertically integrated marketing" because it permits top-down influences from the manufacturer to reinforce bottom-up influences from the retailer.

Two segmentations are typically used to implement the micromerchandising concept. Consumers are segmented into groups so that generalizations can be made regarding the behavior patterns and product assortment needs of each group. Stores are segmented into types—based on a combination of store traits, consumer characteristics, and trade area characteristics—so that sound marketing policies can be developed by store type.

These ideas are implemented using three databases:

1. A *consumer purchase database* (containing volumetric data that reveal purchase patterns at all levels of transaction activity)
2. A *consumer characteristics database* (containing geodemographic data that link consumers to their neighborhoods)
3. A *store facts database* (containing store profile data that characterize different stores within and between chains)

Figure 17.3 provides detail for the three databases (each representing a traditional merchandising perspective) that are integrated in a micromerchandising system. (The exhibit shows the Kraft building blocks. The Spectra system, discussed subsequently, uses PRIZM rather than MicroVision data.) In the Kraft system, Information Resources, Inc., supplies volumetric data via InfoScan's household panel, Equifax Marketing Decision Systems supplies geodemographic data via MicroVision, and Market Metrics supplies store profile data. The next section explains how to build a micromerchandising system. The Kraft system is discussed first and the Spectra system is discussed second.

THE SYSTEM BUILD: KRAFT

Kraft's approach defines a nationally representative set of "shopper groups" (clusters of households) using behavioral data, constructs sets of market specific "store types" using store facts data, and links these two classifications through MicroVision (95) by profiling a store in terms of its shopper group composition. Since certain shopper types tend to frequent certain stores, the number of store types in a given market is usually small. Each store type becomes a specific merchandising target. These steps are explained next.

Shopper Groups

IRI's InfoScan household panel is a nationally representative sample of more than 60,000 U.S. households. (See Chapter 7 for details.) Kraft uses volumetric data to sort these households into a small set of shopper groups so that households within a group exhibit similar in-store shopping behavior, while households in different groups exhibit distinct behaviors.[8]

Consumer Purchase Dbase

Supplier: Information Resources, Inc.
Source: InfoScan
Nature: Scanner Data from 40,000-household panel
in major Kraft product categories
Period: Jan. 1988–Dec. 1989 (2 years)
Facts: Demographics plus:
-penetration/buying rate/purchase cycle
-percent volume bought on (Coupon/Feature/
Display/Price Reduction.)

Consumer Characteristics Dbase

Supplier: Equifax: National Decision Systems
Source: MicroVision (95/50)
Nature: GD results from clustering 19 million
ZIP+4 neighborhoods
Period: Latest available annual update
Facts: Lifestyle, geodemographic measures
crystalized from 200+ census and
financial variables. Linked to major media

Store Facts Dbase

Supplier: Market Metrics
Source: Store attributes, trade areas dbases
Nature: Store environment and trade area data
for approximately 28,000 retail stores
Period: 1989 (most recent at time of system build)
Facts: -Store location/size ($ACV)
-Buying power of nearby neighborhoods
-Drive time/traffic patterns

FIGURE 17.3. Components of Kraft's Micromerchandising System

331

Each IRI household was characterized by its levels on nine measures of in-store purchase behavior:

1. Total shopping trips per quad week
2. Dollars requirements in primary store
3. Dollars spent to purchase items on feature
4. Dollars spent to purchase items on display
5. Dollars spent to purchase price-reduced items
6. Dollars spent using manufacturer coupons
7. Dollars spent on private label brands
8. Dollars total spent per quad week (total trip base)
9. Dollars total spent per quad week (IRI base)

IRI then sorted their household panel into the MicroVision (95) system and summarized each of the 95 segments by its mean score on each of the nine measures. This process resulted in a 95 × 9 data matrix where a given row represents all IRI panel households belonging to that row's MicroVision segment. Entries in a row are the mean levels of each of the nine volumetric measures listed earlier; that is, the mean number of shopping trips per quad week (variable 1), the mean dollar amount spent in each household's primary store (variable 2), and so forth.

The resulting 95 × 9 data matrix was then submitted to a two-step "factor then cluster" procedure (as explained in Chapter 12, Appendix B). The factor analysis of variables recovered four factors that explained 77 percent of the raw score variation in these data. The 95 rows were subsequently clustered—using Ward's Minimum Variance method in SAS—on the basis of four factor scores per household. Six shopper groups emerged, as shown in Table 17.1. This procedure, therefore, aggregates the 95 MicroVision segments "upward" to a six-group solution customized by each segment's packaged goods buyer behavior.

Store Types

Whereas the shopper groups are a "fixed system" nationwide (that is, a full margin shopper in Chicago exhibits approximately the same in-store behavior as a full margin shopper in Seattle), store types are built market-by-market for the 70 major metro markets included in Kraft's system.

The objective in a particular market is to sort all stores into a small set of homogeneous store types. For example, there are about 650 major retail grocery stores in the Chicago metro area. Each store is characterized by its shopper group profile. Thus, a store's record is a six-part vector with the percentage of shopper group $g(g = 1,6)$ as the gth entry.

To form this vector, a store's trade area population is sorted into the shopper group classification. Since the store's trade area is a mosaic of MicroVision (95) neighborhoods, the neighborhoods are first sorted into MicroVision, then aggre-

TABLE 17.1.   Kraft's Shopper Classification

Type	Characteristics
Full Margin Shopper	Mixed middle to older (35–74) Affluent Active, busy Few children Frequent trips; willing to pay Entertain at home
Merchandise-Ables	Middle-aged (30–54) Relatively affluent Active, sports busy lifestyles Traditional family (ages 0–18) Low education levels High $$ per trip/infrequent trips
Planners and Dine-Outs	Mixed middle to older (30–74) Upper-middle income Mixed white and blue collar Some college; few children Very infrequent shopping trips Diverse spending; planned shopping
Frequent Shoppers	Young (19–39) Low to middle income Singles/couples: few children Very frequent shoppers; low $$/trip High total grocery dollars
Minibaskets	Older (60+) Low income; low education Inactive lifestyles Relatively frequent shopping trips
Commodity Shoppers	Mixed age groups Low income/education Many young children High number Black and Hispanic High store loyalty Buy generics/private labels

gated upward to the six shopper groups. The result shows that a given store's trade area is composed of N1 shopper group 1 neighborhoods, N2 shopper group 2 neighborhoods, and so on.

Kraft then clusters the stores in a metro-market by analyzing each store's shopper group profile, this time without an intervening factor-analysis step. Typically, 4 to 6 store types emerge. Usually, results are "clean;" that is, a given store type is dominated by three or fewer shopper groups.

THE SYSTEM BUILD: SPECTRA

The Spectra system, like Kraft's system, combines geodemographic, trade area, and scanner data. Unlike the Kraft system, Spectra uses PRIZM segments (rather than MicroVision segments). It also refines PRIZM's lifestyle model using lifestage information, employs a proprietary trade area model (rather than Super Market Solution's model), and often supplements scanner data with data from other suppliers in order to customize applications. Although Spectra, like Kraft, builds its applications around a base of shopper groups, Spectra's household classification contains 54 cells rather than 6. Where Kraft routinely generates (metro-market) store clusters based on shopper group profiles, Spectra generates store types customized to an application. Resulting store types are, therefore, not necessarily formed from each store's shopper group profile.

Critical elements of the Spectra system are now discussed. Following this discussion, applications of both systems are illustrated.

The Lifestyle/Lifestage Matrix

The lifestyle component of Spectra's shopper classification grid is a reduced form of PRIZM. Recall that PRIZM contains 40 lifestyle segments obtained by factoring and then clustering U.S. census data at the census block group (CBG) level. Spectra's system designers aggregated these 40 segments upward to 9 lifestyles. They argue that repeated applications of geodemography in packaged goods categories show that a significant portion of the variance in buyer behavior can be captured with fewer segments, especially segments exhibiting marked differences in affluence and urbanization.[9]

Results are summarized in Table 17.2. For example, households in the upscale suburbs lifestyle show elevated incomes and superior education levels and tend to live in urban and suburban fringes around major cities such as San Francisco, Dallas–Fort Worth, and Washington, D.C. In contrast, households in the mid-urban melting pot are middle-income and live primarily in urban areas. Each of the other lifestyles is characterized by its particular blend of demographic and geographic traits.

Repeated studies with geodemographic segments alone also revealed that GD systems often distort or mask important differences in grocery purchase behavior among segments. Spectra's designers recognized that grocery purchases are strongly influenced by a household's stage in the family life cycle. By including lifestage in the analysis, much of the distortion could be eliminated. Lifestage can be indexed by crossing the presence or absence of children with the age of the head of household (HOH), as shown in the following list:

1. HOH aged 18–34 with children
2. HOH aged 18–34 without children
3. HOH aged 35–54 with children
4. HOH aged 35–54 without children
5. HOH aged 55–64
6. HOH aged 65 and over

TABLE 17.2. Spectra Lifestyle Segments[1]

	Predominant Characteristics										
	Household Income		Education		Occupation		Urbanization		Race		Region	
Lifestyle Segment	Level	Index	Level	Index	Level	Index	Level	Index	Level	Index	Level	Index
Upscale suburbs	100k+	382	4+	211	UWC	166	Sub Fr	178	Cauc	173	West	133
Traditional families	50–75k	158	some	120	LWC	108	Sub Fr	171	Cauc	111	West	132
Mid/upscale suburbs	75–100k	155	4+	135	UWC	133	Urb Fr	165	Cauc	113	NE	133
Metro elite	75–100k	118	4+	174	UWC	139	Urban	211	Other	120	West	168
Working class towns	20–25k	110	HS	110	Service	106	Rur/Twn	192	Cauc	112	Cntrl	117
Rural towns and farms	20–25k	117	HS	119	Farm	318	Rur/Twn	207	Cauc	114	Cntrl	172
Mid-urban melting pot	15–20k	116	less	110	Service	119	Urban	282	Black	189	NE	178
Downscale rural	< 10k	160	less	164	Farm	217	Rur/Twn	244	Black	165	South	224
Downscale urban	< 10k	187	less	157	Service	157	Urban	225	Black	319	NE	138

Key: income is in thousands of dollars

education: 4+ (years of college), some (college), HS (high school diploma), less (adults who did not finish high school)

occupation: Upper level White Collar, Lower level White Collar, Service occupations, Farming occupations

urbanization: Urban, Urban Fringe, Suburban Fringe, and Rural Towns

race: caucasian, black, other (asian, american indian), hispanic

region: 4 census regions

[1] This table shows only the most distinctive level for each of the six characteristics. For example, in upscale suburbs the indices for the other income levels are $75–100k (330), $50–75k (230), $35–50k (135), $25–35k (76), $20–25k (52), $15–20k (42), $10–15k (33), and less than 10k (25).

Crossing the nine lifestyle segments and the six lifestages yields the 54-cell grid that forms the primary shopper group model for Spectra Advantage.[10]

The Trade Area Model

Micromerchandising requires that each store's trade area be defined and profiled by shopper groups. Kraft uses Super Market Solution's trade area model to define a store's trade area independently from the area's shopper group composition. The trade area is then profiled post hoc using Kraft's six-group solution.

Spectra inverts the procedure; that is, Spectra's trade area model first profiles CBGs by Spectra lifestyle/lifestage shopper groups, then defines a store's trade area in such a way that it exerts more or less pull on a given CBG, depending on that CBG's grocery expenditure patterns. In other words, Kraft defines a trade area polygon, then profiles by shopper group; Spectra profiles by grid cell, then uses these results to help define a store's trade area. More information about Spectra's method is contained in Appendix 17A.

Although details of Spectra's trade area algorithm are proprietary, resulting trade areas are typically irregular in shape and may overlap, as shown in Figure 17.4. Since the algorithm prevents stores from the same chain from competing for the same shoppers, the model accurately reproduces account level market share and sales data. Tests also show that the algorithm results in different trade area definitions than those produced by the Super Market Solutions algorithm. Differences result from inverting the profiling-geography steps and from the way each algorithm treats physical barriers and traffic patterns.

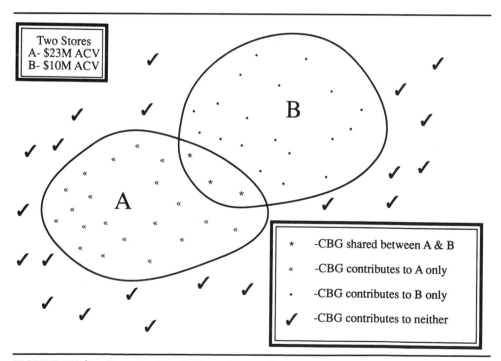

FIGURE 17.4.   Spectra Trade Area Example

In summary, Spectra's micromerchandising model consists of shopper groups with known spending patterns integrated with trade area data. It shares these features with Kraft's system. It differs from Kraft's system in the way shopper groups are formed (Spectra's grid is more detailed than Kraft's) and in the way trade areas are defined (Spectra profiles CBGs prior to assigning them to a store's trade area rather than after). Both systems produce a variety of useful reports, as described next.

REPORTS

Examples from the Kraft System

A micromerchandising system produces reports that facilitate the interaction between manufacturers and retailers. From a manufacturer's point of view, reports facilitate fact-based selling by addressing the unique situation of a given store. Armed with forecasts that indicate how an item's sales may increase as a function of special merchandising events, the manufacturer's representative is well-informed and precisely focused when discussing the item's sales possibilities with the store manager.

However, a retailer can apply micromerchandising in several areas of its business to improve sales, share, and operating performance at the account level, the store cluster level, and the store level. For example, although most retailers adjust their planograms based on store size or format, they generally do not factor in demand-side elements such as differential buying rates for an item among different shopper groups that reside in the local area. Since micromerchandising examines trade area potential, as well as historical sales activity, it can help adjust a store's product assortment with the consumer environment in mind.

Kraft USA's MMS produces an extensive package of reports to support special programs. A thorough discussion of each report would take too much space, but the package contains both market status and market response reports. Market status reports indicate "what happened," while market response reports indicate "what will be" or "what could be," given alternative merchandising programs.[11] One report of each type is reviewed here in order to highlight system applications.

The *Store Profile* report shown in Table 17.3 is a market status report. Three predominant shopper groups frequent this Metromart store located in the midwest: Merchandisables, Commodity Shoppers, and Planners and Dine-Outs. These three groups represent 88.4 percent of the customers living in this store's trade area. The report shows the share of this store's ACV by group, characterizes members of each group, and discusses their shopping propensities.

A Kraft representative might show this report to the Metromart manager in order to quantify the manager's subjective view of his or her store's customers. Note that even though the store profile is a market status report generated routinely by Kraft's MMS, it contains information previously unavailable to either the store manager or to a manufacturer's representative. In this condensed form it is a top-line report, yet because each shopper group is an amalgam of specific

TABLE 17.3. Store Profile

STORE: METROMART #35
ADDRESS: 251 COLLINS RD, ANYTOWN, USA

BACKGROUND INFORMATION:

What Shopper Groups frequent your stores?

MERCHANDISE-ABLES	43.7%	High income, avg education, middle aged, blue collar couples and families. Store and brand loyal consumers. Shop infrequently, but spend a lot per trip. Responsive to all kinds of merchandising.
COMMODITY SHOPPERS	27.8%	Lowest income/education, blue collar families with children. High number of minorities. Heavy TV viewers, especially during the daytime. Buy private label and generic. Store loyal. Low coupon usage.
PLANNERS & DINE-OUTS	13.2%	Conservative middle-aged/older, upper/middle income couples and families. Shop infrequently, low grocery dollars spent per household, tendency to plan shopping trips. Dine out often. Responsive to coupons and features.

KEY INFORMATION:

The above Shopper Groups represent 88.4% of the customers who live in the trading area of your store. Their predominant characteristics include above average: purchase of feature items; purchase of display items; dollars spent per trip.

Indexed demand for a product can be determined by identifying the consumers who shop at your stores. This Micro-Merchandising Consumer Demand Potential Index can then be applied to a category or product case demand. Please call the Micro-Merchandising Hotline if you are interested in this next level of information.

Customer Code	Kraft Product #	Product Description	Merchandising Support	Number of Cases	Profit Per Case	% Gross Profit	Total Profit

RECOMMENDED SHELVING:

_____
_____
_____

EXECUTION:

_____
_____
_____

Source: Kraft USA *Micro-Merchandising System*

MicroVision segments, it can be exploded into a very detailed analysis of each shopper group's media preferences and shopping behaviors.

Kraft's representative would supplement the store profile with an *Increased Item Distribution* report for the items shown in Table 17.4. This is a market response report because it is based on the forecasting model that drives the micromerchandising system. (See Appendix 17B for details.) The report explains in quantitive terms why the store should carry more of these specific items, and suggests appropriate case levels and merchandising support. Projected profits are provided for each merchandising scenario.

These two reports and the others generated by the system place Kraft USA field representatives at a distinct advantage over representatives from competing manufacturers. They show a retail store manager how to increase his or her store's sales of a Kraft item by matching the store's customer base with the item's merchandising and stocking policies. Increased merchandising costs are not necessarily involved since a store's current budget allocation can often be effectively reorganized using programs tailored to the store's clientele. The system is simple to use and allows Kraft representatives to offer (1) a fact-based sales presentation, (2) an integrated solution for the store and its chain, and (3) projectable results based on sound statistical modeling.

Examples from the Spectra System

Kraft's system was developed to support the company's sales force. Reports emphasize case volume forecasts conditioned on various promotion activities for a given retailer. The Spectra system can also be used for fact-based sales, but is flexible enough to assist a manufacturer in developing a complete marketing plan. The system, therefore, supports relationship marketing to the extent that a retailer's interests are factored into the marketing planning process. The example in this section illustrates the flexibility of the Spectra system. Implications for trade relations are discussed near the end of the example to compare the two systems.

Spectra: Marketing Planning

Consider the problem of revising the marketing strategy for a mature consumer packaged good such as Peter Pan peanut butter. Sales had been faltering due to changing consumer habits, increased competition from "natural" peanut butters, and changing national demographics. The product's original marketing plan was not only dated but was developed without a detailed segmentation study. Management wanted a revised plan that (1) selected precise consumer targets; (2) described the targets in terms of key demographic, attitudinal, purchase behavior, and media-use variables; (3) located geographic concentrations of the targets; (4) specified marketing objectives for each target; (5) described media, promotions, and tactics to achieve these objectives; and (6) formulated a trade program that supported the consumer strategy.

To develop such a plan, Spectra indexed InfoScan households by the volume consumed of the item, and then sorted them into the Spectra grid. The

TABLE 17.4. Increased Item Distribution

STORE: METROMART #35
ADDRESS: 251 COLLINS RD, ANYTOWN, USA

BACKGROUND INFORMATION:

What Shopper Groups frequent your stores?

MERCHANDISE-ABLES 47.3% High income, avg education, middle aged, blue collar couples and families. Store and brand loyal consumers. Shop infrequently, but spend a lot per trip. Responsive to all kinds of merchandising.

COMMODITY SHOPPERS 27.8% Lowest income/education, blue collar families with children. High number of minorities. Heavy TV viewers, especially during the daytime. Buy private label and generic. Store loyal. Low coupon usage.

PLANNERS & DINE-OUTS 13.2% Conservative middle-aged/older, upper/middle income couples and families. Shop infrequently, low grocery dollars spent per household, tendency to plan shopping trips. Dine out often. Responsive to coupons and features.

KEY INFORMATION:

The above Shopper Groups represent 88.4% of the customers who shop at your stores. Their predominant characteristics include above average: purchase of feature items; purchase of display items; dollars spent per trip.

Indexed demand for a product can be determined by identifying the consumers who shop at your store. This Micro-Merchandising Consumer Demand Potential Index was then applied for this item based on the Shopper Groups within your store's trading area. Using this index and actual purchase behavior data for the products(s) listed below or a similar product, we were able to project the weekly case potential.

Customer Code	Kraft Product #	Product Description	Merchandising Support	Number of Cases	Profit Per Case	% Gross Profit	Total Profit
	43566789	8 OZ PRODUCT EG	FEATURE	200	$4.20	16.3%	$840.00
	43966231	26 OZ PRODUCT C	FEAT/DISPLAY	193	$3.69	18.11%	$712.17

RECOMMENDED SHELVING:

EXECUTION:

Source: Kraft USA *Micro-Merchandising System*

results—shown in Table 17.5—reveal that when children are present, the product appeals to families that span the entire socioeconomic scale; this comes as no surprise. However, interesting secondary demand is present among families without children in three lifestyles—Working Class Towns, Rural Towns and Farms, and Downscale Rural families.

Once selected, the primary and secondary targets are profiled by demography, purchase behavior, media habits, and other characteristics that enrich management's understanding and help refine media choices and distribution plans. In this case, these analyses also simplified program development. They reveal that the number and ages of children in a household make little difference in Peter Pan consumption. The respective indices for households with one (174), two (184), and three or more children (185) are nearly indistinguishable. Consumption dips only slightly as the children age, from less than 6 years (189), to 6-12 years (182), to 13-17 years (170).

Media consumption and lifestyle analyses offer a refined picture of target households. Heavy users listen to country radio (139), read fishing and hunting magazines (137), and tune in to Spanish/ethnic radio (120). The top three lifestyle activities are "Go Fresh Water Fishing" (131), "Buy Country Music" (130), and "Go Overnight Camping" (127), patterns that match media consumption and suggest commonalities among target households despite socioeconomic differences along the lifestyle dimension.

TABLE 17.5. Spectra Advantage 54 Cell Matrix Peanut Butter Analysis

52 Weeks Ending 10/29/89
EASTERN REGION
Total Peter Pan

Spectra LIFESTYLE	18–34 with kids	18–34 no kids	35–54 with kids	35–54 no kids	55–64	65+	Total Lifestyle
Upscale Suburbs	**122**	90	**94**	38	59	34	73
Trad. Families	**213**	109	**145**	69	79	78	118
Mid Upsc Sburbs	**177**	92	**140**	85	96	61	101
Metro Elite	71	16	81	111	92	49	65
Wkg Class Towns	**251**	85	**226**	**150**	148	94	**160**
Rural Twns/Farm	**272**	84	**236**	**152**	146	92	**167**
Mid Urb Mlt Pot	79	44	93	44	84	39	63
Downscale Rural	**279**	83	**236**	**151**	149	92	**166**
Downscale Urban	**127**	5	89	70	57	48	65
TOTAL LIFESTAGE	167	56	139	85	94	61	100

Equivalized Unit = Pounds
Bold numbers represent high category consumption.

Spectra analysts, using these facts as well as many others, suggested that Peter Pan concentrate on increasing consumption among existing heavy users (franchise building), and on attracting peanut butter switchers. Switchers typically bought either JIF, Skippy, or Peter Pan as a function of in-store promotions and coupon availability. Price deals, coupons, and in-store sampling were suggested to increase penetration among existing customers. Coupons off larger sizes would be sent to targeted "switcher" families along with a multiple purchase rebate to retain their business once they switched to Peter Pan. The coupon program would be supported by in-store displays in targeted stores.

Trade Relations

The foregoing discussion shows how Spectra can be used to develop a unified consumer marketing program. However, a key component of overall strategy is to select appropriate retail accounts in which to distribute the product. Selected accounts are then prioritized to allocate merchandising funds within account. These aspects of the plan could be framed as fact-based sales for the manufacturer's sales force. A broader perspective is to develop an overall trade strategy that involves retailers as part of the manufacturer's plan. Rather than emphasize short-term sales blips related to merchandising events, the plan stresses increased buying penetration, an outcome that helps the retailer (since it avoids cannibalization of other items in the same category) as well as the manufacturer (since it avoids cannibalization of Peter Pan's future sales).

To round out the program, Spectra ranked accounts in each ADI nationwide, identified key accounts, and sorted individual stores in each key account to help the retailer and the manufacturer plan product shipments and merchandising allocations. Table 17.6 shows excerpts from three steps in the process. Step 1 ranks ADIs—here in the eastern United States only—and shows that Buffalo (highlighted) represents opportunity. Step 2 ranks accounts in Buffalo (the Quality Market chain is highlighted), and Step 3 ranks stores within account.[12]

Table 17.6 is based on historical penetration rates. It may reflect a supply-side bias where certain stores have low sales of Peter Pan simply because they did not stock it in sufficient quantities. However, Spectra's link to trade-area geography facilitates carrying out a prospective analysis based on neighborhood profiles. This analysis would identify all stores in neighborhoods with a high incidence of target households regardless of past sales of the item. Conditional forecasting of this sort is routine with the Spectra system.

LIMITATIONS OF EXISTING SYSTEMS

Micromerchandising is a relatively new concept. The two systems reviewed in this chapter represent the vanguard in what promises to be an expanding niche in the field of marketing research systems. To date, system designers have solved a variety of complex theoretical and practical problems, yet present systems are not without limitations. Two of these are reviewed in this section.

TABLE 17.6. Three Step Procedure for Trade Support

Step 1: Rank ADIs by Penetration

ADI Name	Total Eastern ADIs		Peter Pan Heavy Users			
	HHs	%HHs	Tgt HHs	%Tgt HHs	%Pen	Index
Buffalo, NY	**622,432**	**3.19**	**226,232**	**4.12**	**36.3**	**129**
Pittsburg, PA	1,139,116	5.83	400,060	7.28	35.1	125
Springfield, MA	246,020	1.26	79,104	1.44	32.2	114
Providence, RI	568,041	2.91	171,304	3.12	30.2	107

Step 2: Rank Accounts within an ADI

Account Name	Total ACV ($000s)	Peter Pan Heavy Users		
		ACV ($000)	% Pen	Index
Quality Markets, Buffalo NY	**119,997**	**71,998**	**60.0**	**121**
S M Flickinger, Buffalo NY	13,000	6,158	47.4	115

Step 3: Rank Individual Stores within Account

Store Name	ACV	Heavy Users		Address	City	Zip
		% Pen	Index			
Quality Mkt. 18	2,032	67.7	113	20 Center St.	Frewsburg	738
Quality Mkt. 6	4,675	66.8	111	Randolph Plaza	Randolph	772
Quality Mkt. 51	6,629	66.3	110	Chautauqua Mall	Lakewood	750
Quality Mkt. 57	3,258	65.2	109	Washington St.	Ellicottvl.	731

Bold numbers represent maximum opportunity.

Segmentation Model

The first limitation is that neither system was developed from first principles using a nationwide segmentation model designed specifically for packaged goods applications. Both the Spectra and Kraft systems were built by customizing an existing geodemographic system, merging it with volumetric data then collapsing its lifestyle segments to reflect packaged goods purchase behavior. Customizing is a necessity because geodemography does not discriminate well in many packaged goods categories. Use behavior in categories such as toothpaste, toilet paper, or cereal is not strongly related to a household's affluence, education, ethnicity, or mobility, factors that underpin traditional GD-clusters. Both Kraft and Spectra realized this and designed their systems accordingly.

If integrating volumetric data into the process was a necessity, collapsing GD-segments into "shopper groups" is, arguably, less so. Collapsing is designed to reduce system complexity and increase ease of use. (The alternative; for example, using 95 shopper groups in the Kraft system or $(40 \times 6 =)$ 240 cells in the Spectra system would be unwieldy, especially if it can be empirically verified that fewer types will do the job.) Of course, collapsing begs the question of how many shopper segments can do the job.

Thus, although it represents a much more ambitious and expensive alternative, a segmentation model for packaged goods could be developed from scratch. Rather than overlay volumetric data on an existing GD-system, system designers could make volumetric data an integral part of the system build process. Two ways to do this come to mind. First, rather than use all census variables to profile a CBG, select—through extensive empirical study—census variables that show strong relationships to various aspects of packaged goods consumption behavior. Then, using these variables, possibly complemented with other variables needed to complete the system's strategy delivery potential, redo the factor and cluster analyses of CBGs. Second, analysts could cluster InfoScan or SCANTRACK households directly using the extensive array of volumetric data available for each household, and then link results to the census system. This approach reverses the current practice of clustering on the basis of census data, and then linking results to volumetric data.

In summary, micromerchandising is predicated on a valid segmentation model. Existing systems represent a second-hand approach to segmentation because they rely on broad-based geodemographic clusters designed to cut across all consumer goods. Piggybacking on an existing system conserves financial resources, but it may yield a suboptimal system for packaged goods applications.

Manufacturer Interests Predominate

The second limitation is that existing systems stress manufacturer interests over retailer interests. Given the shift in channel power from manufacturers to retailers, it is natural that the first micromerchandising systems would be tools that help manufacturers gain scarce retail shelf space and focus in-store merchandising efforts on their brands. Manufacturers have large research budgets and have traditionally relied on outside consultants for assistance. An even more fundamental reason for choosing manufacturers as primary clients may be that retail problems are an order of magnitude more complex than manufacturer problems. Space allocation, new item addition, and item deletion decisions are particularly pressing for the retailer, yet these problems are nearly intractable. Optimal solutions must trade off uncertain results on the demand side with often poorly measured costs on the supply side. Put another way, the retailer is wedged between the vagaries of human behavior and the precise but often meaningless calculations of cost accountants.

As complex as they are, space allocation problems can be treated with static models. The retailer's other major problem—when, how, and for whom to conduct in-store promotions—requires a valid dynamic model if solutions are to have even modest face validity. Micromerchandising systems can help characterize the enduring component of demand—and, therefore, have relevance for space allocation problems—but they offer no dynamic mechanisms to solve even the most basic promotion questions such as "Should item u be featured two weeks in a row?" As these ideas are discussed in more detail in the next chapter, they will not be pursued here. Chapter 18 presents a dynamic model that resolves the promotion problem.

CONCLUSION

This chapter discusses the micromerchandising concept and reviews two systems for implementing it, the Kraft system and Spectra Advantage. Both systems combine geodemographic data, trade area data, and scanner data to develop a segmentation model suited to the needs of packaged goods manufacturers and retailers. The model—a set of shopper groups in the Kraft system and a set of lifestyle/lifestage cells in the Spectra system—serves as a basis for developing and implementing marketing plans.

The chapter shows how to build and use a micromerchandising system, and discusses certain limitations of existing systems. Despite limitations, existing systems are a significant step toward full implementation of the channel partnership concept currently espoused by leading marketing scholars. Given today's rapidly advancing technical environment, expect to see improvements in existing systems and the emergence of new systems in this specialized subfield.

Notes

1. Super Market Solutions' *Sales Manager* package is a PC-based system for merchandising, store profiling, and other applications. It is a product of Market Metrics, Inc. The system was developed under the auspices of a General Foods/Market Metrics joint venture and was until January 1, 1989, reserved for General Food's exclusive use.

2. See Appendix A for an outline of how Super Market Solutions creates its trade areas.

3. For a review of traditional methods, see Chapter 13 of Dale M. Lewison and M. Wayne Delozier *Retailing*, 2nd ed., Columbus, OH: Merrill, 1986.

4. The major geodemographers have begun to customize their systems for packaged goods applications in an effort to compete in the micromerchandizing niche. For example, National Decision Systems offers InfoMark Merchandising, a special version of its InfoMark System, and Optisel, a second system for consumer package goods applications.

5. See the IRI brochure entitled "PromotionScan: Managing Trade Promotions," p. 3.

6. A. C. Nielsen's SCANTRACK collects data from multiple outlets via its portable scanners. Thus, SCANTRACK can track store-switching behavior among panel members.

7. In the traditional view, a manufacturer offers a retailer a trade promotion— a short-term price discount. To qualify and to ensure that the discount is passed

to the consumer, the retailer is required to comply with certain terms, such as a reduction in shelf price, an allocation of space for an in-store display, and a feature ad in the store's local newspaper. Despite these stipulations, the deal volume passed through is usually less than the volume bought. (See Robert C. Blattberg and Scott A. Neslin *Sales Promotion: Concepts, Methods, and Strategies,* Englewood Cliffs, NJ: Prentice-Hall, 1990.)

8. BehaviorScan households were not used in Kraft's sort process. Thus, the system was build using approximately 40,000 InfoScan households.

9. These arguments are outlined in "Spectra Advantage: Lifestyle/Lifestage Methodology," available from Spectra Marketing Systems, Inc., 1990.

10. In certain categories, Spectra creates special grids to maximize variance in a particular vertical industry segment.

11. For more details about report types, see Chapter 8.

12. The three lists excerpted in Table 17.6 are usually quite long. There are more than 200 ADIs nationwide. The accounts in a given ADI may number as many as 40. A given account, such as Kroger or Dominick's, may contain hundreds of stores.

APPENDIX 17A:
TRADE AREA DEFINITIONS
IN SUPERMARKET SOLUTIONS
AND SPECTRA ADVANTAGE

SuperMarket Solutions/Kraft

Summary: This method builds a store's trade area from surrounding census tracts. It establishes a trade area population quota and adds census tracts to fill this quota. The underlying attraction model assumes that a store draws people living nearby and that certain directions are easier to draw from than others.

The following steps provide more detail.

Step 1 Outline the trade area's geographic boundaries.
  a. Plot each store on a map using longitude and latitude.
  b. Build a specific store's TA from surrounding census tracts. (Two stores located near each other may have identical TAs at this step.)

Step 2 Define a store's trade area population.
  a. Define the total number of shoppers in a store's TA by dividing the store's average weekly sales volume by the prevailing national per capita food expenditure amount. (For example, this amount was $19.75 in 1986.)
  b. Attempt to find this number of shoppers in the store's surrounding census tracts as described in Step 3.

Step 3 Accumulate census tracts to fulfill the shopper quota established in Step 2.
  a. First, assess the directional gradients of attraction for the store by analyzing the population densities in surrounding census tracts, the locations of competitive stores, physical barriers, and traffic patterns.
  b. Next, search surrounding census tracts for the required number of "target" customers. Accumulate census tracts until the total in Step 2 has been accounted for. In some cases, only a fraction of a census tract need become part of a particular store's TA.

Spectra

Summary: Spectra's model profiles CBGs by the 54 lifestyle/lifestage cells and computes the average household food expenditure per year per CBG. Next, it defines a competitive set of stores that could serve a given CBG and assigns the CBG to a given store as a function of distance and store size. Adjustments are made for stores in the same chain and for directional gradients blocked by natural barriers.

The following steps provide more detail.[1]

Step 1   Estimate the annual expenditures on food (by census region) for households in each of the 54 cells in the Spectra grid. Estimates are derived using IRI InfoScan data.

Step 2   Generate the most current count of households for each of the approximately 250,000 CBGs nationwide. Multiply a CBG's household count by the average weekly expenditure on groceries for the grid cells represented in the CBG, sum over all grid cells, and multiply by 52 to annualize the weekly data.

Step 3   Locate each grocery store in the U.S. using its longitude and latitude. Since each CBG is also situated at a fixed location, the distance between any store and (the centroid of) any CBG is known.

Step 4   Define a CBG's competitive set by selecting all stores that are within 15 miles of that CBG.

Step 5   Identify the ACV size of each store using data from Progressive Grocer and Market Metrics grocery store databases.

Step 6   Invoke a retail gravity model that includes, partially includes, or excludes a given CBG from a store's trade area. The algorithm considers a CBG's distance from each store in its competitive set, whether or not two stores in the set are part of the same chain, and each store's ACV size.

Step 7   Add CBGs to a given store's trade area, spiraling out from the store accumulating CBGs to account for the store's historical ACV sales total.

Notes

1. Source: "Spectra Advantage Grocery Store Trading Area Methodology." copyright 1989, Spectra Marketing Systems, Inc.

APPENDIX 17B:
CALCULATING AN INDEX OF
CASE MOVEMENT USING KRAFT USA'S
MICRO-MERCHANDISING SYSTEM

Although Kraft's MMS is designed to support a variety of merchandising applications, one of these—indexing item potential on a store-by-store basis—is key since it underpins other applications. An item's potential is the quantity that could be sold in a given store if the item were supported by an optimum marketing mix program. An item's demand, on the other hand, is the quantity that is sold under a prevailing marketing program. Unlike demand, potential is unobservable. This appendix outlines the model Kraft uses to estimate an item's potential and reports results from an empirical test of the model.[1]

The model is created in two steps: First, the MMS is used to estimate the total units (pound/pints) a given store would sell in a given week. These totals (denoted u_t for store t) are then normalized to apportion total potential among the participating stores.

MMS Case Movement Model

The estimate for item k in store t (denoted $\hat{u}_{kt}$) is built by examining store t's shopper group composition and each group's consumption rate for the item in question. These elements are adjusted to account for the absolute size of each store's trade area, regional differences in the product's consumption rate, and seasonality. The (nonseasonal) model is given in equation [1].

$$\hat{u}_{kt} = \sum_{g=1}^{6} a_{tg} u_{kg} f_{rk} \qquad [1]$$

where:

$\hat{u}_{kt}$ = projected potential units of Kraft item k that could be sold in store t (during a fixed time period)

a_{tg} = number of members of shopper group g living in store t's trade area

u_{kg} = average (per capita) number of lb./pints of Kraft item k consumed by members of shopper group g (during a 1-year period)

f_{rk} = a regional adjustment factor that indexes a region's tendency to deviate from the national per capita consumption average (= 1.00) in category k.

For a given shopper group, this model partitions store t's sales of item k according to the store's composition of shopper groups. The factor $(a_{tg} \cdot u_{kg})$ yields total lb./pints consumed by group g. These subtotals are summed over all six groups to estimate total consumption of k in t's trade area. The term f_{rk} accounts for differing regional consumption rates. For example, people in the southeastern United States may consume 1.14 times the national average of item k.

Another Form of the Basic Model

If $a_t = \sum_{g=1}^{6} a_{tg}$ is the total number of shoppers in a store's trade area, then $a_{tg}/a_t = p_{tg}$ is the proportion of shoppers in group g . When defined this way, the p_{tg} are nonnegative and add up to 1.0. Substituting $a_{tg} = p_{tg} \cdot a_t$ in equation [1], we can write:

$$U_{kt} = \sum_{g=1}^{6} (p_{tg} \cdot a_t) \cdot u_{kg} \cdot f_{rk} \qquad [2]$$

The terms a_t and f_{rk} are constant with respect to the summation over g. They can be factored out of the sum, yielding equation [3].

$$\hat{u}_{kt} = a_t \cdot f_{rk} \sum_{g=1}^{6} p_{tg} \cdot u_{kg} \qquad [3]$$

Equation [3] shows that item k's potential in store t is a weighted sum of expected unit sales of item k among the six Kraft shopper groups, adjusted for the size of the store's trade area (a_t) and the regional consumption factor (f_{rk}). In other words, the term p_{tg} can be interpreted as the probability that a shopper from group g enters store t, and u_{kg} is the amount of item k that such a shopper is expected to buy on average once they are in store t.

A TEST OF SYSTEM VALIDITY

In 1990, Kraft conducted a test of the (full) model in order to benchmark its performance with real data. Since an item's potential is unobservable, the test required that the model produce, on a store-by-store basis, out-of-sample forecasts of demand. This is a stringent requirement, since both theory and empirical evidence show that factors omitted from the model—such as in-store merchandising events—influence an item's demand, but not its long-term potential. Potential is a function of enduring elements, such as product characteristics, that reflect the item's ability to fulfill consumer needs.

The Test Environment

Kraft conducted its test with the cooperation of a major food retailer with outlets concentrated in a major midwestern market. (By agreement, the retailer's identity must remain confidential.) The chain permitted Kraft USA to test its MMS in 90 stores.

Methodology

Three Kraft items—referred to as items x, y, and z—were included in the test. Each store was typed using Kraft's Micro-Merchandising System, and case quantities were forecast by item (by store) for a future two-week period. Actual sales for those two weeks were then collected by item, by store via the retailer's in-store scanners. Actual and predicted sales were compared across stores for each item.

Results

Results are summarized in Table 17.7. Indexed actual volume served as the dependent variable in a regression with predicted volume. Part (a) of the Table shows that both product moment and rank correlations—predicted vs. actual—are high, positive, and statistically significant for all three items. Regressions confirm that the model's estimates are linearly related to actual volumes, and that actual and predicted values are simultaneously zero as expected.

Hit-rate tests were also conducted by dividing both predicted and actual values into two categories—above and below 100—and cross-tabbing. The diagonal cell counts in the resulting two-way table reveal the total correct hits. These can be compared to the total expected by chance. The respective hit rates are listed in the following table.

Item	Actual Hits Using MMS	Proportion Correct	Chance Proportion Correct
x	40 (out of 62)	.645	.502
y	60 (out of 80)	.750	.515
z	66 (out of 81)	.815	.555

In all three cases the model predicts considerably better than would a naive chance model.[2]

TABLE 17.7. Validation Test Results

Item	n	(a) Correlations[1] Pearson (r)	Spearman (rank)
x	62	.347[a]	.329[a]
y	80	.530[b]	.626[b]
z	81	.582[b]	.710[b]
overall	223	.495[b]	.553[b]

Term	x	(b) Regressions[2] y	z
intercept	43.00	−25.52	−31.07
linear	0.63	1.81[b]	1.81[b]
quadratic	−0.00	−0.00[a]	−0.00[a]
R^2	.1212[a]	.3695[b]	.3844[b]

[1] $a : p \leq .05$ $b : p \leq .0001$

Discussion

These results are encouraging considering the nature of the test and the basic objectives of the MMS. Note that a variety of in-store factors affect a store's sales for a given item during a fixed time period—for example, the item's display, feature, and couponing activity and similar activities for competing items. An MMS cannot, nor is it designed to, control for these potentially very strong effects. The system is designed to index each item's potential in a given store conditional on the composition of shopper groups in the store's trade area. Thus, the MMS only controls for each store's shopper group profile and regional differences in an item's seasonally adjusted average consumption rate. Since an MMS is not designed to be a precise forecasting tool, its performance in this test is satisfactory.

Notes

1. At the request of Kraft USA, the appendix conveys the essence of the model without revealing details.

2. Chance is defined as $\text{Prob(chance)} = \sum_{i=1}^{2} P(c_i)^2$ where $P(c_i)$ is the (estimated) marginal probability of the i_{th} category. This is the conservative measure suggested by Morrison (*JMR*, 1969). Analyses were also carried out using low, medium, and high splits. Hit rates exceeded chance at about the same rates as shown here. Statistical tests of association such as chi-square, Fisher's exact test, and contingency coefficients, were all highly significant for these tables, confirming the association between predicted and actual results.

18 CATEGORY MANAGEMENT

One approach to gaining a longer term information advantage is to adopt a process of gaining "real-time" decision-making advantages as an ultimate goal. To do so means committing the company to working toward an integrated decision-making system. This integration will involve uniting the external information provided by research firms with proprietary internal information.

Blair Peters, "The Brave New World of Single-Source Information"

Both brand managers and store managers are interested in how the packaged goods grouped together on store shelves compete with one another; both are also interested in how these products build sales for other products in the same brand family or the same store. That is, both brand managers and store managers practice the art of "category management," although each has different objectives in mind and different variables under his or her control.

Category management starts at the point of purchase—the store shelf. There, a branded product is thought of as a "category entrant" (by the brand manager) or as a "shelf-keeping unit" or SKU (by the store manager). A *category* is a set of entrants, or shelf-keeping units, that have similar product characteristics and are displayed together on the shelf. For example, Renuzit Freshell and

Glade Plug-Ins are both entrants in the air freshener category and Tide Unscented 96 oz., Bright Liquid 32 oz., and Arm & Hammer 28 oz. are entrants in the laundry detergent category. *Category management* refers to the establishment of levels of marketing mix variables for each SKU to control sales and revenues in the category.

Brand managers try to set these variables so that their own category entrants generate profitable sales, often at the expense of competitive entrants. Brand managers control the physical characteristics of their own products, and of marketing communications delivered on their behalf through channels other than the retailer. These communications—delivered through the mass media or direct mail—inform consumers of the product's benefits, enhance the brand's equity, and increase its attractiveness. However, nonstore advertising usually cannot stimulate enough consumer demand to pull the product through the distribution pipeline. In today's packaged goods environment, distribution is controlled by the retailer.

Store managers, who have become the clients for much single-source reporting, want to stock a set of shelf-keeping units that will generate profitable sales for the category as a whole and increase overall store traffic. To achieve these objectives, retailers decide which SKUs will be allotted the limited shelf space available in their stores; they also control price reductions, features, and other promotion activities for the SKUs they stock. In other words, retailers control the most critical aspect of packaged goods marketing, the environment in which the final exchange transaction occurs.

OVERVIEW OF THE CHAPTER

This chapter illustrates a new approach to category management, one based on the mathematical theory of dynamic optimal control. However, mathematical detail is suppressed in favor of intuitive arguments recognizing that the reader is not likely to be the analyst who actually does the mathematical modeling. Instead, the chapter is intended for brand managers and store managers who are knowledgeable about industry practice and interested in the competitive benefits that the new approach can provide.

The chapter first reviews traditional brand management and contrasts it with category management. It is argued that category management is more valid than the traditional approach for two reasons. First, it captures the competitive interactions referred to in this quotation from Guadagni and Little: "Although first priority goes to determining how a product's variables affect its own sales, marketing managers increasingly would like to learn more about product interactions within a category."[1] Second, it captures the dynamics of the marketplace—that is, it shows explicitly how marketing and sales activities in one week are related to previous weeks' activities.

The next section of the chapter outlines how current approaches attempt but fail to capture competitive interactions. The chapter then presents an alternative approach which combines a "state-space" forecasting model with principles of dynamic optimization. Examples illustrate the forecasting power of this model. Three types of forecasts are discussed: unconditional forecasts, conditional forecasts, and impulse responses. Next, optimization principles are presented and illustrated. The chapter concludes with a summary, and an appendix provides further insight into the control framework.

Dynamic optimal control theory may allow managers to make the best use of scanner data for solving problems in packaged goods management, especially in existing (as opposed to new) categories. For example, control theory produces results that multinomial logit analysis—the method now most widely used—cannot obtain: it suggests weekly optimal levels for the marketing mix variables for each category entrant; it shows how these optimal levels would differ for a brand manager and for a store manager; and it suggests the optimal timing both of in-store merchandising activities and of certain non-store marketing communications.

CATEGORY MANAGEMENT VERSUS BRAND MANAGEMENT

Traditional brand management focuses on a single brand, its marketing mix, and its market performance. A brand manager establishes a week-by-week pricing and promotion plan, implements this plan in light of retail constraints, and then reads single-source reports to assess whether or not the plan was effective.

For example, Figure 18.1 shows the weekly volume sold, the regular price, the deal price, and the feature, display, and advertising activity for one brand in a packaged goods category. These data are from a metro-market consisting of about 40 major grocery stores.[2] Brand 1's sales are highly seasonal and the brand manager uses an advertising program pulsed to push sales just before natural seasonal upswings. Moreover, in 1989 and early 1990 the manager increased the marketing effort for this brand. (Note the increase in displays and television advertising beginning in January 1990. The dynamic model will show that the increased advertising dollars were misspent.)

A decision support system for brand management typically produces brand-specific market status reports, often at the expense of comparative summaries or category-wide projections. In some cases, a firm's own multiple entrants in a category are managed separately, though their demand is clearly intertwined and they could be managed more efficiently in unison. For example, in the category studied here, Brands 1 and 2 are produced by the same manufacturer but sold as different lines. As Figure 18.2 illustrates, Brand 2's sales average about one-third of Brand 1's. Although its seasonal sales patterns closely mimic those of Brand 1, the amount and timing of Brand 2's marketing mix activities are somewhat different (not shown).

Category managers should be supported by systems that explicitly reveal competitive dynamics. Such systems focus on the contemporaneous and time-lagged interaction of marketing programs for all category entrants, not just one. A sophisticated category manager, whether she or he works for a manufacturer or a retailer, should use market response reports as well as market status reports. Market response reports can project the consequences of any managerial intervention, whether by a retailer, by the brand manager, or by a competitor.

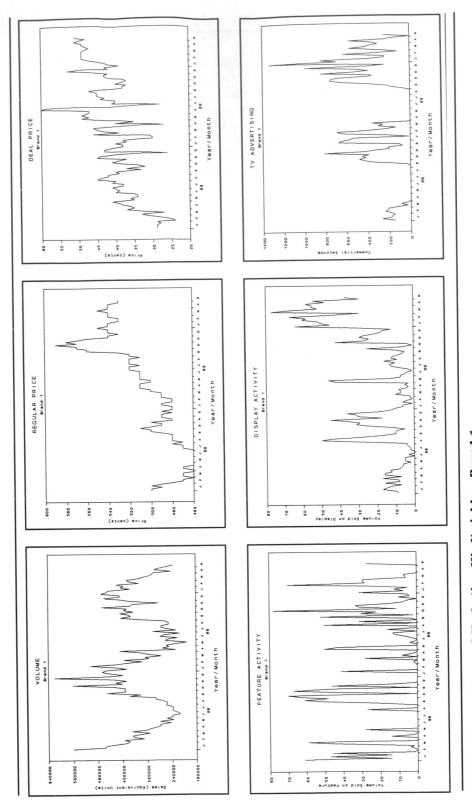

FIGURE 18.1. Sales and Marketing Mix Variables: Brand 1

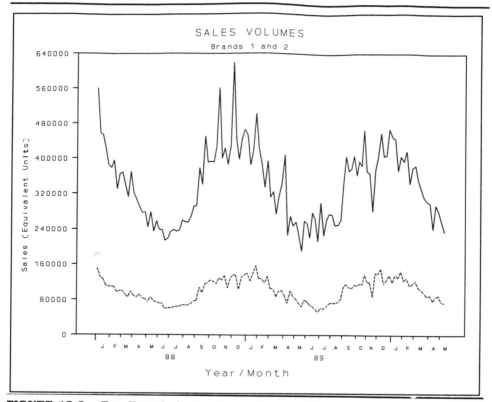

FIGURE 18.2. Two Brands in the Same Product Line

In summary, although the desired outcomes differ, both brand and retail managers must understand total category dynamics to do their jobs properly. Since they control different aspects of the marketing environment, a brand manager and a retailer can accomplish their separate objectives only through mutual understanding and some degree of cooperation.

CURRENT PRACTICE:
CHARACTERIZATION AND WEAKNESSES

Currently, category managers use reports produced from several types of mathematical models, mostly variations of the multinomial logit model. These models summarize the competitive interaction between products, estimating direct and cross elasticities between category entrants.[3] For reference, the top frame of Figure 18.3 shows a logit model that uses each brand's price and feature activity as predictor variables. The bottom frame shows a pooled store level model that uses the same variables as predictors. Both approaches model how one category entrant's marketing activities influence the sales or market share of all entrants. Thus, both approaches model competitive interactions but use different functional forms to do so.

A Multinomial Logit Model

$$(Market) \ Share \ Entrant_k = \frac{Attraction_k}{\sum\limits_{j=1}^{J} Attraction_j} = \frac{A_k}{\sum\limits_{j=1}^{J} A_j}$$

where; $\quad MS^*_{ikt} = \exp\left[\alpha^*_k + \sum\limits_{j=1}^{J} \alpha^*_j F_{ijt} + \sum\limits_{j=1}^{J} \beta_{pj}(P_{ijt} - p_{it}) + \epsilon^*_{ikt}\right]$

A Pooled Store Level Model

$$\frac{S_{ikt}}{S_{ik}} = \left[\prod\limits_{j=1}^{J}\left(\frac{P_{ijt}}{p_{ijt}}\right)^{\beta_{jk}} \prod\limits_{j=1}^{J} \gamma_{jk}^{F_{ijt}} \prod\limits_{t=1}^{T} \delta_{kt}^{x_t} e^{\mu_{ikt}}\right]$$

Notation

Logit

MS_{ikt}	: the market share for brand k in store i, week t
p_{it}	: mean price over brands in store i, week t
ϵ^*_{ikt}	: a random error term for store i, brand k, week t

Pooled Store Level

S_{ikt}	: unit sales — in equivalent units — for brand k in store i, week t
S_{ik}	: the level of base sales for brand k in store i
p_{ijt}	: baseline (regular unit) price for brand j, store i, week t
x_t	: an indicator variable: 1 if the observation is in week t; 0 otherwise
μ_{ikt}	: a random error term (attached to the exponential e) store i, brand k, week t

Common

P_{ijt}	: unit price for brand j in store i, week t
F_{ijt}	: an indicator variable for feature activity in store i for brand j, week t
$\alpha^*, \beta, \gamma, \delta$	: are parameters to be estimated from data (elasticities and multipliers)

FIGURE 18.3. Examples of Competitive Interaction Models

Although a thorough comparison would be too lengthy for the purposes of this chapter, the shortcomings of competitive interaction models may be summarized as follows.[4]

1. They are inherently static—their output is a fixed set of information that cannot be clearly associated with a given week, month, or other period of time.
2. They do not produce true forecasts, but rather "what-if" speculations.

3. They are usually zero-sum models—they assume that the category will not expand or contract as a result of management decisions and market place dynamics.
4. They cannot easily incorporate past values of marketing mix variables. Hence, they tend to concentrate on in-store promotional variables rather than on non-store variables (such as advertising), whose effects carry over from past time periods.
5. They cannot optimize the marketing mix in a single time period, let alone in multiperiod planning horizons or in real time.

The basis for an approach that remedies each of these shortcomings is described next.

PROPERTIES OF A CATEGORY MANAGEMENT SYSTEM

The requirements of a good category management system may be summarized as follows.

1. The system would integrate the competitive effects of the marketing mix levels of all SKUs in a category.
2. The "marketing mix" would include both in-store and nonstore variables.
3. Output from the system would reflect the competitive impact of marketing mix variables in one period—for all SKUs—on sales in that period and in subsequent time periods.
4. The system would forecast future levels for all variables, period by period.
5. The system would forecast the response in any subset of variables to changes in the levels of another subset of variables.
6. The system would establish an optimal marketing mix (for one, several, or all category entrants) once certain objectives were defined.

Points 1, 2, and 3 are model specification issues; they suggest the aspects of marketplace dynamics that a good category management model should capture. Points 4, 5, and 6 distinguish forecasting and control applications: the model must be able to produce unconditional forecasts (point 4) as well as conditional forecasts (point 5), and it must lead to optimal control solutions (point 6).

Example

The category referred to earlier provides a good setting in which to illustrate these ideas. In addition to Brands 1 and 2, a third national brand competes in this metro-market, along with several private label and generic brands. To simplify analyses, private labels and generics are grouped into a single "Brand 4" that accounts for about 10 percent of category sales.

For each of the four entrants, the data supplier tracked weekly sales volumes, prices (regular and deal), features, displays (separately and simultaneously), and advertising activities. Therefore, even for this small category there are four entrants and seven variables per entrant, or 28 variables in the total system. This system will illustrate the previously outlined properties.

UNCONDITIONAL FORECASTS

A model produces *unconditional forecasts* if, once calibrated, the model can generate forecasts without requiring additional data inputs. A model is "calibrated" when its unknown numerical constants, or parameters, are estimated from available data.

Most competitive interaction models cannot produce unconditional forecasts because they do not have the necessary data—namely, the values of competitors' marketing mix variables that will obtain during the forecast period. In academic studies this problem is avoided by calibrating a model on historical data (say, using weeks 1–52, 1989), and then "forecasting" to a subsequent period (also already in the past), for which levels of the marketing mix are known (say, the first 20 weeks of 1990). Guadagni and Little use this technique: "In the forecast period we continue to employ the actual prices and promotions of all the brand sizes (i.e., the model is not attempting to predict what marketing decisions will be made)."[5]

To do real forecasting rather than an academic test, a model must in fact predict what marketing decisions will be made. For example, if one brand's quantity sold in period $t + 1$ is modeled as a function of its price and a competitor's price in period $t + 1$, then both price levels must be "known" so that they can be entered into the model. A manager may (sometimes) know what price he will charge in a future time period, but will not know competitors' prices; these must be forecast. Thus, a logit model or any other competitive interaction model requires subsidiary forecasts of exogenous variables, variables that are needed but not supplied by the model itself.

The model advocated here produces a forecasted value for each (time series) variable in the system each week. In other words, its output is a time-varying vector rather than a scalar. This output is much richer than output from a competitive interaction model which forecasts the quantity sold of each brand, but only once—not weekly—and does not forecast marketing mix variables, even those with time series characteristics such as competitors' prices and advertising levels.

Actual Results

For a 16-week forecasting period, Figure 18.4 shows all four volume forecasts from the dynamic model, along with actual results to permit an assessment of the model's out-of-sample forecasting accuracy. The model tracks sales spikes and dips extremely well. Only for Brand 3 is a major sales spike smoothed over in March and April of 1990.

It is important to recall that these are true out-of-sample forecasts. They only use—as input for parameter estimation—data available prior to the 16-week forecasting period, thereby mimicking a manager's real-world situation. Out-of-

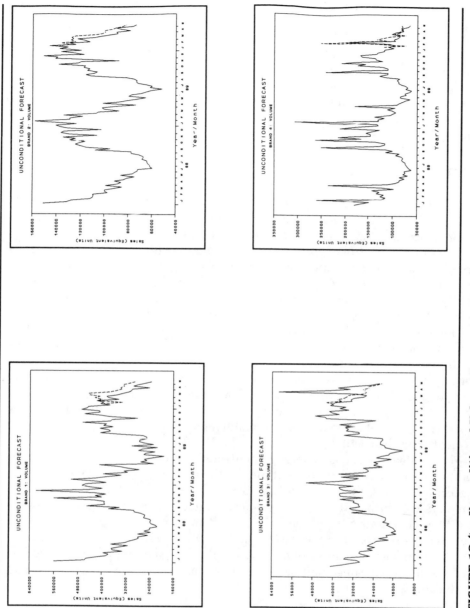

FIGURE 18.4. Unconditional Volume Forecasts: All 4 Brands

sample forecasting is a much sterner test of a model than is R^2, which measures the in-sample fit of a model. In-sample fit can be improved—to perfection ($R^2 = 1.00$) if need be—by adding more terms to a model. However, no matter how many terms are added, out-of-sample accuracy is high only if the model truly captures the real-world process it is designed to mimic.

A second point to remember is that the four forecasts shown in Figure 18.4 (plus 11 others) were generated simultaneously by a single model. The model is, therefore, not only parsimonious but also easier to implement than would be separate models for each time series.[6]

Competitive Advantages

In addition to being self-contained, unconditional forecasts yield competitive advantages. As an example, Brand 1's manager may want forecasts of Brand 4's volume, price, and total revenue. Price in particular is critical since prices are not really under the control of the manufacturer, but are determined by a mixture of retail policies and consumer reactions to those policies. Brand 1's manager wants to anticipate the retailer's pricing policy for private brands because these establish the low end of the category's price spectrum. Total revenue is also needed for subsequent control applications where it will be maximized.

Figure 18.5 shows the 16-week forecasts for these three time series. The left frame shows that volume forecasts precisely track the dip in January of 1989 and the major spike that follows. The middle frame shows that the price cut in February 1989 is tracked accurately, though the model leads slightly and under-estimates the price hikes that follow in March and April. The right frame shows that combining the price and quantity forecasts yields unconditional forecasts of total revenue that are quite accurate, although forecasted spikes and dips are more extreme than actual.

In summary, a category management model should produce accurate un-conditional forecasts, a requirement met by the dynamic optimal control model. To accomplish this, the model treats all variables as part of a unified system. (Modelers call such systems "endogenous.") Endogenous systems are "closed" since they alleviate the need for management intervention in the form of sup-plementary forecasts of exogenous variables. Other benefits of the model are that it accounts for the interaction of the levels established for all marketing mix variables in a given category, it has a parsimonious algebraic representation, and it is dynamic.

CONDITIONAL FORECASTS

A *conditional forecast* is produced when some or all of a model's variables are fixed at certain levels. These levels can be fixed by pure assumption or by logical analysis (for example, "Our price must exceed our marginal cost by 10 percent, therefore set $p = 1.1 \times$ [marginal cost].").

Of course all forecasts are conditional on (1) the algebraic form of the model, (2) the values substituted for the model's parameters, and (3) the values used

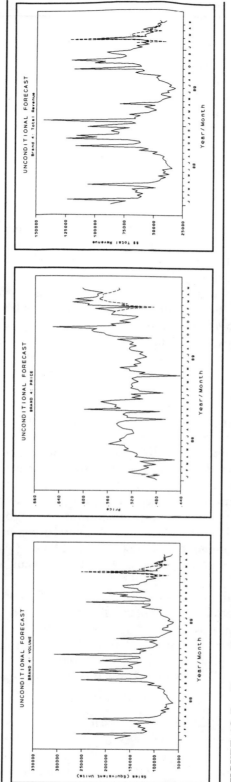

FIGURE 18.5. Unconditional Forecasts for Brand 4: Including Total Revenue

for levels of the model's measured variables. In distinguishing here between unconditional and conditional forecasts, the focus is on point (3), the levels of the variables established for the forecast period. If these levels are forecast by the model itself, then forecasts are "unconditional." If these levels are imposed externally, then forecasts are "conditional."

Competitive interaction models cannot really generate conditional forecasts; they are restricted to a much narrower application called "what-if" (or "if-then") simulation." This point is explored next.

"What-if" Simulators vs. Forecasters

What kinds of conclusions does an if-then simulator produce? First, its *conditions* (the "if" part of the "if-then" analysis) are all exogenously established and completely determine its conclusions. Rerunning a "what-if" simulator under the same conditions will simply duplicate previous output. Second, the conclusions are insensitive to the time sequence of conditions. In other words, if we ask a "what-if" simulator to estimate the incremental sales from a feature of our product this week and then ask the question again next week, results from the two runs will be identical. The fact that a feature is run two weeks in a row will have no bearing on the simulator's output. Third, conclusions drawn from the output may be highly misleading, since the conditions established for the simulation may not be logically consistent.

The model advocated here overcomes each of these flaws. First, because it is both endogenous and dynamic, setting a price at a certain level influences all quantities sold in the current period. These quantity effects then ripple forward to future time periods influencing subsequent prices and quantities sold. Second, because the model explicitly accounts for forward cannibalization, results from (say) featuring a brand two weeks in a row will typically be quite different from those for a one-time feature. More generally, the model links demand among SKUs not only at a given point in time (concurrent effects) but also across time periods (dynamic effects). Third, because the model forecasts all variables *not* set in a conditioning statement, levels of the conditioning variables adhere to the assumptions of the model and are internally consistent, whereas levels set by a manager may not be.

This last point needs clarification. Using a "what-if" simulator, a manager is free to establish any levels for any set of conditioning variables. Because the possibilities are virtually limitless, poor judgment can creep into the model-manager interaction. For example, even with only four SKUs and four marketing mix variables (price, feature, display, and advertising), there are sixteen total variables, eight of which—features and displays—are binary. A one-period conditioning vector looks like this:

$$[\underbrace{p_1, p_2, p_3, p_4}_{\text{prices}} \mid \underbrace{f_1, f_2, f_3, f_4}_{\text{features}} \mid \underbrace{d_1, d_2, d_3, d_4}_{\text{displays}} \mid \underbrace{a_1, a_2, a_3, a_4}_{\text{advertising}}]$$

The binary variables alone can be set at 2^8 or 256 different combinations; for example, f_1 is either "on" or "off," f_2 is either "on" or "off," and so on. Further, even if certain limits are imposed on prices and advertising (say we allow five levels each), there are ($5^8 \times 2^8$), or 100 million possible conditions! It is unlikely that a manager playing "what-if" games will bother to worry about whether a particular set of conditions makes sense.[7]

The new approach works as follows. If a brand manager sets part of this vector—say, the price in one week for the product he or she manages—then the system sets all other variables at their expected levels for that week and for any other week in the conditioning period. Expected levels—as illustrated in the previous section—are unconditional forecasts. These values are nearly impossible to generate by intuition.

Actual Results:
Retrospective Conditional Forecasting

Conditional forecasts can be further classified as either retrospective or prospective. A retrospective conditional forecast answers the question "what would have happened if..." while a prospective conditional forecast answers the question "what will happen if..." Both types are illustrated in this section and the next.

For example, management was interested in what volume would have been sold if an alternative television advertising schedule had been used in the fall of 1989. Two scenarios were played out: a no-advertising scenario, and an average advertising scenario. To exercise these options, values for Brand 1's advertising were reset during a 16-week conditioning period (October–December, 1989). The model was then run under each revised reality to predict what Brand 1's sales would have been during a subsequent 36-week period.

Figure 18.6 shows the results. The left panel compares sales for each scenario to smoothed actual sales. Since differences are small, the right panel shows the cumulated difference between actual and forecast sales. Before March 16, 1990, when it surpasses zero, the no-advertising scenario generates sales superior to what actually occurred. However, Brand 1's actual advertising program eventually wins out, generating incremental sales of 114,398 units. With average advertising, a similar pattern occurs: the actual program loses in early weeks, then overtakes the conditional scenario, winning overall by 39,661 units. The conclusion: the firm's original advertising schedule was only marginally effective, mainly because Brand 1's advertising has little direct effect on its sales.

Actual Results:
Prospective Conditional Forecasts

Table 18.1 shows the results for an 8-week period for two different (future) pricing scenarios for Brand 1. In condition A, Brand 1's price is lowered 10 percent in week 1—from 53¢ to 48¢—and then maintained at 48¢ in week 2 of the conditioning period. In condition B, Brand 1's price is lowered 10 percent in week 1, then lowered 10 percent more in week 2. No other variables are manipulated during the forecasting horizon. In this case the conditioning period consists of the first two weeks of the forecasting horizon.

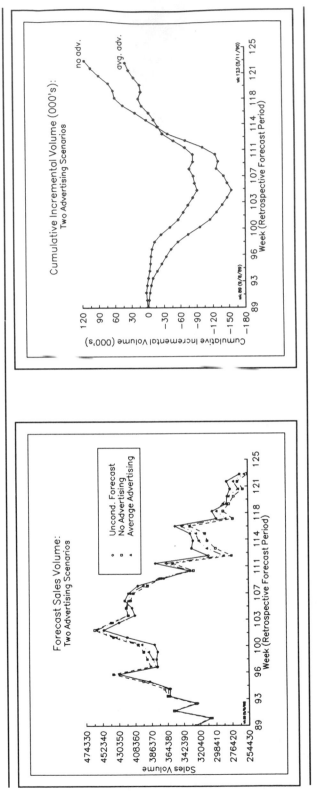

FIGURE 18.6. An Example of a Retrospective Conditional Forecast for Brand 1's Volume

TABLE 18.1. Comparison of Two Conditional Forecasts with Baseline Results

Condition Scenario		Week 1 90:5:18	Week 2 90:5:25	Week 3 90:6:1	Week 4 90:6:8	Week 5 90:6:15	Week 6 90:6:22	Week 7 90:6:29	Week 8 90:7:6	8-week Total
					Forecasted Results					
Baseline	Vol	239,778	242,157	243,412	244,207	244,879	253,460	257,991	260,577	1,986.46
	Pr	.534	.537	.539	.540	.541	.543	.543	.544	0.54
(Uncond.	TR	128,009	129,941	131,111	131,926	132,601	137,526	140,210	141,813	1,073.14
Forecast)	MS	58.4	58.6	58.6	58.7	58.6	58.2	58.6	58.6	58.54
Condition A	Vol	271,210	264,527	256,406	253,193	252,145	260,110	264,505	267,141	2,089.24
reduce	Pr	.480[a]	.480[a]	.486	.490	.494	.497	.499	.502	0.49
price 10%	TR	130,181	126,973	124,540	124,100	124,490	129,218	132,083	134,008	1,025.59
then hold	MS	61.7	59.7	60.3	60.4	60.5	59.9	60.3	60.3	60.39
Condition B	Vol	251,310	286,285	269,195	260,947	258,082	265,340	269,610	272,336	2,133.11
reduce price	Pr	.480[b]	.430[b]	.439	.447	.452	.457	.461	.465	0.45
10% two weeks	TR	120,629	123,103	118,288	116,520	116,721	121,292	124,357	126,608	967.52
in a row	MS	61.7	62.4	60.8	61.8	61.9	61.4	61.7	61.7	61.68

[a,b] These values are fixed by the conditioning scenario.

367

Results show that sales are highest in condition B, although both conditions generate sales increases—146,650 units for B and 102,780 units for A—relative to baseline volume given by the unconditional forecast for the same period. However, neither condition generates higher revenues than the unconditional forecast. If Brand 1's manager considers only these three possibilities, then he or she should use the price trajectory suggested by the unconditional forecast.

The value of the dynamic approach is clear in this example. A static model such as multinomial logit is incapable of comparing these two scenarios. First, it does not generate forecasts of price and, therefore, cannot forecast total revenue. Second, a logit model does not have the flexibility to enter a time-path of price conditions; for example, the phrase "lowering price two weeks in a row" has no meaning in the context of a static model.[8]

Impulse Responses

The approach advocated here supports a third type of conditional forecasting called impulse response analysis. Impulse responses are the time paths of one or more variables as a function of a one-time pulse (rather than a set of enduring conditions) to another variable or set of variables. Impulse responses summarize cause-and-effect relationships in a dynamic system. For example, we might shock the price of Brand 1 by lowering it a certain amount, then trace the week-by-week reactions among all four sales volumes.

As an example, the left panel of Figure 18.7 shows how all four volumes react to a 145-second pulse of Brand 1's advertising; the right panel illustrates volume reaction to an increase of one standard deviation (about 2 cents) in Brand 1's price. These are one-time pulses occurring in a nominal week zero; once a shock is administered, there is no further tampering with the system. (In contrast, a conditional forecast sets conditions for a specific period—not a nominal one—and these conditions endure once set.) The following results are of interest to Brand 1's manager:

Advertising: Although Brand 1's sales eventually respond positively to the advertising shock (a cumulative incremental gain of 1,293 units over 36 weeks), Brand 2 and Brand 4 actually gain more from Brand 1's advertising than does Brand 1. Brand 2—Brand 1's companion brand—gains 3,595 units, while the private labels (Brand 4) gain 2,347 units. Only Brand 3 fails to gain from Brand 1's advertising (a cumulative loss of 38 units).

Pricing: Brand 1's sales fall 20,776 units in response to its price increase, while the other brands gain asymmetrically (Brand 2 gains 10,021 units, Brand 3 gains 4,566 units, and Brand 4 gains 7,421 units).

These dynamics correspond to the known market structure. The positive spillover from Brand 1's advertising to Brand 2's sales seems natural, since Brand 1 and Brand 2 carry the same brand name. Similarly, Brand 3—the only other national brand in the category—should not benefit from Brand 1's advertising but should benefit from its price increase.

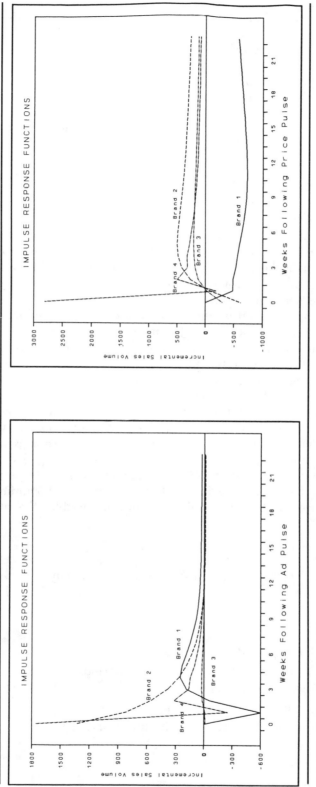

FIGURE 18.7. Volume Responses to an Advertising Pulse and a Price Pulse

DYNAMIC OPTIMAL CONTROL

The model used here not only forecasts future outcomes in a given category, it can also be used for dynamic optimal control. For control applications, three additional components are needed: an explicit objective function, an explicit solution function, and real-time information feedback. These components, described next, are not part of a traditional competitive interaction model.

Objective Functions

Brand managers often say that they want to "maximize sales or market share." Retailers want to "maximize category sales." Both statements require considerable refinement before they can be incorporated into a realistic objective function. Neither goal mentions the costs of control or the time required for interventions to take effect, and neither considers trade-offs between different strategies that might achieve the same end results.

In dynamic optimal control, the objective function typically minimizes the variation around a desired value for sales, market share, or some other process variable. Outcomes are also subject to costs of control. In category management these costs are (a) the costs of setting the marketing mix variables at specific levels (for example, turning a feature on or lowering a price); (b) costs due to negative spillover from one SKU to others; and (c) costs due to price or marketing mix volatility. Further, since interventions at one time affect future outcomes, a valid objective function must explicitly cumulate all future effects. Finally, uncertainty is a factor in dynamic optimal control: one minimizes or maximizes an expected value, not a determined value.

The following equation is an objective function with all these properties, labeled with the letter L since it is a loss function to be minimized. This particular objective function uses only one control variable, the price of the brand.

$$
L = E\left[\sum_{w=0}^{\infty} \beta^{w}\left\{(\mathrm{ms}_{t+w} - \mathrm{ms}_{t+w}^{0})^{2} + \lambda \sum_{k=1}^{q}(p_{t+w} - p_{t+w-k})^{2}\right\}\right]
$$

where:

E = the expected value operator

Σ^{∞} = sums results for all future time periods.

β^{w} = a discounting factor

ms_{t+w} = market share in future period $t + w$

ms_{t+w}^{0} = the target market share in future period $t + w$

λ = a scaling factor: price volatility

Σ^{q} = sums over a volatility "horizon"

p_{t+w} = price in future period $t + w$

p_{t+w-k} = price in (past) period $t + w - k$

Although this objective function is algebraically complex, its meaning can be described fairly simply. First, the manager has a target market share (ms^o) which may be a constant (say 32 percent) but which may also vary on a weekly basis since it is time-subscripted; for example, the manager may desire an upward trending market share. Here both positive and negative variations from the target share are penalized, since the objective function is to be minimized. These variations are time-discounted by the factor β^w and then summed over all future weeks—that is, over an infinite time horizon. Any price put into effect in one week could in theory influence *all* future sales levels; these effects are properly assimilated by this objective function.

Second, the manager wants to minimize price volatility while achieving the market share objective. If prices vary too much from one week to the next, relations with the trade and with consumers might be damaged. Volatility is measured by the sum of squared deviations of prices from lagged values of price during a "price volatility horizon." In other words, the volatility index measures the degree to which current price levels differ from previous price levels. The length (q) of the "price volatility horizon" can be adjusted to avoid pricing policies that whipsaw up and down. (Increasing the length of the horizon tends to smooth the price trajectory of the resulting optimal control policy.)

Finally, the uncertainty associated with forecasting is assimilated by the expected value operator (E), which indicates that the manager is trying to minimize average deviations from target. Thus, the criterion is stochastic rather than deterministic.

Solution Function

The solution to a dynamic optimal control problem is a function, not a fixed plan. A function is an algebraic machine—a formula—that processes data and produces a plan valid for the current planning period. In category management, the data summarize the current state of the category—the latest available sales results and the current levels of the marketing mix variables. Simply put, the optimal plan (from "now on") is formed with full knowledge of "what has happened up until now."

An example will clarify. A family planning a three-day drive from home to Disney World may select a route, meal, and stopover schedule prior to departure. However, en route this schedule may have to be changed in order to meet the trip's overall objective—that is, arriving at Disney World no later than 4:00 P.M. July 10th. The optimal plan at the end of day one must consider the family's status at that time, including the distance already covered and the time and resources spent. If the family failed to cover as much distance in day one as originally planned, then the schedule for days two and three must be revised accordingly.

In the category management problem illustrated here, the optimal price to set in week w depends on what happened in week $w-1$. Thus, a 13-week pricing plan can not be pre-established with 13 prices decided on in advance, to be implemented inflexibly for weeks 1 through 13. A good plan is dynamic, not static, setting next week's price as a function of this week's results.

Marketplace Feedback

Feedback solutions are possible only when analysts have reliable measurements of a system's current state, and they are practical only when the feedback is timely. Single source systems make possible feedback solutions to category management problems. Single source systems report—on a weekly basis—the levels of the marketing mix variables and quantity sold for each SKU in a given product category. These values are used to characterize the state of the category in any given week.

One other requirement of a good category state vector, however, is that it must contain lagged values for certain variables.[9] In the car example, the family really needs to know how far it traveled during day one to plan for the remainder of the trip. This calculation is given by the following formula:

$$\text{distance}_{(\text{day 1})} = [\text{mileage}_{(\text{end of day 1})} - \text{mileage}_{(\text{start of day 1})}]$$

The right hand side of this equation represents one-day "lagged mileage."

In summary, a dynamic optimal control approach to category management consists of five parts: a unified (state-space) model of category dynamics, "old" data to estimate the model's parameters, an objective function, a solution function, and "new" data about the current state of the system. Given these ingredients, sophisticated mathematical techniques are able to solve the problem—that is, to forecast marketing activities and to minimize the objective function in light of the constraints imposed by market dynamics. The resulting solution function uses data from "this week" to establish "next week's" optimal marketing plan.

Actual Results

The objective function used in this application is a variation on the market share example. It balances market share considerations with considerations of total revenue, as shown in equation (2). Equation (2) contains weights (δ and τ), sales terms such as $s_i(w)$ $i = 1, 4$, and total revenue for Brand $1 - p_i(w) \cdot s_i(w)$—as well as a price volatility term.

$$\text{Min} \lim_{N \to \infty} E_o \sum_{w=0}^{N} \delta \left\{ (1-\tau)s_1(w) - \tau \left[\sum_{i \neq 1} s_i(w) \right] \right\}^2 \cdots$$
$$\cdots - p_1(w)s_1(w) + (1-\delta)[p_1(w) - p_1(w-1)]^2 \tag{2}$$

Equation (2) permits management to construct an objective function that reflects specific trade-offs between Brand 1's market share and total revenue, subject to price volatility considerations. The weight δ trades off sales and price volatility. As $\delta \to 1$, more weight is placed on sales and less weight is placed on controlling price volatility. In other words, with high δ's, prices are allowed to vary considerably from week to week to achieve the market share and total revenue goals. The other weight τ allows the manager to place more or less emphasis on Brand 1's market share. For example, when $\tau = 1.0$, the sum of sales of brands 2, 3, and 4—that is, the term $[\Sigma_{i \neq 1} s_i(w)]^2$—is minimized, a result equivalent to maximizing Brand 1's market share.[10]

Table 18.2 shows results for δ varied at five levels and τ varied at two. In each case, forecasted revenue and market share using the optimal feedback rule exceed their baseline counterparts, generating anywhere from $45,546 incremental revenue to $282,108 incremental revenue for a 24-week forecasting horizon.

Expectations about the effects of manipulating δ and τ are also borne out. For example, as δ increases through its five levels, revenues steadily increase because more flexibility is being allowed in the dynamic pricing policy. (Figure 18.8 displays results graphically for conditions 1, 3, and 9, where δ varies while τ is held fixed at 0.6.) Although high levels of total revenue are enticing under the high δ scenarios, the resulting pricing stream may be too variable for sound trade and consumer relations[11]. Brand 1's manager may feel that certain psychological pricing thresholds may be violated by this much price movement. The manager may opt for a more conservative policy.

The market share patterns in Table 18.2 also follow expectations as τ is varied. In each case—holding δ fixed—the market share is at least as large when $\tau = 1.0$ as when it is 0.6. For example, when $\delta = 0.50$, Brand 1's market share averages 0.6103 for $\tau = 1.0$ but only 0.5916 for $\tau = 0.6$.

Summary

The foregoing example illustrates that optimal control theory removes the guesswork implicit in "what-if" conditional forecasting. Optimal control theory finds the feedback rule that establishes a marketing mix trajectory that optimizes a criterion established by management. A feedback rule tells the manager what to do next, given all results to date.

TABLE 18.2. Results from Several Runs of the Optimization Model

Condition			Forecasted Revenue (24 week average)		Forecasted Market Share (24 week average)	
#	δ	τ	Unrestricted	Using Optimal Price Policy	Unrestricted	Using Optimal Price Policy
1	0	0.6	148,926	202,724	.5787	.5923
2	0	1.0	148,926	202,725	.5787	.5923
3	.25	0.6	148,926	200,538	.5787	.5920
4	.25	1.0	148,926	254,378	.5787	.6016
5	.50	0.6	148,926	198,437	.5787	.5916
6	.50	1.0	148,926	309,679	.5787	.6103
7	.75	0.6	148,926	196,416	.5787	.5913
8	.75	1.0	148,926	368,597	.5787	.6184
9	1.0	0.6	148,926	194,472	.5787	.5909
0	1.0	1.0	148,926	431,034	.5787	.6259

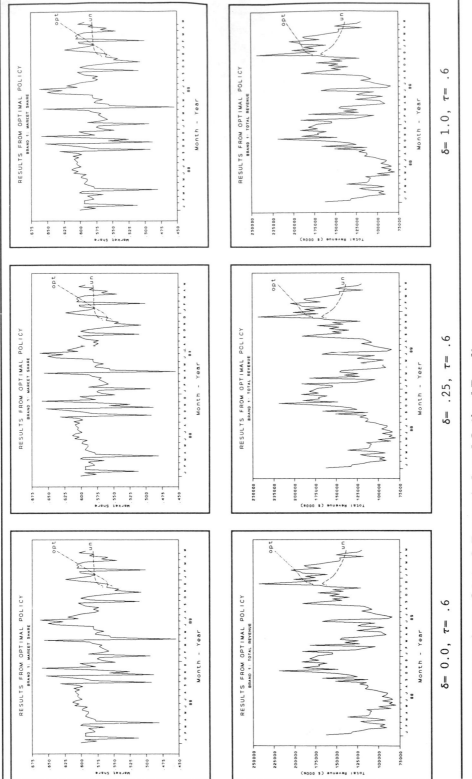

FIGURE 18.8. Comparison of Actual, Forecasted, and Optimal Results

Although the examples used here focus on brand management applications using only price as a control variable, objective functions suited for retail category management can be specified. These functions maximize total revenue for all SKUs in a given product category, subject to certain market share and marketing mix volatility trade-offs.

CONCLUSION

This chapter discusses advanced topics in category management. Although the goals and policy variables differ for brand managers and store managers, the category management viewpoint is valid in both cases because brand managers cannot ignore competitors' activities and store managers cannot ignore substitution effects.

Properties of a good category management model were outlined, including (1) the ability to integrate all competing effects, (2) the ability to model market dynamics, (3) the ability to forecast outcomes, and (4) the ability to exercise control over outcomes. Competitive interaction models—logit, probit, and pooled store level models—fulfill some but not all of these requirements. The weaknesses of competitive interaction models were outlined and an alternative approach based on dynamic optimal control theory was suggested.

Actual output was used to illustrate the model's ability to do unconditional forecasting, conditional forecasting, and impulse response analysis. Even more promising is the model's ability to solve dynamic optimal control problems. Optimal control requires an explicit objective function, an explicit solution function, and data about the current state of the system. These features were discussed and results were provided for a brand management problem, using price as the control variable and a combination of total revenue and market share as the process variable.

Category management using optimal control theory is in its infancy. This chapter provides an intuitive summary of the fundamental ideas. Expectations are that during the next few years the approach will be successfully implemented, especially as standardized software becomes available.

Dynamic optimal control theory appears to tap the strategic potential of today's rich data reserves. It goes beyond data analysis to decision support, suggesting reasonable courses of action regarding the policy variables controlled by a brand or a store manager.

Notes

1. Peter M. Guadagni and John D. C. Little, "A Logit Model of Brand Choice Calibrated on Scanner Data," *Marketing Science*, 2 (Summer 1983), pp. 203–238.

2. By agreement with the data supplier, details must be withheld.

3. For a review of the logit and other random utility models used in packaged goods management, see Lee G. Cooper and Masao Nakanishi, *Market Share Analysis*, Norwell, MA: Kluwer Academic, 1989; and Guadagni and Little, op cit. A related model is presented in Dick R. Wittink, John C. Porter, and Sachin Gupta "Biases in Parameter Estimates from Linearly Aggregated Data when the Disaggre-

gate Model is Nonlinear," working paper, Johnson Graduate School of Managment, Cornell University, January 1991, pp. 1–38. I refer to such models as competitive interaction (CI) models since their output consists of (estimates of) direct and cross elasticities between category entrants.

4. For a statistical comparison of the predictive ability of both the logit model and the pooled store level model with the model presented here, see David Curry and Subir Banyopadhyay, "Static Approximations to Dynamic Processes," working paper No. 8, Center for Integrated Research Systems, the University of Cincinnati.

5. Guadagni and Little, op. cit., p. 225.

6. Statistical tests (Theil Us) comparing these forecasts to those from alternative models show that the dynamic model outperforms all other models tested. Four classes of models were included in comparisons: univariate exponential smoothing, univariate Box-Jenkins, bivariate Box-Jenkins (transfer functions), and mutivariate (non-Bayesian) state-space models. See David J. Curry, Charles H. Whiteman, Suresh Divakar, and Sharat K. Mathur, "Bayesian Vector Autoregression: A New Approach for Modeling Competitive Dynamics in Category Management," working paper, The Center for Integrated Research Systems (June 1992).

7. This is in fact a very small conditioning space. Note that as soon as a time subscript is added to the conditioning vector (permitting a manager to set the marketing mix for several weeks in a multiweek planning period) the conditioning space becomes much larger. In real problems, the conditioning space is effectively infinite.

8. The model can easily generate forecasts conditioned on different time-paths for features and displays of any SKU in the product category. For example, if Brand 1 is featured in various combinations (wkl = 80, wk2 = 0), (wkl = 0, wk2 = 80), and (wkl = 80, wk2 = 80) resulting volumes are less than baseline in all three cases; e.g., −741, −92, −833 units. These losses are slight, since Brand 1's featuring activity has little cumulative impact on its sales, but notable because featuring first creates a sizeable sales spike, then forward cannibalizes enough to make featuring a losing proposition in all three cases.

9. Here we refer to discrete time systems involving difference equations, not continuous time systems involving differential equations. As chapters 6–11 explain, market place feedback arrives weekly even though it is collected continuously. See Appendix A for additional discussion.

10. Equation 2 is a quartic function, or fourth-degree polynomial, rather than a quadratic function, or second-degree polynomial, because it contains the term $[-p_1(w)s_1(w)]^2$. Solutions are derived using the best quadratic approximation to the function in the range of prices under consideration.

11. For example, using the unconditional forecasts, prices range from 40¢ to about 45¢ during the 24-week period. For scenario 7, they range from 46¢ to 57¢, but for scenario 8—when δ is increased from 0.6 to 1.0—they range from 52¢ to $1.24.

APPENDIX 18A:
DYNAMIC MODELS AND LAWS OF MOTION
IN CATEGORY MANAGEMENT

This appendix provides additional information about the dynamic model recommended for category management problems. The appendix is organized as a series of questions and answers, with each question addressing a different aspect of the model. Each aspect is then explained by analogy with a physical system. This format is designed to aid the reader's intuition without presuming any knowledge of stochastic difference equations, the branch of mathematics that underpins the framework.[1] Despite its apparent lack of similarity with category management, the analog system—a space shuttle—accurately illustrates certain properties of category management that are otherwise difficult to grasp.

What Is Meant by the Term "System"?

A system consists of physical objects together with an environment in which the objects interact according to the natural laws of that environment.

For example, the earth, a space shuttle, its crew and cargo, along with the laws of physics constitute a system. Similarly, a set of shelf-keeping units (SKUs) situated in their natural marketing environment together with the economic and psychological laws governing sales and market share constitute a system. The natural marketing environment for a product category consists of its in-store physical environment as well as each SKU's marketing mix (promotional environment), and the ensemble of distributors and consumers associated with the category's geographic markets.

What Is Meant by the Phrase "State of a System"?

A system is characterized by its levels on several dimensions called state variables. For a space shuttle, these dimensions are time plus the three physical coordinates that locate the shuttle relative to its launch site, as well as the shuttle's velocity and acceleration relative to the launch site. (More accurately, we say that the earth launch site is the designated inertial reference frame for the space shuttle.)[2]

For a product category, the relevant dimensions are economic. They include each SKU's price, quantity, and marketing mix variables at a given time. The number of state variables must be sufficient to completely describe the position of the system at a given moment. Further, if energy is introduced into the system—for example, if the shuttle pilot burns the main rocket for two seconds—the information in the state vector plus the information about the input must be sufficient to determine the system's trajectory from that moment onward. More generally, then:

The state of a system at some moment t_0 is the set of information at t_0 that, together with any future input, uniquely determines the behavior of the system from that moment onward.

The state of a system is usually represented mathematically as a vector of numbers. For example, a complete description of a space shuttle's state at any instant in time requires measurements of time, the x,y,z physical coordinates of the shuttle (relative to mission control), a velocity vector (that is, the shuttle's speed in each direction x,y,z), and an acceleration vector (that is, the shuttle's change of speed in each direction x,y,z).[3]

A "complete" description of a product category during any time interval — say, one week — requires measurements of each entrant's price, the quantity sold during that week, and the values of the marketing mix variables in effect during the week. (For now we suppress issues concerning the level of inquiry — store level, metro market level, and so on — as well as corresponding data aggregation issues.)

Just as the shuttle's velocity and acceleration represent, respectively, first-order and second-order changes (lags), lagged values are included in the state vector for a product category. Both cases are shown below.

$$shuttle = [x(t), y(t), z(t), \qquad \Delta x(t), \Delta y(t), \Delta z(t), \qquad \Delta^2 x(t), \Delta^2 y(t), \Delta^2 z(t)]$$

where:

$x(t), y(t), z(t)$ = physical coordinates in three dimensions at time t,

Δ = change; e.g., $\Delta y = y(t) - y(t-1)$ refers to the change in the "y-direction" from one time period to the next,

Δ^2 = change of change; that is, the second difference in the indicated direction.

$$category = [p_i(t), q_i(t), a_i(t), m_i(t), \Delta^j p_i(t), \Delta^j q_i(t), \Delta^j a_i(t)]$$

where:

i is a subscript for SKUs,

$\Delta^j p_i$ means change in price (or quantity, advertising, or any other continuous variable). j stands for the number of lags (differences) in the change

In general a category contains U SKUs and the state vector includes a value for each SKU's price (p), quantity sold (q), advertising (a), and, say, a merchandising variable (m), such as feature.

How Does the System Change from One State to Another?

Changes occur in real time according to the laws of motion governing the system and according to interventions from outside the system.

Laws of motion are expressed algebraically for the space shuttle: that is, force = mass × acceleration, or $F = mA$, and as systems of (difference) equations for a product category. Movements from one state to another must obey "natural laws," and can be summarized using the state vector and a state transition matrix that govern the motion of the state vector in any time interval where system input is identically zero; that is, where the system is coasting, as will be discussed shortly.

What Is Meant by the Term "Natural Law"?

A natural law is an assumption—usually expressed in words or in mathematical symbols—about how a system works.

We think of natural laws as existing apart from human beings, although this is an oversimplification in physics as well as in marketing. For example, Newton's third law states that for every action there is an equal but opposite reaction.[4] This is supposedly a law of nature whose truth or falsity does not depend on human beings.

With marketing and economic phenomena, the idea of a natural law is complicated by the fact that the objects of inquiry (humans) are self-aware and, therefore, may possess free will. Free will blurs the boundary between natural law and self-control; that is, for what aspects and at what scales (individual or social) is human behavior a product of natural laws *not* under the control of one individual? Since much human behavior is predictable, the scientific community searches for lawlike explanations. Thus the scientist speaks of laws of supply and demand, laws of perception, laws of information integration, laws of choice, and other laws that describe people acting alone and interacting with other people. These laws have the following properties.

1. Their existence and effects do not depend on whether or not humans have correctly expressed the laws through the use of prosaic symbols, mathematical symbols or any other form of human communication.
2. Their existence and effects are not under human control or influence; natural laws function independently from the human species—or any other life form, for that matter.
3. Natural laws are pervasive; they are part of the fabric of the universe.[5]

Of course, in both the natural sciences as well as in the social sciences humans seem to intervene to alter certain laws; for example, scientists produce new proteins, or create compounds and elements that do not appear in nature. However, rather than claim that humankind alters laws of nature, it may be more reasonable to say that we simply explore outcomes permitted by the laws of nature but which are not yet or not here realized by nature itself.[6]

Similarly, in marketing we may realize new outcomes from the law of supply and demand by introducing new technology, by using a new production planning process that reduces manufacturing costs, or by running a remarkably persuasive advertising campaign. However, the fundamental laws governing human behavior and market dynamics remain unchanged.

What Is a Law of Motion?

A law of motion is an equation or system of equations that describes time variations of the dimensions constituting the state variables of a system.

Motion need not be interpreted physically. In a product category, we use terms such as "product movement data," "sales increases/plummeting sales," "push-pull strategies," "price drops," and other terms that imply movement or activity in economic reality rather than in physical reality. The critical requirement is that the law of motion uniquely map one state, say x_0 at time t_0 into a new state, x_1 at time $t_1 > t_0$.

What Is the Inertial State of a System?

Inertia is how much opposition a system presents to having its natural state of motion changed.

Systems—be they space shuttles or product categories—consume energy because they meet natural resistance. The idea of inertia allows us to differentiate between the behavior of a system in the absence of energy input—its inertial behavior—and its behavior under the influence of energy interventions.

A system runs in its inertial state given the absence of new energy input. For example, a shuttle—once injected into earth orbit—will orbit according to natural physical laws. Its inertial behavior is a function of the shuttle's mass, velocity, and acceleration, interacting through a law of gravity with the mass of the earth. However, without intermittent energy inputs, the orbit will decay and the craft will be drawn back to earth.

In marketing, an SKU's inertial mass, that is, its natural resistance to sales decays, is a function of its market share, its absolute sales level, and its brand equity. Sales among SKUs in a given product category will continue at a relatively predictable pace if no changes are made to entrant prices or marketing mixes. In other words, without energy inputs such as price decreases or special promotions, each entrant's sales will vary randomly around mutually decaying baseline sales.

What Does the Word "Intervention" Mean?

For a space shuttle, an intervention might be a two-second blast of the main engine or a ten-second burn of smaller side rockets. An intervention is designed to alter the craft's position to establish a new flight trajectory, usually in accordance with a preestablished flight plan. Interventions are designed to control the shuttle's flight path.

In the case of a product category, interventions are in the form of price reductions, features, displays, and other promotions. Just as rocket fuel is costly (and course alterations are resisted by natural forces), sales alterations are costly (and are resisted by lack of consumer interest, distributor skepticism, lack of shelf space, and so on).[7] For example, Guadagni and Little discover a pocket of consumer resistance that they describe as follows: "the picture emerges that a well-entrenched brand size has a set of loyal customers who make its share relatively insensitive to certain marketing actions" (p. 233). Consumer resistance of this sort represents part of the inertial behavior of a product category. Interventions can temporarily overcome such resistance.

What Does It Mean to Say That Event x Causes Event y?

Single-source suppliers assert that they collect causal data: data about interventions such as in-store features or displays that cause a category entrant's sales to increase. However, the idea of causality is problematic, and the principles of causality must be applied carefully or important resources will be wasted.

To illustrate these difficulties, Figure 18.9 shows a space shuttle and a communications satellite in synchronized earth orbits. Measurements taken at equally spaced time intervals (x_i, y_i) would reveal high correlation between the x, y time series, yet neither object is causing the behavior of the other. In fact, each object's orbit was established by earlier rocket launches, and their current trajectories in space-time are both caused (maintained) by natural laws of physics.

In this case, the logical disassociation of orbits could be verified by the following statistical test. First, attempt to predict the shuttle's flight path from past x information alone. Next, attempt to predict the shuttle's path using both

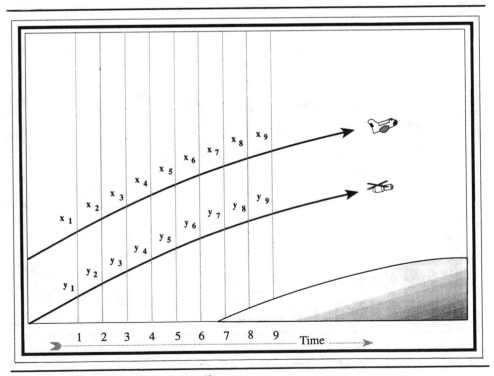

FIGURE 18.9.   Spurious Causality

past x and past y information. A comparison of the forecasts from these two approaches would reveal no improvement in prediction using the y information. Conclusion: the satellite's path does not cause the shuttle's path.

Figure 18.10 shows a different scenario, in which the shuttle and satellite have intersecting orbits and relative speeds that foretell a collision at time t_c. As before, the time series (x_i, y_i) are highly correlated both before and after the collision. In this case, however, the collision causes the flight paths to change: causality that would be revealed by the test suggested earlier. That is, using the y information, along with the satellite's mass and velocity relative to the shuttle, we would improve our ability to predict the postcollision course of each object.[8]

> Generally then, variable y is said to cause variable x if past values of y can help predict future values of x better than past values of x alone can predict future values of x.

In marketing, two time series may be highly correlated; for example sales of two competing SKUs, with neither causing the other. Tests of causality must compare the predictive ability of two forecasting rules. Rule 1 is $x_t = f\{x_{t-j}, j = 1, 2, \ldots\}$, while Rule 2 is $[x_t | Y] = f\{x_{t-j}, y_{t-j}, j = 1, 2, \ldots\}$, where $|Y$ is read as "given all past values of the variable y." If the difference in predictive ability, that is, (Rule 2 − Rule 1) is statistically significant, we say that y caused x.

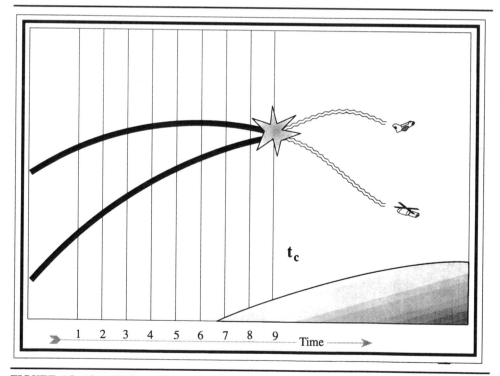

FIGURE 18.10. Weiner-Granger Causality

Are Causes Events or Processes?

This view of and test for causality seems to suggest that one phenomenon (a process) causes another process rather than that an event causes an event. But if processes cause processes, how can an event such as an in-store display for brand x cause sales to change? A display is a binary (on/off) event, not a process for which time series data are available.

Although apparently paradoxical, in fact the collision/shuttle example and the display/sales example have the same properties. To see this, note first that although the course changes shown in Figure 18.10 result from the physical interaction of solid objects during the collision event, the earlier paths of the two objects contain valuable information relevant to the event: for example, will it happen, when, where, and with what force? This insight suggests that causality be viewed from an information perspective rather than a physical perspective. That is, it is not sufficient to ask whether or not the collision per se causes the postcollision courses. One needs to inquire about the relationship between pre- and postcollision information.

The information-theory helps to resolve the paradox of process-process vs. event-event causality. It indicates that the effect of a display for brand x and its effects on x's future volume cannot be divorced from x's past sales (and the past sales of competing brands), or from other activities prior to the display. Put succinctly, the display alone does not cause subsequent sales levels; it simply alters the sales trajectories of x and the other brands. The size of these alterations depends on the sales paths prior to the display (a sort of "sales momentum"), as well as on other aspects of the system prior to the x-display—for example, previous displays for x, previous price reductions for x, x's "marketing mass" (brand equity), and similar information about the competing brands.

In summary, an information-theory view of causality examines time series of data about events in the space-time neighborhood of the process being examined and relative to the system's inertial state. It does not attempt to trace the current state of affairs to an *initial cause*, for example, the rocket launch, the invention of the rocket, the category's creation, the industrial revolution, but assumes that any lingering effects from earlier "causes" will either be or not be contained in current information. If the effects from earlier causes are not detectable in current information, then these earlier causes are no longer relevant. If the effects from earlier causes are contained in current information, then current information is sufficient for prediction.

Theorems

Certain implications of the foregoing arguments are summarized in this section. The label "theorem" is used to punctuate a particular idea, and each theorem is exemplified using parallel examples from physics and category management. Clearly, these conclusions are subject to debate both in physics and marketing. They represent working hypotheses intended to encourage discussion rather than foregone conclusions intended to preclude it.

Theorem 1: *Natural laws, including laws of motion, are unalterable.*

For example, in physics the speed of light is constant. As a consequence, certain laws of time and distance such as the Lorentz transformations are valid.

In category management, the psychological mechanisms governing human choice process—for example, the ability of humans to remember and integrate information, and the competitive dynamics governing a market—are unalterable.

Theorem 2: *A system can change states only within limits imposed by its laws of motion.*

A space shuttle cannot change positions instantaneously; spatial movement must occur over time. Similarly, a shuttle cannot change from one velocity to another without passing through all intervening velocities. Furthermore, a shuttle's velocity cannot exceed the speed of light.

In category management, an entrant's market share cannot move from one level to another level without passing through all intermediate levels. This change takes time and is subject to the laws of motion governing the category.

Theorem 3: *All state changes deviating from a system's inertial trajectory are costly.*

Changing a shuttle's course requires a rocket burn that uses costly fuel. An innovative shuttle design may meet less inertial resistance than would an older design, but does not change a system's laws of motion.

A change in sales or market share for a given category entrant requires costly marketing programs, for example, a price reduction, a feature, an infusion of advertising dollars. A creative advertising campaign may decrease consumer resistance to buying but does not change the laws of supply and demand.

Theorem 4: *Certain changes in a system's trajectory are less costly than others.*

A shuttle that must inject into a higher orbit can accomplish the change via many alternative—but permissible—trajectories. For example, one possibility is to burn fuel heavily using the main rocket—speeding up and then inserting into the new orbit using a heavy burn of retro rockets. Such a "brute force" state change uses less time but is much more costly than a slow, steady burn of the main rocket. A refined technique may require only minor retro rocket adjustments, saving fuel overall.

Similarly, a brand manager can increase his or her brand's share by large infusions of advertising, promotion, and slotting dollars. But this policy may be far more costly than an alternative strategy that takes longer but is technically more refined.

Theorem 5: An optimal (cost/benefit) trajectory exists to navigate from any one state to any other.

Optimal changes in a shuttle's flight path (1) require an explicit criterion to be optimized, and (2) must operate within (or even take advantage of) natural laws. The objective function usually balances cost/time trade-offs and achieves certain trajectories by gravitational slingshot maneuvers around planets, the sun, or other stellar objects.

In category management, an objective function also balances cost/time trade-offs and is usually stated in the form of a quadratic loss function that simultaneously recognizes the discounted present value of money and the presence of uncertainty in the system.

Theorem 6: Systems differ in their degree of controllability.

Not only are certain processes and events uncontrollable by a shuttle pilot—the moon's orbit around the earth, a solar flare, or a meteor shower—but the craft can only be controlled within the limits established by natural laws interacting with the ship's mass, design, and available resources, for example, computer software and fuel.

Marketing management must clearly understand what aspects of the competitive environment they can control (perhaps their brand's price at the trade level but not at the retail level; certainly not competitors' prices). Further, management must recognize the limits on control imposed by the natural laws of the system and the difference between instrumental variables and process variables.

Notes

1. Readers who desire mathematical detail are urged to consult Andrew Harvey, *The Econometric Analysis of Time Series,* 2nd ed., MIT Press, 1990; Thomas J. Sargent, *Macroeconomic Theory,* 2nd edition, Academic Press 1987; or Chi-Tsong Chen, *Linear System Theory and Design,* 2nd ed., New York 1984: Holt, Rinehart & Winston, 1984.

2. Any other physical location—say the moon, or the interior of the shuttle itself—could be chosen as the shuttle's inertial reference frame. The laws of physics would remain the same regardless of this choice, although the ship's coordinates in space-time would change.

3. We usually choose the time dimension as dominant, asking, "what is the state of the system at time t?" However, choosing time in this way is arbitrary since an instant in time must correspond precisely to a place in physical space. Note also that we might note the pitch, roll, and yaw as part of the state of a shuttle if we treat the shuttle as a three-dimensional object rather than as a point mass. These comments suggest that there is no right way to characterize the state of a system, only a best way relative to an analyst's objectives.

4. The standard translation of the *Principia* is Florian Cajori, *Sir Issac Newton's Mathematical Principles of Natural Philosophy and His System of the World,* Berke-

ley: University of California Press, 1966. Cajori translates the second principle as follows (p. 13): "To every action there is always opposed an equal reaction or the mutual actions of two bodies upon each other are always equal and directed to contrary parts."

5. We sidestep important questions about natural laws: their existence, their relationship to human consciousness, their possible local character, and so forth.

6. The term "not here" means not in the (very small) part of the universe that human beings have surveyed. For example, we should not presume that certain types of elements or proteins produced through research on earth do not occur naturally elsewhere in the universe.

7. Note that from the point of view of a given brand manager, the category environment is more analogous to flying a fighter plane in combat than to piloting a space shuttle. However, the analogy used here closely matches a retailer's situation, since a retailer manages all category entrants, not just one.

8. A third rather perplexing variation on the question of casuality is as follows. Suppose the shuttle pilot fires a rocket to avoid collision. (Question: Did the impending collision cause the rocket blast?) Knowing the y data plus the rocket force (and direction) improves our prediction of post- (near-) collision x. In fact, there exists a precise rocket burn that will make the shuttle's postburn trajectory identical to its path after an actual collision. Could an outside observer distinguish between these two types of casuality—one physical and the other psychological?

INDEX